Ellen Mitchell

12.70
H

Understanding and Evaluating Educational Research

Understanding and Evaluating Educational Research

Jean Royer Dyer

RESEARCH DESIGN AND STATISTICAL CONSULTANT,
DEPARTMENT OF THE ARMY

ADDISON-WESLEY PUBLISHING COMPANY
READING, MASSACHUSETTS · MENLO PARK, CALIFORNIA
LONDON · AMSTERDAM · DON MILLS, ONTARIO · SYDNEY

This book is in the
ADDISON-WESLEY SERIES IN EDUCATION

Library of Congress Cataloging in Publication Data

Dyer, Jean Royer, 1941–
    Understanding and evaluating educational research.

    Bibliography: p.
    Includes index.
    1. Educational research. I. Title.
LB1028.D87   370'.78   78-67952
ISBN 0-201-01184-0

TO MY PARENTS

To the Reader

The title of this book, *Understanding and Evaluating Educational Research,* names its two major goals. The first objective is to help you understand and comprehend the research process, especially research as it is conducted within the field of education and described in research reports. Only after this first goal of understanding has been achieved can you attain the second goal of evaluation. Not all research studies are of equal merit, and studies may be excellent for different reasons. It is important that you be able to recognize such distinctions and thereby be able to evaluate the quality of research studies.

It is expected that most of you will be educators who have had little, if any, exposure to the research process. The term "educators" is defined broadly to include teachers at all levels of education (preschool, elementary, junior high, senior high, higher and adult education), administrators, guidance personnel, curriculum developers, and specialists in such fields as mental retardation, reading, speech and hearing, learning disabilities, and vocational education.

Many skills basic to conducting research will be learned while attaining the two goals cited above, and therefore the book is an appropriate introduction to research for individuals who plan to devote part of their professional careers to the actual conduct of research in education. Although most of the examples of research principles are from education, the research principles themselves are basic to all social science research.

The book is divided into four parts. Part I is a general introduction to the process of research in the social sciences, with applications and illustrations from educational research. Part II focuses on basic concepts in the areas of scales of measurement, sampling, reliability and validity of measurement, and descriptive and inferential statistics. Part III focuses upon research designs and methods which are used in educational research and illustrates these procedures with published studies. Studies from different fields within education that illustrate different research designs are listed in Part III so you can easily locate an example of a particular research form within your own field. Part IV presents guidelines to assist you in applying research results. These guidelines are illustrated with several published studies. This section should be particularly helpful to those of you who want to implement or try out research results, but who either cannot or do not want to be directly involved in the actual conduct of research. Study problems and quizzes are included at the end of chapters or within chapters to test your comprehension of the concepts in the book.

A unique feature of the text is the use of a variety of published studies in the field of education to illustrate basic research concepts and forms. These studies are inserted throughout the text so you are immediately and continually exposed to examples of research. Such exposure is essential if the concepts of research methodology, which can sometimes be rather abstract and compli-cated, are to be meaningful to you during your initial exposure to them.

Another important feature of the book is the guidelines that have been developed to assist you in examining and evaluating research studies. These guidelines are presented as a series of questions at the conclusion of most chapters. They also function as chapter summaries. An index to these guidelines is presented within the front and back covers of the text.

In order to understand research reports, you must be familiar with some of the technical procedures used by researchers. Without such knowledge the Method and Results sections of research reports are almost incomprehensible, and you must rely completely upon the researcher's conclusions. Such a depen-dency is undesirable since many times other conclusions could have been made, and since results of particular interest to you may have been ignored by the researcher. Technical procedures used by researchers are described in Part II and in Appendix D. These sections of the text do not require any knowledge of mathematics beyond that which you acquired in high school. All calculations are fully illustrated with sample data. The concepts presented in Part II are referred to again in Parts III and IV. Appendix D contains supplementary information on a variety of statistical techniques to which you or your instructor may wish to refer at various points during the course.

The other appendixes contain information you should find quite helpful if you are required to write a research paper and/or conduct a research study in the course. Appendix A gives suggestions on how to conduct a research study. Appendix B contains information on how to locate research reports and includes a list of research journals in education and of abstracting and indexing journals. Appendix C gives suggestions on how to summarize the information from several research studies, including guidelines for taking research notes. Appen-dix E presents some commonly used statistical tables.

The studies reprinted in this book were carefully selected to illustrate certain principles of research design and to make the research process "come alive." I wish to express my deepest appreciation to those individuals and publishers who gave permission to use their materials. I am also most grateful to Ralph Dunagin who allowed me to select cartoons from his personal file, and to the reviewers and editors for their helpful suggestions. Finally, I must thank my husband Fred, who made it possible for me to take a "sabbatical" to write the book and who reviewed every chapter.

J.R.D.

January 1979

Contents

xi

APPENDIXES

Introduction to the Process of Educational Research

Applying the principles of scientific inquiry to the study of educational problems is not a simple task. Part I of this text will expose you to concepts that are central to all forms of scientific inquiry. Some of these concepts are illustrated by actual reports of educational research in order to provide you, the reader, with a better understanding of the role of these concepts in educational research.

In Chapter 1, the main steps in scientific inquiry are outlined and the importance of research hypotheses is stressed. Several studies have been reprinted to illustrate the impact that research hypotheses have upon the type of conclusions that can be drawn from research results. Chapter 2 focuses on the importance of objectivity in research. The close relationship between scientists' values and the research decisions scientists constantly make is illustrated by a published study. The major points in this introductory section are summarized in an exhibit at the end of Chapter 2 that contains a list of questions you should apply when making your initial analysis of a research report.

1
Scientific Inquiry in Education

Do you believe that students learn more in small classes than they do in large ones, or that juvenile delinquents often have poor reading skills? If so, you could have acquired your beliefs in many different ways. Perhaps you have actually observed or experienced such phenomena. Perhaps you heard about them from an authority in the field. Each of these ways of acquiring knowledge has its disadvantages. For example, personal experiences are limited in number. Not only do we forget much that we have experienced but we also tend to distort what we have experienced. Authorities are not always the experts in a field, and experts are not always right.

Another method of acquiring knowledge is through scientific investigation. The primary advantage of this method is that it is self-correcting. Scientists do not blindly accept a statement as true. They check its accuracy with methods that can be examined, critiqued, and repeated by others. Scientists attempt to control for their personal biases and to eliminate other possible explanations of the event being investigated. They do not claim that they have the only solution to the problem, and realize that alternative answers may be discovered by others, or even by themselves at a later date.

This text focuses upon the scientific methods that are used to investigate educational problems. Its primary *goals* are to enable you *to understand research reports, to evaluate the quality of research,* and *to determine when research findings can be applied to your educational setting.* Guidelines for the critical evaluation of research reports are presented throughout the text to help you attain these goals.

1.1 AIMS OF SCIENCE

Description, prediction, and explanation are goals common to all sciences. However, social scientists study problems that are more complex and events that are harder to predict than are those that typically confront the natural scientist. Predictions and explanations are very difficult to make within the field of education because educational settings are always being changed. For exam-

3

ple, generalizations and predictions in such a basic area as the effects of teachers on students are difficult to achieve when the educational programs within a school vary from year to year and when teachers move from school to school.

1.2 UNITY OF SCIENCE

The three goals of description, prediction, and explanation unite all scientists, as do scientists' attitudes about their work and their methods of investigating a problem. They try to do the "damnedest with [their minds], no holds barred" (20, p. 450) in order to solve a problem. Scientists recognize their need to have others critically evaluate their work. They systematically test their ideas, more formally called hypotheses, knowing that the results of their study may not support these ideas. Scientists know that their methods of investigation must be open to the public so that scientific disagreements can be resolved, and so that other scientists can use their methods and apply the knowledge obtained from their work.

All scientists apply similar *methods,* that is, general procedures and approaches, in studying a problem. These methods include "forming concepts and hypotheses, making observations and measurements, performing experiments, building models and theories, providing explanations, and making predictions" (90, p. 23).

Although different sciences are united by general methods or approaches to problems, they are distinguished one from the other by their subject matter. These subject matter differences require that different techniques be employed in the investigation of problems (e.g., you cannot ask a rock to fill out a questionnaire). It is important that educational researchers determine what is unique about educational problems so that appropriate techniques are used. Many educational research techniques have been borrowed from other social sciences such as psychology and sociology. However, educational research is rapidly becoming a discipline in its own right, and techniques appropriate for investigating complex educational phenomena are being developed (e.g., classroom observation procedures appropriate for preschoolers and for university students).

1.3 SCIENTIFIC INQUIRY

Although the reasoning process used by scientists in studying a problem does not necessarily follow a prescribed sequence and is assuredly not the same for all scientists, certain essential steps in scientific inquiry can be identified. These essential steps are systematically described in research articles. The relationships between the sections of a research report and the steps in scientific inquiry are:

Steps in Scientific Inquiry	*Sections of Research Report*
1. A problem is identified by researchers. Ideally, they find a *theory* applicable to the problem.	1. *Introduction.* The purpose of the study is presented. Background information on the problem is cited,

They then derive consequences directly relevant to their problem that follow from the theoretical principles. These consequences are usually labeled *research hypotheses,* since they indicate what the researchers expect to find at the conclusion of their study.

2. The research hypotheses are subjected to *empirical test* by observation or experiment.

3. *Evidence* regarding the research hypotheses is obtained. In general, it either supports or does not support the hypotheses.

4. Depending on the result that occurs in Step 3, *support* or *lack of support* is shown for the original *theoretical principles* cited in Step 1.

usually in the form of a review of relevant literature. Research hypotheses are usually cited.

2. *Method.* Details on how the study was conducted are cited: characteristics of the subjects, measurement procedures, study design, special materials, etc.

3. *Results.* The data are described and analyzed, usually with statistical tests. This is the most technical section of the report.

4. *Conclusions and Discussion.* Factors that might have accounted for the results are discussed, and major conclusions from the study are presented.

Let us examine these steps in scientific inquiry in more detail. In the remaining sections of the chapter, Steps 1 and 2 are examined more thoroughly than are Steps 3 and 4. In particular, the role of hypotheses in the research process is stressed. Sections of published studies have been included to clarify this role.

1.3.1 THE ORIGIN OF A RESEARCH PROBLEM (STEP 1)

The origins of studies are quite varied: researcher curiosity (a "what would happen if I did this" type of question), an idea that two or more events might be related, a hypothesis derived from a personal experience, an unsolved problem known to many scientists, a conflict in results of previous studies, a test of a theoretical principle, an advance in research methodology, etc. The best research ideas generate much new knowledge, often have many practical applications, and lead to further research. How does a researcher decide if a particular research problem is worth investigating? No definitive guidelines have been developed. Those ideas that have proved worthwhile are best characterized as being the result of the genius of the scientist (127).

1.3.2 THE ROLE OF HYPOTHESES (STEPS 1, 2, AND 3)

Hypotheses are crucial to scientific inquiry because "the scientist cannot tell positive from negative evidence unless he uses hypotheses" (92, p. 26). Without research hypotheses, the steps in scientific inquiry just cited do not exist, and much of the logic underlying the process of scientific inquiry breaks down. Despite the importance of hypotheses, they are omitted in many studies in education. Instead, only a problem statement or question is presented. Problem statements and questions ask only if there is a relationship between two or more variables. In contrast, hypotheses speculate about the nature of the relationship between variables, and thus go beyond problem statements in describing phenomena.

"Does placement of mentally retarded children in special classrooms increase their reading achievement more than placement in regular classrooms?", "What student characteristics are associated with school vandalism?", and "What is the relationship between self-concept and achievement?" are all problem questions. They do not specify a direction to the relationship between variables, as is the case with research hypotheses. Problems, however, can be converted into research hypotheses. For example, the first problem could yield three different hypotheses: (1) mentally retarded children in special classrooms achieve higher reading levels than do those in regular classrooms, (2) mentally retarded children in special classrooms achieve lower reading levels than do those in regular classrooms, and (3) special and regular classrooms for the mentally retarded have the same effects on the reading achievement of the retarded. With the second problem one might hypothesize that students who are bored in the classroom are more apt to vandalize a school than are students who are not bored.

STUDIES WITHOUT RESEARCH HYPOTHESES

Typically, studies without hypotheses are exploratory efforts and are based on little, if any, theory. The review of related literature cited in the introduction of the report serves primarily to document the need for the study, rather than to lay the foundation for making hypotheses or predictions.

The following two studies are presented to illustrate the limiting role of problem statements in research, as well as the type of rationale that usually accompanies studies that do not have a research hypothesis.

EXAMPLE—BYALICK AND BERSOFF STUDY The introduction to Byalick and Bersoff's (25) study illustrates an exploratory effort without research hypotheses. In the first two paragraphs, Byalick and Bersoff cite the lack of data on the type of reinforcers that teachers actually use in the classroom, and note that such information was missing particularly on biracial samples of teachers and students. The major goals of the study are presented in the last paragraph.

> It is now well established that contingent reinforcement by teachers has direct effects on both academic and nonacademic behavior of students. The interaction of variables such as age (Cradler and Goodwin 1971; Rosenhan and Greenwald 1965), sex (Rosenhan and Greenwald 1965; Rucinski 1968), intelligence (Wolfensberger 1960), and social class (Cradler and Goodwin 1971; Shores 1969; Zigler and Kanzer 1962) as they influence reinforcement effectiveness has also been widely studied (though with few findings that are either clear or consistent). Yet, Staats' (1968) indictment that systems of reinforcement in school

situations have never been subjected to systematic study and research remains correct. With very few exceptions (e.g., Meyer and Lindstrom 1969), observations of reinforcing behavior in the natural setting of the classroom are absent from the literature. Thus, while there is a genuine concern over the propriety and utility of concrete, extrinsic, and intrinsic reinforcement as they relate to children's learning, there is a dearth of normative data regarding the actual emission of the variety of reinforcers available to teachers.

If normative data concerning teacher reinforcement emission is scanty, such information is almost nonexistent for biracial samples of teachers. Increasing numbers of black and white teachers are facing integrated classrooms, yet very little empirical data concerning teacher–child interaction in such classes has been published. Reviewing the literature recently, Meyer and Lindstrom (1969) commented that observational studies of teacher behavior toward black and white children were unknown to them. Their own study, comparing the rates of approval and disapproval in biracial classrooms, yielded no differences between black and white teachers toward classes of mixed race/sex children. However, only 13 teachers were studied and only four of those were black.

Lastly, previous research (Bersoff and Moyer 1973) has suggested that teachers have rather clear ideas concerning the kinds of reinforcers they believe to be the most effective in the classroom. What is not known is whether teachers actually use those reinforcers they state they prefer. In the light of the above concerns, the present investigation had three major goals: (1) Begin a systematic inquiry into the reinforcement practices of teachers as they exhibit them under natural classroom conditions. (2) Compare the rate of reinforcement emission of a sizeable sample of black and white teachers in integrated classrooms. (3) Compare the rates of actual reinforcement emission of teachers with their stated preferences (pp. 473–474).

It should be clear that Goal (1) was not a research hypothesis. In fact, it was not even a problem statement, since it cannot be reformulated in terms of a question about the possible relationship between variables in the study. However, Goal (2) was a problem statement that asked if there was a relationship between the race of a teacher and the rate or pace of reinforcement given to children. Goal (3) asked if there was a relationship between actual and preferred rates of teachers' reinforcement. Goals (2) and (3) did not hypothesize what the outcome might be. Apparently the authors had no expectations regarding the reinforcement rates of black and white teachers.

Byalick and Bersoff found that the rate of positive reinforcement was similar for both black and white teachers. Should they have been "pleased" with this result? No; they did not state that they expected similar rates, and therefore the results cannot be used to support such an expectation. On the other hand, should they be "unhappy"? Again, the answer is no. They did not hypothesize that black and white teachers would differ and therefore the results did not contradict their expectations. Thus without a hypothesis the findings of the study cannot be interpreted as either positive or negative evidence.

EXAMPLE—GRIBBONS AND LOHNES STUDY Gribbons and Lohnes cited two problem statements in their study of adolescents' vocational values (paragraph 2 of study): "Is there an important shift in the typal hierarchy of vocational values over five years of adolescence?" and "Is there an important difference between the developed typal hierarchy of vocational values for boys and that for girls?" If hypotheses had been made instead, then the nature of a shift, if any, in values would have been specified, as well as the nature of any differences between values for the two sexes.

Statistical guide.   In Table 1.1 the relationship between various sets of rankings was determined by the Spearman rank-correlation coefficient, sometimes called rho. The twelve values were ranked, 1 through 12, according to their popularity for each sex at each of the three grade levels. If the values had been ranked exactly the same for any two groups, say boys and girls at the eighth grade level, then the correlation or rho coefficient would have been +1.00. If the ranks had been exactly reversed, then rho would have been −1.00. If there had been no relationship between two sets of ranks, then rho would have equaled 0. The positive correlations actually obtained between the various sets of ranks ranged from .46 between the eighth and twelfth grade girl ranks to a high of .95 between the eighth and tenth grade girl ranks, indicating relatively similar orderings of the values for the various groups.

Shifts in Adolescents' Vocational Values
WARREN D. GRIBBONS
PAUL R. LOHNES

[1] Career psychology has attended closely to the emerging vocational interests and aspirations of youth, but little is known about the reasons for the preference patterns which have been described. It has been suggested repeatedly that family press shapes the occupational concepts of youth (e.g., Tiedeman and O'Hara, 1963, p. 83), but the available empirical evidence fails to support this view (Brunkan and Crites, 1964). It seems more reasonable to emphasize, as Super has all along (e.g., Super et al., 1963), that a system of self-concepts provides the matrix for specific occupational concepts, censoring and molding them to a comfortable fit in the matrix, and that the self-concept system itself is a product of a vast congeries of determinants. In this mélange of causes, family related variables contribute to the fomentation of self-concepts, but so do such factors as neighborhood, community and regional influences, educational and religious factors, mass media exposures, and friendships. Taking the system of self-concepts as the immediate control over occupational preferences, then, it seems likely that some hierarchy of values embedded in the system dominates the preference-building process. One career psychologist has expressed this hypothesis as follows:

If there is a single synthesizing element that orders, arranges, and unifies such interactions, that ties together an individual's perceptions of cultural promptings, motivating

Warren D. Gribbons and Paul R. Lohnes, 1965. Shifts in adolescents' vocational values. *Personnel and Guidance Journal* 44: 248–252. Copyright © 1965 by the American Personnel and Guidance Association. Reprinted with permission.

needs, mediating symbols, differentiating characteristics, and sense of resolution, that relates perception to self-concepts, and that accounts most directly for a particular decision or for a mode of choosing, it is here suggested that that element is the individual's value system (Katz, 1963, p. 16).

[2] The authors are involved in a longitudinal study of the career development of 111 boys and girls which was begun in 1958, when the senior author interviewed the subjects first. At that time they were beginning the eighth grade in several junior high schools in metropolitan Boston's outlying cities. They were interviewed again in the last months of the tenth grade (1961), and again late in the senior year of high school (1963). No subjects were lost during the five-year period. Agreeing with Katz, the authors report in this paper on the inferred value hierarchies of these boys and girls, as they have been judged from the interview protocols, and on the changes observed in these value hierarchies over five years of development. Other aspects of the longitudinal study data have been reported in Gribbons (1964) and Gribbons and Lohnes (1964a, 1964b, 1964c). Answers were sought to two questions about values for this study:

1. Is there an important shift in the typal hierarchy of vocational values over five years of adolescence?
2. Is there an important difference between the developed typal hierarchy of vocational values for boys and that for girls?

METHOD

[3] Before attempting to answer these questions from the data, an account of the interview questions that elicited the responses from which the values of the subjects were judged and ranked is in order. Precisely the same interview form was employed in 1958 and in 1961. Of its 43 questions, the following provided the stimuli for expression of values:

1. What made you decide to take X curriculum?
2. What made you decide not to take Y or Z curriculum?
3. Is there any advantage to taking the college curriculum?
4. Why would you like to become an X (occupation)?
5. What particular interests would X occupation satisfy?
6. What interests do you have that will not be satisfied by X?
7. As you know, things that are important to us are called values. Tell me about some of your values.
8. What values of yours would working as an X satisfy?
9. What values of yours would not be satisfied in your occupation as an X?
10. Which of your values will conflict with one another in your choice of an occupation?

The 1963 interview was conducted on the basis of a somewhat different set of questions, from among which the following served to elicit vocational values responses:

1. What is the most important factor to consider in making an occupational choice?
2. Why do you consider this factor important?

3. In the eighth grade you were considering the possibility of becoming an X, and in the tenth grade an X', and now you plan to be an X''. Will you tell me what has strengthened this decision (or caused you to change your mind)?

4. Do you feel that the occupation you will enter is a matter of chance or choice? Can you tell me why?

5. What would you like to get out of life? What do you think would make you happy and satisfied?

6. What would you like to get out of work?

7. Can you tell me something of how you feel about going to work?

8. When you think about work, is there anything you feel to be especially disagreeable about it?

Those responses were classified as values that seemed to provide broad guideposts to action or that entailed a commitment to long-range goals. Because of the high degree of specificity of the instructions for coding protocol materials, this judge had no difficulty in reaching an unambiguous categorization of each response unit. Although no formal reliability study was done, the authors feel that the reliability of categorization must have been very high. It was found that 12 general categories accommodated the responses tallied as value indicators, as follows, with some examples of indicators:

Advancement: opportunity to get ahead; good future in it; can become a manager; can work from bottom up

Demand: good job for later on; it's in demand; teachers are needed

Geographic location, travel: like to fly; able to travel; learning from travel; raises transportation problems

Interest: like to work with my hands; really enjoy it

Marriage and family: get married eventually; be happy with husband and children; want a nice home and kids

Social service: help others; to further society; giving something to humanity; making people happy; like to help children

Personal contact: chance to meet new friends; like to meet people; working with others; get to know people better

Preparation, ability: where abilities lie; what I'm good at; suited to it

Prestige: people look up to you; earn recognition, respectability

Salary: earn enough to support family; good income; bank account

Satisfaction: happy at work; fulfill myself; doing something worthwhile

Personal goals: improve self; get to know myself better

Typal value hierarchies were created for each age and sex by ranking the 12 values according to the number of subjects, mentioning each. The authors are aware that this procedure involves the popularity of a value category rather than the intensity with which it is employed by those who use it. Table 1.1 reports the resulting ranking of the values for each age and sex, and the frequencies on which the rankings are based. It should be noted that some values were employed by almost all the subjects (the maximum possible frequency for any age-sex combination is 55), and others were very seldom employed.

TIME SHIFTS IN THE TYPAL HIERARCHIES

[4] *Satisfaction* and *interest* were far and away the most popular types of values put forward in the eighth grade, and remained so for both sexes in the other

TABLE 1.1   TYPAL HIERARCHIES OF VOCATIONAL VALUES FOR EACH SEX AND AGE

Values	8th grade				10th grade				12th grade			
	Girls (N = 57)		Boys (N = 54)		Girls (N = 57)		Boys (N = 54)		Girls (N = 57)		Boys (N = 54)	
	Rank	f	Rank	f	Rank	f	Rank	f	Rank	f	Rank	f
Satisfaction	1.0	48	1.0	47	2	50	1	51	1.0	51	2.0	50
Interest	2.0	47	2.0	44	1	51	2	47	2.0	49	1.0	51
Marriage and family	7.5	9	11.0	4	7	14	12	4	3.0	30	4.0	22
Personal contact	3.5	24	6.0	11	3	35	5	16	4.0	25	6.5	14
Social service	3.5	24	5.0	12	4	26	8	13	5.0	23	8.0	10
Preparation, ability	9.0	5	7.5	10	9	7	6	16	6.0	15	6.5	14
Advancement	12.0	0	10.0	7	12	4	11	7	7.0	14	9.0	7
Salary	11.0	3	3.0	19	9	7	3	25	8.0	13	3.0	41
Personal goals	5.0	14	7.5	10	6	13	4	20	9.5	8	10.0	6
Demand	10.0	4	12.0	3	11	6	10	9	9.5	8	11.0	4
Location, travel	6.0	12	9.0	8	5	15	9	12	11.5	3	12.0	2
Prestige	7.5	9	4.0	13	9	7	7	15	11.5	3	5.0	16
Girls vs. boys:	Rho = .50				Rho = .52				Rho = .62			

For girls: 8th vs. 10th, Rho = .95; 8th vs. 12th, Rho = .46;
10th vs. 12th, Rho = .52

For boys: 8th vs. 10th, Rho = .84; 8th vs. 12th, Rho = .68;
10th vs. 12th, Rho = .50

interviews. So heavily saturated are these two categories that the authors wish they knew how to break them down into smaller units, but no workable scheme has suggested itself. Our generalization is that the vocational values which were uppermost in the thoughts of our subjects early in adolescence remained uppermost throughout the five-year period.

[5] *Marriage and family* is always employed by more girls than boys, and becomes consistently more popular with both sexes as they advance in years. The boys are persistently interested in *salary* and *prestige;* the girls not so. The girls are persistently interested in *personal contact* and *social service;* the boys less so and decreasingly so over time. There is a decreasing concern with *personal goals, geographic location,* and *travel,* and corresponding increase in concern with *preparation, ability,* and *advancement* on the part of both sexes. There is little or no concern with *demand* at any time. Apart from the sex differences noted, to be discussed below, perhaps the most noticeable trend is from "idealism" in the eighth grade (*social service, personal goals, location and travel*) to "realism" in the twelfth (*marriage and family, preparation and ability, advancement*), which is probably to be applauded. This evidence for the emergence of more mature values somewhat contradicts the findings of Dipboye and Anderson that "little change takes place [in occupational values] during [his] high school career" (1959, p. 124). However, as noted, there are important constancies over the five years in our data also.

SEX DIFFERENCES IN DEVELOPED TYPAL HIERARCHIES

[6] Super included only boys in his Career Pattern Study (1957), and it has been suggested by friends that the sex mix in the small sample of this research may have been rash. Consideration of the developed (i.e., twelfth grade) typal hierarchies of vocational values for the two sexes does reveal an important contrast. Where the boys have given high rank to *salary* and *prestige* values, the girls have given high rank to *personal contact* and *social service* values. This finding lends some support to the theoretical notion of Harrod and Griswold (1960) that girls are people-oriented, in that they like to meet people and help them, whereas boys are career- or extrinsic-reward-oriented in that they are most concerned with salary, security, and prestige.

[7] The comparison of the final hierarchies for the two sexes is dominated by the similarities rather than by the differences, however. There is overwhelming concern with *satisfaction* to be found in vocation and the opportunity to satisfy *interest* particularly. Both groups have arrived at very high concern for *marriage and family.* In line with the result of Astin and Nichols that "men are more likely to give a response with vocational content, whereas women are much more likely to give a response with family or marriage content" (1964, p. 56), it is true that our girls spoke of marriage in terms of husband and children, while our boys spoke of it in terms of providing basic necessities and some luxuries for the family. The two hierarchies are also in near agreement on the position given to *preparation and ability,* and the low positions given in *advancement, personal goals, demand,* and *location and travel.*

CONCLUSIONS

[8] It has been said that "students make choices in terms of the kind of person they believe themselves to be" (Holland, 1964, p. 97). We have argued that the

value categories favored by adolescents in their discussion of vocational issues reveal aspects of their self-concept systems which are crucial in determining occupational preferences. Enough early maturity and constancy in the typal hierarchies of vocation values over five years of adolescence has been shown to warrant challenging Ginzberg's theoretical position that values do not play an important part in early vocational development. Even the eighth grade value statements of our sample of youth are relatively free of "fantasy" elements, although we do discern a shift from "idealism" to "realism" over the five years. Our interpretation of our data is that the constancy it shows bespeaks a maturity of self-concepts early in the eighth grade sufficient to justify close attention from counselors at that time, while the shifts testify to a healthy maturation during adolescence.

[9] Although theoreticians emphasize that career development differs for boys and girls (e.g., Matthews, 1963), and we have noted a bit of a people-oriented (girls) versus career-oriented (boys) differentiation in our developed typal hierarchies, it is our contention that the similarities in our data outweigh the differences, and that our boys and girls appear to be rather alike in their employment of vocational value categories.

[10] It has been shown that school counselors can interfere successfully in the vocational development process (Gribbons, 1960; Shimberg, 1962). It would seem that counselors should assist young people at an early age to an increased awareness of their personal value hierarchies, to the improvement of their values, and to the integration of their values and their aspirations and plans.

REFERENCES

Astin, A. W., and Nichols, R. C. Life goals and vocational choice. *J. appl. Psychol.*, 1964, *48*, 50–58.

Brunkan, R. J., and Crites, J. O. An inventory to measure the parental attitude variables in Roe's theory of vocational choice. *J. counsel. Psychol.*, 1964, *11*, 3–12.

Dipboye, W. J., and Anderson, W. F. The ordering of occupational values by high school freshmen and seniors. *Personnel Guid. J.*, 1959, *38*, 121–124.

Ginzberg, E., Ginsburg, S. W., Axelrad, S., and Herma, J. L. *Occupational choice.* New York: Columbia Univ. Press, 1951.

Gribbons, W. D. Evaluation of an eighth grade group guidance program. *Personnel Guid. J.*, 1960, *38*, 740–745.

Gribbons, W. D. Changes in readiness for vocational planning from the eighth to the tenth grade. *Personnel Guid. J.*, 1964, *41*, 908–913.

Gribbons, W. D., and Lohnes, P. R. Relationships among measures of readiness for vocational planning. *J. counsel. Psychol.*, 1964, *11*, 13–19. (a)

Gribbons, W. D., and Lohnes, P. R. Validation of vocational planning interview scales. *J. counsel. Psychol.*, 1964, *11*, 20–26. (b)

Gribbons, W. D., and Lohnes, P. R. Predicting five years of development in adolescents from readiness for vocational planning scales. 1964, in press. (c)

Harrod, G., and Griswold, Norma. Occupational values and counseling. *Voc. Guid. Quart.*, 1960, *9*, 60–66.

Holland, J. L. A theory of vocational choice; vocational daydreams. *Voc. Guid. Quart.*, Winter 1963–64, *12*, 93–97.

Katz, M. *Decisions and values.* New York: College Entrance Examination Board, 1963.

Matthews, Esther. Career development of girls. *Voc. Guid. Quart.*, 1963, *11*, 273–278.

Shimberg, B., and Katz, M. Evaluation of a guidance text. *Personnel Guid. J.*, 1962, *41*, 126–132.

Super, D. E., et al. *Vocational development: a framework for research.* New York: Bureau of Publications, Teachers College, Columbia Univ., 1957.

Super, D. E., et al. *Career development: self-concept theory.* New York: College Entrance Examination Board, 1963.

Tiedeman, D. V., and O'Hara, R. P. *Career development: choice and adjustment.* New York: College Entrance Examination Board, 1963.

Readers arrived at the end of the method section before they learned the specific vocational values that were studied. If the specific values had been discussed in the introduction (e.g., possible overlap among the values, the generality of each value, the nature of values such as realistic versus idealistic), then hypotheses regarding possible changes in the value hierarchy might have been made. For example, one might expect general values to be cited rather frequently at all time periods. One might also expect changes in the hierarchy to occur primarily with the more specific values.

As with Byalick and Bersoff's study, neither positive nor negative evidence was presented since no hypotheses were made. In fact, the ambiguity of the word "important" in the two problem questions (paragraph 2) makes them difficult to answer. What criterion defines an "important shift" in values—a change in at least two rank positions, in at least five rank positions, a decrease in the rho coefficient between increasing time periods? What criterion defines an "important difference" in the hierarchy for the two sexes? Such ambiguity means that someone else could easily arrive at a different interpretation of the results.

When the characteristics of the major variables in a study are not thoroughly discussed in the introduction of a report, post hoc descriptions and explanations must often be made. For example, Gribbons and Lohnes identified a shift from idealistic values (social service, personal goals, location and travel) to realistic values (marriage and family, preparation and ability, advancement) at the end of the article (paragraphs 5 and 8). Would the same values have been so classified prior to the study? What makes "advancement" realistic rather than idealistic, or "location and travel" idealistic instead of realistic? Prior discussion of such issues would make post hoc interpretations less controversial.

These two studies illustrate that establishing a need for a study does not always generate hypotheses nor provide a theoretical rationale. As a result, possible explanations of the findings, if any are given, follow rather than precede the collection of data. The results cannot be perceived as providing either positive or negative evidence for a position. In studies without hypotheses, the introduction frequently provides an inadequate guide for the reader. Some important variables may be omitted and those variables that are mentioned may not be thoroughly examined.

STUDIES WITH RESEARCH HYPOTHESES

Research hypotheses are generated from previous research and theory, and reflect the *researcher's expectations* regarding the outcome of a study. Research hypotheses should *not* be confused with what are known as *null hypotheses*. Null hypotheses are very precise mathematical statements that describe the results that would occur if only chance factors were operating in the study, and usually state either that there is no difference among the groups being compared or that there is no relationship among the variables being examined. Null hypotheses do not necessarily correspond to the researcher's expectations.[1] For example, a researcher might hypothesize that there are more male than female high school teachers. The null hypothesis, based on the assumption that only chance factors operate, would be that there is no difference between the number of male and female high school teachers. Another research hypothesis might be that students who receive high grades also participate in many extracurricular activities and that students with low grades participate in fewer such activities. The corresponding null hypothesis would be that there is no relationship between grade point average and extracurricular activities.

Frequently, articles contain a list of "no difference" or "no relationship" hypotheses. In the majority of such cases, the author does not really expect such results, but has simply cited the null hypothesis. In a few instances, a research hypothesis does in fact correspond to the null hypothesis. The Sabatino and Dorfman study that follows contain both types of research hypotheses: two that stated that differences in groups were expected and one that stated no differences were expected.

EXAMPLE—SABATINO AND DORFMAN STUDY   The rationale for Sabatino and Dorfman's (124) study was based on the opinion of authorities and the results of previous research. The three hypotheses in the excerpt that follows are examined in detail.

Matching Learner Aptitude to Two Commercial Reading Programs
DAVID A. SABATINO
NANCY DORFMAN

[1] The major problem confronting the teacher of mentally retarded children is to decide on an appropriate instructional objective and then achieve it through teaching materials and behavioral management techniques. One instructional process that has recently received attention is the so-called diagnostic-prescriptive matching of a specific instructional procedure to a given learner aptitude.

---

[1] Refer to Chapter 7 for a more detailed discussion of null hypotheses.

David A. Sabatino and Nancy Dorfman, 1974. Matching learner aptitude to two commercial reading programs. *Exceptional Children* 41(2): 85–90. Copyright 1974 by The Council for Exceptional Children. Reprinted with permission from The Council for Exceptional Children, David A. Sabatino, and Nancy Dorfman.

[2] This approach advocates that particular learning strengths can be specified by measuring or observing certain behaviors (aptitudes) displayed by handicapped children. Several contemporary special educators (Reynolds, 1963; Englemann, 1967; Bateman, 1969) have reported studies which demonstrate significant interactions between selected aptitudes and specific instructional interventions. McClurg (1970) noted that most instruction indicates that "the classroom teacher must find the modality that seems to work best with each child [p. 35]." Most teachers have not, however, developed a systematic means of using psychometric or behavioral data based on observations to match curricular materials to instructional settings (Schiller and Deignan, 1969).

[3] The concern for identifying a particularly strong modality as an aptitude by which handicapped children can learn most efficiently is not a new one. Strauss (1947) attempted to fit instructional materials to the modality of greatest strength some 30 years ago. Gellner (1958) felt that the two primary modalities could be divided into the major information processing styles, visual and auditory, through which children learn. She advocated that children be divided according to strengths within modality functions and that highly specified teaching methods be applied to the children in these clusters. Wepman (1961, 1964). Bateman (1967), Werner and Kaplan (1963) and Sabatino, Ysseldyke and Woolston (1973) have all referenced developmental discrepancies in modality growth and the resulting variation in learning styles. Most educational theorists recommend that children be grouped for teaching on the basis of directing instruction to the strongest avenues for learning.

PURPOSE

[4] The major purpose of this study was to determine if children grouped according to their performance on perceptual aptitude tests would make significant academic achievement gains when commercial curricula materials were matched to the perceptual modality of greater measured strength. The supposition is that by isolating the primary perceptual modality (visual or auditory) teachers may plan instruction and group children accordingly. Three major postulates underlie this research:

1. That children with visual strengths and auditory weaknesses would make significantly greater gains in reading skills than audile subjects following instructional interventions with commercial curricular materials received primarily through the visual modality.

2. That children with auditory strengths and visual perceptual weaknesses would yield significantly greater gains in reading skills than visile children following interventions with commercial materials received primarily through the auditory modality.

3. That subjects who did not show significant discrepancies between visual and auditory perceptual test function would fail to demonstrate statistically significant growth on either of the curricula used in this study.

REFERENCES

Bateman, B. Implication of a learning disability approach for teaching educable retardates. *Mental Retardation*, 1967, **5**, 23–25.

Englemann, R. Relationship between psychological theories and the act of teaching. *Journal of School Psychology*, 1967, 2, 93–100.

Gellner, L. *Teaching devices for children with impaired learning.* Columbus, Ohio: The Parents' Volunteer Association, 1958.

McClurg, W. H. Dyslexia: Early identification and treatment in the schools. *Journal of Learning Disabilities*, 1970, 3, 34–49.

Reynolds, M. C. A strategy for research. *Exceptional Children*, 1963, 29, 213–219.

Sabatino, D. A., Ysseldyke, J. E., and Woolston, J. Diagnostic-prescriptive teaching utilizing perceptual strengths of mentally retarded children. *American Journal of Mental Deficiency*, 1973, 78, 7–14.

Schiller, J., and Deignan, M. An approach to diagnosis and remediation of learning disabilities. *Journal of Learning Disabilities*, 1969, 2, 508–524.

Strauss, A. A., and Lehtinen, L. E. *Psychopathology and education of the brain-injured child.* New York: Grune & Stratton, 1947.

Wepman, J. Interrelationship of hearing, speech and reading. *Reading Teacher*, 1961, 14, 245–247.

Wepman, J. M. The perceptual basis for learning. In H. A. Robinson (Ed.), *Meeting individual differences in reading.* Chicago: University of Chicago Press, 1964.

Werner, H., and Kaplan, B. *Symbol formation.* New York: Wiley & Sons, 1963.

The three hypotheses just cited divided the children into three groups—visiles (children with more visual than auditory strengths), audiles (children with greater auditory than visual strengths), and those with no imbalance in modality. Visual and auditory instructional materials were predicted to have specific effects for each type of child. It is important to note that these hypotheses stated the anticipated direction of difference, not simply that differences were expected to occur. The third hypothesis indicated that children with no imbalance in perceptual modality (nonpreference subjects) would be affected to the same extent by the instructional treatments. Although this hypothesis corresponded in form to the statistical null hypothesis, it was also the researchers' hypothesis because it reflected what they expected to find.

Researchers must clearly specify the hypotheses. Readers must also be aware of researchers' exact meaning so they can check upon the validity of the researchers' conclusions regarding whether or not the data supported the hypotheses. The two variables in the Sabatino and Dorfman study were instructional mode and perceptual mode of the child, yielding the six combinations illustrated in Fig. 1.1. The relationship of the three hypotheses to these six conditions is also illustrated in the diagram.

Sabatino and Dorfman could have made other research hypotheses. A comparison of the hypotheses that were made with the hypotheses that could have been made, but were not, illustrates the importance of fully understanding research hypotheses. For example, no hypotheses were made regarding the relative gains of all types of children in the various curricula. An example of a hypothesis that includes all types of children would be that visiles under the visual curriculum (VV) would gain the same amount as that of audiles in the

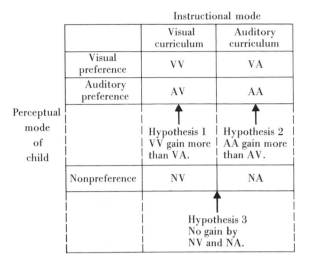

FIG. 1.1 Correspondence between the research design and hypotheses in the Sabatino and Dorfman study.

auditory curriculum (AA), and that both groups would gain more than children would in the other conditions, including the nonpreference children (VA, AV, NV, and NA). Hypothesis 1 stated that the audiles in the visual curriculum (AV) would gain less in comparison to visiles in the visual curriculum (VV), not that the AV group would show no gain. Hypothesis 2 was stated similarly but referred to audiles and visiles in the auditory curriculum. Hypothesis 3 stated that neither nonpreference group would experience any gain. This differs from hypothesizing that the nonpreference groups would have equal increases in reading achievement and therefore similar scores at the end of the study.

SUPPORT REQUIRED FOR MAKING A HYPOTHESIS

Rationales for hypotheses can vary greatly in sophistication, formalization, and empirical and logical support. The Sabatino and Dorfman study just referred to and the Cicirelli and Cicirelli study which follows contain hypotheses that are best labeled "formative" (133), since they were based on relatively little empirical data and theory. Hypotheses can also be generated from much theory and research.

How do researchers decide if the theory and data upon which they generate their hypotheses are valid; if support for these generalizations is adequate or reasonable? Support is inferred through the process of *induction,* i.e., of inferring a generalization from observation of its particular instances. A generalization can be considered to be well supported if it has not been refuted by experience, if it has been confirmed by a number of instances in a variety of conditions, and if competing generalizations have been refuted. Scientists' previous experience, knowledge, and judgment all influence how they evaluate such evidence. One researcher could argue that theory and research support a certain hypothesis; another researcher could argue that the hypothesis is not justified on the basis of the same evidence.

EXAMPLE—CICIRELLI AND CICIRELLI STUDY   The Cicirelli and Cicirelli study that follows illustrates how researchers must frequently base their hypotheses upon a combination of research results and reasoning. Studies of the characteristics of creative individuals and Carl Rogers' notions of client-centered counseling were reviewed. However, not all of this information related directly to the situation of interest to the authors, and they were forced to form their own inferences about what would happen in that situation.

Statistical guide.   Product–moment correlations were used to describe the relationships between creativity, attitude, and counseling behavior (paragraph 17). Such coefficients provide an index of the strength of a linear (a straight line) relationship between two variables and can range in value from −1 to +1. A zero correlation indicates no linear relationship between two variables. Stronger relationships are indicated as the coefficient approaches either −1 or +1, both of which reflect perfect relationships (i.e., an individual's score on one variable can be precisely predicted from knowing his or her score on the other correlated variable). The positive correlation coefficient of .82 between flexibility and fluency cited in Table 1.2 meant that most individuals who scored above the mean on flexibility also scored above the mean on fluency, individuals whose scores were approximately at the mean on flexibility were also similar to the mean on fluency, and individuals below the mean on flexibility were also below the mean on fluency. A lower, yet still positive, correlation of .55 between fluency and originality meant that a similar but weaker pattern of scores existed for these two variables. A negative correlation would indicate the reverse trend, e.g., individuals above the mean on one variable would be below the mean on the other correlated variable (high-low, medium-medium, and low-high pairings). Some negative correlations are reported in Table 1.4.

The statistical significance of these correlations is indicated in the tables by an asterisk. The asterisks refer to the probability of a correlation of a given magnitude occurring if only chance factors were operating. If this probability is very low ($p < .05$, less than 5 out of 100 times or $p < .01$, less than 1 out of 100 times), it is usually stated that the correlation is statistically significant, or statistically different from zero. The .82 correlation between flexibility and fluency was statistically significant, and the authors concluded (paragraph 20) that the two variables were in fact related and the relationship was not simply a chance occurrence.

The last column in Table 1.4 gives the multiple correlation between the behavior measures and a weighted combination of the TTCT fluency and MTAI scores. A multiple correlation coefficient (R) can range 0 to +1 with +1 meaning that scores from a combination of variables can accurately reproduce the scores on one criterion measure, and a correlation of zero indicates no relationship between the set of scores and the criterion.

Counselors' Creative Ability and Attitude in Relation
to Counseling Behavior with Disadvantaged Counselees
VICTOR G. CICIRELLI
JEAN S. CICIRELLI

[1] As a group, socially disadvantaged youth stand to profit greatly from effective counseling. Yet, two obstacles stand in the way of providing effective counseling for such youth: lack of counseling services in disadvantaged areas, and lack of counselors trained in understanding and communicating with disadvantaged youth. Accordingly, much federal support has been given to the establishment and enlargement of guidance programs in disadvantaged areas as well as to training programs for counselors to work with the disadvantaged. Such training programs tend to emphasize study of the cultural mores and values, the intellectual and personality characteristics, and (to some extent) the nonstandard language of the disadvantaged group, along with specific training in counseling skills and counseling field experience. Counselors typically find it difficult, even after much training, to establish satisfactory counseling relationships with disadvantaged counselees due to the cultural gap, the communication problem, and the rather suspicious and withdrawn reactions of the disadvantaged counselee.

[2] The present study involved participants in a National Defense Education Act summer institute for counselors of the disadvantaged. The purpose of the study was threefold: (*a*) to determine the kinds of verbal interaction that went on during counseling sessions with disadvantaged youth, (*b*) to investigate the hypothesis that more creative counselors were able to establish a more effective counseling relationship with disadvantaged counselees than were their less creative colleagues, and (*c*) to investigate the hypothesis that counselors with a more positive attitude toward the student were able to establish a more effective counseling relationship with disadvantaged counselees than were their colleagues with a less positive attitude.

[3] Studies of the creative personality have found that the creative person tends to be more sensitive to problems, more flexible, less rigid, more tolerant of ambiguity, and more open to experience (MacKinnon, 1960; Taylor, 1964). Torrance (1962), in his discussions of creativity in counseling relationships, draws a close parallel between the ideal therapeutic relationship and the creative relationship when he says,

Victor G. Cicirelli and Jean S. Cicirelli, 1970. Counselors' creative ability and attitude in relation to counseling behavior with disadvantaged counselees. *Journal of Counseling Psychology* **17**: 177–183. Copyright 1970 by the American Psychological Association. Reprinted with permission.

...to achieve the relationship...one must enter imaginatively into the thinking and feeling experiences of another. Only by doing this can one participate completely in another's communicating, keep his comments in line with what the other is trying to say, understand his feelings, follow his line of thought, and share his feelings [p. 165].

(Torrance, however, excludes as a possible successful counselor the obvious case of the highly creative individual who is highly absorbed in his own creativity.)

[4] Applying such notions of the creative counselor to the problem of counseling the disadvantaged, it would seem that the more creative counselor should be better able than the less creative counselor to be sufficiently sensitive, open, and flexible to bridge the gap in values and language and to understand, communicate with, and maintain rapport with the counselee. He should be better able to accept and enlarge upon counselee ideas and feelings, and to thereby stimulate greater responsiveness and involvement on the part of the counselee.

[5] Counselor attitudes toward the counselee have an important part in any counseling theory. Most counseling theories assume that positive attitudes toward the counselee are essential for adequate counseling, although they differ as to the degree that such attitudes are sufficient. Rogers' (1957, 1958, 1962) client-centered approach is well known for the central role which counselor attitudes play. For example, "growth and change are more likely to occur the more that the counselor is experiencing a warm, positive, acceptant attitude toward what *is* in the client [Rogers, 1962, p. 420]."

[6] The attitude of the counselor is particularly relevant in dealing with disadvantaged youth. Often suspicious and withdrawn, the disadvantaged youth seems to need special reassurance to let down his defenses and enter into a counseling relationship.

[7] While it is hypothesized that both more positive attitudes and more creative ability should lead to a more effective counseling relationship, there are serious difficulties in the way of attempting to define and measure just what is an effective counseling relationship. Rather than this, the present study seeks to determine whether differences in counselor attitude and creative ability are associated with certain behaviors in the counseling situation: Amidon's (1965) method of interaction analysis of the counseling situation seems well suited to the measurement of different types of behavior in the counseling situation. By recording the kind of verbal behavior going on in the counseling interview at 3-second intervals, one obtains a detailed record of counselor and counselee behavior. Categories of counselor behavior include accepting feelings, praising or encouraging, accepting or building on counselee's ideas, asking questions, giving information or opinions, giving directions or orders, and criticizing or justifying authority. Counselee behavior is categorized into that which he initiates and that which occurs in response to the counselor. And finally, the occurrence of periods of silence is noted. To introduce a further complexity into the analysis, the behaviors can be analyzed in terms of sequences; that is, what kind of behavior follows each of the above types.

[8] A detailed statement of hypotheses involving all possible sequences of behavior would be too tedious but the following are the hypotheses involving behavior categories:

1. Counselors' creative ability is positively related to the following behaviors: (*a*) counselors' acceptance of counselee feelings, (*b*) praise and encourage-

ment of the counselee, (c) acceptance and use of counselee's ideas, (d) amount of counselee talk.

2. Counselors' attitude toward the counselee is positively related to the four aforementioned behaviors.

Some characteristics of creative individuals, based on previous research, were cited (paragraph 3). However, it was necessary for the Cicirellis to conjecture how creative individuals would react in a counseling setting with a disadvantaged client (paragraph 4), since neither existing theory nor research provided guidelines for hypotheses in this particular context. The rationale for the relationship between counselor attitude and counselor-client behavior was developed similarly (paragraphs 6 and 7).

METHOD

Subjects

[9] Subjects of the study were 52 participants in a National Defense Education Act summer institute for counselors of the socially disadvantaged. Of these, 26 already held positions as school counselors and 26 were teachers aspiring to become counselors or at least to develop a guidance orientation to teaching. The institute involved study of the disadvantaged, counseling methods, and a supervised practicum in counseling, part of which was carried out at the university and part in the field. The field work consisted of actual counseling interviews with disadvantaged counselees who were in the Neighborhood Youth Corps summer work program or similar supervised situations. All counseling interviews were tape recorded and reviewed in group sessions at the university. Emphasis of the practicum was on the gaining of skills toward establishing rapport and an effective counseling relationship with the disadvantaged counselee, rather than an approach centered around the counselee's problems.

Measures

[10] Mednick's Remote Associates Test (RAT) and the Torrance Tests of Creative Thinking (TTCT) were used as measures of creativity. The Torrance tests were scored to provide measures of verbal fluency, flexibility, and originality (defined as uncommonness of response), while the Remote Associates Test provided a kind of originality measure defined as "unusual responses which do meet specified requirements."

[11] The Minnesota Teacher Attitude Inventory (MTAI) was administered to provide a measure of teacher attitude related to good interpersonal relationships in the classroom, that is, the maintenance of pupil rapport. According to the manual (Cook, Leeds, and Callis, undated), "it is assumed that a teacher ranking at the high end of the scale should be able to maintain a state of harmonious relations with his pupils characterized by mutual affection and sympathetic understanding [p. 3]."

[12] The creativity and attitude scales were given in the last week of the 8-week summer institute.

Interaction Analysis of Counseling Behavior

[13] Each counselor submitted a tape recording of an interview with a disadvantaged counselee, taken from one of the counseling sessions during the last week of the institute. Ten 1-minute periods were selected at random from each of the taped interviews (excluding the opening and closing 3-minute periods), and subjected to interaction analysis following Amidon's (1965) method. The person categorizing the interaction wrote down an appropriate category number for the verbal behavior going on during the interview at 3-second intervals (shifts to a new category within the 3-second interval were also recorded). The categorization scheme was as follows:

Kinds of counselor talk:

Indirect influence
1. Accepts counselee's feelings
2. Praises or encourages counselee behavior
3. Accepts or uses ideas of counselee
4. Asks questions

Direct influence
5. Gives information or opinion
6. Gives directions or orders
7. Criticizes or justifies authority

Kinds of counselee talk
8. Counselee talk in response to counselor
9. Counselee talk which he initiates

Other interaction
10. Silence

		1	2	3	4	5	6	7	8	9	10
Accepts feelings	1										
Praise	2								A	B	C
Counselee idea	3										
Asks questions	4								D	E	F
Gives information	5										
Gives directions	6								G	H	I
Criticizes	7										
Counselee response	8		J		K		L				M
Counselee initiation	9		N		O		P				Q
Silence	10		R		S		T		U		

FIG. 1.2 Interaction matrix showing areas used for correlation analysis.

[14] Both of the experimenters coded all tapes. Where disagreements in coding occurred, the tape was replayed and the differences in coding resolved.

[15] The total number of verbal behaviors in each of the 10 categories was recorded for each of the counselors to obtain the frequency with which each of the 10 types of verbal behavior occurred during the sampled portions of the interview.

[16] Then sequences of two categories of behavior were plotted as ordered pairs in a 10 × 10 matrix, to yield measures of the frequency with which a certain verbal behavior leads to other kinds of verbal behavior. A separate matrix was prepared for the behavior of each counselor. Certain areas of the matrix were selected as being of special interest for this study, for they were concerned with the sequences in which actual interaction between counselor and counselee took place (e.g., where counselor talk led to counselee talk, or to silence, and so on). These areas, labeled A–U, are presented in Fig. 1.2. Area A, for example, involves the following sequences of behavior: 1,8 (counselor accepting feelings of counselee is followed by counselee talk in response); 2,8 (counselor praising or encouraging counselee behavior is followed by counselee talk in response); and 3,8 (counselor accepting or using ideas of counselee is followed by counselee talk in response). Frequencies of each of the three sequences are summed to give a total frequency of behavior for Area A. Area F, to give another example, involves the behavior sequence 4,10 (counselor asking questions is followed by silence).

Statistical Analysis

[17] Product-moment correlations between the creativity measures, the MTAI score, and each of the measures arising from the interaction analysis (frequency of each of the categories 1–10, and each of the areas A–U) were computed. Significant correlations in the predicted direction were taken as support of the hypotheses of the study.

RESULTS

Creativity and Attitude Measures

[18] The sample of 52 counselors used in the study obtained the following scores on the TTCT (Verbal Form A): fluency—$M = 76.1$, $SD = 27.8$; flexibility—$M = 35.8$, $SD = 10.4$; and originality—$M = 53.4$, $SD = 27.0$. While the manual for the TTCT does not provide full adult norms, examination of the scores reported for the various comparison groups indicates that mean scores and standard deviations for this group of counselors fell within the range of mean scores for the various comparison groups listed in the manual. Thus, this sample of counselors does not deviate markedly in creative ability from other groups measured on the TTCT.

[19] The group mean on the MTAI was 82.8; the standard deviation was 19.3. There is no appropriate norm group reported in the manual; however, the mean score of graduate students in Education at the University of Minnesota was 63.98. This group of counselors also scored markedly above various groups of teachers whose scores were reported in the manual.

TABLE 1.2 *INTERCORRELATIONS OF MINNESOTA TEACHER ATTITUDE INVENTORY (MTAI), REMOTE ASSOCIATES TEST (RAT), AND TORRANCE TESTS OF CREATIVE THINKING (TTCT) SCORES FOR 52 HIGH SCHOOL COUNSELORS*

Item	TTCT		RAT	MTAI
	Flexibility	*Originality*		
TTCT				
Fluency	.82*	.55*	.17	.01
Flexibility	—	.68*	.14	—.10
Originality		—	.07	—.16
RAT			—	.04

* $p < .05.$

[20] Product-moment correlations between the various measures are shown in Table 1.2. While the TTCT measures show substantial intercorrelation, correlations with the RAT and MTAI are nonsignificant.

[21] Table 1.3 presents the percentage of verbal behavior in each of the 10 categories for all 52 counselors. On the average, 62% of the interview was devoted to counselee talk (about half of the talk initiated by the counselee and half in response to counselor questions), 28% to counselor talk, and 12% to silence. Question asking was the most frequent kind of counselor talk, followed by the giving of opinion or information. Praise or encouragement of the counselee and accepting or using counselee ideas each accounted for only 3% of the verbal behavior in the interview. Accepting the feelings of the counselee, giving directions, or criticism were even more infrequent, each accounting for .1% or less of all the talk in the interview. (There was, of course, considerable variation in the verbal behavior of individual counselors. Verbal behavior classified in combined Categories 1, 2, and 3 ranged from .5% to 22%; Category 4 from 1.0% to 35.5%; Categories 5, 6, and 7 from 0% to 51%; Categories 8 and 9 from 30% to 92%; and Category 10 from 0% to 37.5%.)

TABLE 1.3 *PERCENTAGE OF VERBAL BEHAVIOR IN EACH OF TEN CATEGORIES*

Kind of talk	Percent
Counselor talk: Indirect influence	
1. Accepts counselee's feelings	0.02
2. Praises or encourages counselee behavior	3.70
3. Accepts or uses ideas of counselee	3.10
4. Asks questions	11.70
Counselor talk: Direct influence	
5. Gives information or opinion	8.86
6. Gives directions or orders	0.06
7. Criticizes or justifies authority	0.10
Counselee talk	
8. Counselee talk in response to counselor	29.27
9. Counselee talk which he initiates	31.08
Other	
10. Silence	12.13

[22] Table 1.4 presents the correlations of frequencies in each of the categories of behavior (and areas of the interaction matrix) with the measures of counselor creativity and attitudes. (Since Categories 1, 6, and 7 were used quite infrequently, no correlation coefficients were computed for them.)

[23] To summarize the relationships indicated by statistically significant correlations:

1. Counselors with greater verbal fluency scores tend to have less silence in the interview (10), fewer of their questions followed by silence (F), fewer counselee responses followed by silence (M), and fewer silences broken by question asking (S).

2. Counselors with greater flexibility scores tend to have less silence in the interview (10), and fewer of their questions followed by silence (F).

TABLE 1.4　CORRELATION OF VARIOUS MEASURES OF COUNSELOR–COUNSELEE INTERACTION WITH MINNESOTA TEACHER ATTITUDE INVENTORY (MTAI), REMOTE ASSOCIATES TEST (RAT), AND TORRANCE TESTS OF CREATIVE THINKING (TTCT) SCORES FOR 52 HIGH SCHOOL COUNSELORS

	TTCT					
Interaction measure	*Fluency*	*Flexibility*	*Originality*	*RAT*	*MTAI*	*R*[a]
2. Praises, encourages	.10	.11	.05	−.07	.42†	.43†
3. Accepts, uses ideas	−.02	.03	.00	.11	.01	—
4. Asks questions	−.18	−.10	−.05	.10	−.27*	.32
5. Gives information	.06	.04	.19	.12	.18	—
8. Counselee response	−.10	−.05	−.11	.06	−.15	—
9. Counselee initiation	.20	.14	.06	−.10	.12	—
10. Silence	−.29*	−.28*	−.20	−.02	−.12	.31
A. 1,2,3 → 8	.02	.08	.03	.09	.24	—
B. 1,2,3 → 9	.22	.17	.11	.00	.38†	.44†
C. 1,2,3 → 10	−.01	−.05	−.01	−.15	.24	—
D. 4 → 8	−.14	−.07	−.02	.13	−.19	—
E. 4 → 9	.07	.10	.04	−.20	.07	—
F. 4 → 10	−.35†	−.32*	−.16	.10	−.28*	.45†
G. 5,6,7 → 8	−.06	.01	.10	−.01	.10	—
H. 5,6,7 → 9	.16	.19	.21	.22	.22	—
I. 5,6,7 → 10	.11	.00	−.03	−.12	.10	—
J. 8 → 1,2,3	−.01	.05	.06	.01	.23	—
K. 8 → 4	.02	.09	.05	.14	−.17	—
L. 8 → 5,6,7	−.07	.03	.17	.05	.16	—
M. 8 → 10	−.35†	−.25	−.16	.07	−.30*	.46†
N. 9 → 1,2,3	.19	.15	.09	−.01	.40†	.44†
O. 9 → 4	.18	.12	.10	.14	.07	—
P. 9 → 5,6,7	.14	.16	.16	.20	.26	—
Q. 9 → 10	−.11	−.14	−.18	−.09	−.06	—
R. 10 → 1,2,3	−.13	−.15	−.07	.03	.14	—
S. 10 → 4	−.29*	−.24	−.14	.04	−.28*	.40†
T. 10 → 5,6,7	−.02	−.06	−.01	.06	.05	—
U. 10 → 8,9	−.26	−.25	−.27*	−.09	−.10	.28

* $p < .05$.
† $p < .01$.
[a] Multiple R computed between Fluency and MTAI scores and the criterion measure.

3. Counselors with greater originality scores tend to have fewer silences in the interview broken by the counselee (U).

4. Counselors with more positive attitude scores on the MTAI tend to have more use of praise and encouragement of the counselee (2), more behavior sequences where praise, encouragement, and acceptance of the counselee is followed by counselee-initiated statements (B), or where counselee-initiated statements are followed by praise, encouragement, and acceptance of the counselee (N), less question asking in the interview (4), less questioning followed by silence (F), less use of questioning to end silence (S), and less silence following counselee responses (M).

In order to clarify the correspondence between these statements and the correlations in Table 1.4, go back to Table 1.4 and circle the significant correlations (those with asterisks and daggers). Point 1 in paragraph 23 described the significant fluency correlations (the correlations in the first column that you just circled) with silence ($-.29$), with category F ($-.35$), with category M ($-.35$), etc. Point 2 described the significant flexibility correlations (those in the second column), etc.

[24] No correlations with RAT scores were large enough to be statistically significant.

[25] Multiple correlation coefficients were computed between the fluency and MTAI scores and the criterion measures; values of R ranged from .40 to .46 (for measures 2, B, F, M, N, and S).

DISCUSSION

[26] It was hypothesized earlier that counselors with more creative ability and more positive attitude scores would show greater acceptance of the counselee's feelings and ideas, greater use of praise and encouragement, and more counselee talk during the counseling session.

[27] While the hypotheses were not fully verified, verbal fluency and flexibility as measured by the TTCT did show a relationship to the amount of counselee talk, and positive attitude scores on the MTAI showed a relationship to the use of more praise and encouragement during the interview as well.

[28] (The lack of relationship between the TTCT—especially the originality measure—and the RAT indicates the difficulty in identifying the meaning of creativity. However, one can identify fluency and flexibility as abilities important to the counseling relationship regardless of whether or not these abilities are truly dimensions of creative thinking.)

[29] It is somewhat surprising to find that creativity and positive attitude are not related, since it was expected that the creative person would be more open and would have a more positive regard for others. This finding implies that creativity and attitude should be considered in an additive rather than an interactive way in relationship to the counseling process.

[30] Neither creative ability nor positive attitude were related to the acceptance

of the counselee's feelings or his ideas, although this apparent lack of relationship stems from the fact that there was almost no counselor talk in these categories. Since almost all counseling theories stress the importance of acceptance of the counselee, it would seem that these counselors were not using these categories as much as might be desired. Is this an indication of lack of rapport with the disadvantaged counselee or is this the behavior of high school counselors in general? In any event, it points to the need for further training in this area for high school counselors working with the disadvantaged. While the wary nature of the disadvantaged counselee makes him timid about expressing his own feelings or ideas in a counseling interview, specific training of the counselor in the skills of reflecting or using these feelings and ideas when they are advanced by the counselee would do much toward moving the counseling sessions into more meaningful areas.

[31] Assuming that a more effective counseling relationship exists when the counselee is able to talk and express himself, the interview sessions sampled for this study reveal that these counselors were able, in general, to establish such a relationship with the disadvantaged counselee. Further research appears to be needed to determine the relationship between effective counseling and the ratio of counselor-counselee talk during the interview sessions.

[32] In conclusion, the results of this study indicate that the counselor with a strong positive attitude and with verbal fluency and flexibility is in a more favorable position in terms of establishing and maintaining conversation during the interview. When there is increased talk between counselor and disadvantaged counselee, there is a greater chance for true communication and subsequent growth of the counselee during the counseling experience. It is recommended that high school counselors who work with the disadvantaged be selected for their fluency, flexibility, and positive attitudes (in addition to other characteristics normally considered in the selection of counselors), or that special training be given to improve the verbal abilities and to modify attitudes.

REFERENCES

Amidon, E. A technique for analyzing counselor-counselee interaction. In J. F. Adams (Ed.), *Counseling and guidance: A summary view.* New York: Macmillan, 1965.

Cook, W. W., Leeds, C. H., and Callis, R. *Minnesota Teacher Attitude Inventory: Manual.* New York: The Psychological Corp., Undated.

MacKinnon, D. W. What do we mean by talent and how do we test for it? *The search for talent.* New York: College Entrance Examination Board, 1960.

Mednick, S. A., and Mednick, M. T. The associative basis of the creative process. (Cooperative Research Project No. 1073) Ann Arbor: University of Michigan, 1965.

Rogers, C. R. The necessary and sufficient conditions of therapeutic personality change. *Journal of Consulting Psychology,* 1957, **21,** 95–103.

Rogers, C. R. The characteristics of a helping relationship. *Personnel and Guidance Journal,* 1958, **37,** 6–16.

Rogers, C. R. The interpersonal relationship: The core of guidance. *Harvard Educational Review,* 1962, **32,** 416–439.

Taylor, C. W., and Holland, J. Predictors of creative performance. In C. W. Taylor (Ed.), *Creativity: Progress and potential.* New York: McGraw-Hill, 1964.

Torrance, E. P. *Guiding creative talent.* Englewood Cliffs, N.J.: Prentice-Hall, 1962.

Torrance, E. P. *Torrance Tests of Creative Thinking: Norms-technical manual.* Princeton, N.J.: Personnel Press, 1966.

The Cicirellis clearly stated that the criterion for determining whether the results supported the hypotheses was the existence of "significant correlations in the predicted direction" (paragraph 17). Unfortunately, the hypothesis regarding acceptance of the counselee's feelings could not be tested due to the very low incidence of this behavior (Table 1.3, paragraphs 21 and 22). The other hypotheses referred to categories 2 (praise, encouragement), 3 (accepts, uses ideas) and 8 and 9 (counselee talk, response and initiation). From all the correlations of these behaviors with the creativity and attitude scores, only one hypothesis was supported (Table 1.4); the significant correlation of .42 between praise and attitude (MTAI).

Relationships which were *not* hypothesized were also examined, specifically correlations between sequences of behavior and the counselor traits (Table 1.4). Previously (paragraph 8), the authors implied that they had formulated hypotheses regarding these relationships, but simply did not present them. The results would have been clearer if the authors had mentioned which hypotheses were supported by the correlations.

Consider how the results and conclusions would have changed if creativity had been measured only by the RAT. The results of the test of any hypothesis always depend heavily on the adequacy with which the variables are measured. With variables like creativity, the measurement of which has just begun, it was wise of the authors to avoid "putting all their eggs in one basket," and to use more than one test. No matter what the hypothesis, using more than one measure of each variable will enable the researcher to be more confident of conclusions.

Careful reading of this article is necessary in order to clearly distinguish the statements that reflect the hypotheses actually tested from those that go beyond the hypotheses. The tone of the article becomes more speculative in the concluding paragraphs (31 and 32) when the authors assumed that high amounts of praise, counselee talk, etc. created an effective counseling relationship. Because there was no direct support for these statements, other inferences can easily be drawn. Recommendations by researchers are usually even further removed from the data. In this case, the authors advised selection and/or training of counselors on the basis of such traits as creative fluency and flexibility. Do you think the data warranted such recommendations?

1.3.3 INDUCTIVE AND DEDUCTIVE REASONING (STEPS 1 AND 2)

As stated previously, researchers determine if there is enough support for their rationale through the process of induction. The conclusions or generalizations they derive from this evidence can usually be systematically organized into what is known as a *hypothetico-deductive system*. This is a logical system in which more comprehensive generalizations serve as premises for more specific generalizations. Research hypotheses are simply the logical consequences of the principles within the particular hypothetico-deductive system created by the researcher.

The power of such a deductive system derives from its logic of proof. A single piece of contrary evidence is sufficient to disprove or refute a hypothesis. On the other hand, one piece of positive evidence is not sufficient to prove a hypothesis. Even though a hypothesis could yield a true prediction, there are always other hypotheses that could produce the same prediction. For example, if a boy has chicken pox, it can be logically deduced that he will run a fever. But if a boy is running a fever, it cannot be logically inferred that he has chicken pox. When the research evidence does not contradict the hypothesis, the usual procedure is to say that the data tend to support, confirm, establish, or make it reasonable to accept the hypothesis, but *never* that it *proves* the hypothesis, since the hypothesis is not a logical consequence of the evidence.

In actual practice, scientists rarely follow exactly the hypothetico-deductive model, although it may be the goal they wish to achieve. A careful examination of the introductory sections of research reports will sometimes reveal an incomplete presentation of the scientist's reasoning. Little reference is usually made to *auxiliary assumptions* (i.e., assumptions regarding the nature of the research techniques). Yet explicit statements of all such assumptions are necessary in order to determine exactly what problem was investigated in a study. For example, a researcher may have initially believed that his or her creativity test really measured creativity. Later investigation indicated, however, that it measured persistence instead. Since an auxiliary assumption was false, the original hypotheses involving creativity were never tested.

1.3.4 THE EMPIRICAL TEST (STEP 2)

The process by which the research hypotheses are subjected to empirical test is described in the method section of a report. The procedures should be reported in sufficient detail so that another investigator could replicate the study. The characteristics of the participating subjects, how the subjects were selected, materials used by the subjects and experimenter, special equipment, the physical setting of the study, etc. all need to be described.

1.3.5 ANALYSES AND CONCLUSIONS (STEPS 3 AND 4)

Statistical tests are usually employed to determine whether the results coincide with the research hypothesis. Yet the final decision regarding whether the data support or do not support the research hypothesis involves more than the results of a statistical test. The underlying logic of the study and the research techniques also strongly influence this decision. As such, researchers often disagree on the specific conclusions that are justified by the study results.

STUDY PROBLEMS

1. Locate five studies in an area of interest to you.

a) In how many of these studies were research hypotheses stated? What was the primary justification for each hypothesis—previous research findings, theory, or logic? For each research hypothesis, determine whether the data supported or failed to support it. When a hypothesis was not supported, how did the researcher explain the result?

b) In how many studies were only problem statements/questions given? Rephrase each problem statement in terms of a research hypothesis.

2. Identify a teaching method or device that you are using in your classroom or one that has been recommended to you. Does the research literature justify its use?

3. Indicate whether each of the following statements is a problem statement, a research hypothesis, a result, a conclusion, or a recommendation.

a) Academic performance in high school is a better predictor of college performance for females than for males.

b) High schools should provide a remedial computer-assisted instruction course in reading for those students reading below the sixth grade level.

c) Nonverbal IQ scores had less stability than verbal IQ scores over a ten year period.

d) Students who have a high need for social affection and approval will prefer small group discussion courses to lecture courses.

e) The relationship between teaching experience and attitude toward labor unions will be examined.

f) Underlining is an effective way of improving recall and comprehension of text material.

g) Students who were highly anxious took longer to complete the test than did those who were not anxious.

4. A researcher hypothesized that girls are less likely to take four years of high school math than boys are because junior high counselors do not advise most girls to take that much math. The results supported his hypothesis (few girls took four years of math while most boys did). Do the data also support the researcher's explanation of this phenomenon? Why or why not?

2
Objectivity in Educational Research

One of the hallmarks of science, no matter what techniques are used, is objectivity. In some contexts, objectivity refers to the fact that several individuals agree that they have experienced the same event, although group consensus does not guarantee that truth has been attained. In other contexts, objectivity is achieved when events have been confirmed or are reliable, as when replications of studies are required before a finding is widely accepted by the scientific community. Objectivity can also be achieved by controlling for personal biases when hypotheses are tested.

Let us examine how this goal of objectivity affects the way scientific observations are made, how the need for objectivity leads to the use of operational definitions to define theoretical terms, and how the values of the researcher can influence the objectivity of the research process.

2.1 OBSERVATION

It is often assumed that observations are simply matters of fact; that everyone sees the same thing and therefore that observations are objective. However, "there is more to seeing than meets the eyeball" (69, p. 7). What one "sees" depends on one's past experience and knowledge. A microscopist sees very different things through a microscope from what an eighth grade student sees.

The observations made in a research study must meet certain criteria in order for the study to be methodologically acceptable. What is observed in one study must also be observed in subsequent studies even though the original observer is no longer present. In order to increase the likelihood that findings will be replicated, the researcher can *minimize errors in observation* with one of three general procedures (90).

First, the researcher may try to *insulate the observation,* to separate or isolate it from extraneous factors. Examples of this procedure include testing of questionnaires, controlling experimental settings for observations, and training of observers. In Hosie, Gentile, and Carroll's (79) study, special observation sessions and materials were used to determine the time children spent in painting, modeling clay, and writing reports. No interruptions were permitted during the observation period, and only materials relevant to the study were allowed in order that the timed observations would be uncontaminated by extraneous factors.

Second, in cases in which elimination of error is not feasible or possible, controls may be instituted to *cancel* error. For example, multiple observers may be used to cancel each other's biases. In Rubin's (121) study, judges classified research articles into one of three categories: (1) favorable to first-borns, (2) favorable to later-borns, and (3) equally favorable to first- and later-borns. In a deliberate effort to cancel any rating biases due to the birth order of the judges themselves, their birth order was systematically balanced, i.e., a first-born, a later-born, and a last-born judge were used.

Third, the researcher may attempt to *discount* error by considering the direction and extent of the error when examining the data. In the Jackson and Cosca (86) study (presented later in this chapter), the authors speculated on the possibility of distortion in the data and discussed how such error affected their conclusions. In brief, teachers were observed to differ in the way they interacted with Chicano and Anglo students. Classroom observers were from a civil rights agency. The authors concluded (paragraph 23) that

> there are two reasons to suspect that the actual average disparities in teacher's behaviors toward Chicano and Anglo students are even greater than observed in this study. First, most teachers knew the classroom observer was from a federal civil rights agency, a factor which probably influenced many of the teachers to be particularly careful about how they related to their minority group pupils during the period of observation. Second, the sample excluded schools in districts with records of federal investigation or prosecution for civil rights violations; on the average, these schools probably have somewhat worse disparities in teacher behaviors than those visited (p. 227).

In this case no precise estimates of the degree of potential error or bias in the observations were available. One possible way to obtain an estimate of the degree and direction of error would have been to observe a small sample of teachers over a longer time using observers who were not from a civil rights agency. A longer period would allow the teachers to adjust to the presence of an observer. Discrepancies between early and later observations and between civil rights and noncivil rights observers would provide estimates of potential error in the original data. Without such data you can easily disagree with the author's suggestion that error occurred and was in the conservative direction. In discounting error, researchers should attempt to directly measure its magnitude and adjust their results accordingly. Nevertheless, at the present, it is often difficult to obtain such estimates in educational research, and error is often discounted in a manner similar to that presented in the Jackson and Cosca study.

2.2 OPERATIONAL DEFINITIONS

Educational terms such as intelligence, creativity, a warm classroom atmosphere, the whole child, and punishment lack precise meaning. Such ambiguity

DUNAGIN'S PEOPLE   by Dunagin

DUNAGIN'S PEOPLE BY RALPH DUNAGIN, COURTESY OF FIELD NEWSPAPER SYNDICATE

"SURE I KNOW WHAT H²O MEANS __ TWO PARTS HYDROGEN AND ONE PART OIL."

must be reduced for scientific purposes, since findings cannot be replicated unless the meaning of a term remains constant from one study to the next, and agreement upon what is observed within a single study cannot be achieved until concepts are precisely defined. Operational definitions of terms reduce this ambiguity and thereby increase the objectivity of the study. In operational definitions, the precise *activities* or *operations* used by the researcher in measuring or manipulating each variable are specified.

A major variable in the Hosie, Gentile, and Carroll (79) study was preference for either painting or working with modeling clay. Preference was operationally defined as the time spent at these activities. However, preference was determined in slightly different ways in the two experiments that were conducted. Strictly speaking, since the operations used to define preference differed in the two experiments, the meaning of the term "preference" also differed. The operational definitions were as follows:

> In Experiment I each S was observed for two 20-minute sessions, while in Experiment II each S was observed for two 5-minute sessions. . . . As a result of these observations each S was classified as preferring either painting or modeling clay, depending upon which activity he or she spent more free time on, summed across both observation days. . . . Experiment II added the more stringent classification criterion that a S had to spend at least twice as much time in one activity as any other to be labeled as preferring one activity (pp. 242–243).

The two operational definitions differed in terms of total time allowed with the activities and in the time criterion used to determine whether one activity was preferred over another. Apparently the authors disregarded these differences and assumed that the meaning of preference was basically the same in both experiments.

Such assumptions are necessary and commonplace. Replications of studies would not be possible without such assumptions, for changes in even the time and place of measurement would create different concepts. One solution to this problem is to treat operational definitions as the same if they yield the same result (71).

2.3 VALUES

It is frequently assumed that science must be "value-free"; that the values of the scientist must be eliminated in order to avoid distortion and bias. But values cannot be eliminated from the research process because they play an essential role in the decisions a researcher must constantly make. When values bias the research process, then problems do arise. *Bias* occurs when values interfere with scientific objectivity; that is, when a proposition is accepted not on the basis of the evidence that supports it, but because it is in agreement with the research- er's personal beliefs and opinions. When bias cannot be eliminated, then it should be controlled, just as errors in observation are controlled. To clarify the relationship between values and bias in the research process, the following research stages are examined: selection of the problem for study, development of the study, and the assessment of evidence.

2.3.1 VALUES IN SELECTION OF THE PROBLEM

Selection refers not only to the initial choice of a problem to investigate, but also to the priorities scientists place on the problems they would like to inves- tigate, the resources they allocate for investigation, etc. Obviously, the interests and values of scientists play a role in such decisions. Yet the involvement of values in the problem selection stage does not mean that the scientific proce- dures of investigation will be contaminated or subject to bias.

2.3.2 VALUES IN DEVELOPMENT OF THE STUDY

Values influence scientists' decisions as they explore the problem in greater depth, attempt to determine the most fruitful way of examining it, and finally decide on a specific approach. At this point scientists are concerned with the way in which basic concepts are to be defined, the various hypotheses and theories that are considered, the choice of measuring instruments, weighing the pros and cons of data from previous research, determining which design will be most appropriate, etc. It is not necessarily the personal interests or desires of the scientists that enter at this stage, but values related to the methods of scientific inquiry. Scientists want to employ the most sensitive instruments and the best design in order to conduct an excellent study. However, every researcher needs to be constantly aware that many approaches are possible and might be as fruitful as the one that was chosen. It is the blindness to such alternatives and the failure to recognize their merits that constitute bias.

2.3.3 VALUES IN ASSESSMENT OF EVIDENCE

In assessing evidence scientists must determine the following: what the "facts" are, what statistical tests are appropriate, if the evidence is sound, the seriousness of a mistake in reaching one conclusion as opposed to another, etc. Crucial decisions are made when scientists determine the meaning of their data and what conclusions are warranted. Since no research hypothesis is ever completely verified and it is often difficult to determine which auxiliary hypotheses might be incorrect, scientists must evaluate their data. The recent national publicity and controversy surrounding some major educational studies (for example, the Westinghouse report on Head Start (30), Rosenthal and Jacobson's (120) investigation of teacher expectations, the Coleman (32) report on equality of educational opportunity, and Jensen's (87) review of the relative importance of heredity and environment in determining intelligence) underscore the impact of such decisions, although at the time the decisions are made, they may not seem so important to researchers.

Finally, researchers may make some general recommendations. At this point, they may also make some of their own values explicit. Two types of value judgments exist (110), those that *characterize* and those that *appraise*. Characterizing value judgments *describe* actions, objects, or individuals, while appraising value judgments express *approval or disapproval* of such phenomena. You can characterize someone as being a "good politician" without necessarily meaning that being a politician is good or desirable. A teacher can be characterized or described as one who frequently praises students without implying that praise is a desirable teaching technique. The ambiguities of the English language often make it difficult to distinguish between these two value statements. Many terms in educational research could be used in both appraising and characterizing statements. Consider, for example, the following phrases: gifted, retarded, bureaucracy, abnormal, authoritarian, gain in achievement, inequality, and creativity.

Bias can creep into appraisal statements. Should appraisals therefore be eliminated from scientific reports? No, but it should always be clear to the readers and to the scientists themselves when they switch hats; when they change from describer/characterizer to evaluator/appraiser. The following study by Jackson and Cosca shows the interplay between scientists' values and the research process.

The Inequality of Educational Opportunity in the Southwest:
An Observational Study of Ethnically Mixed Classrooms
GREGG JACKSON
CECILIA COSCA

[1] Civil rights activities have long put heavy emphasis on achieving equal opportunity in education. Frequent studies of educational opportunity have repeatedly shown that in many school districts, minority group children attend school in older, less well maintained facilities, and have less equipment, older materials, and less educated and experienced teachers than majority group children (Guthrie, 1971). But the quality of educational opportunity is probably most importantly affected *by what actually happens* in the school setting; the instruction, guidance, and encouragement provided to the students would seem to be of essential importance to the quality of educational opportunity. A comprehensive review of studies focusing on educational opportunities does not include a single study which has assessed educational opportunities arising from the classroom teaching process (Guthrie, 1971). This is partly due to the fact that assessing the teaching processes is a much more difficult and expensive task than assessing school facilities, materials, and qualifications of teachers. However, it is also partly due to the impression that the amount of training and experience of a teacher determines the quality of the teaching process. Unfortunately, education research has failed to find strong relations between these or other teacher status characteristics, and teacher effectiveness. Consequently, in order to assess fully the quality of educational opportunity afforded different groups of students, it has become imperative to study directly the actual classroom instructional processes.

[2] The objective assessment of the teaching process has been a small but growing area in educational research over the last decade. In this research, teaching is conceptualized as a series of actions and reactions by both the instructor and students. Systematic analysis of these behaviors is frequently known as "interaction analysis." During the last decade hundreds of classroom interaction studies have been conducted; however, a review of the research indicates that there have been only a very few studies which compared teacher-pupil interactions among students of different ethnic groups. Those studies which could be located are of little use for broad generalizations because of their very small, nonrandom samples (Biddle and Loflin, 1971; Brophy and Good, 1971; Powell and White, 1970).

[3] The present study was specifically designed to help remedy the dearth of data on possible ethnic disparities in classroom behaviors. It focused particularly on possible disparities between Mexican American and Anglo pupils. Data were collected on blacks and students of other ethnic groups as well, but the number of these students included in the sample proved inadequate for statistical analysis.

Gregg Jackson and Cecilia Cosca, 1974. The inequality of educational opportunity in the Southwest: an observational study of ethnically mixed classrooms. *American Educational Research Journal 11* (3):219–229. Copyright 1974, American Educational Research Association, Washington, D.C. Reprinted with permission.

[4] Mexican Americans, also referred to as Chicanos, are the second largest minority group in the U.S. They constitute about 3 percent of the U.S. population and 18 percent of the public school enrollment in the five Southwestern states (Arizona, California, Colorado, New Mexico and Texas). The term "Anglo" is used in the Southwest to refer to white persons who are not of Spanish-speaking background.

Jackson and Cosca's introductory statements and the fact that they were employed by the U.S. Commission on Civil Rights both reflect an interest in and commitment to equality of educational opportunity. However, the existence of such a value does not mean that their research techniques were biased or that the data were distorted.

METHOD

Sample

[5] Classroom observation was conducted in three states. Within each state, limited geographical areas were selected that included rural, urban, and suburban schools with substantial numbers of Mexican American students. The areas selected were: Santa Clara County including the city of San Jose (California); the metropolitan areas of San Antonio and Corpus Christi, the area between these two population centers, and the area 30 miles south of Corpus Christi (Texas); and the Albuquerque area and the south central part of New Mexico.

[6] All schools in these areas were considered eligible to be sampled except (1) special schools (such as those for the handicapped), (2) schools not likely to have at least two classes at each grade level, or (3) schools in districts which had recently been or were about to be investigated by federal civil rights agencies or subject to court orders for civil rights violations. Fifty-two schools were randomly sampled from the 430 eligible schools in the selected areas.

[7] The classrooms were sampled from all the 4th, 8th, 10th, and 12th grade classes in which English language arts were being taught. Where English classes were not taught at the desired grade levels, social studies classes were sampled. Complete data were available for 429 visited classrooms.

[8] District superintendents and principals were requested to allow staff members of the U.S. Commission on Civil Rights to visit the school, interview school personnel, and observe classrooms. No superintendent or principal refused access to a school, and no teacher refused to be observed in her or his classroom. In most cases the teachers had been informed by the principal that they would be visited by federal civil rights staff.

[9] Efforts were made to assign all observers equal proportions of Spanish surnamed and Anglo teachers, male and female teachers, classrooms of varying track characteristics (untracked, and low, medium, or high tracked), and classrooms at each grade level observed. The only other information known when assigning observers to classes was the time and room number of the class and the name of the teacher. Chi-square tests indicate no significant differences in the assignment of observers to those characteristics of observed teachers and classrooms.

Data Collection

[10] The Flanders Interaction Analysis system was used to code teacher-pupil interactions. The Flanders system codes the predominant verbal classroom behavior once every three seconds according to the most appropriate of ten categories. There are seven categories of teacher behavior: accepts students' feelings, praises or encourages, accepts or uses ideas of students, asks questions, lectures, gives directions, and criticizes or justifies authority. The other three categories are: student response talk, student initiated talk, and silence or confusion (Flanders, 1970).

[11] The Flanders system is normally used to code behaviors without reference to whether they involve individual pupils or a group of pupils. The coding procedure was modified for this study so as to distinguish among behaviors associated with individual students of various different ethnic groups. Behaviors directed to or from the whole class or a subgroup of the class were also coded, but are not discussed in this report.

[12] Five persons were used as observers. They were given four days of intensive training by a researcher experienced with the use of the Flanders coding system. Before starting the data collection, all five observers were checked for their coding reliability with the trainers own coding of actual classrooms. The reliabilities using the Scott's Pi Coefficient exceeded .85 except in one case (.78) which the trainer thought involved a class session that was particularly difficult to code. The observers were twice checked in the same manner during the course of data collection; their reliabilities were somewhat higher in these checks than in the first one.

[13] Possible differences in the actual coding practices of observers when they were in the field were examined on a post hoc basis. Each of the twelve measures used as criteria in the analyses of possible disparities in classroom interaction was tested in a one-way analysis of variance using the observers' identity as the classifying factor. There was a significant difference between coders on only one behavior, praise and encouragement. Contrasts using Dunn's method showed that the difference was significant only between the observer who coded the disparity as being most unfavorable for Mexican Americans and the observer who coded the disparity as being least unfavorable for Mexican Americans.

[14] Classroom observers spent about 45 minutes in each class. They would temporarily stop coding when the teacher and students were not interacting, such as when students were doing assigned work at their desks, handing in papers, or watching a film. A total of ten minutes of coding was done for each classroom. This ten-minute segment of a classroom's instructional process is not considered to be representative of the instructional process in any individual class. However, a sample of ten-minute observations from a large number of classrooms is likely to be representative of the interactions of classrooms in the sampled universe.

[15] Classroom observers also collected information on a number of characteristics of teachers and classrooms. Other data on several characteristics of the visited schools were also collected. There was a total of 22 such characteristics. They are listed in Table 2.1.

The method section of any report is written in a straightforward manner that conceals the multitude of decisions the researcher makes when selecting

---

TABLE 2.1   *TEACHER, CLASSROOM, AND SCHOOL CHARACTERISTICS*

School characteristics
1. Mexican American percentage of school enrollment
2. Anglo percentage of school enrollment
3. Degree of ethnic concentration within school (measured by the variance of the Anglo percent composition of the classroom)[a]
4. Average socio-economic status (SES) of Mexican Americans in the school (principal's estimate)
5. Average SES of Anglos in the school (principal's estimate)
6. Difference in Mexican American and Anglo SES
7. Average SES of the school (weighted average of Mexican American and Anglo SES)
8. State in which school is located

Classroom characteristics
9. Grade level of class
10. Track level of class (as reported by teacher)[b]
11. Subject matter of course
12. Criteria used to seat students (as reported by the teacher)[c]
13. Seating priority index of Mexican Americans in the classroom (based on observed seating positions)[d]
14. Seating priority index of Anglos in the classroom (based on observed seating positions)[d]
15. Mexican American percentage of enrollment in the class
16. Anglo percentage of enrollment in the class
17. Total number of students in the class

Teacher characteristics
18. Extent of teacher's formal education
19. Teacher attendance at any inservice training sessions related to teaching Mexican Americans (as reported by the teacher)
20. Teacher's ethnicity
21. Teacher's age
22. Teacher's sex

---

[a] This indicates the extent to which Anglo and minority students in a given school are separated into different classrooms.
[b] Tracking is the practice of assigning students to classrooms so as to make class enrollments more homogeneous in respect to some purported measure of the students' ability or performance.
[c] Seating criteria were divided into five categories: student choice, student choice with teacher modification (teacher modification was usually to correct discipline problems), alphabetical order, homogeneous "ability" grouping, and other methods of teacher choice.
[d] The seating priority index indicates how close, on the average, students of a given ethnic group were to the teacher's primary location for the period of coded interaction.

specific procedures. The following questions can be asked regarding Jackson and Cosca's decisions:

1. Why were the three states of California, Texas, and New Mexico selected (paragraph 5)? Why not Arizona?
2. Why were specific types of schools eliminated (paragraph 6)?
3. Why were two classes at each grade level required (paragraph 6)?
4. Why were 52 schools chosen from the 430 eligible schools (paragraph 6)? Did this size give the desired statistical precision? Was it determined by the desired statistical precision? Was it determined by the money that was available?

5. Why were grades 4, 8, 10, and 12 selected (paragraph 7)? The selection criterion appeared to be every other grade level. Why were grades 2 and 6 not included?
6. Why were English language arts classes chosen (paragraph 7)? Were English teachers assumed to be representative of all other teachers or were they assumed to be different on some important dimension? Were English classes chosen because of the verbal nature of the Flanders observation scheme? Were both ethnic groups of students more likely to be found in English than in other classes?
7. Why were social studies classes the substitute for English classes (paragraph 7)?
8. Why was the Flanders observation system chosen from among the many other systems in existence (paragraph 10)? Was it because it is well known, because it focuses on the verbal behavior of teachers, and/or because some normative data are available at different grade levels?

Such "why" questions are practically endless and they usually cannot be answered in the limited space of a journal report. Yet each time a decision is made, the researcher employs some criterion. That criterion may be based upon principles of experimental design, sampling theory, measurement theory, previous research, or may simply reflect the researcher's guess about what technique is most appropriate. The criterion may be totally different from the one that the reader thinks to be the case, and without additional information it is extremely difficult to determine if bias has occurred.

Data Preparation and Analyses

[16] The raw data from the Flanders interaction coding was modified in five ways to allow for sensitive analysis of possible disparities among students of different ethnic groups. First, the measures were corrected for variation in the total number of tallies made for each observed classroom. Observers were supposed to make one tally every three seconds for a period of ten minutes, but for a number of reasons not all observation sessions resulted in exactly 200 tallies. This was corrected by multiplying each tally for a given classroom by 200/total number of tallies for the observation of that class. Second, category 10 of the Flanders system was dropped from the analysis (because it was always coded in reference to "part or all of the class," not in reference to student ethnicity), and three compound categories of behavior were constructed from the other Flanders categories (listed as categories 10 through 12 in Table 2.2). Third, the Mexican American interaction measures and the Anglo interaction measures for each class were converted to average per pupil measures by dividing the total number of tallies for each interaction behavior for each ethnic group by the number of students of that ethnicity in that class. This was necessary because different classrooms had different numbers of Mexican Americans and Anglos. Fourth, the Mexican American and Anglo per pupil measures were corrected for each class size. The total number of tallies would not be affected by class size, but per pupil measures would be. This is because teachers have a relatively fixed amount of time to interact with individual students, and thus the more students there are in the class, the less time the teacher will have to interact with each one. The pur-

pose of controlling for class size is not to deny its importance, but rather to control its pervasive impact on the per pupil measures. The correction for class size was made by multiplying each per pupil interaction measure by (class size/25). Lastly, difference scores were constructed for each classroom from each of the 12 per pupil measures for Mexican Americans and the corresponding per pupil measures for Anglos.

[17] The major question for analysis was whether or not Mexican American and Anglo students were equally often involved in each category of interaction. This was tested using the difference scores for 12 matched-sample t tests, one for each category of interaction. It was also of interest to know if the significant disparities in teacher-pupil interaction involving Anglo and Chicano pupils varied across levels or categories of the 22 teacher, classroom, and school characteristics. This was examined by one-way analysis of variance tests. All hypotheses were tested at the .01 level of significance.

RESULTS AND DISCUSSION

[18] Six of the 12 measures of interaction showed substantial and statistically significant differences between Chicano and Anglo students. These differences were for teacher praise or encouragement of students, teacher acceptance or use of students' ideas, teacher questioning, the teachers' giving of positive feedback, all noncriticizing teacher talk, and all student speaking. The results are shown in Table 2.2.

TABLE 2.2   AVERAGE FREQUENCY OF CODED BEHAVIORS ASSOCIATED WITH
AVERAGE INDIVIDUAL MEXICAN AMERICAN AND
AVERAGE INDIVIDUAL ANGLO STUDENTS[a]

Teacher and student behaviors	Average Mexican American student	Average Anglo student	t value
1. Teacher acceptance of students' feelings	.004	.008	1.73
2. Teacher praising or encouraging students	.137	.186	2.95*
3. Teacher acceptance or use of students' ideas	.156	.219	3.32*
4. Teacher questioning	.525	.636	2.41*
5. Teacher lecturing	.584	.710	1.87
6. Teacher giving of directions	.146	.141	.20
7. Teacher criticizing or justifying authority	.055	.052	.37
8. Student response speaking	.771	.948	1.99
9. Student initiated speaking	.796	1.034	1.66
10. Teacher giving of positive feedback	.296	.413	3.73*
11. All noncriticizing teacher talk	1.551	1.901	2.99*
12. All student speaking	1.567	1.982	2.45*

[a] The values in the first two columns represent the number of times during a ten-minute period that the average individual student of the indicated ethnicity was coded as involved in the specified interaction; coding was done at a fixed rate of 20 times per minute.
* t is statistically significant at .01 level for a one-tail test with 428 degrees of freedom when equal to or greater than 2.326. The one-tail test was used because prior to seeing the data the authors had hypothesized that all measures except the teacher's giving of directions and teacher criticizing would be greater for Anglos than for Mexican Americans.

TABLE 2.3 *AMOUNT OF PRAISE OR ENCOURAGEMENT GIVEN PER PUPIL TO INDIVIDUAL MEXICAN AMERICAN AND ANGLO STUDENTS, BY TEACHERS USING THE SPECIFIED CRITERIA FOR ASSIGNMENTS OF SEATS AND BY TEACHERS OF SPECIFIED ETHNICITY*

	Chicano students	Anglo students	Disparity
Criteria for assignment of seats			
Teacher choice	.179	.198	+.019
Alphabetical	.161	.183	+.022
Homogeneous by ability	.121	.559	+.438
Student choice	.125	.179	+.054
Student choice with teacher modification	.110	.103	−.007
Teacher ethnicity			
Mexican American teachers	.136	.326	+.190
Anglo teachers	.138	.172	+.034

[19] Only three of the significant disparities in teacher-pupil interactions involving Chicano and Anglo students varied significantly across any of the 22 investigated characteristics of schools, classroom, and teachers. The disparities in the amount of praise or encouragement given to Chicano and Anglo students varied significantly across categories of student seating assignment criteria and teacher ethnicity. The disparities in the amount of acceptance or use of students' ideas varied significantly across levels of ethnic concentration within the school. And the disparities in the amount of all positive feedback given to Chicano and Anglo students varied between categories of student seating assignment criteria and levels of ethnic concentration within the school. The mean values for these significant differences are shown in Tables 2.3 through 2.5. Caution should be used when relying on these latter five statistically significant results. They came from 132 hypotheses (six behaviors times 22 characteristics) tested at the .01 level, therefore, one or two of the results probably is a type I error rather than an indication of a real difference in the population.

TABLE 2.4 *AVERAGE AMOUNT OF ACCEPTANCE AND USE OF STUDENT IDEAS GIVEN PER PUPIL TO INDIVIDUAL MEXICAN AMERICAN AND ANGLO STUDENTS, BY TEACHERS IN SCHOOLS WITH VARIOUS DEGREES OF ETHNIC CONCENTRATION*[a]

	Chicano students	Anglo students	Disparity
Degree of ethnic concentration			
Low	.140	.327	+.187
Medium	.177	.189	+.012
High	.145	.188	+.043

[a] The degree of ethnic concentration within the school represents the extent to which there is variation in the ethnic composition of classrooms within a school. In low ethnic concentration schools, Anglo students appear to be distributed evenly among the classrooms. In high ethnic concentration schools, Anglos and non-Anglos are assigned to different classes.

TABLE 2.5   *AVERAGE AMOUNT OF POSITIVE FEEDBACK GIVEN PER PUPIL TO INDIVIDUAL MEXICAN AMERICAN AND ANGLO STUDENTS, BY TEACHERS USING THE SPECIFIED CRITERIA FOR ASSIGNMENT OF SEATS AND BY TEACHERS IN SCHOOLS WITH VARIOUS DEGREES OF ETHNIC CONCENTRATION*

	Chicano students	*Anglo students*	*Disparity*
Criteria for assignment of seats			
Teacher choice	.318	.422	+.104
Alphabetical	.335	.375	+.040
Homogeneous by ability	.308	1.062	+.754
Student choice	.284	.391	+.107
Student choice with teacher modification	.284	.380	+.096
Degree of ethnic concentration			
Low	.280	.569	+.289
Medium	.350	.362	+.012
High	.255	.374	+.119

[20] A decade of research has investigated the relationships between teacher behaviors and gains in student achievement. Rosenshine has conducted the most comprehensive review of classroom interaction studies. He has found the results of these studies to be somewhat inconsistent but, of all the behaviors examined, certain forms of praise, the acceptance and use of student ideas, and questioning of students were most strongly and consistently related to student gains in achievement (Rosenshine, 1971).

[21] Rosenshine is hesitant to conclude that these behaviors *generally* have a positive relationship to student gains because only half of the reviewed studies showed statistically significant positive differences. His hesitancy, however, is based on an invalid procedure for drawing inferences from a set of findings from different studies. For inferences to be validly based directly on the relative frequency of a given statistically significant finding across replicated studies, the studies must have approximately equivalent probabilities of finding significant results when differences actually exist (statistical power). Unfortunately, it is not possible to estimate the relative power of the studies from the data Rosenshine provides in his reviews. Nor would the original reports of the studies provide the needed data, because statistical power in classroom interaction studies is importantly influenced by intercoder reliability *under actual field conditions* and few researchers have made an effort to assess this. Without information on the relative power of the reviewed studies, it is impossible to know if the nonsignificant findings are a result of the treatment variable having varying degrees of impact under different scope conditions or a result of the studies differing in their statistical power. Consequently, the consistency of the relationships between these teaching behaviors and student achievement is best judged at this time by the ratio of positive findings to negative ones. Rosenshine indicates the direction of only the statistically significant findings; for the three behaviors together there have been 33 significant positive findings and only one significant negative finding. Thus, the available evidence shows great consistency in the relationship between student achievement and teachers' behaviors involving certain forms of praise, the acceptance and use of students' ideas, and the questioning of pupils.

[22] This study found large and significant disparities in all three of these be-haviors. Teachers praised or encouraged Anglos 35% more than they did Chi-canos, accepted or used Anglo's ideas 40% more than they did those of Chicanos, and directed 21% more questions to Anglos than to Chicanos. Thus, Chicanos in the Southwest receive substantially less of those types of teacher behavior pres-ently known to be most strongly related to gains in student achievement.

[23] There are two reasons to suspect that the actual average disparities in teachers' behavior toward Chicano and Anglo students are even greater than ob-served in this study. First, most teachers knew the classroom observer was from a federal civil rights agency, a factor which probably influenced many of the teachers to be particularly careful about how they related to their minority group pupils during the period of observation. Second, the sample excluded schools in districts with records of federal investigation or prosecution for civil rights viola-tions; on the average, these schools probably have somewhat worse disparities in teacher behaviors than those visited.

[24] In addition, there is reason to think that the disparities in teacher behaviors which were found in this study have more effect on student achievement than is suggested by previous research. Most previous research has analyzed the relation between interaction data coded for the whole class and the classrooms' average gains in student achievement. In contrast, this study investigated disparities in teacher behaviors between different groups of students within the same class-room. Because disparities within classrooms are more visible to students than dis-parities among classrooms, they probably have more impact on students' motiva-tion and achievement.

[25] The average school achievement of Mexican Americans is substantially be-low that of Anglos in the Southwest. The proportion of Chicano students reading below grade level is approximately twice that of Anglos. Furthermore, 40% of Chicanos, as compared to only 15% of Anglos, fail to complete high school (U.S. Commission on Civil Rights, 1971). This study cannot prove whether the dis-covered disparities in teacher behaviors are a cause of these disparities in stu-dent achievement. But three factors, the previously discussed research on teacher behaviors and student achievement, the magnitude of the discovered disparities in teacher behaviors, and the discussions in the above two paragraphs, together suggest that the behaviors of teachers in the Southwest are at least partly con-tributing to the poor academic achievement of many Chicano students.

[26] It can be conjectured that the poor academic performance of many Chicanos in turn influences the disparities in teachers' behaviors. This may be true to a limited extent, but the data clearly demonstrate that these disparities are not the *inevitable* result of differences in the academic performance levels of Chicano and Anglo students. Pupils who are having academic difficulties may offer the teacher fewer than normal opportunities for praise, but they need more than the normal amount of encouragement; yet the data show that teachers gave Anglos 35% more praise and encouragement (coded as one behavior category) than they gave to Chicanos. In addition, teacher's questioning of a student *need* not be dependent on the pupil's achievement, yet teachers directed 21% more ques-tions to the average Anglo pupil than to the average Chicano pupil.

[27] It seems likely that at least four other factors, together, are contributing to both the disparities in teacher behaviors and the generally poor academic per-formance of Chicano pupils. They are: (1) the linguistic and cultural differences

of Chicano pupils, (2) the lack of school programs in the Southwest to accommodate these differences (U.S. Commission on Civil Rights, 1972), (3) the tendency of teachers to respond differently to identical behaviors by students of different racial, SES, or achievement characteristics (Brophy and Good, 1969; Good, Brophy, and Mendosa, 1970), and (4) the failure of teacher training institutions in the Southwest to provide course work and supervised experiences specifically designed to prepare prospective teachers to instruct Chicano pupils (U.S. Commission on Civil Rights, 1974). Further research will be needed to verify the actual extent to which these factors and others influence the disparities in teachers' behaviors and the disparities in student achievement.

[28] This study, however, provides clear evidence that teachers in the Southwest behave differently toward Chicano and Anglo pupils. This finding, together with previous research on the effects of teacher behaviors, suggests that the instructional processes in the classrooms of the Southwest must be changed if Mexican American youth are to be afforded educational opportunities equal to those available to Anglo students. The finding also raises an important question of whether similar inequities in the classroom instructional process exist for other minority group children throughout this nation's schools.

REFERENCES

Biddle, B., and Loflin, M. Verbal behavior in black/ghetto and white/suburban classrooms: An overview. Paper presented at the meeting of the. American Educational Research Association, New York, February 1971.

Brophy, J. E., and Good, T. L. Teachers' communication of differential expectations for children's classroom performance: Some behavioral data. (Report series No. 25) Austin, Texas: Research and Development Center for Teacher Education, University of Texas, 1969.

Brophy, J. E., and Good, T. L. Dyadic teacher-child interaction: Variation across social class and racial groups. Paper presented at the meeting of the American Educational Research Association, New York, February 1971.

Flanders, N. A. *Analyzing teaching behavior.* Reading, Mass.: Addison-Wesley, 1970.

Good, T. L., Brophy, J. E., and Mendosa, S. Who talks in the classroom. Austin, Texas: Research and Development Center for Teacher Education, University of Texas, 1970.

Guthrie, J. W., Kleindorfer, G., Levin, H., and Stout, R. *Schools and inequality.* Cambridge, Mass.: M.I.T. Press, 1971.

Powell, E. R., and White, W. Learning climate correlates in black and white rural schools. Athens, Georgia: Research and Development Center in Educational Stimulation, University of Georgia, 1970.

Rosenshine, B. Teaching behavior related to pupil achievement: Review of research. In I. Westbury and A. A. Bellack (eds.), *Research into classroom processes: Recent developments and next steps.* New York: Teachers College Press, 1971, pp. 51–98.

U. S. Commission on Civil Rights. *The unfinished education.* (Report II of the Mexican American Education Study) Washington, D.C.: U. S. Government Printing Office, 1971.

U. S. Commission on Civil Rights. *The excluded student.* (Report III of the Mexican American Education Study) Washington, D.C.: U. S. Government Printing Office, 1972.

U. S. Commission on Civil Rights. *Toward quality education for Mexican Americans.* (Report VI of the Mexican American Education Study) Washington, D.C.: U. S. Government Printing Office, 1974.

In the results and discussion section, Jackson and Cosca described the results, weighed their strength, and finally discussed their impact and possible implications for education in the Southwest. Despite some significant differences that occurred when certain characteristics of the sample were examined (paragraph 19), the authors decided that such complex differences could have been the result of chance fluctuations in their data and did not discuss these particular results further. However, the results presented in paragraph 18 were considered to be other than chance and were discussed at length. Would all researchers agree with these two decisions regarding the strength of the evidence? Probably not, and it is at this point that researchers' interests, previous background and training influence what they say about their results.

The arguments and information presented in the remaining paragraphs (20–28) are devoted to supporting the conclusion that the observed differences were important enough to recommend that the "instructional processes in the classrooms of the Southwest must be changed if Mexican American youths are to be afforded educational opportunities equal to those available to Anglo students" (paragraph 28). This statement is an appraising value judgment because it implies that the instructional processes were deficient enough to create educational inequalities, and such inequalities were undesirable. Does this conclusion follow from the study? Does it reflect the authors' preconceived determination of the results and is it therefore bias? The answers to these questions are not indicated in the article, but the questions should be raised by the reader.

In paragraph 21, the authors conclude that "the available evidence shows great consistency in the relationship between student achievement and teachers' behaviors involving certain forms of praise, the acceptance and use of students' ideas, and the questioning of pupils." Is the use of the term "great" descriptive or evaluative? Does it simply state that a ratio of 33 positive findings to one negative finding can be described as high or large, or does it indicate a judgment that such consistency is of considerable importance and is worthy of notice?

Let us examine some other statements. In paragraph 22, the authors conclude that "Chicanos in the Southwest receive substantially less of those types of teacher behaviors." Does "substantially" simply characterize or describe the 35 percent more praise, the 40 percent more acceptance of ideas, and the 21 percent more questions that the Anglos received? Or does it indicate an evaluation of the practical importance of such discrepancies and that receiving fewer of these teacher behaviors was bad? What are the implications of using the phrase "disparities in teacher behavior" (paragraphs 23 and 24) as opposed to the more neutral phrase "differences in teacher behavior"? Why did the authors suggest that the differences in teacher behavior may actually be greater than that observed and that the impact of such behavior within classrooms may be stronger than indicated by other studies? Additional statements could be examined, but these illustrations should alert the reader to the types of questions that should be raised when critiquing research reports.

Appraisal or evaluative statements should not be omitted from the discussion sections of research reports because such judgments are important. Yet in any discussion section, the reader needs to be conscious of when the author's statements may be appraisals rather than descriptions. Explicit statements of the author's values would help readers to identify possible bias in such appraisals.

2.4 MORAL VERSUS SCIENTIFIC QUESTIONS

Another major value issue remains: can moral or ethical questions also be scientific questions? Can science answer such problems as: Should the school system adopt textbook A? Should more elementary teachers be men? and should physical punishment be prohibited in the schools? The prevailing point of view (90, 92, 144) is that such problems are beyond the scope of direct scientific inquiry because "an empirical science cannot tell anyone what he *should* do—but rather what *he can do*" (144, p. 508). Any recommendations made by educational researchers are based not only on research findings but also on their philosophy of education and their personal values.

2.5 QUESTIONS TO ASK WHEN ANALYZING RESEARCH ARTICLES

When reading research articles, the reader must make a careful analysis of the underlying logic, the research procedures, and the conclusions. The questions in Exhibit 2.1 reflect the major points discussed in Chapters 1 and 2 and should be posed by the reader in an initial critique of an article.

STUDY PROBLEMS

1. Suppose Jackson and Cosca had hypothesized that: (1) teachers would allow Anglo students to speak more than Mexican-American students, and (2) teachers would praise the Anglo students more than the Mexican-American students. Develop a rationale or explanation for each of these hypotheses; that is, why such hypotheses might be made.

2. What were the major variables in the Jackson and Cosca study? How were they defined? Were the labels for the Flanders categories sufficient to clarify what was observed, or did you feel a need to refer to the original description of the observation system for clarification?

EXHIBIT 2.1   *ANALYSIS OF RESEARCH ARTICLES*

A. What was the specific *problem being investigated?* State it in your own words. See if you can describe clearly the purpose to another person.

B. Were the origins of the problem presented? If so, summarize the *rationale for the study.* Were there inconsistencies in the author's rationale? What *research hypotheses* were made? What was the primary justification for each hypothesis— previous research findings, theory, or logic? Specify the major auxiliary assumptions made by the researcher.

C. Identify the *operational definitions of the major variables.* Did these definitions stand on their own, or did they assume some prior knowledge on your part, e.g., that you had read related literature or had examined the tests in use? If the definitions assumed prior knowledge, then you may find it necessary to study additional material in order to understand and to adequately critique the article.

D. Did the *research methods* actually test the problem or the hypothesis specified?

E. What *controls* were instituted to *minimize errors in observation?* Did the controls insulate, cancel, or discount error?

F. Did the *data* support the research hypotheses? When a hypothesis was not supported, how did the researcher explain the result?

G. At what points did the *author's values* influence the study? Did the author present a complete and unbiased review of related literature? Which decisions made by the researcher probably reflected methodological concerns rather than personal values or interests? What *appraisal statements* were made? Did the data support these appraisals?

---

3. Construct two operational definitions for each of the following concepts:

discovery learning	leadership
achievement in algebra	student attention to subject matter
creative students	authoritarian teacher
conformity	authoritarian principal

4. What types of observation error might occur in administering individualized intelligence tests to the Mexican-American and Anglo students in the Jackson and Cosca study? What specific techniques could be used to control each error? Classify each control technique as an attempt to either discount, insulate, or cancel error.

5. Locate a study of interest to you and identify all the instances in which the researcher had to decide what specific research techniques to employ.

a) Did any of these techniques introduce bias?

b) Identify all possible appraisal statements. Rewrite each of the appraisal statements in the form of a descriptive or characterizing statement.

PART II

Technical Concepts and Procedures Used in Conducting Research

As you have probably already discovered in reading the research articles in Part I, researchers have a technical language of their own. Phrases such as the following are examples of this language: "since the data were ordinal, the Spearman rank order correlation coeffient was applied," "the test-retest reliability coefficient was .78," "significant differences were found among the four treatments (F (3,76) = 10.51, p < .01)," and "study participants were randomly selected from ten psychology classes." Such terms and concepts are most evident in the Method and Results sections of research reports. Your ability to understand and evaluate an entire study is greatly dependent on your ability to understand the Method and Results Sections.

Most of the technical concepts used by researchers come from the areas of measurement, sampling, and statistics. The information in Part II should help you understand some of the basic concepts in each of these areas. The chapters which focus on each of these areas are as follows:

Measurement
    Scale of Measurement—Chapter 3
    Reliability of Measurement—Chapter 8
    Validity of Measurement—Chapter 9
Sampling—*Chapter 6*

Statistics
> Descriptive Statistics (one variable)—
> Chapter 4
> Descriptive Statistics (two variables)—
> Chapter 5
> Inferential Statistics—Chapter 7

The chapters have been sequenced according to the relationships among the concepts in these areas. It is recommended that you examine the chapters in sequence. (However, Chapters 8 and 9 on reliability and validity can be read after Chapter 5, and Chapter 6 on sampling can be read before Chapters 3, 4, and 5). Dependencies among the chapters are given in Fig. II.1. Note that the concepts in Chapter 7 on inferential statistics are dependent on information in all the previous chapters.

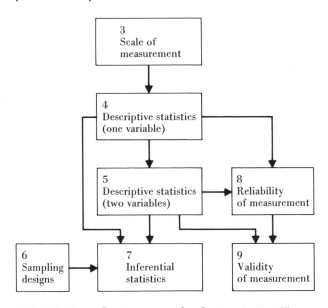

FIG. II.1 Dependencies among the chapters in Part II.

Specific concepts *that* must *be understood in a particular chapter before proceeding to later chapters are noted at the beginning of the appropriate chapters. Quizzes are inserted periodically within the chapters so you can check your mastery of the concepts.*

3

The Level or Scale
of Measurement [1]

Once investigators have clearly identified the variables they propose to study, they must "measure" each one. Measurement to the layperson means measuring the distance between cities, the height of individuals, the weight of an automobile, or the body temperature of a hospital patient. What is measured is not the object itself, but a property or attribute of that object (89); that is, the weight or length of an automobile is measured, not the automobile itself. This measurement process assumes that a *unit* of measurement exists, e.g., pounds, miles, centimeters, and that the measured variables are *quantifiable;* that differences in the property being measured reflect differences in amount, magnitude, or quantity.

However, many variables of interest to educational and social science researchers either cannot be quantified (that is, they are *qualitative*), or are *semiquantifiable.* Examples of qualitative variables are sex, college major, and occupation. Examples of semiquantifiable variables are intelligence, achievement in English, attitude toward school, and interest in a specific occupation.

To distinguish among the types of measurement appropriate for variables common in the behavioral sciences, Stevens (137) proposed four scales or levels of measurement: nominal, ordinal, interval, and ratio. The numbers associated with each of these scales have different meanings, as illustrated below.

3.1 NOMINAL SCALES OR CLASSIFICATION

At the nominal level, variations in the attribute being measured are classified into distinct categories. The simplest instance is dichotomous classification (voting for or against an issue, male/female). More complex classifications involve more than two categories and ordered categories.

At this lowest level of measurement, the "measurement" process requires

---

[1] The concepts in this chapter must be mastered before progressing to Chapters 4 and 5 on descriptive statistics.

DUNAGIN'S PEOPLE

DUNAGIN'S PEOPLE BY RALPH DUNAGIN, COURTESY OF FIELD NEWSPAPER SYNDICATE

"WE'VE ARRANGED THE BEST-SELLERS INTO THREE CATEGORIES... LEGISLATIVE, JUDICIAL, AND EXECUTIVE."

clear definition of each category so that *each* individual or object is placed in *only one* classification. In other words, the categories must be *mutually exclusive*. The following categories of high school teachers (physical science, English, foreign language, chemistry, and Spanish) are not mutually exclusive because a chemistry teacher can be classified under both the physical science and chemistry categories and a Spanish teacher as either a foreign language teacher or a Spanish teacher. In addition, the categories must be *exhaustive*, so that *all* cases can be classified. The previous categories are not exhaustive since teachers in history, biology, mathematics, etc. cannot be placed.

All cases within a category are treated the same in analyses of the data. Assignment of numbers to the categories, if made at all, is arbitrary since the numbers simply code the categories. For example, the numerical code for males could be 0 and the code for females be 1, or vice versa.

When a variable is either semiquantifiable or quantifiable, *ordered categories* may be constructed (e.g., weight: very heavy, heavy, normal, light, very light; opinion: strongly agree, agree, undecided, disagree, strongly disagree). Strictly speaking, such measurement falls between nominal measurement and ordinal measurement.

3.2 ORDINAL SCALES

At the ordinal level of measurement, *each* individual or object can be ordered relative to *each other* individual or object on the variable of interest. It is possible to determine if one individual or object possesses *more* of a variable than another. Since no unit of measurement exists, it is *not* possible to speak of *how much more*. Rudimentary as such comparisons are, they are impossible with qualitative variables. Ordinal measurement is achieved when teachers rank students on achievement. In Gribbons and Lohnes's study (Chapter 1) twelve occupational values were ordered in terms of their importance to students.

Although ranks increase in increments of one (first, second, third), this does not mean that the property being measured also increases in equal units. For example, if 30 students were ordered by their weight, the difference between the weight of those individuals ranked first and second cannot be assumed to be equal to the difference between the students ranked 20th and 21st, even though the difference in numerical rank is one in each case. In addition, ranks are not fixed. They vary with the other cases in the set to be ranked. A student may rank first in achievement in the high school graduating class, but 50th in achievement among the graduating seniors in the entire school district. Thus the meaning of any rank is confined to the particular set of objects or individuals from which it is obtained and may not apply when objects or individuals are added to or removed from the set.

3.3 INTERVAL SCALES

Nominal and ordinal measurements are probably novel concepts to you because measurement usually refers to an interval or ratio scale. With an interval scale, the closeness of objects or individuals can be determined, as well as their rank order. A fixed *unit* of measurement exists throughout the scale that makes addition and subtraction of scores on the scale meaningful. Thus in measuring the height of a building, the difference of 2 feet between the 10- and 12-foot heights is equal to the 2-foot difference at the 100- and 102-foot heights. If intelligence tests were to yield an interval scale, then the unit of one IQ point would be fixed throughout the scale. The difference between individuals with IQ scores of 90 and 100 would be numerically and substantively equivalent to the difference between individuals with IQ scores of 140 and 150. If intelligence scores were viewed as having only ordinal properties, then one could only conclude that the individual with a score of 150 is more intelligent than individuals with scores of 140, 100, and 90; that an individual with 140 ranks higher than individuals with scores of 100 and 90; etc.

A major controversy in social science measurement is whether an ordinal or interval scale applies to such variables as intelligence, achievement, attitude, and personality traits. Strictly speaking, these are ordinal scales, although Gardner (54) placed many of them somewhere between ordinal and interval. Special scaling techniques have been developed to yield interval scales for such variables. Psychological and educational tests are often treated as yielding interval scales because most of them "approximate interval equality fairly well" (92, p. 440).

3.4 RATIO SCALES

At the highest level of measurement, an absolute or natural zero point exists, which makes ratios of scores on the scale meaningful. A zero point means that "there is a basis for saying that some object has none of the property being measured" (92, p. 438). Weight and height possess a zero point (absence of weight or height). Thus we can say that an individual who weighs 100 pounds is twice as heavy as an individual who weighs 50 pounds.

A zero score on a test (as in no items correct on a math test) does not necessarily mean that a ratio scale exists. At present, the concept of an absolute zero level of achievement, intelligence, attitude, or personality has no meaning. Therefore, we cannot conclude that a person with an IQ score of 160 is twice as intelligent as an individual with an IQ of 80.

Number of objects does, however, constitute a ratio scale (e.g., number of plants in the garden, number of students in an auditorium). A common procedure in observation studies is to count the number of times a certain act is performed. In such cases, there is a zero point—no acts. If the number of positive reinforcements given by a teacher were tallied, and researchers confined their interpretation of this measure to the number of positive reinforcement acts, then a ratio scale exists. If the researchers claimed to measure teacher effectiveness instead, then the number of reinforcements loses its ratio properties since zero reinforcements cannot necessarily be interpreted as reflecting an absence of teacher effectiveness. Since the variable being measured changed, the level of measurement also changed.

3.5 COMPARISON OF SCALES OF MEASUREMENT

The four scales just discussed form a hierarchy, in that ordinal scales have nominal properties, the characteristics of nominal and ordinal scales apply to interval scales, and the properties of nominal, ordinal, and interval scales are also properties of ratio scales. A variable that can be measured at the highest or ratio level can also be measured at each of the other levels, but the converse is not necessarily the case. In addition, more information is provided about the variable being measured at the higher levels of the hierarchy.

No scale is inherently better than another. The central question facing the researcher and the reader is the appropriate meaning to attach to the numbers obtained from the measurement process. In addition, as indicated in later chapters, the scale of measurement influences the statistical analysis of the data.

STUDY PROBLEMS

Determine the level or scale of measurement for each of the following variables.

a) Rate of performance, as measured by number of minutes to complete a five-page essay.

b) Suppose the same criterion (number of minutes to complete the essay) had been used as a measure of task interest. What would be the level of measurement for the variable of task interest?

c) The observational variables cited in Table 2.2 of the Jackson and Cosca study.

d) Instructional method: lecture, tutorial, small group discussion, combination of lecture/discussion, other methods.

e) Teacher attitude regarding good interpersonal relations in the classroom, as indicated by scores on the Minnesota Teacher Attitude Inventory (Cicirelli and Cicirelli study, Chapter 1, paragraph 11).

4
Describing the Distribution of a Single Variable[1]

There are many steps researchers must go through before they can say they have completed the analysis of their data. The first step is to "get a feeling" for the data. That is, researchers must carefully examine *how individuals* in the study *were distributed on each variable.* For example, did they all have quite similar scores, were there great discrepancies in the scores, or did several clusters of individuals occur? Such information is crucial to researchers for it determines what statements can be made about each variable and also how each variable is likely to relate to other variables in the study.

A summary of the results of this "first-stage" analysis can be found in most research reports. This chapter focuses on the most common ways of describing the distribution of scores on a single variable. The distribution of a variable can be described with graphs and tables or with numerical summaries. Since each form of description contains unique information, researchers use both forms in examining their data. The different modes of description are illustrated with the data in Table 4.1. Six demographic variables on students enrolled in a master's level educational research course are presented in this table: the student's major, age, sex, height, weight, and whether or not the student had previously taken a course in the area of tests and measurements. Three of the variables are clearly qualitative in nature and reflect a nominal scale of measurement: major, sex, and previous testing course. Each of the other three variables is clearly quantifiable and reflects a ratio scale of measurement: age, weight, and height. The scale of measurement determines which graphs and which numerical summaries are appropriate descriptions.

---

[1] The concept of a frequency distribution, and of the normal distribution in particular, is central to much of the material in Chapter 7 on inferential statistics, as are the concepts of the mean, standard deviation, and variance. These last three concepts are also referred to in Chapter 5 when the product–moment correlation is discussed. The concept of the variance is central to the discussion of the reliability of measurement in Chapter 8. Calculation of the median is an optional section.

4.1 GRAPHIC AND TABULAR REPRESENTATIONS

4.1.1 QUALITATIVE VARIABLES

Data on qualitative variables can be represented easily in either tabular or graphic form. Data on the variable of graduate major are tabulated in Table 4.2. The frequency of occurrence and the corresponding percentage for each category are given. Note that the categories meet the nominal scale requirements of being mutually exclusive and exhaustive.

Graphic illustrations of the distributions of qualitative variables come in many varieties: bar graphs, circles or pie charts, and pictograms. Although graphs can sometimes be misleading, standards for constructing accurate and unambiguous graphs have been adopted by journal editors. A graph often illustrates the distribution of data better than tabular forms do, but space limitations in journals reduce the use of graphs. A bar graph representing the percentage of students with different majors is given in Fig. 4.1.

4.1.2 QUANTITATIVE VARIABLES

Let us now turn our attention to quantitative variables measured on either an ordinal, interval, or ratio scale. With most ordinal scales, each individual can be assigned a unique rank number and tabular representations simply show the order of the individuals. When ties in rank order occur, the corresponding individuals are simply assigned an average rank, indicating that no distinctions can be made among them.

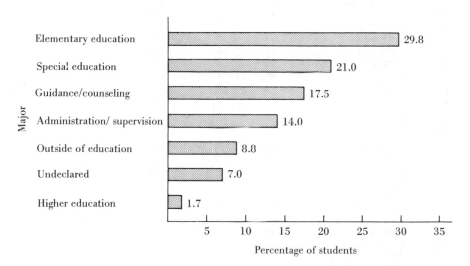

FIG. 4.1 Bar graph showing percentage of graduate students classified by major.

TABLE 4.1   *DEMOGRAPHIC DATA ON STUDENTS ENROLLED IN A MASTER'S-LEVEL COURSE ON EDUCATIONAL RESEARCH*

Student number	Major	Age (in years)	Sex	Weight (in pounds)	Height (in inches)	Prior testing course
1	Higher Education	23	M	180	70	No
2	Elementary Education	29	F	105	62	No
3	Elementary Education	21	F	120	65	No
4	Elementary Education	22	F	135	66	No
5	Guidance/ Counseling	32	F	114	62	Yes
6	Social Work	40	F	185	70	No
7	Elementary Education	54	F	110	62	Yes
8	Elementary Education	23	F	130	64	Yes
9	Administration/ Supervision	23	M	165	67	Yes
10	Elementary	23	F	125	66	Yes
11	Emotionally Disturbed	41	F	123	67	Yes
12	Elementary	23	F	140	65	No
13	Guidance/ Counseling	56	M	140	70	Yes
14	Elementary	22	F	118	67	No
15	Administration	38	M	180	72	Yes
16	Administration	44	M	205	73	Yes
17	Elementary	25	F	135	65	No
18	Learning Disability	23	F	107	61	Yes
19	Elementary	24	F	130	69	No
20	Special Education	40	F	97	60	Yes
21	Social Work	51	F	110	61	Yes
22	Administration	28	F	130	62	No
23	Hard of Hearing	29	F	124	65	Yes
24	Supervision	44	M	160	71	Yes
25	Special Education	23	F	115	65	Yes
26	Guidance/ Counseling	28	F	155	65	Yes
27	Special Education	29	M	197	71	No
28	Special Education	25	M	140	59	No
29	Guidance	34	M	150	66	Yes
30	Administration/ Supervision	34	M	142	66	Yes
31	Elementary	38	F	120	63	No
32	Elementary	38	F	135	64	Yes
33	Home Economics	31	F	150	67	No
34	Special Education	21	F	112	63	No
35	Perceptually Disabled	35	M	170	71	No

Student number	Major	Age (in years)	Sex	Weight (in pounds)	Height (in inches)	Prior testing course
36	Administration/ Supervision	30	M	187	76	No
37	Guidance	23	F	120	63	No
38	Elementary	22	F	110	64	No
39	Undeclared	26	F	125	66	No
40	Elementary	31	F	132	66	No
41	Mentally Retarded	31	F	150	68	No
42	Elementary	23	F	106	62	No
43	Undeclared	24	M	175	72	No
44	Undeclared	26	F	117	66	No
45	Undeclared	31	F	118	63	Yes
46	Social Studies	25	F	91	61	No
47	Guidance	43	M	170	70	Yes
48	Guidance	45	F	116	60	Yes
49	Elementary	28	M	175	72	Yes
50	Elementary	44	F	110	60	Yes
51	Counseling	37	F	115	65	Yes
52	Guidance	46	F	108	62	Yes
53	Administration	28	M	193	72	No
54	Counseling	36	M	183	71	Yes
55	Home Economics	29	F	130	65	No
56	Special Education	29	M	160	67	No
57	Perceptually Disabled	34	F	200	69	No

With interval and ratio scales, a tabulation of the frequency with which each score occurs is made, called a *frequency distribution*. All possible scores are listed from high to low and the number of times each score occurs is tallied (its frequency). The frequency for each score is symbolized by f, and the total number of scores by n. Table 4.3 gives the frequency distribution for the age variable. Note that all ages in year increments between the highest and lowest age in the sample were recorded. Those ages that did not occur in the sample had a frequency of zero.

A quick examination of a frequency distribution indicates where the majority of scores occur, and if any scores are unusual by being separated from the other scores or by having a low frequency of occurrence. Sometimes the *cumulative frequency* (cf) is also tabulated, by totaling the number of scores at and below each score (see Table 4.3).

A graphic representation of the frequency distribution can be made by what is known as a *frequency polygon*. A portion of the frequency polygon for the age scores is presented in Fig. 4.2.

TABLE 4.2   *NUMBER AND PERCENTAGE OF GRADUATE STUDENTS CLASSIFIED BY MAJOR*

Major	Number	Percentage
Education		
Administration/supervision	8	14.03
Elementary	17	29.82
Guidance/counseling	10	17.54
Higher education	1	1.75
Special education	12	21.05
Outside of education	5	8.77
No major (undeclared)	4	7.01

Note: Total $n = 57$.

In a frequency polygon the horizontal axis represents the variable of interest, and the vertical axis, the frequency of the scores on that variable. An examination of Fig. 4.2 indicates that the horizontal axis represents the age variable. It is marked off in equal increments of one year, starting with zero years. The slash marks in the axis after zero is a convention used to conserve space when the zero point of the scale is really not part of the scores observed. The zero point must be indicated since the intersection of the two axes represents the origin. The vertical axis represents the frequency of the scores in increments of one unit starting at zero.

To finish a frequency polygon, a point is located above each score at the proper height corresponding to the frequency of that score. All these points are then joined by straight lines. In Fig. 4.2 only the points through age 35

TABLE 4.3   *FREQUENCY AND CUMULATIVE FREQUENCY DISTRIBUTIONS OF THE AGES OF THE GRADUATE STUDENTS IN TABLE 4.1*

Age	f	cf	Age	f	cf	Age	f	cf
56	1	57	44	3	52	32	1	36
55	0	56	43	1	49	31	4	35
54	1	56	42	0	48	30	1	31
53	0	55	41	1	48	29	5	30
52	0	55	40	2	47	28	4	25
51	1	55	39	0	45	27	0	21
50	0	54	38	3	45	26	2	21
49	0	54	37	1	42	25	3	19
48	0	54	36	1	41	24	2	16
47	0	54	35	1	40	23	9	14
46	1	54	34	3	39	22	3	5
45	1	53	33	0	36	21	2	2

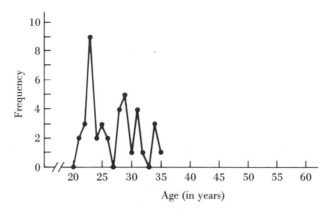

FIG. 4.2 A portion of the frequency polygon of the ages of the graduate students cited in Table 4.1.

have been graphed and joined. Note that the value just below the lowest score that actually occurred in the sample was marked as zero frequency, indicating that the value of 20 did not occur in the sample. The value just above the highest score should also be marked as having zero frequency. These two markings enclose the polygon at the horizontal axis. By referring to the frequency distribution in Table 4.3, you should be able to complete the frequency polygon in Fig. 4.2.

Instead of a frequency polygon, a *curve* is sometimes used to illustrate the frequency distribution. A curve approximates the polygon by smoothing out the angles and jags.

Graphing the distribution of a variable clearly *illustrates its shape*. Often it is important to determine whether the distribution is symmetric. Symmetry is indicated if there is a point about which one half of the distribution is a mirror image of the other half. Otherwise the distribution is asymmetric or skewed. Note that the distribution of age scores is asymmetric.

Several examples of symmetric and asymmetric distributions are given in Fig. 4.3. Distributions (a), (b), and (c) are each symmetric distributions. Note that each of these distributions can be divided in half so that one half is the mirror image of the other half. Distribution (a) is a "bell-shaped" distribution with most scores falling in the middle of the distribution, and with few very high and few very low scores. Distribution (b) is a uniform distribution; all scores occur with the same frequency. In Distribution (c), two clusters of scores exist, with each cluster being the same distance from the middle of the distribution. On the other hand, Distributions (d), (e), and (f) are each asymmetric or skewed. These distributions cannot be divided in half so that one half is the mirror image of the other half. In Distribution (d), there are few low scores but many high scores. The opposite relationship holds in Distribution (e); there are few high scores but many low scores. In Distribution (f)

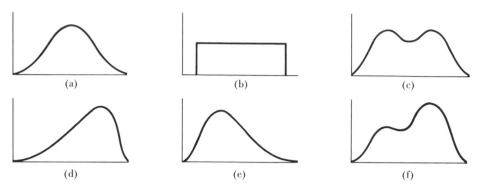

FIG. 4.3 Illustrations of (a, b, and c) symmetric and (d, e, and f) asymmetric distributions.

two clusters of scores exist, yet the number of scores in these two clusters is not the same since there are more high than low scores. The two clusters of scores in Distribution (f) are not balanced about the mid-point of the distribution as they are in Distribution (c).

One assumption in the construction of a frequency polygon is that the scores constitute an interval scale. Otherwise it would not be legitimate to represent the distance between scores on the horizontal axis as being equal. If, in fact, the distances between scores were unequal, then the shape of the frequency polygon would change. With variables such as achievement, IQ, and personality, inequality of intervals may exist. One simply hopes the distortion in shape is not great.

It is important that the researcher and the reader not be misled by graphs of a single variable that involve more than one dimension. For example, the age graph in Fig. 4.2 combined two distinct groups, males and females. As you will discover in Quiz 4.1, there is a distinct difference in the age distribution for these two groups. Researchers usually report such differences when interpreting their data. Because tabular and graphic representations of frequency distributions consume much space, researchers use summary statistics, such as those described in the remainder of this chapter, to convey much of the descriptive information about a distribution.

QUIZ 4.1

1. Construct both the frequency and cumulative frequency distributions for the height and weight scores given in Table 4.1. Plot the frequency polygons for the height and weight scores.

2. Construct separate frequency polygons for males and females on the age variable. What are the differences, if any, between these two distributions?

4.2 CENTRAL TENDENCY

One way to describe the distribution of a variable is to report the *typical or central score*. The three most common indices of this central tendency of a distribution are the mode, median, and mean. Other indices such as the geometric and harmonic means are described in most statistics texts.

4.2.1 MODE

The mode is the *most frequent score* in the distribution. In the distribution of age scores, the mode was 23 (see Table 4.3 and Fig. 4.2). This was the peak of the distribution. The age of 23 occurred nine times and every other age occurred five times or less. When two distinct peaks occur in a distribution, the distribution is usually called bimodal. With nominal data, the mode is simply the category that occurs most frequently. For the variable of graduate major, the modal category was that of elementary graduate major (Fig. 4.1).

4.2.2 MEDIAN

The median (Md) is the *point* that divides the set of scores in half; 50 percent are above or larger than the median and 50 percent are below or smaller. It is the 50th percentile.

In order to determine the median, the scores must be ordered from high to low. When the distribution is simple, the median is easy to calculate. For example, if the number of scores is even and no ties exist, then the median is the halfway point between the two central values (Md = 5 when the scores are 1, 4, 6, and 10). When simple distributions do not occur, the calculation of the median is more complicated, requiring what is called interpolation. For your information, a guide to calculating the median is given in Exhibit 4.1.

EXHIBIT 4.1 (OPTIONAL) *CALCULATION OF THE MEDIAN*

Step 1. Tabulate both the frequency and the cumulative frequency distributions of the scores. Be sure to cite all possible scores that could occur between the top and bottom values. Scores that do not occur between these two values are tabulated as having zero frequency.

Step 2. Consider each score as the midpoint of an interval. Determine the width of the interval. In many educational contexts the interval width equals one unit.

Step 3. The median is the point below which 50 percent of the cases fall or the $(n/2)th$ point from the bottom score.

Step 4. Identify the interval in which the median is located. Determine the following four values or numbers associated with this median interval.

    a) Its lower bound or limit
    b) Its width (number of units)

   c) The cumulative frequency of scores *up to* the median interval
   d) The frequency or number of scores *in* the median interval

Step 5. Calculate the median with the following formula:

$$Md = \begin{bmatrix} \text{lower limit} \\ \text{of median} \\ \text{interval} \end{bmatrix} + \begin{bmatrix} \text{width of} \\ \text{median} \\ \text{interval} \end{bmatrix} \left[\frac{(n/2) - \left(\begin{matrix} \text{cumulative frequency up} \\ \text{to median interval} \end{matrix} \right)}{\text{frequency in median interval}} \right]$$

Example

Number correct on a ten word spelling quiz for 18 students:

$$1, 1, 1, 1, 3, 3, 4, 4, 5, 5, 5, 5, 5, 5, 7, 7, 9, 9.$$

Step 1. Frequency Distribution

Score	f	cf	
9	2	18	
8	0	16	
7	2	16	
6	0	14	
[5	6	14]	← Median lies within
4	2	8	this interval.
3	2	6	
2	0	4	
1	4	4	

Upper limit = 5.5 →
Lower limit = 4.5 →

Step 2. The width of each interval is 1 unit. (The number 9 is considered the midpoint of the interval 8.5 to 9.5; 8 is considered the midpoint of the interval 7.5 to 8.5; etc.)

Step 3. The median is the $(n/2)th = 18/2 = $ 9th point from the bottom score of 1.

Step 4. The median is located in the interval from 4.5 to 5.5. Up to that interval, 8 scores or cases have occurred and just after that interval 14 scores have occurred. Therefore, the ninth score exists within that interval.

   a) The lower limit of the interval is 4.5.
   b) The interval width equals 1.
   c) The cumulative frequency up to the interval is 8.
   d) The frequency of the scores within the interval is 6.

Step 5.

$$Md = 4.5 + (1) \left(\frac{(9-8)}{6} \right) = 4.5 + (1)(1/6) = 4.5 + .17 = 4.67.$$

Discussion

Fifty percent of the scores fell below 4.67 and 50 percent were above 4.67. Equivalently, 50 percent of the students spelled at least 4.67 words correctly and 50 percent of them spelled less than 4.67 words correctly. Note that the median was only slightly greater than 4.5, the lower limit of the median interval. Only one more score was needed in that interval to reach the median, i.e., 1/6th of the cases in the interval.

QUIZ 4.2

Verify that the median for the following distribution is 4.67, the same as for the distribution in Exhibit 4.1: a score of 9 occurs four times, a score of 5 occurs six times, and a score of 1 occurs eight times.

4.2.3 MEAN

The most frequently used index of central tendency is the mean. It is the *average* of all the scores in a distribution. Simply add the scores and divide by the number of scores. For scores of 2, 2, 1, 5, 4, and 4, the mean is 18/6 or 3. With large volumes of data, such calculations are easily performed on a computer. The symbolic notation for the mean in journal articles is usually M or $\overline{X}$ (sometimes read "X bar"). The notation in this book is $\overline{X}$.

Some statistical notation must be introduced at this point to symbolize the processes involved in calculation of such statistics as the mean. First, we need a symbol to represent a single score. This is X_i (read as "X sub i," short for "X with the subscript of i"). X refers to any score or number; i indicates that it is the ith number. When the subscript of i is given a particular value, say 3, then X_3 refers to the third number; X_{10} refers to the tenth number; etc. Assignment of such subscripts to the scores is arbitrary for the subscripts simply identify each score. X_1 is the first number in the list and X_n is the last number (recall that n refers to the total number of scores). With the scores in the preceding paragraph, we could make the following assignments: $X_1 = 2$, $X_2 = 2$, $X_3 = 1$, $X_4 = 5$, $X_5 = 4$, and $X_6 = 4$.

One way of symbolizing the calculation of the mean of these six numbers is as follows:

$$\overline{X} = \frac{X_1 + X_2 + X_3 + X_4 + X_5 + X_6}{6} = \frac{2 + 2 + 1 + 5 + 4 + 4}{6} = \frac{18}{6} = 3,$$

or in more general terms:

$$\overline{X} = \frac{X_1 + X_2 + \cdots + X_n}{n}.$$

Such notation is cumbersome and further symbolization summarizes the process of addition. This is the Greek capital letter of Σ (read as "sigma"). $\Sigma_i X_i$ means "$X_1 + X_2 + \cdots + X_n$" or "add whatever follows the Σ." In other words, add all the scores in the distribution. Thus the process for obtaining the mean is symbolized by:

$$\overline{X} = \frac{\Sigma_i X_i}{n}.$$

Tables of means were presented in the Jackson and Cosca study (Chapter 2). A careful examination of a table of means before reading the text of the results section of a research report gives the reader a good summary of the results, and enables the reader to check his or her impressions of the results with the author's version.

QUIZ 4.3

1. Calculate the means of the following distributions:

Distribution A		Distribution B		Distribution C	
Score	f	Score	f	Score	f
10	1	10	2	20	1
6	1	6	1	6	1
5	1	5	4	5	1
4	1	4	2	4	1
3	1	3	1	3	1

2. Given the set of scores: 1, 2, 3, 4, and 5, calculate the following numbers:

a) $\Sigma_i X_i^2$ b) $(\Sigma_i X_i)^2$ c) $\Sigma_i (X_i - 3)$

4.2.4 COMPARISON OF INDICES OF CENTRAL TENDENCY

When data are nominal, only the mode is applicable. When order exists, the median can be calculated. When equal intervals occur, then the mean is also applicable, and the researcher must decide which index or indices to report. All three indices are identical only when the distribution is symmetric and has one mode. When such conditions do not exist, as with skewed distributions, the researcher may need to report more than one index.

When a distribution is skewed and unimodal, the three indices differ from each other in predictable ways. If the majority of scores is higher than the peak or mode, then the mean will be the highest value, followed by the median, and then the mode. The distribution of age scores in Fig. 4.2 illustrates this relationship. The mode was 23, the median 29.2 and the mean 31.6. If the distribution is skewed in the opposite direction, then the relationship among the indices is reversed, with the mode being the highest value and the mean being the lowest.

A discrepancy between the mean and median of a skewed distribution occurs because the size of each score effects the mean, while this is not the case with the median. For example, consider Distributions A and C in the preceding quiz (4.3). The only difference between the two distributions is the maximum scores (10 versus 20). The medians of both distributions are the same (5), but the means differ (5.6 for Distribution A and 7.6 for Distribution C). The mean was affected by a change in one score (10 versus 20), while the median was not. When a distribution is skewed, the median is often a better index than the mean of central tendency. Distribution C illustrates this principle in that the mean is higher than all but one of the scores.

Since the distributions of many educational variables are symmetric and unimodal, researchers typically report the mean and not the median or the mode. However, when distributions are skewed, flat, or U-shaped, the researcher will present a different index or more than one index of central tendency in order to describe the variables adequately.

4.3 DISPERSION

It is rare for all the scores in a distribution to be identical. The scores *vary*, and an index of this scatter, dispersion, or variability is required. The range, interquartile range, variance, and standard deviation are common indices of dispersion and are discussed below. Other indices such as the semi-interquartile range, the average deviation, and the index of qualitative variation (109) can also be calculated.

4.3.1 INDICES OF RANGE

The crudest measure of the scatter of scores is simply the difference between the maximum and minimum scores; technically called the *inclusive range*. For example, the range on the variable of age (Table 4.1) is 35 years (56 minus 21). Sometimes researchers simply report that the scores range from point *a* to point *b*; e.g., from 21 to 56 years of age.

One major limitation of the range is that it depends on only two scores and is therefore unstable. Another limitation is that two distributions can have the same range but be entirely different in shape, e.g., scores distributed uniformly throughout the distribution vs. scores concentrated at one point.

The *interquartile range* indicates where the middle 50 percent of the scores lie (i.e., from the 25th to the 75th percentile). With the age scores, the interquartile range was approximately 14 years with 50 percent of the individuals falling between the ages of 24 and 38. Generally speaking, if two distributions have similar values for the interquartile range, they are apt to be more similar than if the values for the range were the same. Therefore the interquartile range is preferred to the range as an index of dispersion.

4.3.2 VARIANCE AND STANDARD DEVIATION

Neither of the indices of range considers every score in the distribution. However, both the variance and standard deviation are affected by each score. The central concept involved in these indices is a *deviation score; that is the deviation or difference of each score from the mean.* As the individual scores deviate more from the mean, indicating more dispersion or spread, the variance and standard deviation increase in size. At one extreme, if all the scores in a distribution were the same, there would be no variability. The scores would not deviate from the mean but would be identical to it, yielding a variance of zero.

In calculating the variance and standard deviation on a sample of scores, the deviation scores are first squared and then added together. This sum is then divided by the number of scores minus 1, yielding the *variance*, symbolized by s_x^2. The *standard deviation*, symbolized by s_x or SD, is simply the positive square root of the variance. Exhibit 4.2 illustrates the calculation of these two values. Other formulas for calculating the variance can be derived from the formula in Exhibit 4.2 and are cited in statistics texts.

EXHIBIT 4.2   *CALCULATION OF THE VARIANCE AND STANDARD DEVIATION*

Variance

$$s_x^2 = \frac{\Sigma_i(X_i - \bar{X})^2}{n-1} = \frac{(X_1 - \bar{X})^2 + (X_2 - \bar{X})^2 + \cdots + (X_n - \bar{X})^2}{n-1}.$$

Step 1. Find the mean, $\bar{X}$.

Step 2. Find $(X_i - \bar{X})$, the deviation of each score from the mean.

Step 3. Square each of the deviation scores and then find their sum, $\Sigma_i(X_i - \bar{X})^2$.

Step 4. Divide this sum by $(n-1)$. This yields the variance.

Standard Deviation

Step 5. Take the positive square root of the variance.

Example

Scores: 1, 2, 3, 4, 5.

Step 1. $\bar{X} = 3$.

Steps 2 and 3.	*Scores*	*Deviation Scores*	*Deviation Scores Squared*
	1	$1 - 3 = -2$	4
	2	$2 - 3 = -1$	1
	3	$3 - 3 = 0$	0
	4	$4 - 3 = +1$	1
	5	$5 - 3 = +2$	4
		(Step 2)	$\Sigma_i(X_i - \bar{X})^2 = 10$ (Step 3)

Step 4. Variance. $s_x{}^2 = 10/4 = 2.5$.

Step 5. Standard deviation: $s_x = \sqrt{s_x{}^2} = \sqrt{2.5} = 1.58$.

The variance is disproportionately affected by extreme, outlying scores. Such distortion is particularly noticeable in small samples with skewed distributions. You are given an opportunity to examine the effect of extreme scores on the variance in the next quiz (4.4).

Researchers usually report the standard deviation rather than the variance because the standard deviation can be directly related to the original distribution of scores. The percentage of scores that lie within 1, 2, or 3 standard deviations of the mean is a useful index. For example, the standard deviation of the age scores in Table 4.1 was 8.9, meaning that scores or ages lying within one standard deviation above and below the mean ranged from 22.8 to 40.6 years of age. More discussion of this use of the standard deviation occurs in the section on z scores. Sometimes it is also useful to compare the standard deviation of different groups in the study. A major result of the Sullivan et al. study cited later in Chapter 19 was the discrepancy in variability between the two experimental groups (see Table 19.3 in that article).

QUIZ 4.4

1. Calculate the inclusive range, variance, and standard deviation for Distributions A, B, and C in Quiz 4.3.

2. Explain why Distribution B has the smallest variance and standard deviation and why Distribution C has the largest variance and standard deviation.

3. For each distribution, which index (or indices) of variability best describes the dispersion or scatter of scores? Consider the interquartile range, the range, the standard deviation, and the variance.

4. Would any of the measures of dispersion present a distorted picture of score variability for any of the distributions?

4.4 THE NORMAL DISTRIBUTION

Many distributions approximate what is known as the normal distribution. It is a theoretical distribution with certain mathematically defined properties, among them:

1. Unimodal and symmetric, making the mean, mode, and median identical.

2. 68.3 percent of the scores lie within ± one standard deviation of the mean.

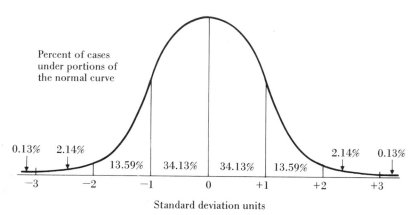

Percent of cases
under portions of
the normal curve

0.13%   2.14%   13.59%   34.13%   34.13%   13.59%   2.14%   0.13%

−3   −2   −1   0   +1   +2   +3

Standard deviation units

FIG. 4.4 Properties of the normal curve.

95.4 percent of the scores lie within ± two standard deviations of the mean. 99.7 percent of the scores lie within ± three standard deviations of the mean.

3. The maximum and minimum scores are infinite.

These properties are illustrated in Fig. 4.4 and yield the familiar bell-shaped curve.

The normal distribution should not be perceived as an ideal distribution, for it is only one of many theoretical distributions. Other families of distributions such as Chi-square, t, F, and Poisson exist. The normal distribution is emphasized because many theoretical distributions as well as the observed distributions of many educational and psychological variables approximate it, and because it possesses important mathematical properties.

4.5 SKEWNESS AND KURTOSIS

Two other indices complete the description of a frequency distribution; skewness and kurtosis. As discussed previously, the degree to which a distribution is not perfectly symmetric is its *skewness*. Distributions can be skewed either positively or negatively. Figure 4.5 illustrates both these tendencies. Although the degree of skew can be calculated, a graphic representation of the distribution is frequently sufficient to indicate the degree of skew. Numerically, no skew would be reflected by a value of zero. A positively skewed distribution has scores that extend further above than below the mean. In a positively skewed, unimodal distribution (Fig. 4.5(a)), the mode is below the median, which in turn is below the mean. The opposite relationships hold for a nega-

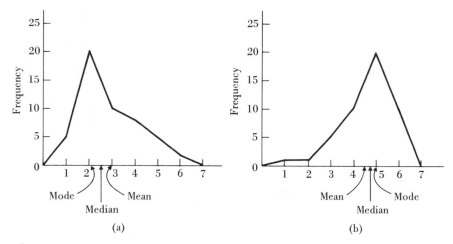

FIG. 4.5 Examples of positively skewed and negatively skewed distributions; (a) positively skewed, skewed to the right; (b) negatively skewed, skewed to the left.

tively skewed distribution. Generally, measures of skew will range between −3 and +3.

The degree to which a unimodal distribution is peaked or flat near its mode refers to its *kurtosis*. A very peaked distribution is called leptokurtic, a very flat distribution is called platykurtic, and a distribution with an intermediate amount of curve like the normal distribution is called mesokurtic. Indices of kurtosis are applicable only to unimodal distributions, equaling 3 for the normal distribution, greater than 3 for a very peaked distribution, and less than 3 for a flat distribution. Generally speaking, it is unusual to find the degree of skewness or kurtosis presented in research articles.

4.6 USE OF THE NORMAL CURVE TABLE

When a distribution approximates the normal curve, the percentage of scores that fall between or beyond any points of interest can be easily determined. However, in order to use the normal curve to make such calculations, it is first necessary to transform the original scores into what are known as *z scores*.

A *z* score is obtained by subtracting the mean from each score, and dividing this difference by the standard deviation of the distribution. In terms of an equation, the transformation is:

$$z_i = \frac{(X_i - \overline{X})}{s_x}.$$

The main advantage of z scores is that they directly reflect standard deviation units. For example, the following set of scores (2, 4, 5, 5, 6, and 8) has a mean of 5 and a standard deviation of 2. The z score corresponding to the original score of 2 is -1.5 or $(2–5)/2$. The z score corresponding to the score of 4 is $-.5$; 5 corresponds to a z score of 0; 6 to a z score of $+.5$; and 8 to a z score of $+1.5$. In other words, the score of 2 is one and a half standard deviations below the mean, and the score of 6 is half a standard deviation above the mean. A distribution of z scores always has a mean of zero and a standard deviation of 1, and the shape of the original distribution of scores is not changed in the transformation process. Thus the mean of the original distribution of scores will always correspond to a z score of zero.

Table E.2 in Appendix E is a table of the normal distribution. It is organized by z scores. The first column in the table cites the z values themselves, which can be treated as being either positive or negative. The second column gives the proportion of the area between a particular z value and the mean. The third column presents the larger area under the normal curve that falls beyond a particular z value. The fourth column presents the smaller area under the normal curve that falls beyond the z values. Figure 4.6 illustrates the meaning of the second, third, and fourth columns for z scores of $+1$ and -1. In determining the proportion or percentage of scores that fall in a particular location on the normal curve, as is required in Quiz 4.5, it is always helpful to first draw a sketch of the normal curve and then locate the corresponding z score values on it. These z score concepts are referred to again in Chapter 7 on statistical inference.

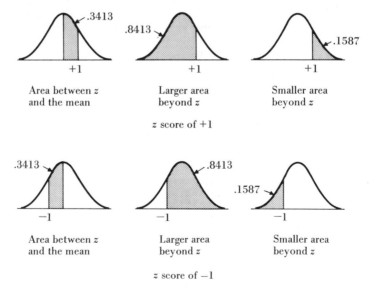

FIG. 4.6 Application of the normal curve table in Appendix E for z scores of $+1$ and -1.

QUIZ 4.5

A normal distribution has a mean of 60 and a standard deviation of 10.

1. Determine the z scores corresponding to the raw scores of 40, 50, 65, and 76.

2. What percentage of scores falls below each of these scores?

3. What percentage of scores falls above each of these scores?

4. What percentage of scores falls between scores of 40 and 50, between 50 and 76, and between 65 and 76?

5

Describing the Association between Two Variables[1]

When more than one variable is observed and measured, it is common to determine the nature of the relationship between pairs of variables; to ask whether knowing how an individual scores on one variable gives any information regarding the individual's position on a second variable; to ask if increases in one variable are associated with increases or decreases in another; if predictions can be made from one variable to another; etc. The direction of the relationship *and* the strength of the relationship are both of interest.

The scale of measurement for each of the two variables being examined could be nominal, ordinal, interval, or ratio, with the corresponding relationship between them being any one of 16 possible combinations: ratio–ratio, interval–interval, interval–ordinal, interval–nominal, etc. Ways of graphing and numerically summarizing the association between two variables at the interval level of measurement and between two nominal variables are presented in this chapter.

5.1 GRAPHIC AND TABULAR REPRESENTATIONS

5.1.1 INTERVAL–INTERVAL RELATIONSHIPS

When two variables are each measured at least at the interval level, a quick indication of the nature of their association can be obtained by plotting what is called a *scatter diagram*. Each person (or unit) must have a score on each of the variables. The set of data given in Table 5.1 cites scores for 11 individuals on an intelligence test and on a reading achievement test. A scatter diagram of these scores is given in Fig. 5.1.

---

[1] The product–moment correlation coefficient is central to much of the discussion on reliability and validity of measurement in Chapters 8 and 9. Both the product–moment correlation coefficient and the Chi-square test are mentioned in Chapter 7 on inferential statistics.

TABLE 5.1 *SCORES ON AN INTELLIGENCE TEST AND A READING TEST FOR 11 STUDENTS*

Student	Intelligence test score (X)	Reading test score (Y)
A	90	18
B	100	16
C	105	24
D	121	23
E	124	22
F	130	35
G	117	26
H	111	20
I	98	25
J	120	36
K	127	30

In a scatter diagram the horizontal axis represents the X variable and the vertical axis represents the Y variable. Each person in the sample is represented by *one* point determined by the individual's scores on the two variables. In Fig. 5.1 the point corresponding to Student A is at the intersection of two straight lines; one drawn perpendicular to Student A's IQ score of 90 on the X axis and the other drawn perpendicular to Student A's reading score of 18 on the Y axis. These two lines intersect at the point identified as A. A similar procedure is followed in plotting the points for each of the remaining students. Several of these points have been identified so you can check your ability to make a scatter diagram.

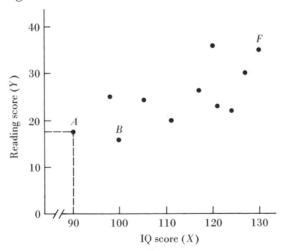

FIG. 5.1 Scatter diagram between intelligence (X) scores and reading (Y) scores in Table 5.1—a positive linear relationship.

The association depicted in Fig. 5.1 indicates that, in general, as IQ scores increase so do reading scores, reflecting what is called a positive linear relationship. Other types of relationships also exist: negative linear relationships sometimes called inverse relationships; curvilinear relationships; and, of course, no relationship of any form. Examples of these types are presented in Fig. 5.2.

A scatter plot provides a clear picture of the association between two variables: the shape and direction of the relationship and indirectly the strength

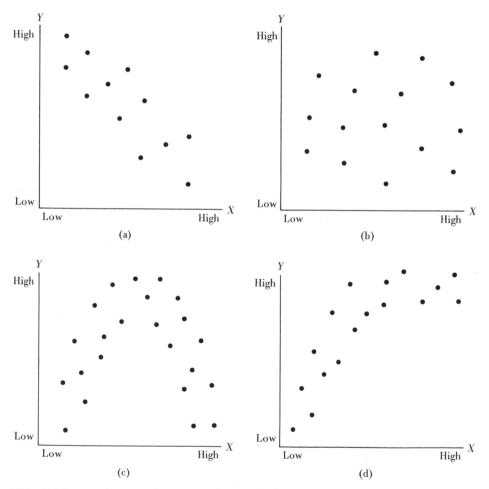

FIG. 5.2 Scatter diagrams for various forms of relationship between two variables: (a) Negative linear relationship; as scores on X increase, scores on Y decrease; (b) No relationship, scores on X are not associated with any particular level of Y score and vice versa; (c) Curvilinear relationship; low and high scores on X are associated with low Y scores, and intermediate X scores are associated with high Y scores; (d) Curvilinear relationship; as scores on X increase, Y scores increase and then level off.

of the relationship. One numerical index of association strength, the product-moment correlation coefficient, is discussed later in the chapter.

5.1.2 NOMINAL–NOMINAL RELATIONSHIPS

If both variables are at the nominal level, a quick way of identifying possible associations between the two classifications is to construct a *cross-tabulation table* that shows the joint frequency distribution of the two variables. One variable is used to generate the columns of the table and the other to generate the rows. Within each cell (i.e., the intersection of a row and column), the frequency of occurrence of that particular combination of categories is tabulated.

A cross-tabulation of the variables of sex and graduate major cited in Table 4.1 is presented in Table 5.2. It indicates that from the sample of 57 individuals, one was a male majoring in elementary education, 16 were females in elementary education, yielding a total of 17 elementary education majors; the only higher education major was a male; etc. Sometimes researchers convert the original cell frequencies to percentages in order to clarify the pattern of association.

TABLE 5.2   *JOINT DISTRIBUTION OF THE VARIABLES OF SEX AND MAJOR CITED IN TABLE 4.1*

Major	Sex		
	Male	*Female*	*Total*
Elementary education	1	16	17
Higher education	1	0	1
Administration/supervision	7	1	8
Guidance/counseling	4	6	10
Special education	4	8	12
Outside of education	0	5	5
Undeclared	1	3	4
Total	18	39	57

QUIZ 5.1

1. Plot a scatter diagram of the height and weight variables cited in Table 4.1. Is there a relationship between height and weight? If so, is this relationship positive and linear, negative and linear, or curvilinear?

2. Construct a cross-tabulation table representing the joint frequency of the major and the prior testing course variables cited in Table 4.1. Describe the nature of the association between the two variables.

5.2 NUMERICAL INDICES OF ASSOCIATION

5.2.1 PRODUCT–MOMENT CORRELATION COEFFICIENT

The product–moment correlation coefficient (r_{xy} or simply r) is the most common index of association you will encounter in published research reports. Generally speaking, when researchers refer to the correlation between two variables, they are referring to the product–moment correlation coefficient. It indicates the strength of a linear or straight-line relationship between two variables at the interval level of measurement (such as that in Fig. 5.1 and in Fig. 5.2(a)). It is not applicable to variables that possess a curvilinear relationship (Fig. 5.2(c) and (d)).

If a straight line can be reasonably fitted to a scatter diagram, the *size* of the correlation coefficient reflects the degree of scatter about that line and the *sign* of the coefficient indicates whether the line slopes upward or downward. A positive coefficient reflects high–high and low–low pairings of scores on the two variables (Fig. 5.1). A negative coefficient reflects high–low and low–high pairings of scores (Fig. 5.2(a)). The correlation coefficient can range in value from -1 to 0 to $+1$, with both $+1$ and -1 indicating a *perfect* linear relationship in which all points in the scatter diagram fall on a straight line. A value of zero indicates no linear relationship between two variables (Fig. 5.2(b)). As *correlation coefficients deviate from zero*, either positively or negatively, the *relationship between the two variables increases*.

CALCULATION

The factor that most directly affects both the size and sign of the correlation coefficient is the deviation of each score from its mean. (You will recall that the deviation score was also the central concept underlying the calculation of the variance and standard deviation.) If pairs of deviation scores tend to have the same sign ($++$ pairings, above the mean on both variables, and $--$ pairings, below the mean on both variables), the correlation will be strong and positive. If pairs of deviation scores tend to have unlike signs ($+-$ pairings, scores above the mean on one variable and below the mean on the other), then the correlation will be strong and negative.

Exhibit 5.1 shows how to calculate the correlation coefficient using the deviation scores obtained from the IQ and reading achievement data reported in Table 5.1. Other formulas for calculating r exist and are more efficient on large sets of data.

**EXHIBIT 5.1   CALCULATION OF THE
PRODUCT–MOMENT CORRELATION COEFFICIENT**

$$r_{xy} = s_{xy}/s_x s_y \qquad \text{where} \qquad s_{xy} = \frac{\Sigma_i(X_i - \bar{X})(Y_i - \bar{Y})}{(n-1)} \quad \text{(covariance between } X \text{ and } Y\text{)}$$

s_x = standard deviation of the X scores.
s_y = standard deviation of the Y scores.

Step 1. Find the mean and standard deviation for each of the variables.

Step 2. Find the deviation score for each individual on both variables; that is, calculate both $(X_t - \bar{X})$ and $(Y_i - \bar{Y})$.

Step 3. Find the product of the deviation scores for each individual $(X_i - \bar{X})(Y_i - \bar{Y})$. Remember that the product of two positive or two negative numbers is positive, the product of a positive and a negative number is negative, and the product of zero and any other number is zero.

Step 4. Find the sum of these products: $\Sigma_i(X_i - \bar{X})(Y_i - \bar{Y})$

Step 5. Find the covariance between X and Y by dividing the sum obtained in Step 4 by $(n-1)$; the number of individuals in the sample minus 1, *not* the number of scores minus 1.

Step 6. Divide the covariance by the product of the two standard deviations, yielding the product–moment correlation coefficient, r_{xy}.

Example

Scores on intelligence (X) and reading (Y) cited in Table 5.1.

$\bar{X} = 113$; $s_x = 13.14$.
$\bar{Y} = 25$; $s_y = 6.45$.

Student	X Intelligence	Y Reading	Step 2 $(X_i - \bar{X})$	Step 2 $(Y_i - \bar{Y})$	Step 3 $(X_i - \bar{X})(Y_i - \bar{Y})$
A	90	18	−23	−7	161
B	100	16	−13	−9	117
C	105	24	−8	−1	8
D	121	23	8	−2	−16
E	124	22	11	−3	−33
F	130	35	17	10	170
G	117	26	4	1	4
H	111	20	−2	−5	10
I	98	25	−15	0	0
J	120	36	7	11	77
K	127	30	14	5	70

Step 4: $\Sigma_i = 568$

Step 5. Covariance: $s_{xy} = 568/(n-1) = 568/10 = 56.8$.

Step 6. Correlation coefficient: $r_{xy} = 56.8/(13.14)(6.45) = .67$.

Discussion

The correlation coefficient was positive and "rather strong." Note that most of the products of the deviation scores were positive, reflecting consistency in deviation scores for most individuals (negative/negative and positive/positive pairs of deviation scores).

INTERPRETATION

In order to appropriately interpret a correlation coefficient, one must know how each variable is scored. When there is a positive correlation between intelligence and achievement, this means that high *numerical* scores on one variable are associated with high numerical scores on the other. Since tests are usually scored for the number of correct answers, high numerical scores also indicate high performance levels. What would happen to the sign and the strength of the correlation coefficient if the achievement test were scored for the number of incorrect answers? The correlation coefficient would then be negative, yet the strength of the association would remain the same. The basic nature of the association also remains unchanged, since high performance levels on achievement are still associated with high performance on intelligence.

There are many ways of determining whether the strength of an association is "high" or "low." No absolute criteria exist. One criterion, testing for statistical significance, is discussed in Chapter 7. Other criteria include (1) the relationship between the two variables as reported in the research literature, (2) the decisions or actions to be made on the basis of the correlation, and (3) the square of the correlation coefficient.

As research in a field grows, relationships between variables are documented. Researchers aware of this literature know immediately if the correlations they obtain are typical or atypical. If the correlation is used in some way to make decisions about individuals (e.g., placement in particular education programs, job selection), then the precision of the test as reflected in correlation coefficients should be above .90 (112).

Another way of examining the strength of the correlation coefficient is to square it. The squared value gives the *proportion of error variance that is eliminated* in predicting one variable by knowledge of the other variable. What does error variance mean? Suppose you were asked to guess individual achievement test scores in English (the Y variable) for a class of 30 students. Your best guess in each case would be the mean ($\overline{Y}$). However, you would be in error in each instance by an amount equal to the deviation of each individual's score from the mean (your guess); that is, $Y_i - \overline{Y}$. This discrepancy between your guess and the actual score constitutes error.

What would happen if you used your knowledge of the relationship between math (X) and English (Y) to predict the English scores? If a sizeable relationship exists, you can make a much better estimate than the Y mean.[2] You can now examine the difference or error between the actual Y scores and these *new* guesses, (that is, $Y_i -$ estimated Y_i) and determine the variance of these errors. In comparison to the error variance obtained without knowledge of the math (X) scores, the error variance will now be reduced by an amount equal to the square of the correlation between the math and English scores, r^2_{xy}.

If the correlation between math and English is .50, then $r^2 = .25$. In other words, 25 percent of the error in predicting one variable has been eliminated by knowledge of the other variable. If $r^2 = .80$, then the error variance has been reduced by 64 percent. At the extremes, if $r = 0$, then $r^2 = 0$, resulting in no error reduction; we are no better off by having knowledge of the second variable. If $r \pm 1$, then $r^2 = 1.00$, resulting in 100 percent error reduction; absolutely no error in prediction.

Just as r_{xy} is symmetric ($r_{xy} = r_{yx}$), so is r^2. Thus in the preceding example, the words "math" and "English" could have been interchanged. Table 5.3 illustrates the increase in r^2 values as r increases by units of .10. Note that it is not until a correlation equals $\pm .50$ that the error variance is reduced by one-fourth; and it requires a correlation greater than $\pm .70$ to eliminate half the error variance. For descriptive and decision-making purposes, the r^2 value is most useful.

The size of the correlation coefficient is sensitive to many factors: (1) a few extreme pairs of scores can inflate the correlation, (2) imprecise measurement of the two variables lowers it, (3) it can be at its maximum only when the X and Y distributions have identical shapes, (4) it is frequently reduced in size when the range on a variable is restricted (consider the correlation between achievement and intelligence within a highly intelligent sample as compared with a sample with a broad range of intelligence scores), and (5) pooling of

TABLE 5.3 *CORRESPONDENCE BETWEEN r_{xy} AND r^2_{xy}*

r_{xy}	r^2_{xy}	r_{xy}	r^2_{xy}
$\pm.00$	.00	$\pm.60$	.36
$\pm.10$	.01	$\pm.70$	.49
$\pm.20$	.04	$\pm.80$	.64
$\pm.30$	.09	$\pm.90$	.81
$\pm.40$	.16	±1.00	1.00
$\pm.50$	.25		

[2] The following formula can be used to determine the new estimates:

$$\text{Estimated } Y_i = \left[\frac{r_{xy}\, s_y}{s_x} \right] \left[X_i - \overline{X} \right] + \overline{Y}.$$

distinct groups with different means may inflate the correlation. Ordinarily readers of a research article cannot determine whether inflation or reduction in correlation coefficients has occurred, and they must rely on the author to present results related to these issues.

QUIZ 5.2

1. Calculate the correlation between the following two variables and describe the nature of the relationship.

Student	Math quiz (number correct)	Number of days absent per month
A	10	0
B	9	1
C	9	1
D	8	4
E	6	2
F	6	4

2. Below are several statements regarding associations between variables. Indicate whether each statement reflects a positive linear, negative linear, curvilinear, or no relationship between the two variables.

   a) Anxiety inhibits academic performance.
   b) My son Billy gets high marks because he is bright.
   c) It's good to get a little worried before making a public speech, but no concern or too much worrying produce a poor speech.
   d) Individuals who can climb a 20-foot rope fast can also do a lot of chin-ups in 10 seconds.
   e) Knowing how a student performs in social studies gives little information about his or her artistic ability.

3. Cicirelli and Cicirelli (Chapter 1) in paragraph 20 of their report briefly described the nature of the correlations among the teacher attitude and creativity variables presented in Table 1.2. Try to explain why the correlations in that table were of that size and of that sign.

5.2.2 CRAMÉR'S V-STATISTIC AND THE CHI-SQUARE TEST FOR INDEPENDENCE

Another common form of association encountered in educational research is that between nominal variables. Cramér's V-statistic (35) can be used in such instances. It is based on the Chi-square (χ^2) test for independence (70, 99). V ranges between 0 and +1, with 0 reflecting no association between two variables and +1 indicating a perfect association. Frequently researchers report only the Chi-square value, but the V-statistic is easily obtained from it.

The central concept underlying the Chi-square test for independence is the frequencies that would be expected if the two variables were unrelated; that is, independent of each other. Suppose you know the number of males and females in a particular sample and also the number of individuals with blue, brown, and green eyes. You could determine the number of individuals you would expect to be blue-eyed females, brown-eyed females, etc., if eye color and sex were unrelated. Case I in Table 5.4 gives some sample data in which only the totals for sex and eye color are presented. From this information you know that there are equal numbers of males and females in the sample and that 20 individuals have blue eyes. Assuming that sex has nothing to do with eye color, we would expect an equal number of males and females to have blue eyes; in this instance the expected frequencies would be 10 and 10. Applying the same logic to the individuals with brown eyes, the expected frequencies would be 25 for each sex. What are the expected frequencies in the green eye column?

TABLE 5.4 *CROSS-TABULATION TABLES REPRESENTING VARYING DEGREES OF ASSOCIATION BETWEEN TWO NOMINAL VARIABLES AS INDICATED BY THE CHI-SQUARE TEST FOR INDEPENDENCE AND CRAMÉR'S V-STATISTIC*

Case I

		Eye color			
		Blue	Brown	Green	Total
Sex	Male	?	?	?	50
	Female	?	?	?	50
	Total	20	50	30	100

Case II: $\chi^2 = 0$; $V = 0$

		Eye color			
		Blue	Brown	Green	Total
Sex	Male	10	25	15	50
	Female	10	25	15	50
	Total	20	50	30	100

Case III: $\chi^2 = 100$; $V = 1.00$

		Eye color			
		Blue	Brown	Green	Total
Sex	Male	0	50	0	50
	Female	20	0	30	50
	Total	20	50	30	100

Case IV: $\chi^2 = 16.34$; $V = .40$

		Eye color			
		Blue	Brown	Green	Total
Sex	Male	5	35	10	50
	Female	15	15	20	50
	Total	20	50	30	100

In determining the Chi-square value, these expected frequencies are then compared with the actual or observed frequencies in the sample. When the expected and observed frequencies are identical, then the Chi-square value is zero, as in Case II. To the extent that the expected and observed frequencies differ from each other, then the Chi-square value increases, reflecting more association and less independence between the variables, as in Cases III and IV.

The V-statistic is based on this Chi-square value and is equal to:

$$V = \sqrt{\frac{\chi^2}{n \, (\min, \, r - 1, \, c - 1)}},$$

where n refers to the total number in the sample, and r and c refer to the number of rows and columns respectively. The term "min" means to determine the minimum of these two values, $r - 1$ and $c - 1$. The total "row" and the total "column" are not included in these calculations. Exhibit 5.2 cites the steps involved in calculating V, including determination of the χ^2 value.

EXHIBIT 5.2 CALCULATION FOR THE CHI-SQUARE TEST FOR INDEPENDENCE AND CRAMÉR'S V-STATISTICS

$$\chi^2 = \frac{\Sigma_i \, \Sigma_i (O_{ij} - E_{ij})^2}{E_{ij}}$$

$$V = \sqrt{\frac{\chi^2}{n(\min, \, r - 1, \, c - 1)}}$$

where $(\min, \, r - 1, \, c - 1)$ refers to the minimum of the two values, $r - 1$, and $c - 1$.

where

$r =$ number of rows excluding the row that gives total values

$c =$ number of columns

$O_{ij} =$ observed frequency in the ith row of the jth column excluding the column that gives total values

$E_{ij} =$ expected frequency in the ith row of the jth column. E_{ij} is determined by multiplying the two marginal totals common to a specific cell and then dividing the product by the total number of cases. Expected frequencies are calculated only for each "cell," not for the "total" row and the "total" column.

Example

Case IV in Table 5.4.

Eye color

		Blue	Brown	Green	Total
	Male	5	35	10	50
Sex	Female	15	15	20	50
	Total	20	50	30	100

Step 1. Determine the expected frequencies for each cell, E_{ij}, as described above. Beginning with the first row and first column, we have the following:

$E_{11} = (50)(20)/100 = 10,$
First row, second column, $E_{12} = (50)(50)/100 = 25,$
First row, third column, $E_{13} = (50)(30)/100 = 15,$
Second row, first column, $E_{21} = (50)(20)/100 = 10,$
Second row, second column, $E_{22} = (50)(50)/100 = 25,$
Second row, third column, $E_{23} = (50)(30)/100 = 15.$

Step 2. For each cell determine the difference between the observed and expected frequencies, square this difference, divide it by the expected frequency for that cell:

$$\frac{(O_{ij} - E_{ij})^2}{E_{ij}}$$

Step 3. Find the sum of all the values in Step 2 ($\Sigma_i \Sigma_j$). This is the *Chi-square* value.

Starting with the first row, first column and ending with the second row, third column:

$$\chi^2 = \frac{(5-10)^2}{10} + \frac{(35-25)^2}{25} + \frac{(10-15)^2}{15} + \frac{(15-10)^2}{10} + \frac{(15-25)^2}{25}$$
$$+ \frac{(20-15)^2}{15}$$

$$= 2.5 + 4 + 1.67 + 2.5 + 4 + 1.67$$
$$= 16.34.$$

Step 4. V is then equal to the square root of the ratio of the Chi-square value to the product of the total number of cases and the minimum of r-1 and c-1.

$$V = \sqrt{16.34/(100)(1)} = 4.04/10 = .404.$$

Discussion

The expected and observed frequencies did differ somewhat for each cell. A perfect association was not found between eye color and sex, but there was some association as reflected in the V value of .40.

QUIZ 5.3

The association between two nominal variables, enrollment in different foreign language courses and sex of the student, is presented below.

1. Compute the Chi-square value and the V-statistic.

2. Describe the strength and pattern of the association.

		Foreign language				
		French	Spanish	German	Russian	Total
Sex	Male	25	25	25	25	100
	Female	75	75	25	25	200
	Total	100	100	50	50	300

5.3 QUESTIONS TO ASK OF DESCRIPTIVE STATISTICS IN RESEARCH ARTICLES

Appropriate interpretation of research results requires an extensive examination of the nature of each variable. The statistical concepts and techniques presented in this chapter and the two previous chapters are basic to further analyses of data. When extensive descriptive information is presented in a journal article, the reader is in a good position to evaluate the researcher's interpretation of the data. The following checklist can be used to determine the extent of the descriptive statistical information in research reports.

EXHIBIT 5.3   CHECKLIST: STATISTICAL DESCRIPTION OF VARIABLES IN RESEARCH REPORTS

Description of Individual Variables

1. Was the measurement procedure described so that you could determine the *level or scale of measurement,* or did the researchers themselves indicate the level of measurement?

2. Were there any graphic or tabular *representations of variable distributions?* (Variables at the nominal level are more apt to be represented than variables at the interval or ratio level.)

3. Was there any information on the *central tendency* of each variable?

4. Was there any information on the *dispersion* of variable scores?

5. For quantitative variables, was there any indication of the degree of skew and kurtosis?

Description of the Relationship between Variables

6. Were there any graphic or tabular *representations of the association* between variables? (Cross-tabulation tables are more common than scatterplots.)

7. Was there any numerical index of the *strength of the association?* (For a more complete list of such indices, refer to Appendix D.)

6

Sampling Designs[1]

Researchers want their data to apply to groups other than the study sample itself. However, such generalizations can be made only when researchers use appropriate sampling procedures. Ideally, the *sample* is representative of the group or population from which it was drawn, i.e., the *population accessible* to the researcher. In turn, this accessible population should be representative of an even larger group that researchers want to understand better or to which they want to apply their conclusions, known as the *target population* (18, 132). The primary focus in this chapter is upon sampling techniques that are typically applied to the accessible population.

Sampling from a population does not necessarily mean that the population elements of interest are single individuals, although this is true of much educational research. The population elements of interest can also be groups of individuals and other entities. If the intent is to determine the average classroom size within a school district, the population elements are the classrooms. When the aim is to determine the proportion of districts with fewer than 10,000 students, the population elements are school districts. School buildings are the population elements if the focus is on the average square footage in elementary school buildings.

Numerical indices computed on samples and populations are given different labels. These indices are called *statistics* when a sample is involved, but are called *parameters* when a population is involved. All the indices presented in Chapters 4 and 5 were statistics. In general, statistics are represented by Roman letters and parameters by Greek letters. For example, the symbol $\bar{X}$ represents

---

[1] The concept of simple random sampling is central to the concept of statistical inference as presented in Chapter 7. The sections on other forms of probability sampling (6.4) and on combinations of sampling designs (6.5) may be treated as optional material at this point since they are not referred to again in Part II. However, the material in these two sections (6.4 and 6.5) is referred to in Parts III and IV. Therefore these sections should be examined at a later time, if they are not examined now.

the sample mean, and the Greek letter μ represents the population mean. The symbolic notation for other common statistics and parameters is given in Table 6.1.

TABLE 6.1 *SYMBOLIC NOTATION FOR DESCRIPTIVE INDICES COMPUTED ON SAMPLE AND POPULATION*

Index	Sample: Statistic	Population: Parameter
Mean	$\overline{X}$	μ (mu)
Standard deviation	s	σ (sigma)
Variance	s^2	σ^2
Product–moment correlation	r	ρ (rho)

6.1 PROBABILITY SAMPLING

No guarantee can be made that the sample will be a mirror image of the population. All the researcher can hope for is that the sample will not differ too greatly from the population from which it was obtained. *Only probability sampling plans provide an estimate of how much the sample might differ from the population.* Such estimates are possible with probability sampling because every element in the population not only has a chance of being selected but also the probability of its being selected is known to the researcher. In contrast, *nonprobability sampling techniques* provide no way of estimating the chances of selecting each population element and provide "no assurance that every element has some chance of being included" (29, p. 516).

Most probability sampling designs are modifications of simple random sampling. Simple random sampling is discussed first in this chapter, and is then compared with three common nonprobability sampling procedures (haphazard/accidental, purposive/expert choice, and quota). Variations of simple random sampling (stratified random, systematic, and cluster) conclude the chapter.

6.2 SIMPLE RANDOM SAMPLING

With *simple random sampling, each element in the population has an equal chance of being included in the sample. In addition, every sample of the desired size has an equal chance of being selected.* Suppose a population consists of only four elements: A, B, C, and D. How many combinations of two elements are possible in this population? There are six pairs: AB, AC, AD, BC, BD, and CD. With a simple random sampling procedure, each of these six pairs of samples has the same chance of being selected (i.e., 1 in 6), and each of the four elements has the same chance of being selected (i.e., 1 in 4). The same principles apply if the sample were to consist of three population elements. But then only four combinations are possible: ABC, ABD, ACD, and BCD.

DUNAGIN'S PEOPLE

DUNAGIN'S PEOPLE BY RALPH DUNAGIN, COURTESY OF FIELD NEWSPAPER SYNDICATE

"WITH SEVENTEEN VOTES IN, WALTER, WE DEFINITELY HAVE A TREND..."

How does one actually select a sample through a random process? Obviously, as the population increases in number, it becomes impossible to list all the possible samples of a given size and then to select one of them. If we wanted to select a sample of five individuals from a population of 20 individuals, there would be 15,504 possible samples of size five. If the population size were doubled to 40, there would be 6,580,080 possible samples of size five. Writing out all possible combinations, placing them in a hat, stirring well, and drawing a combination blindfolded is not feasible. Instead, a table of random numbers is used to accomplish the same goal where individuals or units, rather than samples of a certain size, are selected randomly one by one until the desired sample size is reached. Table E.1 in Appendix E presents a table of random numbers or digits. Such tables have been carefully prepared to have no systematic order in the sequence of digits.

The steps in selecting a simple random sample using such a table are as follows:

1. List all the elements in the population and assign them consecutive numbers from 1 through N, where N represents the total number of population elements.

2. Decide upon the desired sample size or n.

3. Enter the table of random numbers at some random starting point (e.g., by a blind pencil stab at the page), and begin reading down the column of numbers.

4. Select *n different* numbers, corresponding to the numbers given the population elements. (If N is a two-digit number, then n successive two-digit numbers within the 01 to N range are selected. If N is a three-digit number, then n three-digit numbers within the 001 to N range are selected. Ignore numbers greater than N.)

5. The n numbers selected from the random number table must be unique, so disregard any number previously encountered (because the corresponding population element has already been selected for the sample).

6. The elements in the population that correspond to these n random numbers then constitute the sample.

With this procedure, selection of any element places no restriction on what other elements may be drawn. At the end of each successive drawing, the probability of drawing any of the remaining unselected elements is the same, thus making equally possible the selection of any of the possible combination of cases.

Table 6.2 lists a population of 100 students with data on their sex, school, intelligence scores, and a short math quiz. Each student or population element has been assigned a unique number. The exercise in Quiz 6.1 tests your skill in using a random number table with the population in Table 6.2.

QUIZ 6.1

> Using the table of random numbers and a simple random sampling procedure, select a sample of 20 students from Table 6.2. Recall that according to the steps just cited, any number between 001 and 100 can be chosen; numbers greater than 100 are ignored; and any number can be selected only once. Call this sample "A."
>
> What is the proportion of males and females in Sample A? What is the average IQ of the sample? Are these the same values as the population values cited at the bottom of the table?
>
> Would you expect the same values if you drew another sample? Select two more samples of size 20 and determine the sex distribution and average IQ of these samples. Call these samples "B" and "C." Compare the results of the three samples.

The individuals chosen for samples A, B, and C in Quiz 6.1 should have differed, unless you happened by chance to start at the same place in the random number table each time. Of course, a few individuals might have been selected again, but the total composition of the samples should have differed. As a result, the sample statistics (e.g., proportion of males and females, mean IQ) for the three samples were probably not identical. If other samples were drawn, other values would occur. This variation in sample estimates, which results simply from the fact that different samples are drawn, is called *sampling*

TABLE 6.2   POPULATION OF 100 STUDENTS WITH DATA ON THE VARIABLES OF SEX, SCHOOL, INTELLIGENCE, AND MATHEMATICS ACHIEVEMENT

Student Number	Sex	School	IQ	Math	Student Number	Sex	School	IQ	Math
01	F	1	123	3	51	M	1	142	4
02	F	1	120	3	52	M	1	137	9
03	F	1	118	3	53	M	1	119	5
04	F	1	115	3	54	M	2	134	1
05	F	1	115	3	55	M	2	130	7
06	F	1	133	4	56	M	2	122	6
07	F	1	131	6	57	M	3	128	4
08	F	1	116	7	58	M	3	131	4
09	F	1	133	7	59	M	3	125	4
10	F	2	146	7	60	M	3	125	5
11	F	2	121	5	61	M	3	125	5
12	F	2	117	5	62	M	3	115	4
13	F	1	107	1	63	M	1	114	3
14	F	1	106	5	64	M	1	106	5
15	F	1	106	3	65	M	2	114	6
16	F	1	110	6	66	M	2	114	3
17	F	2	110	5	67	M	2	113	3
18	F	2	106	2	68	M	2	111	1
19	F	2	105	5	69	M	3	111	2
20	F	2	113	7	70	M	3	109	3
21	F	2	112	5	71	M	3	114	2
22	F	2	108	2	72	M	3	110	9
23	F	2	107	3	73	M	3	106	4
24	F	2	106	5	74	M	3	112	3
25	F	1	104	7	75	M	1	105	3
26	F	1	102	1	76	M	1	101	1
27	F	1	102	0	77	M	1	101	3
28	F	1	98	3	78	M	1	105	3
29	F	1	98	4	79	M	1	102	6
30	F	1	99	5	80	M	1	100	5
31	F	2	102	4	81	M	2	105	2
32	F	2	103	2	82	M	2	98	3
33	F	2	99	1	83	M	2	103	3
34	F	2	98	3	84	M	2	100	6
35	F	3	102	1	85	M	3	105	0
36	F	3	104	7	86	M	3	104	3
37	F	1	98	1	87	M	1	97	1
38	F	1	92	1	88	M	1	87	4
39	F	1	94	1	89	M	1	97	2
40	F	2	97	3	90	M	1	95	3
41	F	2	91	2	91	M	2	95	3
42	F	2	85	1	92	M	2	93	2
43	F	2	90	4	93	M	2	95	5
44	F	2	97	3	94	M	2	94	2
45	F	2	93	3	95	M	2	94	3
46	F	2	90	2	96	M	2	89	1
47	F	2	87	3	97	M	3	96	3
48	F	3	97	6	98	M	3	89	5
49	F	3	114	1	99	M	3	116	5
50	F	3	114	3	100	M	3	116	6

Parameters. Means: IQ = 107.83; Math = 3.62. Proportions: M = .50, F = .50;
School 1 = .37, 2 = .40, 3 = .23.

variation or error. It indicates error since the sample is not the entire population and what occurs for a sample differs to some degree from what is true for the population.

6.3 NONPROBABILITY SAMPLING

Despite the advantages of probability sampling procedures, many educational researchers employ nonprobability sampling techniques because of the convenience and usually lower cost. While the journal article description of probability sampling designs is usually quite detailed and specific, the description of nonprobability procedures may be quite brief and inadequate.

6.3.1 HAPHAZARD OR ACCIDENTAL SAMPLING

With haphazard or accidental sampling researchers take the cases at hand until the desired number is reached or until they obtain all the cases available. Samples consisting of volunteer subjects are obtained by such procedures. A researcher relies on accidental sampling procedures when it is impossible to construct a list of population elements or when such lists could be constructed only with great difficulty. This is especially true of such fields as archeology, history, and astronomy.

6.3.2 PURPOSIVE OR EXPERT CHOICE SAMPLING

In purposive/expert choice sampling, experts choose "typical" or "representative" cases on the assumption that with judgment and reason a satisfactory sample can be chosen. For example, a few students are chosen as typical or representative of the student body as a whole; a principal selects a typical teacher to be interviewed by the press; one city is chosen to illustrate communities of a given size; a reporter describes the plight of one cattle farmer in the Midwest as typical of that experienced by other Midwest cattle farmers.

In some cases expert choice may be used to select an atypical sample or a sample with particular characteristics. In the study by Marascuilo and Dagenais (see Chapter 19), the researchers deliberately selected a large city that had undergone voluntary racial integration by busing of students.

6.3.3 QUOTA SAMPLING

In quota sampling, researchers ensure that certain types of population elements are represented. For example, they may want both male and female elementary teachers. They decide on the desired number of each and select teachers until this criterion is reached. It is not necessary that the quotas for each characteristic be proportional to the existence of those characteristics in the population as a whole. In some cases, researchers may want a certain characteristic to be overrepresented in their sample. To obtain a large sample of highly gifted students, it may be necessary to select proportionately more gifted students for the sample than exist in the population. The sample may have 10 percent gifted students whereas the population may only have 1 percent.

6.3.4 COMPARISON WITH SIMPLE RANDOM SAMPLING

None of these three procedures fits the definition of probability sampling; i.e., that each element in the population has a known nonzero probability of being selected. In most cases the population elements are not known and even if a list of the population elements were available, the likelihood of selecting each element is not known. Some elements have no chance of being selected. You do not know *a priori* the likelihood of someone being a volunteer or the likelihood of someone being at the corner of First and Maple where the interviewer is standing. People who do not volunteer for activities have no chance of being selected. Some individuals simply do not fit the judge's stereotype of typical or representative.

The major advantage of simple random sampling is that the selection procedure itself is not biased; it is a *representative sampling plan*. The procedure is unbiased in the sense that it is "blind." The random process selects elements by chance, rather than because the elements possess certain traits, as in "being available" with accidental sampling. Thus *all* characteristics of the population elements have a chance of being represented, which is not the case with nonprobability plans. However, there is no guarantee that a particular sample is not biased, because by chance an unusual sample can occur.

In some cases nonprobability samples are justified. A researcher may not be interested in generalizing to a population. Purposive sampling of economic experts may be used in order to obtain critical expertise, rather than the opinion of economists as a whole. In other cases, probability sampling is simply not feasible. If you want to study the Chinese educational system, you would probably need to rely either on informants who have spent some time in the country or on government reports. It is highly unlikely that you would be able to randomly select a sample of schools to visit or pupils to interview.

6.4 OTHER FORMS OF PROBABILITY SAMPLING (OPTIONAL)

6.4.1 STRATIFIED RANDOM SAMPLING

With stratified random sampling the population is first divided into desired groups or strata on one or more criteria such as sex, socioeconomic status or age. The population elements are then randomly selected from each stratum, and these subsamples are combined to form the total sample. Stratification is used when it can produce more accurate estimates of population characteristics than simple random sampling designs. Increased precision occurs only when the stratification variable is related to the characteristic being measured (e.g., amount of education is related to voter preference for presidential candidates but color of eyes is probably not related). Another reason for stratification is that different sampling procedures or different methods of observation may be needed in various segments of the population. Finally, comparisons among the strata levels may be a major objective of the study.

In some cases stratification is introduced *after* population elements have been selected by simple random sampling. Such *poststratification* is often used when the stratifying variable is unavailable prior to the selection of the sample. Stratification on such variables as personality, attitude, and motivation must usually be done this way. Poststratification requires an initial simple random sampling plan, and is not synonymous with subgroup comparisons made on samples collected in a haphazard manner or through any other nonprobability design.

6.4.2 SYSTEMATIC SAMPLING

Systematic sampling consists of taking every *k*th sampling unit from a list of population elements after a random start. The random start qualifies it as a probability sampling design, since the first case is chosen at random placing no limitation in advance upon the chances of an element being selected for the sample. If the start were not random, then it would be a nonprobability design. Systematic sampling is well known and frequently used because of its ease of application by a clerk or an interviewer in the field.

Whatever stratification exists in the ordering of the population list will be reflected in the sample. If the population list is thoroughly shuffled, then the systematic sample is equivalent to a simple random sample. However, many population lists have some order: student records may be kept by grade level and by classroom, schools may be numbered or filed by geographic region or by size, lists of teachers may be ordered by school or by subject taught, etc. When trends or periodic fluctuations exist in the population list, then systematic selection can provide misleading results. These problems can be reduced by changing the random start several times.

6.4.3 CLUSTER SAMPLING

Often it is difficult to obtain a list of every population element, but lists of groups or clusters of elements are available. For example, lists of schools in a school district and homeroom classes in those schools are easier to construct than is a list citing every child in the district. In cluster sampling the sampling unit is a group of population elements. The clusters can be selected by any of the previous probability techniques.

Cluster sampling is frequently used to reduce cost and to increase the ease of conducting a study. If the population is spread over a large geographic area, the expense and time involved in locating a simple random sample may be quite high. In other cases, it may be extremely difficult to satisfy the conditions of simple random sampling whereas cluster procedures are feasible. The principal of a school may allow several entire classes, randomly selected, to participate in a study, but may not allow students to be randomly selected from all classes.

Cluster sampling requires a larger sample size than does simple random sampling to obtain the same degree of precision, since clusters of individuals are usually not created by a random process. People live in a particular area of a city because they can afford to or because they want to, not because they were randomly placed there. Neither teachers nor students are usually randomly assigned to classrooms, nor are principals randomly assigned to schools. A number of clusters of small size are likely to produce more precise estimates than fewer clusters of a larger size.

QUIZ 6.2

1. Divide the population in Table 6.2 into strata of female and male students. Randomly select ten female and ten male students from their respective groups. Calculate the mean IQ for each sex. Then average these two IQ values and compare the result with the mean IQ obtained for samples A, B, and C selected previously in Quiz 6.1 and to the population IQ cited in Table 6.2.

2. Suppose researchers used a cluster sampling design on the population cited in Table 6.2. They used schools as the sampling unit, and randomly selected School 3. Calculate the proportion of males and females in this school. Do these values differ greatly from the population parameters and from the values obtained from the simple random samples previously drawn in Quiz 6.1?

6.5 COMBINATIONS OF SAMPLING DESIGNS (OPTIONAL)

Sampling can also be done in stages, i.e., *multistage sampling*. At each stage either a probability or nonprobability sampling design is used. The population elements that actually form the sample are selected at the final stage.

The annual Gallup Poll of public attitudes toward education published in the *Phi Delta Kappan* illustrates multistage sampling techniques (basically a combination of cluster and stratification designs). Gallup (53) stated that the sampling design was developed "to produce an approximation of the adult civilian population, 18 years and older, living in the United States, except for those persons in institutions such as prisons or hospitals" (p. 50). In each survey a minimum of 1500 individuals is interviewed, and an independent sample is drawn. Gallup's condensed description of the sampling procedure indicated four stages. Some form of probability sampling is employed at each stage and all but the last stage involve cluster sampling. If you are interested in how samples are selected for national polls, you should read Gallup's description.

The Jackson and Cosca Study (Chapter 2) illustrates two-stage sampling. The accessible population was defined as English teachers/classes at "rural, urban, and suburban schools with substantial numbers of Mexican American students" (paragraph 5). Areas that met this criterion were identified and the population of schools was further restricted by other criteria (e.g., no special schools for the handicapped (paragraph 6)). The accessible population then consisted of 430 schools. At the first sampling stage, 52 schools were randomly selected from the population of 430. Cluster sampling was used at this stage, since the schools were clusters of the population elements (teacher/class) and the clusters were selected at random. The sampling design at the second and final stage was not fully described, although grade level was used as a stratifying variable (only grades 4, 8, 10, and 12 were selected). The selection procedures within each grade at each school were also not described. One might assume, however, from the statement in paragraph 8 referring to the fact that no teacher refused to be observed, that all teachers/classes at each of these grade levels were included in the sample.

6.6 DETERMINING THE SAMPLE DESIGN IN RESEARCH ARTICLES

The questions in Exhibit 6.1 will help you identify the sampling design employed in any study.

EXHIBIT 6.1   *IDENTIFICATION OF SAMPLING DESIGNS*

A. Was *any* type of *probability sampling* employed at *any* point in the selection of the sample? (Read the section of the research report that describes the sample very carefully. In instances in which little information is given, nonprobability techniques were probably used. When probability sampling is involved in educational studies, random sampling is likely to be employed at some stage.)

If *no*, go to section B.
If *yes*, how *many stages of sampling* were involved?

1. If there was *only one stage*,

   a) Was the sample selected through *simple random sampling* procedures?
   b) Was the sample selected through *stratified random sampling* procedures? If yes, what were the strata on which the sample was divided? Was post-stratification applied?

      c) Was the sample selected through *systematic sampling* procedures? If yes, what was the nature of the list from which the sample elements were drawn?

    2. If there was *more than one stage* of sampling, various combinations of the probability techniques cited above and nonprobability techniques, cited in B, could have been employed. Attempt to determine the nature of the sampling design at each stage. Most likely some form of clustering of elements is involved, although the clustering may or may not be associated with random selection of the clusters.

B. No form of probability sampling was used. *Generalization* beyond the sample involves *risk* and the amount of error associated wih sample estimates of population characteristics cannot be determined accurately. Which form of nonprobability sampling best describes the procedure employed?

1. Haphazard/accidental
2. Expert choice/purposive
3. Quota

7

Inferences from Sample to Population: Selected Elementary Statistical Techniques[1]

You have probably encountered such phrases as "the correlation coefficient was statistically significant" and "significant differences were found between the two means" in research reports. In such instances the researcher is reporting the results of the *test of a statistical hypothesis*. The area of hypothesis testing is indeed large; many statistical tests exist. (See Appendix D for a list of some commonly used statistical procedures.) The purpose of this chapter is to explain to you the logic of hypothesis testing. This logic applies to practically every statistical test you will encounter in research articles, although the specific hypothesis tested and the specific mathematical calculations involved will vary from test to test. Hypothesis testing is illustrated in this chapter with tests of the mean. Brief comments are also made about statistical tests involving correlation coefficients and cross-tabulation tables. First, let us examine a situation in which hypothesis testing could be used.

Suppose you are a school superintendent faced with the following problem. You want to determine whether the intelligence level of the students in your school district can be considered to be like the norm; that is, to have an average IQ of 100. You randomly select a sample of 225 students and compute the mean for the sample $(\overline{X})$. It is 105. What decision would you make about all the students in your district based on this sample? Are they like the norm? At this point, the only decision you can make is a subjective one.

Suppose you had some additional information. You knew that *if* the mean IQ of all your students was really 100, and *if* you had taken the time to *randomly select all possible samples* of size 225 from your school district and had calculated the mean on *each* sample, that 68 percent of these means would fall between 99 and 101. In addition, 95 percent of them would be between 98 and 102, and 99 percent between 97.4 and 102.6. Now you can make a more informed decision. You know that only one in 100 times would you randomly select

---

[1] Most of the material in Chapters 3 through 6 has provided the prerequisite concepts for this chapter. Information in this chapter is not a prerequisite for Chapters 8 and 9.

a sample with a mean of 105 from such a population (i.e., students with a mean IQ of 100). Since the chances of this situation occurring are so small, you are pretty safe in deciding that your students do not come from such a group; that they are above the norm, on the average. On the other hand, if the sample mean had been 101.5, you know that the probability of selecting such a sample (from a population with a mean of 100) is quite high, and therefore that your students could easily be like the norm of 100.

In this example, the superintendent wanted to make an inference or generalization about a population on the basis of a single sample. In particular, inferences were made about a *population parameter* (μ, the population mean) on the basis of a *sample statistic* ($\bar{X}$, the sample mean). *Researchers test statistical hypotheses in order to determine what type of statements can be made about the population of interest based on the research sample.* The focus is no longer upon the sample per se, but upon the population which the sample represents. The following discussion of statistical inference assumes that the sample has been randomly selected from the population.

7.1 INFERENCES REGARDING THE POPULATION MEAN (μ)

7.1.1 SAMPLING DISTRIBUTION OF THE MEAN ($\bar{X}$)

In the superintendent example, no informed decision could be made until the superintendent had information on how the means from all possible samples of

DUNAGIN'S PEOPLE   by Dunagin

DUNAGIN'S PEOPLE BY RALPH DUNAGIN, COURTESY OF FIELD NEWSPAPER SYNDICATE

"DEAR, THERE'S A FORTY PERCENT CHANCE I'LL BE LATE FOR DINNER."

a specific size were distributed. This distribution is called the *sampling distribution of the mean* (X). Only when the characteristics of this distribution are known or assumed can hypothesis testing of the mean begin. Luckily such information can be estimated from just one sample. In fact, if a large sample is selected from a population with mean μ and standard deviation σ_x, the sampling distribution of the mean ($\overline{X}$) will approximate the normal distribution. This sampling distribution will have a mean equal to the population mean of raw scores μ denoted by μ_x) and a standard deviation equal to $\sigma_x/\sqrt{n}$ (the population standard deviation of raw scores divided by the square root of the sample size), called the *standard error of the mean,* abbreviated here as $\mathrm{SE}_{\overline{x}}$). The information given to the superintendent involved this concept of the sampling distribution of the mean. Let us examine the example in more detail.

Given the large sample of 225, it was assumed that the sampling distribution approximated the normal distribution. The next important assumption or hypothesis that was made was that the population mean μ (the mean IQ of all the students) was 100 (making the mean of the sampling distribution $\mu_{\overline{x}}$ also equal to 100). This hypothesis, that $\mu = 100$, is called a *statistical* or *null hypothesis,* and it is this hypothesis which is actually tested by the sample data. The general form of this particular null hypothesis is that μ equals some constant value, $\mu = c$.

Null hypotheses are usually denoted by H_0. The convention of calling these hypotheses "null" came from the "fact that statistical hypothesis testing procedures arose within a philosophy of science that conceived of its role as gathering evidence in attempts to *nullify* hypotheses" (56, p. 280). Null hypotheses often state that there are no differences among parameters or that the value of a certain parameter is zero. Other examples of null hypotheses are H_0: $\mu_1 = \mu_2$, the means of two populations are equal, and H_0: $\rho_{xy} = 0$, the population correlation coefficient between variables X and Y equals zero. It is important to remember that null hypotheses are symbolic statements about population parameters, while research hypotheses are general statements about the nature of the results expected by the researcher.

One more piece of information was provided to the superintendent, the standard error $\mathrm{SE}_{\overline{x}}$ of the sampling distribution (i.e., its standard deviation). It was assumed that the population standard deviation of IQ scores, μ_x, equaled 15 (as is the case with WAIS intelligence test norms), making the $\mathrm{SE}_{\overline{x}}$ equal to 1 ($\mathrm{SE}_{\overline{x}} = \sigma_x/\sqrt{n} = 15/\sqrt{225}$).

Thus the information given to the superintendent assumed that the sampling distribution of the mean ($\overline{X}$) was normal with a mean equal to 100 (the population mean) and with a $\mathrm{SE}_{\overline{x}}$ of 1. In other words, it was assumed/hypothesized that if samples of size 225 were repeatedly selected from the population of IQ raw scores, the means themselves would be normally distributed with a mean of 100 and a standard deviation of 1. Figure 7.1 illustrates this sampling distribution.

The final information presented to the superintendent was the chances of randomly selecting a sample with an average IQ of 105 from a population whose mean was hypothesized to be 100. This information was determined by

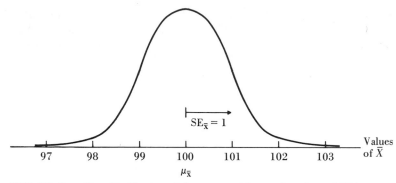

FIG. 7.1 Sampling distribution of the mean with samples of size 225 from a population with $\mu = 100$ and $\sigma_x = 15$.

examining the probabilities associated with the normal curve (Table E.2, Appendix E). The use of the normal curve table was discussed in Chapter 4. From this table we know that 68 percent of the sample means would fall between 99 and 101 (that is, within one standard deviation above and below the mean, corresponding to z scores of ± 1). In addition, 95 percent of the sample means would fall between 98.04 and 101.96 (corresponding to z scores of ± 1.96), and that 99 percent of the sample means would fall between 97.4 and 102.6 (corresponding to z scores of ± 2.57). Thus the likelihood of randomly selecting the sample mean of 105 was less than 1 in 100.

7.1.2 TESTING THE NULL HYPOTHESIS

How do you make the final decision regarding the similarity of the sample results to the condition specified by the null hypothesis? If the sample outcome has a *high* probability of occurring under the conditions specified by the null hypothesis, then the evidence indicates that the null hypothesis is feasible. However, if the sample result has a *low* probability of occurring, the researcher has reason to reject or doubt the null hypothesis. How does the researcher decide if the probability level is high or low? It is customary for educational researchers to define an unlikely outcome as one which occurs 5 percent of the time or less at random (by chance). This probability is called *alpha* (α) and is specified when the researcher designs the study. When analyzing data, the actual probability of the sample result occurring by chance (sometimes called the *significance level*) is then compared to the alpha value to determine whether the null hypothesis is rejected or accepted. It is customary to represent the significance level in research articles by the symbol "*p*." A statement that "$p < .05$" means that the probability of the sample value occurring by chance under the null hypothesis was less than 5 times in 100. If alpha were set at .05, then the null hypothesis would be rejected.

Figure 7.2 illustrates how setting alpha at .05 applies to the sampling distribution in the superintendent example. Since the probability of selecting a sample with a mean of 105, under the null hypothesis specification of $\mu = 100$, was less than .05 (quite unlikely), the null hypothesis was rejected. In other words, it was reasonable to assume that the population from which the sample was drawn did not have an average IQ of 100, but probably had a higher IQ, given the sample mean of 105.

Quiz 7.1 tests your comprehension of the hypothesis-testing concepts presented so far in this chapter.

QUIZ 7.1

1. Using the superintendent example (with H_0: $\mu = 100$, $\sigma_x = 15$, $n = 225$, and $SE_{\bar{x}} = 1$), what is the probability of randomly selecting a mean:

   a) greater than or equal to 101.5?
   b) less than or equal to 99?
   c) less than or equal to 93?

   Assuming that an unlikely event is defined as one that would occur 5 out of 100 times or less under the null hypothesis ($\alpha \leq .05$), in which of the above instances would you reject the null hypothesis?

2. Suppose a sample of only 25 were drawn, with both the null hypothesis and the population standard deviation remaining the same as in Problem 1. What is the probability of randomly selecting a mean:

   a) greater than or equal to 105?
   b) greater than or equal to 101.5?
   c) less than or equal to 99?
   d) less than or equal to 93?

   Setting alpha at .05, in which of the above instances would you reject the null hypothesis? In which instances would you reject the null hypothesis if alpha were .01?

3. The standard error of the mean, SE, was less in Problem 1 than it was in Problem 2 because of the change in sample size. Why would the SE be greater as the sample size decreases? Are you more likely to reject the null hypothesis with large or small sample sizes? Why?

4. Why are you more likely to reject the null hypothesis when alpha is set at .05 than when it is .01 or .001?

7.1.3 ALTERNATIVE HYPOTHESES

When the null hypothesis (H_0) is rejected, an *alternative hypothesis* (H_1) is accepted. Usually the alternative hypothesis specifies all possible values of the parameter of interest not specified by the null hypothesis. If H_0 specifies $\mu =$

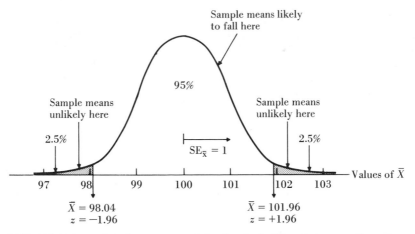

FIG. 7.2 Relationship between an alpha level of .05 and the sampling distribution of the mean with samples of the size 225 from a population with $\mu = 100$ and $\sigma_x = 15$.

100, then H_1 specifies $\mu \neq 100$. If H_0 states $\rho_{xy} = 0$, then H_1 states $\rho_{xy} \neq 0$. If H_0 states that $\mu_1 - \mu_2 = 0$, then H_1 states that $\mu_1 - \mu_2 \neq 0$. Such alternative hypotheses are called *nondirectional* or two-tailed since an extreme value in either direction of the hypothesized null value leads to rejection of the null hypothesis. In some studies, *directional* or one-tailed hypotheses, which specify only one direction of deviation, are used. Examples of directional hypotheses are $\mu < 100$; $\mu_1 - \mu_2 > 0$; and $\rho_{xy} < 0$.

7.1.4 THE TEST STATISTIC

The procedures used in examining a statistical hypothesis are formalized in what is called a *test statistic*. In the particular case of the mean discussed in sections 7.1.1 through 7.1.3 it is the z test. The symbol z equals

$$\frac{\bar{X} - c}{\sigma_x / \sqrt{n}}$$

where c is the value of μ specified in the null hypothesis and z refers to a point on the normal distribution. The z value is calculated from the data. It is then compared to the critical z values obtained from the normal curve table corresponding to the preset alpha value to determine if the null hypothesis is rejected or accepted. If the *calculated z value* is *greater than or equal to the critical z values* from the normal curve table, then the *null hypothesis is rejected.*

If the *calculated z value* is *smaller than the critical z values,* then the *null hypothesis is accepted.* When alpha is set at .05, the critical z values are ± 1.96. When alpha is .01, the critical z values are ± 2.57.

Let us apply the z-test statistic to the previous example where H_0: $\mu = 100$, H_1: $\mu \neq 100$, $\sigma_x = 15$, $n = 225$, and $\overline{X} = 105$. Let us set alpha at .01. The value of the test statistic, z, equals 5 (that is, $(105 - 100)/(15/\sqrt{225}) = 5/1$). Since this calculated z value of 5 is greater than the critical z values of ± 2.57, the null hypothesis is rejected at the .01 level.

QUIZ 7.2

1. Translate the following null hypotheses from symbols to words: H_0: $\mu_1 = \mu_2$. H_0: $\mu_1 - \mu_2 = 0$. H_0: $\mu_1 = \mu_2 = \mu_3 = \mu_4$. H_0: $\rho_{xy} = \rho_{yz}$.

2. Calculate the z-test statistic values corresponding to each of the sample means given in Problems 1 and 2 of Quiz 7.1. Which of these z values are above the critical z values, when alpha equals .05 and .01, and which are below? Based on this information, in which cases is the null hypothesis rejected; in which cases is it accepted?

7.1.5 INFERENCES REGARDING THE MEAN WHEN THE POPULATION STANDARD DEVIATION IS UNKNOWN

When the population standard deviation is unknown, the sample standard deviation (s_x) is used to estimate it. However, the sampling distribution of the mean then corresponds to what is known as the t distribution rather than the normal distribution. The t distribution is symmetric and approximates the normal distribution with large sample sizes. The null hypothesis, $\mu = c$, is then tested by means of the following test statistic:

$$ t = \frac{\overline{X} - c}{s_x/\sqrt{n}}. $$

How do we know if this calculated t value represents an extreme value under the null hypothesis? By examining a table that contains percentile or critical points of the t distribution (Table E.3, Appendix E). This t table introduces a new concept, degrees of freedom (symbolized by df). Degrees of freedom are associated with most test statistics. A good explanation of the df concept, provided by Walker and Lev (141), is as follows:

> Suppose you are asked to write three numbers with no restrictions upon them. You have complete freedom of choice in regard to all three. There are three degrees of freedom.

Now suppose you are asked to write 3 numbers with the restriction that their sum is to be some particular value, say 20. You cannot now choose all 3 freely, but as soon as 2 have been chosen, the third is determined. Your choices are governed by the necessary relation $X_1 + X_2 + X_3 = 20$. In this situation there are only 2 degrees of freedom. The number of variables is 3, but the number of restrictions upon them is 1, and the number of "free" variables, or independent choices, is $3\text{-}1 = 2$. . . .

In every statistical problem in which degrees of freedom are involved, it is necessary to determine the number of "free variables" by first noting the total number of variables and reducing that number by the number of independent restrictions upon them (p. 90).

The number of degrees of freedom in the t test just cited is $n - 1$, the number of individuals in the sample minus 1.

The entries in the t table are points on the t distribution corresponding to the appropriate df beyond which a particular percentage or proportion of the curve falls. Since the t distribution is symmetric about zero, only positive values are cited. Significance levels corresponding to both directional and nondirectional alternative hypotheses are indicated in the table. For example, the t value of $+1.753$ at the intersection of the 15 df row and the .05 column for a one-tailed test refers to the point on a t distribution with 15 df *above* which 5 percent of the scores fall. A t of -1.753 refers to the point *below* which 5 percent of the scores fall. When both points are considered, as is the case when the alternative hypothesis is nondirectional, the corresponding percentage of area is 10 percent, referring to a significance level of .10. When a calculated t value is greater than or equal to the appropriate critical value in the table (i.e., corresponding to the correct df and the desired alpha value), then the null hypothesis is rejected. When the calculated t value is smaller, the null hypothesis is accepted.

Suppose researchers tested a sample of 25 children with the Lorge–Thorndike Intelligence Test and found the sample mean to be 107 and the sample standard deviation to be 20. They decided to determine whether this sample differed from the norm and thus established H_0 as $\mu = 100$ and H_1 as $\mu \neq 100$. The researchers computed the t test as defined above, setting α at .05. They knew that a computed t value $\geq \pm 2.064$ would lead them to reject the null hypothesis. They obtained a t value of 1.75 for their sample:

$$t = \frac{107 - 100}{20/\sqrt{25}} = 1.75.$$

Since this value of t was smaller than the critical values, they accepted the null hypothesis, concluding that their particular sample could have come from a population with a mean of 100.

None of the articles in Chapters 1 and 2 examined the hypothesis that the population mean was equal to a certain value. Quiz 7.3 illustrates one such application. A t test is also used to test the difference between two population means. This version is discussed in Appendix D.

QUIZ 7.3

In Cicirelli and Cicirelli's study (Chapter 1) the Minnesota Teacher Attitude Inventory was given to a group of 52 counselors-in-training. The mean for the group on the inventory was 82.8 with a standard deviation of 19.3 (paragraph 19). The authors mentioned that the mean for the graduate students in Education at the University of Minnesota was 63.98. Test the hypothesis that $\mu = 64$ (i.e., H_0: $\mu = 64$; H_1: $\mu \neq 64$) with α at .05.

1. What is the value of the test statistic, that is, the computed t value?

2. What are the degrees of freedom?

3. What are the critical values of t at the .05 level?

4. Is the computed t value larger than these values?

5. Is the null hypothesis rejected or accepted?

6. State a conclusion that can be drawn on the basis of this statistical result.

7.2 SUMMARY OF THE STEPS IN STATISTICAL INFERENCE

The logic underlying hypothesis testing can be summarized as follows:

1. Assumptions are made about the distribution of the variable of interest in the population of interest. In particular, a precise statement is made regarding the value of *population parameters* (e.g., that the population mean equals a certain value or that two subgroups within the population have identical means). This assumption about population parameters is called the *null hypothesis*.

2. A *sample* is selected from the population and data from the sample are examined. Descriptive statistics are then computed on the variable of interest (e.g., the sample mean or the difference between two sample means).

3. The following question is raised: *What is the probability of randomly selecting a sample with these particular characteristics from the population specified by the null hypothesis?* The answer to this question is determined by applying *inferential statistical techniques, a statistical test.*

4. If the *probability* of selecting such a sample is *high,* i.e., larger than the alpha value which was preset by the researcher, then the researcher will conclude that the sample came from the designated population. The null hypothesis is accepted. If the *probability* is *low* (less than or equal to the alpha value), then the researcher will conclude that the sample came from a population with different characteristics. The null hypothesis is rejected and an alternative hypothesis is accepted.

It is important to remember that the decision made on the basis of statistical techniques may not necessarily correspond with the substance of the original *research hypothesis,* which was derived from theory and previous studies.

7.3 TYPES OF ERROR IN STATISTICAL DECISIONS

No matter what decision is reached regarding the null hypothesis, this decision involves a degree of risk. The contingencies surrounding the researcher's decision are shown in Fig. 7.3.

Consider first the situation in which researchers *reject the null hypothesis* and accept the alternative hypothesis. The population condition may or may not correspond to the null hypothesis. If it does, then a correct decision has been made. If it does not, then an incorrect decision has been made. The dilemma facing the researchers is that they never know whether they have reached a correct or an incorrect decision, since the actual population condition is not known to them. However, they can determine their chances of making a correct or incorrect decision. The probability of erring in rejecting the null hypothesis (i.e., rejecting the null hypothesis when in fact it is true) is equal to the *alpha value* established by the researchers. Such an error is called a *Type I error.* By decreasing the alpha value, say from .05 to .01 or from .01 to .001, researchers also decrease the likelihood of committing a Type I error. The probability of correctly rejecting the null hypothesis equals what is called the *power* of the statistical test. Calculations of the power of a statistical test can be found in advanced statistics texts.

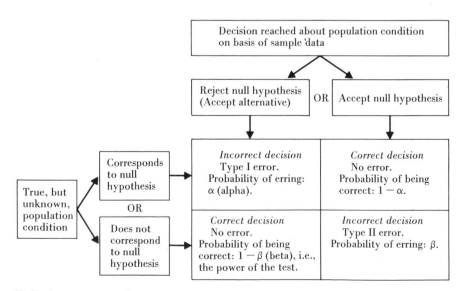

FIG. 7.3 Decision making in hypothesis testing.

When the *null hypothesis is accepted,* a similar dilemma confronts the researchers. They do not know if their decision to accept the null is correct or incorrect. If the true population condition corresponds to the null hypothesis, then the decision to accept the null is correct. The probability of being correct is equal to one minus alpha. On the other hand, if the population does not correspond to the null hypothesis, then the researchers have committed a *Type II error* (accepting the null hypothesis when in fact it is false). The probability of committing such an error is equal to one minus the power of the test and is referred to as beta, β.

Ideally, researchers would like to minimize the likelihood of reaching an incorrect decision. The likelihood of a Type I error can be reduced simply by decreasing the value of alpha. Decreasing the likelihood of committing a Type II error or, equivalently, increasing the power of the test is harder to achieve. Increased power can be obtained, however, by using a larger sample, more reliable measuring instruments, and good research designs.

7.4 CONFIDENCE INTERVAL ESTIMATION

Sometimes the purpose of selecting a sample is to obtain an estimate of the population mean, rather than to test a hypothesis about it. Obviously, one estimate is the sample mean. This is called a point estimate because it specifies only a single number. An interval estimate can also be obtained—a range of values within which the population mean may fall—called a confidence interval. When pollsters talk about being accurate to within two or five percentage points, they are referring to confidence interval techniques. In a close political race, the room for error in prediction is small and a high level of confidence in the prediction is desired. Details on such procedures can be found in statistics texts.

7.5 INFERENCES REGARDING THE PRODUCT–MOMENT CORRELATION COEFFICIENT

The null hypothesis most frequently tested regarding the population correlation coefficient between two variables is that the population correlation coefficient equals zero, H_0: $\rho_{xy} = 0$, with H_1 being $\rho_{xy} \neq 0$. When $\rho_{xy} = 0$ and the sample size is relatively small, the sampling distribution of r_{xy} is a t distribution. The test statistic for H_0 is:

$$t = \frac{r_{xy} \sqrt{n-2}}{\sqrt{1-r_{xy}^2}} \qquad \text{with } n-2 \text{ df.}$$

Tables of critical values of r_{xy} (Table E.4, Appendix E) exist, making it unnecessary to calculate the t statistic just mentioned. All that is required is to compute the sample correlation coefficient and determine if its absolute value (i.e., ignoring its sign) is larger than or equal to the appropriate critical value in the table. If so, then the null hypothesis is rejected. For example, if $r_{xy} = .34$ between anxiety and achievement on a sample of 27 individuals and alpha is set at .05, the critical value of r_{xy} according to the table is .381. Since the correlation of .34 is less than the critical value, H_0 is accepted. Based on the sample, the correlation between anxiety and achievement is not significantly different from zero. If r_{xy} had been .50, then the null hypothesis would have been rejected and the alternative hypothesis, H_1, accepted; meaning that the correlation was significantly different from 0 at $\alpha \leq .05$.

As with other statistical tests, this test depends on the size of the sample. Note that the critical values of r decrease as the df increase. If researchers employ a large sample, they may find many "small" correlation coefficients significantly different from zero. If they use some other mode of interpretation, such as r^2 discussed in Chapter 5, they may conclude that a strong relationship does not exist. Researchers routinely conduct significance tests on correlation

QUIZ 7.4

A battery of six tests was given to 62 high school students and correlation coefficients among all the tests were calculated. The matrix of correlation coefficients presented below contains errors regarding the significance level of the correlation coefficients. (All of the data are hypothetical.)

	Self-concept	Respect for parents	Anxiety	Intelligence	Math achievement	Science achievement
Concept	. . .	.83†	−.10	.40	−.22*	.08
Respect		. . .	.17	.35*	.17	.26
Anxiety			. . .	−.30	−.62*	−.46†
IQ				. . .	.47	.51†
Math					. . .	.76†
Science						. . .

* $p < .05$; † $p < .01$

Note. High numerical scores on the self-concept and respect for parents tests represent a positive self-concept and much respect for parents; high scores on the anxiety scale represent high levels of anxiety; and high scores on the other tests represent high performance levels.

1. Correct all errors regarding significance levels in the matrix.

2. Describe the results of the study as indicated by the corrected significance level of the correlation coefficients.

3. Describe the results of the study using an arbitrary r^2 value of .25 as the point for establishing a linear relationship between two variables.

coefficients, although they may employ additional criteria in determining the strength of the correlation and in making their final conclusions.

Cicirelli and Cicirelli's study (Chapter 1) tested the significance of correlation coefficients. Tables 1.2 and 1.4 in that study indicated the level of significance of r_{xy} by asterisks and daggers, with the probability level cited in the tables' footnotes. For example, the ".82*" notation between flexibility and fluency with "*$p < .05$" at the bottom of Table 1.2 indicated that the correlation of .82 between flexibility and fluency was significant at the .05 level. When no asterisk or dagger followed the correlation coefficient, the null hypothesis was accepted. The daggers in Table 1.4 indicated significance at a higher level, the .01 level. Such notation is commonly used in tables of correlation coefficients.

7.6 INFERENCES ABOUT INDEPENDENCE OF CLASSIFICATIONS

In Chapter 5, the Chi-square test for independence of two modes of classification was presented and used to obtain Cramér's V statistic. The Chi-square value itself is frequently tested for significance. The null hypothesis is that the two classifications are independent of (unrelated to) each other. The alternative hypothesis is that the two dimensions are not independent, but are dependent upon or associated with each other in some way.

To determine whether the Chi-square value calculated on a sample is significant at a specified level, a table of critical values of the Chi-square distribu-

---

QUIZ 7.5

The following cross-tab table shows the relationship between persistence at a task and achievement/anxiety levels (i.e., high/low refers to high-achievement and low-anxiety individuals). The values in the table refer to the numbers of individuals who fit the description of each cell.

		Achievement/Anxiety			
		high/low	high/high	low/low	low/high
Task	Above median	75	40	40	25
Persistence	Below median	25	60	60	75

1. Verify that the expected frequency for each cell is 50. Refer to Exhibit 5.2 for details.

2. Calculate the Chi-square value.

3. Determine the df.

4. Determine whether the null hypothesis of independence between the two classifications is rejected or accepted at alpha equal to both .05 and .01.

tion is used (Table E.5, Appendix E). The number of df is $(r-1)(c-1)$, where r is the number of rows and c is the number of columns (the "total" row and columns are ignored in calculating the df). The Chi-square table gives the points above which a given percentage of the Chi-square distribution falls. Significant calculated Chi-square values are those that are greater than or equal to the critical values in the table at the preset alpha value.

For the three cases in Table 5.4 of Chapter 5 that depicted different degrees of association between eye color (3 levels) and sex (2 levels), the df in each instance were 2 or $(3-1)(2-1)$. Setting alpha at .05, the critical Chi-square value cited in Appendix E, Table E.5, is 5.991. Any calculated Chi-square value greater than or equal to 5.991 would lead to rejection of the null hypothesis. In Case II, $\chi^2 = 0$ and therefore the null hypothesis of independence was accepted. In Cases III and IV, the χ^2 values were 100 and 16.34, respectively, and the null hypothesis was rejected, implying lack of independence between the two dimensions of sex and eye color.

7.7 ADDITIONAL COMMENTS ON THE PRINCIPLES UNDERLYING STATISTICAL INFERENCE

7.7.1 THE DECISIONS AND RISKS IN HYPOTHESIS TESTING

A significant test of the null hypothesis simply gives the probability of randomly selecting a sample with a certain characteristic (e.g., mean, correlation) from the population specified by the null hypothesis. It *does not tell the researcher what course of action to take,* for such actions involve considerations other than the probability of an event. For example, just because the correlation between high school GPA and college GPA is significant at the .05 level does not mean that an administrator should automatically use high school GPA to determine who is and is not admitted to the college. A significant difference between the mean achievement of two educational programs does not necessarily imply that the program with the highest mean should be adopted and the other program abandoned. "Statistical significance is a statement about the likelihood of the observed result, nothing else. It does not guarantee that something important, or even meaningful, has been found" (70, p. 384). It is a means of indicating that "here is something relatively unlikely given the situation initially postulated, but which is rendered relatively much more likely under an alternative situation. The probability is remote of this being a chance occurrence under the initial hypothesis, and something interesting may be here" (70, p. 353).

Although the primary focus in educational research articles is upon the likelihood of a Type I error (of incorrectly rejecting the null hypothesis), the reader and researcher should also be concerned about the *power* of the test. Power is the probability of correctly rejecting the null hypothesis, H_0. Statistical power "is not unlike the power of a microscope. . . . Just as a high-powered microscope lets us distinguish gaps in an apparently solid material that we would miss with low power or the naked eye, so does a high-powered test of H_0 almost insure us of detecting when H_0 is false" (70, p. 357–358).

Researchers should decide whether a Type I or II error is more costly, and plan their study and analysis accordingly in order to reduce the likelihood of the type of error that they feel is the more serious. Is it more serious to conclude there are differences (or there is a relationship) when in fact there are no differences (a Type I error), or is it more serious to conclude there are no differences (or no relationship) when a difference really does exist (a Type II error)?

For example, if a new educational program is very expensive in comparison with an existing program, then before deciding to adopt the new program, it is quite important that the probability of a Type I error be minimized. The cost (in terms of money) of incorrectly concluding that there is a difference between the two programs could be very high. If researchers are attempting to determine if a test administered in high school is a good predictor of academic achievement in college, in order to advise students on how they might perform in college, a strong relationship between the two variables must exist before the researchers can use the test as a predictor. The likelihood of giving students the wrong advice by assuming the test is a good predictor when it is not (a Type I error) should be minimized.

On the other hand, if researchers are exploring a new problem or area, it is important to use a powerful test of differences between groups or of relationships between variables (that is, minimize the likelihood of a Type II error). Overlooking such results could produce a costly error, in terms of ignoring further research possibilities and discoveries or a promising educational program. Similarly, in investigating the effects of therapy and counseling programs, it is important to reduce the likelihood of incorrectly concluding that the therapy has no effect, when in fact it does have an effect, either positive or negative.

7.7.2 RELATIONSHIP TO SIMPLE RANDOM SAMPLING

As stressed throughout this chapter, decisions regarding whether to accept or reject the null hypothesis are based on the chances of randomly selecting a sample with a particular characteristic from the population specified by the null hypothesis. If the sample is in fact *not* randomly selected from a population, then it makes no sense to make decisions regarding the likelihood of its being randomly selected from the population specified by the null hypothesis. Strictly speaking, inferences to any population are not warranted. However, sometimes inferences can be made "with caution" to a "population" like the sample.

Despite the problems in generalizing from nonprobability samples, such samples are more common than probability samples in social science research, and inferences beyond the sample are made all the time. Kerlinger (92, p.

197) recommended the following approach when random sampling cannot be used.

> Be circumspect about interpretations and conclusions; they may be in error. Because of such possibilities of error, it has been said that statistics are misleading, and even useless. Like any other method—consulting authority, using intuition, and the like—statistics *can* be misleading. But even when statistical measures are biased, they are usually less biased than authoritative and intuitive judgments. It is not that numbers lie. The numbers do not know what they are doing. It is that the human beings using the numbers may be informed or misinformed, biased or unbiased, knowledgeable or ignorant, intelligent or stupid. Treat numbers and statistics neither with too great respect nor too great contempt. Calculate statistics and act as though they were "true," but always maintain a certain reserve toward them, a willingness to disbelieve them if the evidence indicates such disbelief.

7.7.3 INTERPRETATION OF RESULTS

Once researchers go beyond probability statements regarding the null hypothesis, such as "the correlation coefficient was significant at the .05 level" or "the Chi-square value was not significant," they are doing more than simply reporting results. They are deciding what the results "mean." They have reached a conclusion about those results, a conclusion with which other researchers as well as the reader of the article could disagree.

One example of why individuals might disagree on the interpretation of the results of a study involves the size of the sample. Recall how the test of significance for a correlation coefficient depended on the sample size. Although two correlation coefficients may both be significant, other measures of the strength of that association, such as r^2, may indicate substantial differences in the degree of association reflected by the two coefficients.

"Good" or "important" results should not be equated with statistically significant results, as is often the case. If a study is carefully conducted, a finding of no association between two variables may be just as important, either theoretically or practically, as a finding of a significant association. "Overemphasizing the role of statistical significance in research is like confusing the paint brush with the painting. This form of statistical inference is a valuable tool in research, but it is never the arbiter of good research. . . . Careful observation is the main business of empirical science, and statistical methods are useful only so long as they help, not hinder, the systematic exploration of data and the cumulation and coordination of results" (70, p. 385–386).

8
Reliability of Measurement Procedures[1]

Any measurement technique should be *accurate or reliable* if interpretations derived from the measurement procedure are to be sound or valid. The researcher must be as concerned about these issues as a counselor or teacher who uses tests to make decisions about pupils.

When a characteristic of an object or individual is measured repeatedly, no measurement ever exactly duplicates the other measurements. Each contains a certain amount of error. The amount of error, no matter what its size, creates what is called *unreliability*. On the other hand, despite the lack of duplication from one measurement to another, there is some degree of consistency in the results. *The greater the consistency, the greater the reliability.*

Reliability is particularly important when decisions are made about individuals on the basis of their test scores. If the score from an unreliable achievement test were used to determine whether a student should be placed in a high, medium, or low ability class, the decision maker cannot be very confident that the student is in the proper class. If an unreliable interest inventory were used to advise students regarding vocational plans, then the counselor's advice could be quite misleading.

Similarly, researchers need to employ reliable measuring procedures because they need to be confident that comparable results would occur upon retest of the sample. Unreliability also lowers the magnitude of the maximum possible relationship between variables. A high correlation cannot be obtained if the measures are unreliable.

The first part of this chapter discusses the types of reliability coefficients that are used by researchers with traditional testing procedures. The last part presents reliability techniques associated with measurement procedures that require an observer or coder.

---

[1] The concepts in this chapter are prerequisites for Sections 9.2.1 and 9.4 in Chapter 9. Section 8.3 on coefficients of generalizability is an optional section.

8.1 TESTS AND OTHER SELF-REPORT MEASUREMENT TECHNIQUES

8.1.1 SOURCES OF TEST SCORE VARIATION

Ideally, the scores obtained by individuals on a test are the result of the trait being measured by the test and nothing else. Since this trait represents lasting and fairly general characteristics of the individuals, the individuals should score similarly on the test when they take it again. Yet test scores are influenced by factors other than the trait being measured, e.g., health and motivation of the individuals taking the test, the procedures used to administer the test. These factors also affect the test's reliability.

A list of six major factors that can affect how individuals perform on tests is presented on Table 8.1 (136, 138). The factors are ordered in terms of

---

TABLE 8.1   *SOURCES OF SYSTEMATIC AND ERROR VARIANCE IN TEST SCORES*

1. *Lasting and general* characteristics of the individual: Level of ability on one or more general traits (verbal comprehension, math ability), general skills of taking tests, general ability to comprehend instructions.

2. *Lasting but specific* characteristics of the individual:
   a) Specific to the test as a whole (and to parallel forms of it): Ability on traits required by the test but not by other tests, skills specific to the form of the test items, stable response sets.
   b) Specific to particular test items: The "chance" element of knowing or not knowing a particular fact, item types with which examinees are unequally familiar.

3. *Temporary but general* characteristics of the individual (factors which affect performance on many or all tests at a particular time): Health, motivation, fatigue, emotional strain, external conditions of heat, light, and ventilation.

4. *Temporary and specific* characteristics of the individual:
   a) Specific to the test as a whole: Momentary "set" for a particular test, comprehension of the specific test task, techniques of dealing with specific test materials, level of practice on skills involved in the test.
   b) Specific to particular test items: Unpredictable fluctuations in human memory and attention.

5. Factors affecting the *administration* of the test or appraisal of test performance: Conditions of testing (adherence to time limits, clarity of instructions), interaction of personality, sex, or race of examiner with examinee performance, bias in grading or rating performance.

6. *Chance:* Luck in selection of answers by sheer guessing, momentary distractions.

---

generality or scope and the degree to which they persist over a period of time. *If a factor is constant when reliability is being estimated, then it has a systematic effect on scores and contributes to reliability. If a factor varies, then it has an unsystematic effect and contributes to unreliability.*

8.1.2 PROCEDURES FOR ESTIMATING RELIABILITY OF TESTS

Many techniques can be applied to estimate the reliability of a test. Ideally, researchers select the technique that corresponds to the type of inferences they wish to make with the test results (e.g., whether they wish to generalize over time and testing conditions). As indicated in the following paragraphs, the sources of variation cited in Table 8.1 have different impacts upon the different reliability techniques.

REPEATED ADMINISTRATION OF THE SAME FORM ON DIFFERENT OCCASIONS

Retesting individuals with the *same form* of a test at a later time is one way of estimating reliability, and is sometimes referred to as an estimate of stability. The correlation coefficient between the two sets of scores provides a numerical index of reliability, referred to as a reliability coefficient. Obviously, high positive values of the correlation coefficient reflect high reliability; that is, consistency in the relative standings of individuals on the two testings.

The size of a test–retest reliability coefficient depends on the relative impact of the systematic and unsystematic (error) sources of variance cited in Table 8.1. Characteristics of the individual that are stable over time and relate to the test itself have a systematic effect on scores. On the other hand, temporary characteristics of the individual such as health, motivation, and level of practice vary from one testing to the next, and lower the reliability coefficient and therefore reflect error variance. If the test interval is short, the test itself is short, and/or the test items are distinct, then the memory of previous responses and of items may make the results on the two testings unusually similar, representing a source of systematic variance. Whether factors relating to the administration of the test reflect systematic or error variance depends on whether or not these conditions change upon retest (e.g., different examiner, time of day or testing room; variation in adherence to instructions).

ADMINISTRATION OF PARALLEL FORMS

Parallel forms of the test can be constructed and administered to the same individuals either on *one occasion* or on *different occasions*. The correlation coefficient between the two sets of scores is the reliability coefficient, and is sometimes referred to as a coefficient of stability and equivalence.

Equivalent or parallel forms of a test are defined "as forms built according to the same specifications but composed of separate samples from the defined area of behavior" (139, p. 182). Parallel forms are appropriate for most achievement, attitude, and personality tests since the items in any particular form are a sample from a large domain or universe of items. If test results are used to generalize about how individuals will do on similar tasks in the future, as is typical of many educational contexts, then administering parallel forms of a test on different occasions is the appropriate procedure by which to evaluate the test's reliability.

In contrast with test–retest procedures, knowledges and skills associated with particular test items no longer have constant effects nor contribute to unreliability since the test items vary on the different forms. When the forms are administered on different occasions, the reliability estimate will usually be lower than it is when the forms are administered on one occasion.

ADMINISTRATION OF ONE FORM

When a single *test* can be administered only *once,* two approaches can be used to obtain a reliability estimate. One procedure is to construct the test so it can be divided into equivalent halves, correlate the scores on the two halves, and then apply what is known as the Spearman–Brown formula to the correlation coefficient to obtain an estimate of the reliability for the full length of the test. The other procedure is to consider each item as a test of the same variable and obtain an estimate of the consistency among items, what is called a measure of *internal consistency.* Such indices are usually reported in terms of a Kuder–Richardson formula (KR–20 or KR–21), coefficient alpha, or Hoyt's analysis of variance procedure. These reliability coefficients will range between 0 and 1.[2]

When only one test is administered, temporary factors such as health, fatigue, practice, and momentary set are relatively constant for individuals and become a source of systematic variance. In general, internal consistency estimates yield the highest reliability coefficients because most of the sources of variation cited in Table 8.1 have systematic or constant effects on test performance.

8.1.3 SATISFACTORY LEVELS OF RELIABILITY

Although no minimum level of reliability can be established to fit all occasions, it is well known that decisions about individuals require higher reliabilities than decisions regarding the average characteristic of a group. In making individual decisions, Davis (42, p. 24) specified that reliability coefficients below .75 were "inefficient." Nunnally (112) concurred with this level as a minimum, yet stated that "in such cases where important decisions must be made about humans on the basis of test scores, even a reliability of .90 is not high enough" (p. 10). When examining the average of a group of size 25 to 50, as is the case in many research studies, tests with reliabilities as low as .50 may still be acceptable (42).

---

[2] With the KR–21 formula, it is mathematically possible to have a reliability index less than 0 when a test is very easy (a high mean and low standard deviation) or very difficult (a low mean and low standard deviation).

The structure of the test may also affect the degree of reliability required from the various estimation procedures. If the test items are intended to reflect only one dimension, then high internal consistency estimates are essential. On the other hand, if the test content is intended to be heterogeneous in nature, then very high internal consistency estimates are not desired, but high test–retest and parallel forms estimates are desired.

8.1.4 SELECTED MEASUREMENT TECHNIQUES

NORM-REFERENCED VERSUS CRITERION-REFERENCED MEASUREMENT

The previous procedures for estimating reliability' were developed from a theory of testing that makes fine discriminations among individuals on the trait being measured. Such tests are referred to as norm-referenced since the meaning of each score depends on a comparison with scores obtained by other individuals on the test, a normative group. Most standardized tests of achievement, ability, personality, motivation, creativity, etc. are norm-referenced.

Another approach to testing achievement is criterion-referenced measurement. In contrast to norm-referenced measurement, the meaning of an individual's score depends on comparison with a previously specified standard of performance on the domain of tasks. Such tests are often used to indicate mastery of subject matter content. A written driver's license test is an example. Whether or not you pass a driver's license test depends on whether your score exceeds a certain standard of performance, not on how your score compares with that of other applicants.

Determining the reliability of criterion-referenced tests is at present a much debated issue. The central issue in this debate is the concept of variability. Variability in scores is not necessary for criterion-referenced tests to have high reliability. For example, when all students achieve mastery, there is no variance in the scores. With no score variability, traditional reliability estimation procedures yield a reliability coefficient of zero. However, a criterion-referenced test would be highly reliable if all students achieved mastery on both test and retest. Thus replicability or repeatability of scores is a necessary condition for a reliable criterion-referenced test.

Many reliability indices have been developed for criterion-referenced tests. A researcher may use an index of agreement that reflects the consistency with which individuals remain at a state of mastery, an index that reflects the discrepancy in scores on parallel tests, a comparison of the percentage of individuals who reach criterion from two comparable groups, or some other index.

QUESTIONNAIRES AND INTERVIEWS

Estimating the reliability of questionnaires and interviews creates special problems since repeated measurements on subjects are extremely difficult to obtain and internal consistency estimates are usually inappropriate (i.e., when the purpose of the questionnaire is to measure more than one dimension or trait). Even when retesting is possible, it is usually very costly.

Techniques for enhancing the reliability of questionnaires typically focus on how to write good questions and on accuracy in coding and tabulating the data. Payne (113) has shown how the wording of questionnaire items can greatly influence how individuals respond. One procedure that examines the effect of word-order, of the order of alternative choices, and of specific wording is the split-ballot technique in which different versions of the question are given to equivalent groups. Researchers usually report when they have used such procedures in developing questionnaires. In cases in which no preliminary testing has been conducted and the questionnaire itself is not included in the research article, the reader has no way of detecting faults in question construction that could lead to unreliability.

8.2 MEASUREMENT TECHNIQUES REQUIRING AN OBSERVER AND/OR CODER

8.2.1 ADDITIONAL SOURCES OF VARIATION

Up to this point measurement techniques that require routine recording of behavior or responses have been considered. However, recording is no longer routine when the measurement requires the observation of ongoing behavior, the rating of behavior, many forms of interviewing, or analysis of the content of documents and of responses to projective tests. The recorder then becomes a major source of unreliability. In fact, the observer/interviewer/coder together with the observation schedule/interview schedule/coding or category system constitute the measuring instrument. The observers/coders are as essential to the measurement process as are the items in a traditional test. Another discrepancy between traditional procedures for estimating reliability and those applicable to techniques that require a coder is that parallel forms of the instrument are rarely constructed.

With observation techniques, two other factors enter the picture. Many different types of situations can be observed, and within each type of situation many repeated observations of the same behavior are possible. The influence of the setting on behavior can be viewed from two conflicting perspectives (145): (1) the setting imposes minimal constraints on behavior and therefore it can be ignored, or (2) the setting coerces behavior and therefore it cannot be changed if meaningful data are to be collected. Some individuals (104, 105) feel that the situation has an important influence on many behaviors typically observed in research on teaching. These additional sources of variability are listed in Table 8.2.

TABLE 8.2 *ADDITIONAL SOURCES OF SYSTEMATIC AND ERROR VARIANCE IN DATA FROM TECHNIQUES REQUIRING AN OBSERVER AND/OR CODER*

1. Factors associated with the administration of the schedule or the appraisal of behavior or content.

    a) Changes within one observer/interviewer/coder within a session or at one time period: Fluctuations in attention, fatigue, boredom, memory errors, observational load, clarity of category definition.

    b) Changes within one observer/interviewer/coder between sessions: Experience or practice with the schedule or system, assimilation to prior coding or behavior observed (plus all factors in a).

    c) Discrepancies between observers/interviewers/coders on same session: Meaning attributed to coding categories, inference level of the category, discrepancies in practice or training with the system, degree to which responses to open-ended questions are recorded by interviewers, depth of interviewer probes, bias such as halo effect or central tendency error (plus all factors associated with a).

    d) Differential changes in observer/interviewer/coder across time sessions (all of the above are applicable as sources of variability).

Observations only

2. Length and number of observation sessions.

3. Factors associated with time itself or change in the observation setting when more than one observation is made: Sensitivity of the subject to the observer, sensitivity of different behaviors to changes in the observation setting, degree of similarity of one setting to another, changes in the subject associated with the intervening time period.

8.2.2 PROCEDURES FOR ESTIMATING RELIABILITY

INTERVIEWS, CONTENT ANALYSES AND RATINGS

One form of reliability estimate for interviews, content analyses, and ratings involves determining the *agreement* among different coders/interviewers/raters in *categorizing the same content or in interviewing or rating the same individuals.* This procedure primarily reflects the clarity or objectivity of the categories in the instrument itself, and is frequently referred to as *interrater, interjudge, or intercoder agreement.* Factors that affect the degree of agreement are the amount of training given to the coder or interviewer, the degree of complexity of the categories, the precision and completeness of the coding rules, the fullness of category illustrations, and the degree of discrimination among categories. When open-ended questions are posed by interviewers, discrepancies in results can occur because interviewers differ in the extent to which they record the respondent's answers, the degree to which they probe ambiguous responses, etc. Disagreement among raters can easily occur. Unreliable ratings can be the result of errors of leniency, errors of central tendency, the halo effect, and contrast errors.

One index of intercoder agreement is Scott's (126) π (pi) coefficient. It reflects the extent of coder agreement corrected for the number of categories to be recorded and the frequency with which each category is used. When quantitative data is obtained, the correlation coefficient between scores obtained by the coders on a set of individuals or documents also reflects the degree of intercoder agreement.

No definitive guidelines exist regarding the minimum level of intercoder agreement. Reliabilities below .70 have been described as poor (55), and those above .85 and .90 as desirable (55, 148). Some individuals (73, 78) have been reluctant to specify a minimum level, stating that the desired level depends on the particular research problem and the way the scores will be used.

Another common reliability estimation techniques is to determine the *consistency in results* obtained by a coder/interviewer/rater when recording the *same content or interviewing/rating the same individual a second time,* called the *stability or consistency of the coder/interviewer.* This index is similar to test–retest estimates of reliability. However, in instances in which the behavior being coded can change, as with a second interview, low stability or consistency coefficients could reflect such different factors as instability in the trait of interest, real changes in the respondent, or inconsistencies in recording by the interviewer.

OBSERVATION

Since observation systems are usually constructed to measure several dimensions, separate reliability indices should be cited for each score actually used in the data analysis. In addition, it is important to check the agreement among observers as the data are collected throughout the study.

Since the observer's role is similar to that of the interviewer/coder, the previously discussed coefficients of coder agreement and coder stability are also applicable to observation instruments. Both the Cicirelli and Cicirelli study (Chapter 1, paragraph 14) and the Jackson and Cosca study (Chapter 2, paragraph 12) checked for interobserver agreement. Although interobserver agreement is the most frequent technique used by researchers, this index does not reflect the consistency of the subject's behavior over time or the consistency with which the observation instrument distinguishes among individuals.

High levels of interobserver agreement and/or stability of observer agreement are viewed by Medley and Mitzel (105) and McGaw *et al.* (104) as minimal conditions for determining the "reliability" of observation procedures. Medley and Mitzel argued that reliability of observation really involves determining the *agreement* between data from *at least two observations* of the *same situation* as recorded by *at least the same two observers;* that is, the correlation between scores based on observations made by different observers at different times. Only indices of this type reflect consistent differences among individuals' behavior over time, regardless of the characteristics of the observer.

Yet they yield the lowest reliability estimates since time and observer characteristics both contribute to error variance. Medley and Mitzel cited several studies that yielded high interobserver agreement indices but relatively low reliability estimates as defined above.

The fact that each observation is confounded with a change in the observation situation itself complicates the interpretation of reliability estimates based upon more than one observation. If the situation has little effect upon the behavior of interest, then this problem is lessened. However, if the situation has an effect, estimates of reliability need to reflect the similarity of situations so the researcher can describe the specific conditions that yielded stable estimates of the behavior of interest. For example, teacher behavior may not be stable across different subject matter areas, but may be stable across different groups of students exposed to the same subject matter.

Estimating the reliability of observations is further complicated by the fact that some behaviors may have such a low frequency of occurrence that even many and long observation sessions may provide an inadequate context for establishing reliability. Reliability estimates may vary because some behaviors may be more stable than others. Ideally, every observation system should be developed so that it can be communicated to and reliably applied by other social scientists. But this is not easily achieved nor frequently attempted.

8.3 COEFFICIENTS OF GENERALIZABILITY (OPTIONAL)

The most recent developments in the area of reliability come from what is known as the theory of generalizability (38, 39). The traditional concepts of reliability are embedded within the larger framework of generalizability. Different coefficients of generalizability are generated corresponding to the degree to which one can accurately generalize about the consistency of behavior over the various conditions of interest (e.g., test items, occasion of testing, scorers, the subjects themselves).

Reliability problems associated with classroom observation instruments illustrate the usefulness of this approach. With such systems it is easy to identify at least four important sources of variability: the subjects themselves, the observer, the occasion or time of observation, and the type of situation observed each time. It is possible to determine coefficients of generalizability corresponding to the reliability or consistency of teachers' behavior within situations (regardless of observer and time), the reliability with which situations themselves may be distinguished, the reliability with which observers can detect systematic variations among teachers' behavior from one situation to the next, etc. Coefficients of generalizability will become more common in the research literature as more researchers assimilate these techniques into their repertoire of skills.

8.4 QUESTIONS TO ASK ABOUT THE RELIABILITY OF MEASUREMENTS IN RESEARCH ARTICLES

Guidelines for examining the reliability of measurements in research articles are presented in Exhibit 8.1.

EXHIBIT 8.1 *GUIDELINES FOR EXAMINING THE RELIABILITY OF MEASUREMENT TECHNIQUES*

A. Did the researcher report any reliability estimates calculated on the sample in the study?

1. If *no,* is the procedure so standardized, e.g., taking a measure of blood pressure, that it can be assumed to have high reliability?
   If *no,* is the test or instrument published commercially so that some form of reliability estimate would be reported in the test manual and/or in critical reviews of the test as in the *Mental Measurements Yearbook* by Buros?

   a) If yes, it would be advisable to check on the reliability estimates reported in the measurement literature.
   b) If no, was this the first time the test was used?

      1) If yes, then you cannot be confident that the instrument is reliable, and the results should be interpreted with caution.
      2) If no, then you should examine previous studies which used the test, and use the guidelines for evaluating reliability presented in Sections B and C below if reliability estimates are reported in previous studies.

2. If *yes,* is the measurement technique best classified as: (1) a test or other measure of self-report in which the coding of responses is fairly routine, or (2) a procedure that involves complex coding or tallying of responses as is typical of most observation and rating schedules, content analysis, and some interviews?

   If (1), go to Section B.
   If (2), go to Section C.

B. Which type of reliability estimate was reported?

   test–retest
   parallel forms—two occasions
   parallel forms—same occasion
   internal consistency
   a coefficient of generalizability

1. Was this estimate appropriate to the questions being asked? (E.g., questions regarding predictions require estimates of reliability over time.)

2. Was a satisfactory level of reliability achieved? (Decisions regarding individual children require much higher levels than do inferences about the mean of an entire group.)

3. Did the researcher consider the reliability/unreliability of the variables in his or her interpretation of the data?

C. Which type of reliability estimate was reported?

intercoder/interjudge/interobserver agreement
coder/observer stability
agreement between different observers/judges at different times
a coefficient of generalizability

1. When was an interjudge/interobserver agreement obtained—during training only, at the initial phases of the study, throughout the study?

2. Were reliability estimates obtained on the variables that were examined in the analysis of the data?

3. Was the form of reliability estimate appropriate to the questions being asked?

4. Was a satisfactory level of interjudge/interobserver agreement or coder/observer stability achieved?

5. Did the researcher consider the reliability/unreliability of the variables in his or her interpretation of the results?

STUDY PROBLEMS

1. Find the latest edition of the *Mental Measurement Yearbook* by Buros and summarize what it says about the reliability of a particular achievement test and a particular personality test. What types of reliability indices have been calculated for each test?

2. Locate the technical manual for a standardized achievement test used in your school. What reliability data are reported in the manual? Would you recommend that additional reliability indices be calculated? Why?

3. What are the disadvantages and advantages to a researcher of relying only on internal consistency reliability estimates for a test?

4. What are the disadvantages and advantages to a researcher of relying on interobserver indices of agreement when estimating the reliability of classroom observation schemes?

5. Which of the following statements reflect likely outcomes of reliability estimation procedures and which reflect unlikely outcomes? Explain your answers.

a) A researcher reported that the test–retest reliability coefficient over a two-month period for his test of science achievement was .84 and that his internal consistency estimate of reliability was .60.

b) The reliability estimate (i.e., correlation coefficient) on a reading achievement test was .81 between parallel forms of the test administered one month apart and was .91 between the same parallel forms administered on the same day.

c) Two observers rated all the teachers in an elementary school on the teachers' interest in young children. The observers simultaneously observed each teacher for half a day and then rated the teachers. The principal had also rated the teachers on the same dimension earlier in the year. There was a stronger agreement between the ratings from the two observers than between each observer's ratings and the principal's ratings.

6. Locate a research study in which at least one reliability estimate was determined for either a test, a questionnaire/interview, rating, or an observation scheme. What factors could have contributed to unreliability of the measurement procedure? Did the researcher consider reliability data when interpreting results? What other reliability estimates would have been appropriate for the study?

9
Validity of
Measurement Procedures

Most debates about the use of tests center on the issue of *validity;* that is, the *soundness of interpretations made about the test and the degree to which the test fulfills the function for which it is used.* For example, whether aptitude tests measure "potential" or "achievement" is a question of validity. Similarly, controversies about the appropriateness of existing IQ tests for minority groups or for grouping students in schools focus on the validity of IQ tests. For many, the validity of measures is more important than their reliability.

The soundness of test interpretation depends on the entire measurement procedure; including the form of the items, the characteristics of the examiner, the nature of the instructions, whether the test is administered in a group or an individualized setting, and the type of response required by the subject (verbal, written, gesture). A change in any one of these conditions may alter the validity of the test. A test may be valid for one purpose but not for another, making broad generalizations about a test's validity difficult. "In the end, the responsibility for valid use of a test rests on the person who interprets it" (37, p. 445). When there is a direct correspondence between the measurement and the attribute being measured (e.g., measuring physical properties such as height and weight), the validity of the result is usually not questioned. However, this is not the case with most measures used in educational research.

This chapter presents three types of validation procedures—content, criterion-related, and construct. The type of validity information usually presented in research articles is also examined.

9.1 VALIDATION PROCEDURES

In most research studies, tests *describe* individuals. Of primary concern is the validity of such descriptions; that is, "when persons are described in [a particular way] on the basis of [test] data, *how much confidence can be placed in each of the implications of the description?*" (37, p. 448). In other studies tests are used to *make decisions* about individuals: (1) to select particular types of individuals or (2) to place individuals in certain conditions of the study. The researcher must be convinced that the test is an appropriate or valid one for such decisions.

Evidence regarding the appropriateness of descriptions made from tests is usually provided by both content and construct validation procedures. Evidence regarding the soundness of placement decisions is usually provided by criterion-related validation techniques, although construct validity is also important in such contexts.

9.1.1. CONTENT VALIDITY

Content validity focuses on whether the test items truly sample all the tasks the test developer intended to measure. Does the test "re-present" the universe of content to be assessed (98)? Content validity is critical for achievement tests.

The content universe of a test is defined by both the *tasks/stimuli* of interest (the appropriate setting, the questions, the examiners, the objectives of interest, the relative importance of each observation, etc.) and the *form of response* that is required. *The task of content validation is to determine whether the final test product fits these specifications.* Content validation does *not* include determining whether the content of the test corresponds to what others think the test should measure.

Ideally, the stimuli are specified so well that everyone can agree on the tasks that are sampled by the test. When the test is restricted to information in a short two- or three-page passage read by the subjects during an experiment, the content is clear. In contrast, in a comparison of the effect of different biology curricula on achievement, the content universe is much larger. In fact, it may be broader than the lessons and textbooks themselves if the ability of students to apply knowledge to new areas is important.

The form of response is specified by the external or observable responses which the test taker must make. "Reads printed numbers aloud" and "circles one of four multiple-choice alternatives" describe such external, observable behaviors. The form of the response is not specified by internal processes (e.g., evaluate, reason, recall, comprehend) that the test taker may use in answering a test item.

Once the test has been constructed, the usual content validation process is a logical analysis—obtaining independent judgments from reviewers on the degree to which the test items meet the content specifications. Cronbach (37) proposed a more stringent test of content validity, that of duplicate-construction. The rules for selecting test content would be described as completely as possible. On the basis of this information a test would then be developed by each of two independent teams of item writers and reviewers. If the description of the content universe is adequate, the two teams should arrive at approximately interchangeable tests. The actual equivalence of the two tests would then be examined by administering the tests to a suitable sample of individuals and comparing the test results.

9.1.2. CRITERION-RELATED VALIDITY

Researchers often use test results in making decisions about the design of a study. A pretest may be used in order to ensure that individuals who have varying degrees of a trait are distributed equally among the experimental conditions of the study. Such placement increases the precision of the design when the test scores are related to the study outcomes. A researcher may need to decide whether a new test is an appropriate substitute for an old test. These decisions assume there is a relationship between the test and a criterion measure, e.g., the test for which a substitute was developed, the outcome of the study.

The question of the *criterion-related validity* of the test is *whether the test does in fact correlate with the criterion of interest*. The size of the correlation coefficient between the test and the criterion is generally accepted as reflecting the strength of the criterion-related validity of the test. Different degrees of criterion-related validity are often found for different groups of individuals, and a particular test will not predict all important outcomes to the same degree.

In instances in which the test whose validity is being examined is given prior to the criterion measure, the term *predictive validity* is used; e.g., using high school achievement tests to predict grades in college or using reading readiness tests to predict reading achievement in the elementary grades. In cases in which the two measures are made simultaneously, the term *concurrent validity* is used, e.g., examining the relationship between the classroom behavior of teachers and the criterion of supervisor's ratings or determining whether a test will substitute for another.

9.1.3 CONSTRUCT VALIDITY

Construct validation involves examining the nature of what has been measured. *A high degree of construct validity means that the instrument measures the construct or trait it claims to measure*. A theory about the construct provides numerous predictions about how individuals who possess varying amounts of the trait should behave. Studies of the trait should yield results consonant with those predictions. In addition, any counterinterpretations of what the test measures must be examined. Cronbach's (37) analysis of the construct validity of reading comprehension tests illustrates possible counterinterpretations of such test scores: do uncommon words appear in the passage implying that the score reflects vocabulary more than comprehension, or can well-informed students answer the questions without reading the passage, reflecting a test of information. Because most constructs have many facets, a multitude of methods can be used to obtain evidence on various counterinterpretations. The validation process is never completed, for all alternatives are never adequately explored.

One basic principle of construct validation is that "persons who score high on the test ought to score high on other indicators of the same construct" (37, p. 466). In other words, different measures of the same construct should *converge*, should correlate with each other, should yield similar results (26). *Convergent validity* should be obtained across different measurement techniques (e.g., ratings, observation, paper-pencil tests).

Not only should different indicators of the same construct converge, but also measures of different constructs should *diverge* (26); not correlate with each other. Evidence of *discriminant validity* should exist. The labels of "math computation" and "math problem solving" imply different processes. If researchers treat measures of these two constructs differently, they should have evidence to support this distinction.

Suppose researchers used two procedures for measuring math computation (a paper-pencil test and a teacher-rating system) and used the same two procedures for measuring math problem solving. They then "tested" a group of students with all four procedures to determine whether convergent and discriminant validity existed. One possible result could have been a high correlation (e.g., $r = .80$) between the two measures of computation and a high correlation between the two measures of problem solving, but a low correlation (e.g., $r = .30$) between the paper-pencil measures of computation and of problem solving and a low correlation between the rating measures of computation and of problem solving. Both the convergent and discriminant validities of the measurement procedures are supported by this result, since the traits being measured, rather than the measurement procedures, appear to account for the result. On the other hand, if the correlations between the two measures of computation and between the two measures of problem solving were low, then convergent validity would not exist. If the correlations between the two rating measures and between the two paper-pencil measures were high, then discriminant validity would not exist. In this case, the measurement procedures have a more powerful effect on the result than do the traits being measured.

Studies of the specific process being measured can also provide information on construct validity; e.g., asking persons why or how they responded, observing behavior during the test. In other cases attempts can be made to experimentally change individuals' scores in order to determine factors that influence test performance (e.g., giving instructions on test-taking strategies to examine the sensitivity of the test to coaching). If a college aptitude test, which purports to measure verbal and mathematical abilities, is shown to be quite sensitive to coaching, then the test may be measuring the test-wiseness of the student rather than his or her verbal or mathematical ability.

In a very broad sense, any research study reflects to some degree upon the construct validity of its measurement procedures—what treatments influence or do not influence test scores, other tests with which the test does or does not correlate, how different groups perform on the test. The Stanford–Binet Intelligence scale has probably been used in more research studies than any other test available to social scientists. To summarize the evidence on the construct validity of the Binet would mean summarizing all the studies conducted since the early 1900s in which the Binet has been employed. It has been used in many different populations (e.g., a wide range of age groups, in many different cultures), in studies in which attempts have been made to change the intelligence score of the participants (as in some Head Start studies), in numerous correlational studies examining the relationship of the Binet to other constructs such as academic achievement, anxiety, creativity, and the need to achieve, in studies examining the change in intelligence as individuals age, etc. Each of these studies has provided evidence on the meaning of the test itself. Despite all these data, controversies still surround the construct validity of intelligence tests, including the Binet.

The importance of construct validation should be obvious when one reflects upon the numerous constructs involved in educational and social science research; e.g., anxiety, self-concept, authoritarianism, comprehension, spatial ability, creativity, persistence, curiosity, conformity, aggressions, sociability. Construct validity is also an important factor in determining researchers' selection of tests. In order to adequately examine hypotheses, researchers must select the most appropriate measures of the constructs embedded in those hypotheses. Too often researchers must conclude that their hypotheses were not adequately examined because a certain test apparently did not measure the construct of interest. *It is ironic that construct validity is the most important type of validity, yet is the most difficult and complex to establish.*

9.2. SELECTED MEASUREMENT TECHNIQUES

9.2.1 CRITERION-REFERENCED MEASUREMENT

With criterion-referenced measurement, the test's sensitivity to the growth or change in students is needed as evidence of construct validity. Since such tests correspond closely to the content of the curriculum, they should be quite sensitive to changes in pupils' knowledge of that content. If little gain in test performance occurs in situations in which great growth is expected, then there is evidence against the test's validity.

9.2.2 OBSERVATION

In general, little validity data exist on most classroom observation schemes, although all three validation procedures are applicable. Without such data, inferences that go beyond the observation categories are risky; e.g., inferring that few smiles implies a "harsh" teacher or concluding that certain classroom activities of a student will predict that student's performance on achievement tests. An approach that lessens the probability of such inferential errors is to pose counterinterpretations of the observation data, a crucial part of the construct validation process. As particular observation systems are used by more and more researchers, evidence regarding the soundness of various interpretations will accumulate. Eventually, critical reviews of observation schemes may be as much a part of the measurement literature as are reviews of published tests.

9.2.3 INTERVIEWS AND QUESTIONNAIRES

When a questionnaire or interview item taps information available in public records, it is possible to use this information as the validity criterion. In studies in which the anonymity of the subject is guaranteed and/or studies in which individual data are not in the public record, it is sometimes possible to examine potential bias by comparing the aggregate response with figures from an outside source (e.g., the distribution of formal education experience or the income level for specific groups). The random probe technique can be used to examine the validity of closed interview questions (multiple-choice, yes–no, agree–disagree items). In this procedure the interviewer randomly selects a prespecified number of items for follow-up questioning, requesting the respondent to explain his or her choice. This information is then used to compare the intended meaning of the question with the meaning as actually perceived by the respondent.

9.3. REPORTING EVIDENCE ON VALIDITY

Validity information in research articles is frequently restricted to the title of the test and perhaps a short summary of the test. When a published test is used, evidence of its validity should be found in the test manual or a technical report. The *Standards for Educational and Psychological Tests* (5) states that "evidence of validity for each type of inference for which use of the test is recommended [should be reported in the test manual.] If validity for some suggested interpretation has not been investigated, that fact should be made clear" (p. 31). Unfortunately, test manuals can be misleading. It is tempting to publish only favorable results and overlook validity investigations that were not confirmatory. When necessary, researchers will cite additional evidence on validity that is crucial to their study. The reader should not rely on the popularity of the test or its name as indicators of its quality.

The researcher does not need to repeat validation results cited in the test manual. However, an extra burden is then placed on the reader who must go beyond the research report itself in order to adequately evaluate the test interpretations made by the researcher. Additional information on validity may be found in some measurement texts and in validation studies reported in such journals as *Educational and Psychological Measurement*. The best known and most extensive source of critical reviews of tests is Buros' (24) *Mental Measurements Yearbooks*. Books that review tests in special areas are also available.

Sometimes the research study is itself primarily a report of a validation effort. In other instances, researchers select tests that have not been published formally. They then rely on validity evidence accumulated by the test developer, as cited in research reports, to determine the suitability of the test.

Finally, researchers may develop a test specifically for the study. In such instances little or no validity data are usually reported. Frequently, more importance is attached to establishing test reliability. The complexity of collecting validation data diminishes the likelihood that the researchers will investigate validity problems in addition to conducting the study itself. However, the study can be viewed as an initial investigation of the construct validity of the test, since it represents the first time that the relationship of the test to other measures has been documented and therefore sheds some light on the nature of the test.

9.4 SATISFACTORY LEVELS OF VALIDITY

In critiquing research articles, the reader must consider the types of validity appropriate to the researcher's purpose, and whether the author kept his or her interpretation of the test scores within the bounds of the validity information available. What is a satisfactory level of validity? No matter what the approach used to obtain validity data, the more conclusive the data are, the better.

Valid measures must be reliable ones. "A test must measure *something* before it can measure what we want it to measure" (139, p. 189). However, the converse is not the case. Test reliability does not guarantee validity of inferences about test scores.

In instances in which the trait or content domain being measured is heterogeneous, test–retest and parallel forms reliability estimates are more appropriate than are internal consistency estimates. In fact, for the validity to be high on such tests, internal consistency estimates cannot be high since high values reflect homogeneity among items.

When validity is reported in terms of the correlation between the test and another test, as in criterion-related validity, the maximum size of the validity coefficient depends on the reliability of the two tests. This maximum or theoretical value is equal to the square root of the product of the two reliabilities (139). If the reliability of the predictor test were .60 and that of the criterion were .70, then the maximum validity coefficient between the two sets would equal $\sqrt{(.60)(.70)}$ or .65. It is unusual for a validity coefficient to exceed .60, and in some instances coefficients as low as .30 are of practical value (36).

9.5 QUESTIONS TO ASK ABOUT THE VALIDITY OF MEASUREMENTS IN RESEARCH ARTICLES

Guidelines for examining the validity of measurements in research articles are presented in Exhibit 9.1.

EXHIBIT 9.1 *GUIDELINES FOR EXAMINING THE VALIDITY OF INFERENCES MADE FROM MEASUREMENT TECHNIQUES*

A. Is the attribute that is claimed to be measured so congruent with the measurement technique itself that validity is not an issue?

1. If *yes,* stop here.

2. If *no,* go to Section B.

B. Is the instrument published commercially, so that validation data are likely to be found in the test manual or a technical report?

1. If the answer is *no* or you do not know the answer to this question, go to Section C.

2. If *yes,* was the investigation itself another validation study of the measurement procedure?

   a) If yes, then the study must be evaluated in terms of the adequacy with which it investigated either the content, construct, or criterion-related validity of the instrument.

   b) If, no,

      (1) What types of validity are required for the function served by the instrument in the study?

         (a) To select individuals with certain characteristics as the sample of interest—construct validity

         (b) As a pretest in order to classify individuals or to serve as a control variable—construct and criterion-related validity

         (c) To describe individuals or organizations—content and construct validity

      (2) Does the test manual or critical reviews of the test present any evidence regarding these types of validity?

      (3) Did the author cite any relevant validation studies?

      (4) Was the author cautious in his or her inferences regarding the meaning of the test scores? Did he or she present alternative interpretations? Can you think of counterinterpretations that the author did not discuss?

C. Was any reference to validity data presented in the study; that is, data collected by the author or by others in previous studies?

1. If yes, then the guidelines presented under Section B.2.b are appropriate. If in doubt about some of the author's interpretations, you may wish to read some of the cited research on the instrument yourself.

2. If there was no information on validity, then:

    a) If the instrument was developed specifically for the study, the study itself provides some construct validity data.

    b) If the instrument was not original with the author, then literature on its validity exists, although it is probably not a part of a systematic validation program. The author should have referred to this literature, for you will probably have difficulties locating it. Again, the study itself provides some validity information.

    c) In either of the instances above, the meaning assigned to test scores should be viewed with caution and counterinterpretations should be considered.

STUDY PROBLEMS

1. Find the latest edition of the *Mental Measurements Yearbook* by Buros and summarize what it says about the validity of a particular achievement test and a particular personality test. What forms of validity have been examined for each test?

2. Locate the technical manual for a standardized achievement test used in your school. What types of validity were examined by the test developers? Would you recommend additional studies of validity? If so, what type of studies would be desirable?

3. What form(s) of validity is (are) reflected in each of the following statements?

    a) High school dropouts scored lower than high school seniors on an enthusiasm-for-education scale.

    b) The correlation between scores on a college entrance test and grade-point average at the end of the freshman year in college was .69.

    c) A panel of teachers examined the content of the social studies test for its relevance to the school curriculum.

    d) Two different measures of student intellectual curiosity and ability to learn were obtained: teacher ratings and parental ratings. The two measures of intellectual curiosity correlated with each other as did the two measures of ability to learn. However, both teacher ratings failed to correlate with each other as did the two parental ratings.

    e) The responses required on the manual dexterity test represented the types of behavior required by car mechanics rather than by telephone switchboard operators.

    f) Mexican-American students scored higher on the science test when it was administered in Spanish than when it was administered in English.

4. Locate a research study in which the validity of at least one measurement procedure was examined in some way. Was the validity achieved high or low? What factors might have contributed to the level of validity attained? Did the researcher consider the degree of validity in his or her interpretation of the results? What other validity studies would be appropriate for the particular instrument that was examined?

5. Determine whether the following statements are correct.

a) This reading comprehension test really measures comprehension because the test–retest reliability is so high.

b) The validity of my social studies test must be low because my internal-consistency estimate of reliability is low.

c) The validity of this test of artistic ability must be high since professional artists developed it.

PART III

The Questions Answered by Research

Research can be used to examine three major types of questions: questions of description, association, and causation. Since the design of studies to investigate causal questions depends on many of the principles of association and of descriptive study design, and studies of association questions depend on many of the principles of descriptive study design, descriptive questions are examined in detail first (Chapters 11 and 12), followed by association questions (Chapters 13 and 14), and lastly causal questions (Chapters 15, 16, and 17). For each research question the general principles of research design are presented first (that is, in the first chapter; Chapters 11, 13, and 15). The specific methods and procedures commonly used to investigate each question are presented in the other chapters (Chapters 12, 14, 16, and 17). Studies illustrating the different forms of research have been reproduced and are discussed in detail. Guidelines for evaluating the quality of each type of research are given at the end of each chapter. Lists of a variety of published educational studies that exemplify the research techniques associated with descriptive, association, and causal questions are presented for reference purposes. Statistical tests/procedures commonly applied in each form of research are described in Appendix D.

10

The Distinctions among Descriptive, Association, and Causal Questions

There are three forms of research questions:

1. Descriptive questions—questions aimed at identifying the characteristics of an individual, a group, several subgroups, a phenomenon, a system, or an object.
2. Association questions—questions that focus on the pattern or the degree of association or covariation between two or more variables.
3. Causal questions—questions that ask if one (or more than one) variable has a role in causing or producing another variable(s).

In general, scientific questions focus on the relationship between at least two variables. Only questions of simple description, in which the characteristics or attributes of an *entire* group, phenomenon, or system are *individually* described, do not reflect relationships between variables.

Some problem statements and questions specify very clearly that the intent is to study relationships among variables; e.g., the relationship between creativity and intelligence, and whether high school grades predict college grades. Problem questions that involve comparisons or differences among existing groups also take this relational form. For example, a question such as "Are there sex differences in high school dropout rate?" is another way of asking if there is a relationship between the variables of sex and dropout rate. An alternative way of viewing this same problem is that the intent is to describe two major sub-groups in the population, males and females, on one characteristic, the frequency with which they drop out of high school. Such studies, which could be classified as examining relationships, but which focus primarily on dividing the sample or population into various naturally occurring subgroups (e.g., age, geographic region, grade level in school, race, religious preference, sex, size of family, socioeconomic level) and on reporting selected characteristics of these subgroups, provide what can be called differentiated description of the

141

population of interest and are therefore classified as descriptive studies. Some disagreement may arise in classifying studies as either descriptive or associational depending on how one views the nature of the variables that are used to subdivide the study sample.

Finally, other research questions refer to a causal relationship between variables; e.g., does career counseling affect the career choices of high school students or does smoking cause cancer. Causal relationships are difficult to establish and some researchers prefer the term "functional" relationships in order to avoid misleading statements about cause. However, the author agrees with the position taken by Blalock (16) and Ennis (44), that elimination of the notion of cause is self-defeating and would

> detour us away from most of the central problems that justify educational research. The education enterprise attempts to bring about changes in students. *Bringing something about* is unavoidably a causal thrust (44, p. 4).

Causal research questions refer to the intent of the study, not to what is actually achieved. In later chapters the difficulties in identifying a causal relationship are discussed, and research designs that provide different degrees of evidence for causal statements are examined.

Some dependencies exist among these three types of questions. Descriptive information is necessary in order to interpret adequately the nature of the relationship between variables, whether causal or noncausal, since the interpretation always depends on knowing the characteristics of the individual variables in the relationship. It is frequently desirable or necessary to establish the existence of an association between two variables before attempting to establish if one variable causes the other or what other factor might have caused the relationship. In addition, some studies may focus on more than one question, making it difficult to classify the entire study, although the principles involved in interpreting descriptive, association, and causal questions still pertain to those respective sections of the study.

10.1 DESCRIPTIVE QUESTIONS

As defined here, *descriptive questions refer to studies that report, classify, or paint a picture of the characteristics of an individual, group, subgroups of individuals, phenomenon or system; or that describe a sequence of events.* The focus is not on the existence or the strength of a relationship between variables, but on description of a population of interest the study sample presumably represents. Sometimes information is presented on the sample as a whole. However, frequently the sample is divided into various groups on the basis of demographic variables (variables that reflect the personal status of an individual and are determined by questions of fact), and the description involves reporting the characteristics of each subgroup and comparing subgroup differences. Such classification variables (sex, occupation, religion, marital status, etc.) are usually measured rather easily but cannot be generated easily or manipulated by the researcher. Subdivision by itself does not indicate that adequate description has been achieved. Division of the sample should be predicated on some level of theory and the results should generalize beyond the sample. Trow (140) called studies without such design characteristics "pseudo" studies.

The Jackson and Cosca study (Chapter 2) is an example of descriptive research. The authors compared the pattern of teacher–pupil interaction that occurred in two ethnic groups, Mexican-American and Anglo students. For example, the data in Table 2.2 presented answers to a series of questions; e.g., were there differences in teacher acceptance of students' feelings in the two groups, in teacher praising or encouraging in the two groups, in teacher acceptance or use of students' ideas, in teacher questioning, etc. The study is not classified as focusing upon association questions, since the variable of ethnic group served primarily to subdivide the student population into two naturally occurring groups, which were then compared on each classroom variable. Nor was there any attempt made to examine the interrelationships among the classroom interaction variables. The questions asked are not causal since the researchers focused first on determining if such differences occurred and on the nature of those differences, not on why or what caused teachers to interact differently with Mexican-American and Anglo students.

The Gribbons and Lohnes study (Chapter 1) is a longitudinal description; that is, it followed a group of individuals over a period of years in order to describe what changes occurred within that group with time or age. The variable of time was reflected by the grade levels of the students.

The variable of time can be introduced into practically any study. In order to distinguish between descriptive and association studies that include the time variable, the following guidelines are given. If the primary focus of the study is to describe what exists or the status of an individual or group at various points in time, then the study is classified as descriptive. If the primary focus is the changing pattern among variables with time (e.g., relationship between intelligence and creativity at different time points), then it is called one of association. The variable of time can also be used in causal studies, as in investigations of the long-term effects of a phenomenon.

The first question in the Gribbons and Lohnes study focused on describing the changes in the hierarchy of adolescent values at three points in time (three grade levels). The second question, "Is there an important difference between the developed typal hierarchy of vocational values for boys and that for girls?" (paragraph 2), specified the additional variable of sex and the sample was divided into males and females at each of the grade levels, yielding six subgroups whose value rankings were reported and compared with each other. In essence, the authors described the changes in values that occurred for males and females over a five-year period. Some individuals, however, might classify the study as one of association since the authors examined the correlations among the value rankings of these six subgroups.

10.2 ASSOCIATION QUESTIONS

Association questions focus on whether variables are linked, correlated, or associated with each other and on the strength of this association. Such questions are not restricted to studies that use some type of correlation coefficient for statistical analysis, but refer to the general issue of the existence, form, and strength of associations among variables, no matter what the statistical technique.

Although it is sometimes difficult to distinguish between association and descriptive studies, studies that investigate association questions often focus on the interrelationships among variables within one group of individuals, or at least within very few groups. An example of an association study would be determining the relationships among the three variables of attitude toward school, academic achievement and number of days absent within a sample of seventh grade students. Another distinction is that the variables identified in association questions usually are not considered to be demographic in nature. Such nondemographic variables include academic achievement, opinions, aptitudes, types of interactions among individuals, etc. However, demographic or background variables are not excluded from association problems. For example, asking if size of family, birth order, and sex jointly predict college grades would be an association question. When some of the variables are demographic, descriptive and association questions can be distinguished from each other by determining whether the researcher is primarily describing a characteristic of the subgroups created by background variables or is determining the strength of the association of the background variables to other variables.

The simplest form of association question is that which identifies only two variables; e.g., "What is the relationship between high school grades and college grades, or between age and political party preference?" This question form may be repeated many times in one study, as when several variables are measured and the association between every pair is determined. A more complicated form is that which examines the joint or combined relationship of two or more variables to one criterion variable, e.g., "To what extent do high school grades and college entrance exam scores jointly predict college grades?" Another form of association may focus on the relationship between two set of variables, e.g., between a set of achievement variables such as high school grades and standardized test performance and a set of affective variables such as liking for school and self-concept. Yet another type may focus on the underlying dimensions or commonalities within a set of variables.

In many correlational studies, researchers attempt to explain after the fact why an association occurred. Such post hoc explanations do not mean that the study was causal, since it was originally designed to determine if a relationship existed, not the reason for the existence of a relationship.

Two major association questions were posed in Cicirelli and Cicirelli's study (Chapter 1): (1) the relationship between creativity of the counselor and counselor–client behavior and (2) the relationship between counselor attitude toward client and counselor–client behavior. None of these three variables was demographic in nature and the relationships among the variables were examined for only one group of individuals ("counselors" at a summer institute). Some of the associations were of the simplest form, i.e., between only two variables (those described in Table 1.2 and the majority of those reported in Table 1.4). The multiple correlations (R) reported in Table 1.4 reflected a more complicated association problem—the joint relationship of creativity and attitude scores to the individual counselor–client behavior variables. It is important to note that some descriptive information on the entire group was also reported, e.g., average creativity scores, percentage of time devoted to the various categories of counselor–client verbal behavior (paragraphs 18, 19, and 21, Table 1.3). Some individuals might think that causal questions were implicit in the research questions that were asked. For example, did the authors mean to investigate the idea that more creative counselors produce certain types of counselor–client behavior? Apparently not, since they rejected this inference in paragraph 7, and stated that they were trying to identify or isolate behaviors associated with, not produced by, counselor creativity and attitude.

10.3 CAUSAL QUESTIONS

Causal relationships not only assume that a relationship exists between at least two variables, but also that one variable produces the other; that a change in one causes or produces a change in the other; that there is a directional nature to the relationship. The presumed cause is termed the *independent variable*, and the presumed effect is called the *dependent variable.* In any causal study, the independent and dependent variables should be easy to identify.

Association is a necessary, but not a sufficient, condition for causation, or as the saying goes "correlation does not imply causation." For example, the fact that the number of pupils per teacher and the number of books in the school library are positively associated does not mean that changes in one will produce changes in the other. Causal questions usually assume some prior descriptive and associational information. The researcher then focuses on why that situation or phenomenon exists. A researcher may find that sex of the student is related to dropout rate, with more boys than girls dropping out. The researcher then asks why; what produced or caused this situation. Studies that examine causal questions are not restricted to experimental methodology in which the researcher establishes or manipulates the independent variable, but include all procedures that attempt to isolate probable causes.

Much causal language is implicit rather than explicit (44). Such terms as "'brings about,' 'results in,' 'produced,' 'contributed to,' 'helped,' 'effected,' 'affected,' and 'consequence'" (p. 4) should be recognized for their causal connotation. Even the terms "teach" and "taught" imply causal relations. Researchers do not have to explicitly state that they are investigating whether Variable A causes or partially causes Variable B in order to be studying a causal question. However, when the causal language is implicit, it is sometimes difficult to distinguish between association and causal studies.

Bishop's study (presented in Chapter 19) focuses on a causal question: the effect of different reading training procedures (the independent variable) upon pronouncing letter-sound combinations and reading new words (the two major dependent variables). The problem in the Sullivan et al. study (also in Chapter 19) is similar, and includes the additional independent variable of student ability. In both studies the independent variable of reading instruction was created by the researcher since he deliberately established different training procedures. In the Sullivan et al report, the independent variable of student ability was not created by the researchers since they worked with the existing differences in ability that occurred in the sample. Some independent variables are easier to create than others and are therefore investigated more frequently, even though scientists may be just as interested in the effects of variables that are less manipulable.

The approach in this text differs from one that classifies studies by their methods or techniques of investigation. In these texts historical research, whose methodology is distinguished by the fact that researchers cannot generate data themselves but are dependent on what data has been generated in the past, differs from experimental research, where researchers have control of the independent variable. In turn, experimental research differs from survey research, which is frequently characterized by the use of questionnaires, or interviews. However, descriptive, associational, and causal questions can be investigated by both historical and survey techniques. Causal questions are associated with nonexperimental as well as with experimental methods. In addition, the same statistical procedures can be used to analyze data pertaining to descriptive, association, and causal questions. Since specific techniques are used to answer more than one research question, the approach in this text focuses first on the form of the question and then on specific research techniques.

10.4 HOW TO IDENTIFY THE RESEARCH QUESTION IN RESEARCH ARTICLES

Exhibit 10.1 provides guidelines for determining the type of question(s) underlying research studies.

EXHIBIT 10.1 *IDENTIFICATION OF THE RESEARCH QUESTION*

A. Identify the variables investigated.

B. Did the investigation focus on the influence of one variable on another; that is, in determining whether one variable causes, produces, or brings about another?

1. If *yes*, then a causal question was investigated. Such studies include those in which the researcher deliberately manipulates one variable in order to observe its effects as well as studies in which the researcher has no control over the causal variable.

2. If *no,* then the question is either descriptive or one of association. Go to Section C.

C. Did the investigation focus on describing or identifying the characteristics of a phenomenon, group, or individual?

1. If *yes,* then a descriptive question was investigated. Such description may involve a routine division of the sample according to demographic variables such as sex, age, or socioeconomic status in order to provide a complete picture of the phenomenon. If the variables of time or age are involved, then descriptions of changes with time or age must be the primary focus if the study is to be classified as descriptive.

2. If *no,* then the question was one of association. Go to Section D.

D. Association questions focus on the strength and pattern of relationships between variables. Questions of prediction fall in this category. If the variable of time or age is included, then the focus must be on the relationship among variables at different times/ages or across time/age to be classified as a study of association. Similarly, if demographic variables are included, then the focus must be on the strength of associations among them, rather than describing differences among demographic groups.

Caution: Of course more than one research question may be involved in a particular study. The research questions can be determined only by a careful, logical analysis of the study's purpose. Do not resort to a quick examination of an article for terms such as "independent" and "dependent" variables, or "experiment" to tell you accurately what question was asked. Such terms are not used consistently by researchers. "Independent" and "dependent" variables can be used in association studies and some researchers label any study an experiment. In addition, statistical techniques are not an infallible guide to the underlying focus of the study. For example, although analysis of variance is frequently used in causal studies, it is just as easily applied to descriptive and association questions.

STUDY PROBLEMS

Randomly select three research articles in an area of interest to you from each of two journals. Identify the major variables in each study and determine whether each study was primarily descriptive, associational, or causal.

1. If descriptive, cite the variables that were used to subdivide the sample and the characteristics of the subgroups in the sample that were described.

2. If associational, state explicitly the variables involved in each question, and whether the association was of the simplest form (between two variables only) or was of a more complex form.

3. If causal, identify the independent and dependent variables.

11

The Design of Studies
to Describe Phenomena

Description is essential to the understanding of situations and individuals. It clarifies our images of events and people; e.g., of what it means to be well or poorly educated, to be a teacher or a student in a high school that is relatively free of vandalism or in one that has a high rate of vandalism, to be a success or a failure in academic subjects, to be a success or failure as an athlete.

A good descriptive design clearly specifies *who and what are to be measured*. Much of the logic and methodology of descriptive research originates from the fields of sociology and anthropology. The research principles described below are important because they apply not only to descriptive research but also to the inquiry of association and causal questions.

11.1 CONCEPTUALIZATION OF THE PHENOMENON TO BE DESCRIBED

Educational phenomena such as juvenile delinquency, teacher behavior in the classroom, the educational values held by the public, and characteristics of individuals who choose the educational field as a career need to be described in order to better understand the educational process and to make informed decisions in educational contexts. Yet the complexity of such phenomena makes description difficult. If a study is to yield an adequate description, the researcher must define very carefully what he or she wishes to describe before determining how to collect data. Hyman (82) has called this initial planning stage *conceptualization*.

Descriptions are often partial and/or misleading when the conceptualization stage is skipped or given only cursory attention. Only after all dimensions of the problem have been considered can the researcher decide which are irrelevant and which are central to the study's objective. For example, attitudes, knowledge, and behavior should be distinguished from each other in the study of psychological phenomena. An individual's knowledge and/or behavior cannot always be predicted from his or her attitudes, and vice versa.

The adequacy of conceptualization in descriptive studies is best determined by examining the measurement procedures used by the researchers and their description of instrument development. When an entire questionnaire or observation scheme is reported, it is easy for the reader to determine which dimensions have been stressed by the researcher. With standardized tests, the researcher has apparently accepted the test developer's conceptualization as being adequate, and the reader should know something about the rationale for the development of the test in order to fully comprehend the type of description that it can provide. In addition, the introduction to the study and the data analysis provide valuable information regarding conceptualization.

11.2 DEFINING THE NATURE OF THE TARGET POPULATION

The description of an event or group must apply to some defined population at some point in time, unless the researcher is interested in an isolated case. It is within the context of such boundaries that the phenomenon assumes reality. Selecting an inappropriate population or an atypical or irrelevant point in time may result in wasted effort and/or a misleading description. "The most unbiased sample of a given population cannot rectify the [initial] mistake that might be made in choosing that [particular] population to sample" (82, p. 110).

When the target population is not described by the author, the reader must determine the nature of the target population from the description of the sample. Sample descriptions can vary from a citation of the sample size to an extensive description of the location from which the sample was obtained (see 107, pp.7–9, 12–16). One study that contains a discussion of the issue of the appropriate target population is that by Gottlieb (61, p. 536) on the career expectations of college seniors.

> The data discussed here are based upon a survey of 1860 male and female graduating seniors (classes of 1972) from five different colleges and universities in Pennsylvania. The sample schools were selected in order to maximize a student population which would be representative of varying religious, ethnic, racial, regional, and socioeconomic backgrounds.
>
> While we cannot assume that our sample is representative of all college seniors in Pennsylvania, much less all college seniors who graduated in the spring of 1972, whatever general data dealing with the characteristics of college seniors that we have been able to locate leads us to believe that our sample students are not too unlike college seniors in four-year colleges and universities throughout the country. We feel that our sample is sufficiently representative to make tentative generalizations; at the same time we are fully aware of methodological considerations and hence recognize the need for caution in the making of such generalizations.

11.2.1 TIME LIMITATIONS

Phenomena have different degrees of stability. Your sense of well-being can vary with the time of day. Your involvement in political issues probably increases every presidential election year. Your interest in local educational policies may be relatively high and constant while your children are in school and then decline when your children graduate. Researchers must consider the influence of such factors when deciding the appropriate time period for their study.

In cases in which changes over a period of years or changes that occur with age are of interest, a study may be greatly extended in time by examining the same individuals over a period of years. Some studies (e.g., Terman's study of gifted individuals) have followed several generations of families. The researcher must decide whether the period of time for the study is unrepresentative, and whether such bias can be handled through careful interpretation of the data or whether it would be better to conduct the study at another time. In all cases, the time period covered in collection of the data must be specified, possible distortions created by this certain period discussed, and limitations on generalization to other time periods cited.

11.2.2 THE POPULATION UNIT

In the majority of educational studies, the population unit is the individual. In some cases collectivities are of interest (families, classrooms, school districts). The data must be collected on the appropriate unit since individual data cannot always provide the required information on the group as a whole nor can group data be translated into individual measures.

11.2.3 DIFFERENTIATION OF THE POPULATION

The description of a large, heterogeneous population is usually abstract and general. In order for findings to be more concrete, breakdowns of the population into subgroups are required. In this way the description becomes more precise and is more likely to enhance understanding and to aid in decision making. Such specification provides a *differentiated description* of the population (82); called a form of "social bookkeeping" in sociology by Glock (58). Typical variables used to create subgroups in sociological studies are sex, race, religion, age, education, income, marital status, rural–urban residence, birth-order, and place of birth. The demographic variables should be selected theoretically rather than routinely as in census-type reports. An extensive conceptualization of the phenomenon will usually identify relevant background variables.

Usually the results of differentiated description are shown for the sample as a whole, then for the subgroups created by each demographic variable, and finally for the subgroups created by the crossing of two or more variables. Possible crossings of variables are limited, however, when small sample sizes are employed. Although the purpose of a descriptive study is not to explain why the differences or similarities in subgroups occur, the researcher may legitimately speculate on such reasons in the discussion section of a report.

11.3 INTERPRETING RESULTS OF DESCRIPTIVE RESEARCH

Accuracy of data is crucial to all forms of descriptive research. The importance of reducing and detecting error becomes especially obvious when the goal is to determine "the facts," as in census-type studies (the percentage unemployed, the number of high school dropouts, the median income). However, the simple reporting or listing of results provides an inadequate description. The results must acquire some meaning, some reality; they cannot be left in the abstract. Techniques used by researchers to give their data some meaning are presented in this section.

11.3.1 EMPIRICAL ESTIMATES OF ERROR

When the reliability and validity of the measurement techniques are known to be high, researchers can be confident in their data; they can assume that the techniques provide consistent responses and measure what they intended to measure. The estimates of reliability and validity provide indications of the type and magnitude of the errors that researchers must consider in interpretation of the results. However, this prior information on reliability and validity does not reduce the need for checking on possible errors during the conduct of the study itself.

With respect to survey research, a distinction is made between *internal* and *external* checks for error, a distinction similar to that made between the concepts of reliability and validity. Internal checks involve comparison of items from the same questionnaire or interview to determine the consistency among responses. Among the internal checks are techniques that require the respondent to elaborate on his or her answer, special items which tap the general trustworthiness of the respondent, and comparison of subgroups under study that should differ in some known way on certain items. External checks provide independent estimates of error. Among such checks are comparison of the results with similar findings collected by others or on other samples from the same population, use of criterion data such as those in public records for comparison, an extensive reinterview of a portion of the respondents by interviewers of superior quality, use of interviewer reports on the survey, and the split-ballot technique.

Nelson and Sieber (111, pp. 218–219 an association study) used both internal and external checks in their national survey of the use in secondary schools of instructional innovations such as language labs, teaching teams, programmed instruction, and resource centers. An internal check on the number of implemented innovations reported by the school principals was its relationship to two other questions: (1) a question regarding the extent to which school priorities had changed in the last five years, expecting and finding a change in priorities related to many innovations, and (2) a question regarding program complexity (the number of different programs and special courses), expecting and finding that many innovations were related to a "complex" program. An external check on the same variable involved its relationship to ratings by a national panel of secondary school experts on the "durability" of each innovation; that is, the degree to which the innovation would be implemented as originally designed. A strong relationship was found between durability and reported implementation. Such results led Nelson and Sieber to conclude that the self-reports of principals on the number of innovations in use in their schools were reliable measures of actual use.

There is no general solution to the issue of how errors affect the data or how errors should be treated in the interpretation of the data. Errors are usually not independent of each other. They often distribute themselves so that it is difficult to determine their impact. For example, they may balance each other, or they each may be very small but collectively create a large error.

11.3.2 NORMS FOR EVALUATION

Suppose a study reveals that 65 percent of the public feels that the public schools are doing a good job. What sort of meaning can be attached to this statement? If the researcher does not appraise it, readers will most likely make their own evaluation. Which of the following statements best reflects the meaning of the 65 percent figure: that the public is *overwhelmingly* satisfied with the public schools, that *nearly* two-thirds of the public is satisfied, that *as many as* one-third is not satisfied, that *only* one-third is not satisfied? Does the response indicate a serious criticism of the schools or is such a level to be expected given the general mood of the public at the time? "Evaluations [of data] are bound to be capricious in the absence of norms for deciding whether such findings are large or small, frequent or rare" (82, p. 127).

Data can be collected on *parallel or related phenomena* from the same individuals to provide norms for evaluation. In the previous case, questions could also be asked about the quality of private schools, about the quality of other tax-supported services requiring professional staffs, or about the quality of higher education. If 50 percent of the public feels that private schools are doing a good job, then the satisfaction with public schools appears in a favorable light. Yet if 90 percent of the public rates private schools positively, then the public school rating appears unfavorable by comparison. One problem with this procedure is the arbitrariness in the choice of related phenomena. The choice should not be restricted to comparisons that are expected to present the major results in a favorable light, but should include a wide spectrum of parallel phenomena. When standardized tests are administered, the subjects' scores can be compared to the test norms in order to appraise test performance.

Another way to obtain comparative data is to examine the results on the subgroups created by differentiated description of the sample. Such comparisons can be made on both the related phenomena and the major variables. Particular subgroups may be selected as important reference points. In the previous example of attitudes toward the public schools, the satisfaction of the parents of children in the public schools (the group directly serviced by the schools) may be contrasted with other groups: parents of children who are in private schools, parents of children who have already graduated from public schools, recent high school graduates, parents of preschool children, public school teachers, etc. Even with such comparisons, problems in interpretation can arise. Hirschi and Selvin (75) cited a tendency of researchers to exaggerate the differences between subgroups, which they labeled the synecdochic fallacy.

A technique frequently employed by researchers in the area of special education is to compare the results on the group of primary interest with a contrast or "normal" group. For instance, the behavior of mentally retarded children is often compared with the behavior of two other groups of children: one of the same mental age but different chronological age (a younger group), and one of the same chronological age but different mental age (a more intelligent group).

11.3.3 ESTABLISHING THE GENERALITY OF THE PHENOMENON

By measuring related phenomena it is also possible to determine whether individuals show consistent tendencies across a number of areas or if the responses are peculiar to particular variables. Is a tendency to rate public schools as satisfactory part of a general tendency to perceive institutions as adequate or is it a distinctive response, restricted primarily to the public school domain? Such comparisons are also useful in interpreting results across time. Is a decline in reaction time with age associated with a decline in other physiological functions or does it tend to be unique? Does this decline parallel the age changes that occur with cognitive functioning? Such relationships should not, however, be used to explain the existence of the phenomenon under study.

11.3.4 STATING THE CONCLUSIONS

Any factors that influence the interpretation of individual variables should be discussed in the study. With survey research this includes such factors as any unusual directions to the coders and the problems encountered with open-ended questions. With observation schemes, problems in interpreting observation categories are important.

To summarize results on a series of variables, a profile of the "average" respondent is sometime presented. Profile descriptions usually state that the typical subject is characterized by trait A, B, C, D. For example, the "typical" elementary teacher might be described as more likely to be married than single and more likely to be female than male. Is it then appropriate to assume that most elementary teachers are married females? Suppose the results indicated that 60 percent were married and 60 percent were female. Unless the joint distribution of both traits is examined, we cannot infer what combination is most characteristic. In Table 11.1 are two possible cross-tabulations of the joint

TABLE 11.1   *TWO HYPOTHETICAL CROSS-TABULATIONS OF MARITAL STATUS AND SEX ON A SAMPLE OF ELEMENTARY TEACHERS*

	Case I				Case II		
	Married	*Single*			*Married*	*Single*	
Female	60%	0%	60%	Female	30%	30%	60%
Male	0%	40%	40%	Male	30%	10%	40%
	60%	40%			60%	40%	

distribution of these two variables, both of which maintain the 60 percent restriction on each variable. The description of the joint distribution of these two variables is quite different in the two cases. In Case I, most elementary teachers are both married and are female, whereas that is certainly not the situation in Case II. Thus assumptions about the nature of the joint distribution of variables may be false when profile descriptions simply list the results on each trait, called the *profile fallacy* by Hirschi and Selvin (75). Only an examination of the joint relationship among variables can provide such a description.

Another error in descriptive studies is an illegitimate shift in the unit of analysis; that is, collecting data on groups and using it to describe individuals, called the *ecological fallacy* (75). A study may focus on the characteristics of classrooms whose mean score on standardized tests is above that of the norming group. In these classrooms 60 percent of the students have an older sibling. However, it would be erroneous to infer that the individuals who score above the mean on standardized tests are also the same ones who have older siblings. The reverse of the ecological fallacy is the *individualistic fallacy* (130), in which data are collected at the individual level and it is assumed that such individual characteristics will hold for the groups or organizations of which the individuals are members.

11.4 QUESTIONS TO ASK ABOUT THE DESIGN AND INTERPRETATION OF DESCRIPTIVE STUDIES

A checklist on the design and interpretation of results from descriptive studies is presented in Exhibit 11.1.

EXHIBIT 11.1   *ANALYSIS OF DESCRIPTIVE STUDY DESIGN*

A. Did the author present in detail the dimensions of the phenomenon to be studied (conceptualization)? Refer to the introduction (references to theory, previous approaches to the problem) and the presentation of measurement techniques (specific questions, observation and coding categories) for such information.

B. Was the target population to which generalization would be appropriate discussed?

1. In terms of the time period of generalization?

2. In terms of the size of the population unit?

3. In terms of specific characteristics of the population (differentiated description)?

C. What techniques were used to ensure an appropriate interpretation of the results?

1. Were any internal checks for error reported?

2. Were any external checks for error reported?

3. What norms were used for evaluation of the results (data on related phenomena, test norms, subgroup comparisons)?

4. Were data collected that indicated that the phenomenon of interest was not unique but part of a more general phenomenon?

5. Did the author avoid the profile fallacy?

6. Did the author describe the appropriate unit (individual vs. group); that is, did he or she avoid the ecological and individualistic fallacies?

STUDY PROBLEMS

1. Read one of the descriptive survey studies cited at the end of Chapter 12. Analyze the design of the study using the series of questions in Exhibit 11.1 Evaluate the quality of the research design. How would you improve upon the following design elements: conceptual phase of the study, the definition of the target population, and the interpretation of the results?

2. What is differentiated description and how can a researcher use such information to interpret results?

3. Give an example of both the profile and the individualistic fallacies.

4. In what ways do external checks for error provide information on the validity of survey items?

12

Techniques Associated with Descriptive Questions: Research Studies

No definitive classification of descriptive research methodology exists. Some research methods are distinguished primarily by the measurement or data collection technique, some by the nature of the sample, and others in terms of the time span encompassed by the study. Furthermore, most of these methods can be used to examine questions of association and of cause as well as of description. The classification in this chapter includes a wide variety of methods, but is not exhaustive of all methods that can be used in a descriptive study. Furthermore, any particular study may use a combination of techniques.

Most of the chapter focuses on descriptive studies characterized by the method of *data collection*. Descriptive surveys, which employ questionnaires and interviews, and observational studies are discussed in detail. Collection of data through existing records and tests is also mentioned. The last part of the chapter focuses on classifying descriptive studies according to their *purpose*. In particular, studies of change, of different cultures, and of individual cases are presented.

12.1 TECHNIQUES OF DATA COLLECTION

12.1.1 DESCRIPTIVE SURVEYS

Descriptive surveys are restricted here to studies that use some form of questionnaire or interview to describe a predefined population. They should employ the criteria of descriptive research cited in Chapter II. The previous discussions on sampling in Chapter 6 and on reliability and validity in Chapters 8 and 9 must also be considered in critiquing descriptive survey research. The sampling design is particularly important when it is assumed that the sample represents a specific population. Pretesting of instruments, training of interviewers, etc. all contribute to the reliability and validity of the data.

DUNAGIN'S PEOPLE

DUNAGIN'S PEOPLE BY RALPH DUNAGIN, COURTESY OF FIELD NEWSPAPER SYNDICATE

"YIPPEE!! THIS YEAR'S OFFICE PARTY IS 17.316 % MORE FUN THAN LAST YEAR'S."

QUESTIONNAIRES VERSUS INTERVIEWS

In contrast with interviews, questionnaires administered either through the mail or in the context of a group setting have the following advantages. They (1) are usually less costly to the researcher (although telephone interviews are less expensive than face-to-face interviews), (2) are easier to administer, (3) do not create problems of interviewer turnover and training, (4) may create more trust in the anonymity of the respondent's answer to personal or embarrassing topics, (5) can include items such as checklists and ratings that are sometimes too time-consuming or unwieldy when read by the interviewer, (6) are not affected by characteristics of the interviewer, and (7) create less pressure for an immediate reply, especially mail questionnaires. On the other hand, interviews (personal or telephone) have their advantages: (1) the literacy or educational level required of the participants is usually low, (2) they have a higher completion rate than mail questionnaires, (3) interviewers can increase the respondent's motivation to give complete and accurate answers, especially in face-to-face situations, (4) they permit greater flexibility—the respondent can ask for questions to be clarified and the interviewer can probe for more detail when the response is ambiguous or incomplete, (5) the interviewer controls the sequence in which questions are posed, (6) complex or emotion-laden topics that are difficult to express in writing can be examined,

(7) the interviewer can ensure that each question is answered, and (8) call backs on telephone interviews are simple and economical.

Partly because of low cost, the mail questionnaire is used very frequently in educational research. However, one major weakness in this approach is that the return rate is less than 100 percent. "Response rates of less than 50 percent are common. However, in the more sophisticated studies, response rates of 75 percent are usual, and rates as high as 95 percent have been reported" (72, p. 1402). Researchers usually report the procedures they used to increase the return rate of mail questionnaires and the way in which the actual respondents differed from the nonrespondents on demographic characteristics, when such data are available.

TYPE OF QUESTION

Interviews can be *unstructured*, including situations in which the respondent is allowed to talk with a minimum of guidance or direction from the interviewer and also situations in which the interviewer is guided only by predetermined topics. More frequently, however, some *structure or standardization* of the interview/questionnaire process exists. The *questions may be closed*, with both the question itself and the response that the respondent is allowed to make predetermined. Or only the questions may be predetermined and the respondent can answer freely, called *open questions*. Examples of both question forms illustrate the variety of descriptive information that each can provide.

CLOSED QUESTIONS   Many types of closed questions exist. Perhaps the most popular type is the *intensity scale* through which respondents are asked to rate a concept, event, or experience on a dimension of intensity of feeling, importance, agreement, etc. The familiar Likert continuum of "strongly agree" to "strongly disagree" illustrates an intensity question.

Similar to intensity questions are questions that require the respondent to estimate the *quantity* (how much, how many) of some phenomenon. In a study of the use of and reactions to intelligence tests, Goslin and Glass (60) asked teachers this question (p. 123): "Have you ever given a student specific information about his intelligence? (a) to most or all of my students, (b) to many students, (c) to some students, (d) to a few students, (e) No, although I have access to the scores, and (f) No, I do not have access to the scores."

Story identification items present a hypothetical situation to which the respondent must react in terms of his or her personal position, or in terms of what decision might be made. Hyman, Carroll, Duffey, and Manni (85, pp. 188–189) presented hypothetical conflict situations regarding classification of children, such as: "The psychologist states that a student is retarded-trainable while the learning disabilities specialist feels the data indicate the child to be retarded-educable with specific learning disabilities." The respondents, composed of learning disability specialists, school psychologists, and social workers, were then asked how such a conflict would be resolved by the child study group in their school.

Sometimes respondents are asked to *rank* a series of options in accordance with their personal preference, the option's importance, or some other standard. Rokeach (116) used this technique in his study of values (subjects ranked such values as equality, freedom, maturity, wisdom, and respect for others in terms of their personal importance). The ranking technique increases in difficulty for the respondent as the number of possibilities to be ranked increases. In such cases, the researcher may ask that the subject give only his or her first three or five choices. Another closed item form is the *checklist* on which the respondents check as many descriptions or alternatives as are applicable.

Closed questions are easy to code and analyze, make answers comparable from individual to individual, and define rather clearly the intent of most questions. However, in some cases they may force an opinion on an issue on which there is none, even with a "don't know," "no opinion," or "other" option. Even though the researcher's frame of reference is usually clarified by the question stem and alternatives, unless extensive pretesting is conducted it may be risky to accept the responses at face value.

OPEN QUESTIONS   With open questions, unexpected responses or effects can be revealed and the respondent's frame of reference, knowledge and/or experience can be detected. In interview situations ambiguities about the question itself or the respondent's answer can be resolved. On the other hand, coding the responses to open questions is often difficult and too many questions can tire the interviewer and/or respondent. The following examples illustrate some situations in which open questions are advisable.

Lortie (101) in his study of the sources of shame among teachers used the following interview question: "Most of us have some occasions, hopefully rare, when we feel ashamed about something we have done. What kind of things have happened which you regretted having done?" (p. 156). One teacher response cited by Lortie (p. 160) was as follows:

> This youngster raised his hand, and I said, "Not now, dear," and he said "But, Mrs. ——————," and I said, "NOT NOW, DEAR!" Honestly, I wasn't as gentle as that, but I lost my temper, and that's the first time that has happened to me. . . . I just can't imagine doing that to a child, because, I mean, a child is helpless. You're standing up there so important, and that child is absolutely helpless, and there is no need to shout at him [Interview 27; fourth grade, female].

The depth of the teacher's feelings and reactions was captured with this open question. The difficulties of using a closed question to describe such feelings, or even an open question in a questionnaire format, should be obvious.

A study by Graves (63) illustrates another research context in which open questions were more appropriate than closed. Graves combined observation and interview techniques in his study of how seven-year-old children write. The observer intervened while the child was writing to ask such questions as (pp. 233–234): "Tell me what you are going to write about when you finish your drawing" (prewriting phase), "Tell me what you are going to write about next. Tell me how your story is going to end." (composing phase), and "Which sentence do you like best? Tell me about it." (postwriting phase).

PROBING THE RESULTS

Data from educational surveys are often examined in a superficial way. Too many articles simply report the nature of the distribution on each variable. This lack of analytic treatment of the data may be partially attributed to an inadequate conceptualization of what is to be described, and to a failure to anticipate how the results are to be interpreted so that a meaningful, coherent, and comprehensive description is not achieved.

EXAMPLE OF A DESCRIPTIVE STUDY

The following descriptive survey illustrates many of the descriptive design factors cited in Chapter 11, and how a wealth of descriptive information can be obtained from a carefully planned study.

*Teaching Styles: Parental Preferences and Professional Role Definitions**
SAM D. SIEBER AND DAVID E. WILDER

[1] All aspects of public education are matters of public interest and concern both by law and by tradition. Public participation in school-related activities however, has often been shown to vary from one social setting to another. Generally, whether the activity is voting in school elections or membership in the PTA, participation is higher in communities or among individuals with relatively high socioeconomic status.[1] This tendency has been interpreted by some observers as reinforcement for inequalities which already exist in the schools and as a barrier to improved education in working-class settings. In recent years, civil rights leaders and poverty area workers have attempted to provoke high participation from parents, particularly in urban slum areas; and school protests (such as the ones in New York City during 1966–1967) have been one of the outgrowths of this movement. Some schools, in turn, have gone on record as favoring decentralization of administration and direct public involvement in school

Sam D. Sieber and David E. Wilder, 1967. Teaching styles: parental preferences and professional role definitions. *Sociology of Education* **40**: 302–315. Reprinted with permission of the American Sociological Association, Sam D. Sieber, and David E. Wilder.

* This study was made possible by a grant from the U.S.O.E. We are indebted to Professor William S. Goode for his helpful comments on the first draft of this article.

[1] For a summary statement of the social characteristics of voters and nonvoters in school elections see R. F. Carter, *Voters and Their Schools*, Stanford University, California 1960. For evidence regarding differential participation in P.T.A., see especially P. C. Sexton, *Education and Income*, N.Y.: Viking, 1961, and R. E. Herriott and N. H. St. John, *Social Class and the Urban School*, New York: John Wiley & Sons, Inc., 1966. A doctoral dissertation is being written by Nathalie Schacter Friedman based on data from this study which further elaborates and corroborates these relationships and investigates some of the consequences of differential parental observability and participation in the schools.

matters.[2] These recommendations are directed at the improvement both of education and of school–community relations. However, it is possible that there are differences in the values and expectations of parents and educators which will lead to open conflict as parental involvement in the schools increases, and as parents and educators become more aware of their differences.[3]

[2] One area of potential conflict between parents and educators is that of the appropriate role behavior of teachers. The role behavior of teachers can be regarded as reflecting instrumental processes as distinguished from terminal goals or the eventual outputs desired from education. It seems probable that the purposes of education must be diffuse in order to accommodate the different values and expectations of the different interested groups. Indeed, the ultimate goals of education are often stated in platitudes. As a result, there are seldom public disputes between parents and teachers over the purposes of education. In contrast, instrumental processes concern the daily behavior of teachers and students. Both parents and teachers may have rather specific ideas about what this should be like, and open disputes may more readily result.[4]

[3] The preferences and images of parents regarding instructional practices has been a subject of considerable debate in the past ten years. Spokesmen on both sides of the "great debate" concerning the most suitable kind of education for the post-Sputnik era have imputed attitudes to the community to support their own preferences. Thus, the critics of progressive education have claimed that parents are dismayed by the poverty of instruction in the basic subjects, while the defense has argued that current instructional approaches reflect the desires of local publics, and that parents are highly concerned about the school's contribution to the emotional and social development of their children.[5]

[4] In the midst of this controversy, some educators have become worried that teachers themselves have been misled by a vocal minority of prominent critics. They fear that teachers wrongly believe that parents favor more academic pres-

---

[2] Two notable examples are the New York City schools (see the minutes of the Board of Education, December 21, 1966) and the recommendation made to the schools of Washington, D.C. by A. Harry Passow as a result of an extensive and much publicized study. (See A. H. Passow, *A Study of Washington, D.C. Schools,* forthcoming.)

[3] The larger study of which this is part will explore several of the areas of possible conflict in a forthcoming report. Some of the normative differences between teachers and parents have been described by D. Jenkins, "Interpersonal Perception of Teachers, Students, and Parents," N.E.A. 1951, and John M. Foskett, *The Normative World of the Elementary School Teacher,* U. of Oregon, Eugene: The Center for the Advanced Study of Educational Administration, 1967.

[4] Traditionally, educators have maintained that the purposes or terminal goals of education should be determined by the citizenry, but that professional educators should be left to decide how subject matter will be taught. Citizens have not always shared this definition of the situation judging from the controversies over methods of teaching reading, for example, and the pronouncements of popular critics of American education, including Admiral Rickover and Martin Mayer. The limits of lay authority become especially relevant when parents participate in school activities: and in New York, parents have recently demanded the right to participate in the selection of professional school personnel.

[5] See, for example, Winfield C. Scott, Clyde M. Hill, and Hobert W. Burns, *The Great Debate—Our Schools in Crisis,* Englewood Cliffs, N.J.: Prentice-Hall, 1959.

sure on pupils at the expense of other kinds of growth.[6] By examining how parents feel about various styles of teaching, we hope to furnish a partial answer to the practical question of what sorts of instruction are preferred by what types of parents. And by juxtaposing self-images of teachers against the expectations of parents, we should be able to see how parents desires compare with teachers' own role-definitions.

METHODS

[5] Styles of teaching can be thought of in many ways—for example, authoritarian versus permissive, pupil-directed versus content-oriented, or businesslike versus unplanned. Several writers have developed lists of teaching styles.[7] But just what teachers actually do is still very much an open question.[8] The main reason for the lack of research evidence on what teachers do in the classroom is the difficulty of measuring classroom behavior. But despite the absence of empirically documented styles, a number of ideal-constructs have been derived from "philosophies" of teaching, from controversies over progressive versus traditional education, and from the everyday discourse of practitioners and parents.

[6] Two especially important aspects of the teaching role are widely discussed in the literature: (1) the extent to which subject matter is emphasized, and (2) the extent to which adult authority is exercised. By dichotomizing and combining these two dimensions, we obtain four distinct styles of teaching:

		Emphasis on subject matter	
		High	Low
Relations between teacher and child	*Adult-centered* (authoritarian)	Content-oriented	Control-oriented
	Child-centered (permissive)	Discovery-oriented	Sympathy-oriented

---

[6] This study of parents' and teachers' opinions about the roles and goals of education was originally prompted by precisely this concern on the part of officials in one of the State Education Departments.

[7] The most extensive list of dimensions for classifying teacher behavior has been developed by Ryan as part of the Teacher Characteristic Study, *Characteristics of Teachers*. Washington, D.C.: American Council on Education, 1960. More sociologically oriented conceptualizations can be found in Orville Brim, *Sociology and the Field of Education*. Philadelphia: Russell Sage, 1958; W. W. Charters, Jr., "The Social Background of Teaching," in N. L. Gage, editor, *Handbook of Research on Teaching*, Chicago: Rand McNally & Co., 1963, pp. 715–813, and Charles E. Bidwell, "The School as a Formal Organization," in James G. March, *Handbook of Organizations*, Chicago: Rand McNally & Co., 1965. Bidwell's recent restatement of Waller (W. Waller, *The Sociology of Teaching*, New York: Wiley, 1932) in terms of two conflicts faced by teachers, the use or nonuse of affect in controlling students, and whether to emphasize nurturance or student achievement, produces four types very similar to those we have used.

[8] Normal E. Wallen and Robert M. W. Travers, "Analysis and Investigation of Teaching Methods," in N. L. Gage, editor, *Handbook of Research on Teaching*, Chicago: Rand McNally, 1963, pp. 448–505.

The four styles singled out for study are not exhaustive of the popular conceptions of teaching and are not wholly accurate reflections of behavior patterns, but they do represent some of the most common images that are held of teaching at the elementary and secondary levels.

[7] The four styles of teaching were presented to first, fifth, and tenth grade *teachers,* to the *mothers* of many of these teachers' pupils, to the *pupils* of selected tenth grade English teachers, and to *principals* of the schools where the teachers were located. (The sample design is discussed below.) The questions that were posed were the following:

Mothers and students—	Although teachers have to concern themselves with many different things in their jobs, some teachers emphasize certain things more than others. Suppose there were four first (fifth, or tenth) grade teachers in (school) and you could choose the one you wanted to be (M: child's teacher; S: your 10th grade English teacher). Which of these would be your first choice?
	Which of these best describes (M: child's teacher; S: name of English teacher)?
Teachers—	Although teachers have to concern themselves with many different things in their jobs, some teachers emphasize certain things more than others. We would like to know which one of the following four types of teachers you think best describes you.
	Which of these four types of teachers do you think most of the mothers of the students in your class prefer?
	How about your principal? Which type do you think he (she) prefers?
Principals—	(Same basic question as above, but:) Which of these four types of teachers do you prefer having as a teacher in (school)?

[8] The four teaching styles were described as follows:

(Control-oriented)	Teacher #1 is most concerned with maintaining discipline, seeing that students work hard, and teaching them to follow directions.
(Content-oriented)	Teacher #2 feels it's most important that students know their subject matter well, and that he (she) cover the material thoroughly and test their progress regularly.
(Discovery-oriented)	Teacher #3 stresses making the class interesting and encourages students to be creative and to figure things out for themselves.
(Sympathy-oriented)	Teacher #4 thinks it's most important that a teacher be friendly and well liked by students and able to understand and to handle their problems.

Of the many possible ways of classifying teaching styles, Sieber and Wilder identified four that varied on two important dimensions indicated by the research literature. The merit of this two-dimensional *conceptualization* of teaching styles was shown later in the analytic comparisons made of the data. The brief, yet clear and distinct descriptions of the four styles (paragraph 8) probably made it relatively easy for the respondents to discriminate among them. On the other hand, some may have found it difficult to respond if they preferred a combination of styles. It is important to note that the authors did not claim to describe all teaching styles, and therefore generalizations beyond the four classifications are unwarranted.

The primary focus was on the mothers' preference of teaching style and the teachers' perception of the teachers' own styles. As is illustrated in the results section, the additional questions asked of both groups as well as the questions posed to students and principals provided *norms for evaluation* of these two central issues.

[9] School attendance areas were selected in order to maximize the homogeneity of certain social and ecological characteristics. (See Table 12.1 for profiles of the communities and numbers of respondents.) A city school system provided four elementary attendance areas. Three of these were predominantly working-class areas: one was mostly white, one was mostly Negro, and one was mixed. The fourth elementary attendance area in the city was mainly composed of white middle-class residents. In the same city a high school which received the students from the schools already mentioned was also selected. Outside of the city, four suburbs, two small towns, and one rural community were chosen. The suburbs were selected according to both SES of the residents (middle versus working class) and rate of growth (stable versus growing). The two small towns were selected according to SES and commuting rate.

[10] All the mothers of pupils in the classrooms of two teachers in each school building at each of three grade levels (first, fifth, and tenth) were in the sample. Wherever possible, the two teachers in each grade represented a slow and a fast track, or a noncollege and a college track. The tenth grade teachers were teachers of English. All teachers in the elementary schools were also interviewed; all English teachers were interviewed in each high school. All principals and all tenth grade English students were also respondents.[9]

The authors used census track data to *describe the population* from which the sample was selected. This procedure is in contrast to one that requires asking questions about income and educational level of each participant. This is a useful approach and one that should be employed more often in similar contexts when such individual data are difficult or impossible to obtain. When reading the remainder of the article, it is important to recall that the *population unit* for the background variables was groups of individuals defined by the geographic areas of the school district. The population unit for the remaining set of data was the individual.

The interview technique employed in the study yielded a very high response rate (footnote 9).

---

[9] For a detailed discussion of the sample design, including problems in its development, see David E. Wilder and Nathalie Schacter Friedman, *Project Memorandum #1*—"Selecting Ideal-Typical Communities and Gaining Access to Their Schools for Social Research Purposes," October, 1965, Bureau of Applied Social Research, Columbia University. Response rates for the various groups were as follows: mothers, 83%; teachers, 99%; principals, 100%; and students, 97%. Interviews with mothers were conducted in the homes by Roper Associates. The interviews lasted 90 minutes on the average. Teachers and students were interviewed in the schools, and interviews averaged 60 minutes.

TABLE 12.1 PROFILES OF ATTENDANCE AREAS AND NUMBERS OF RESPONDENTS*

	Median family income	% in white-collar occupations	Median yrs. of school completed	% Negro	% Increase in school pop. (1960–1963)	Number of interviews			
						Mothers	Teachers	Students	Principals
City neighborhoods									
White middle-class (el.)	$10,000	55	12	>5		92	13	0	1
White working-class (el.)	$6,000	40	8	>5		92	18	0	1
Mixed Negro and white (el.)	$4,500	20	8	40		84	9	0	1
Negro (el.)	$4,500	15	8	90		66	16	0	1
Cross-section (high school)						138	29	157	1
Suburbs									
Stable middle-class	$15,000	75	13	>1	5	131	22	59	2
Growing middle-class	$10,000	70	13	>1	15	128	31	48	2
Stable working-class	$6,000	30	9	>1	1	111	25	49	3
Growing working-class	$7,000	35	11	>1	41	142	48	45	2
Small towns									
Middle-class (pop. 4,000)	$6,300	50	12			154	23	45	2
Working-class (pop. 6,000)	$6,200	40	10			125	30	56	2
Rural community (pop. 2,500)†						127	19	49	2

* All census figures are approximate in order to preserve community anonymity. The 1960 U.S. Census was used.
† Census data not provided.

At this point, it is easy to visualize various ways in which the authors can partition the population to provide *differentiated description*. Four types of individuals were studied: teachers, mothers of the students in those teachers' classrooms, students of the teachers (tenth grade only), and the teachers' principals. Three grade levels were identified. Various types of communities were included (rural vs. urban, middle vs. lower class, different community sizes, different racial composition).

RESULTS

[11] Before looking at the correlates of preferred teaching styles, it needs to be emphasized that the expectations that mothers hold are by no means of minor importance to them. For if mothers do not believe that teachers are meeting their role expectations, they tend to be dissatisfied with the teacher.

[12] As noted above, the mothers were asked to select the style that they preferred and also the style that "best describes" the teacher. By matching the mothers' *preferences* with their *perceptions* of teachers, we are able to designate mothers who desire a teaching style that is at odds with what they believe the teacher is actually doing in the classroom. As a measure of satisfaction with the teacher's performance, we have employed the following question:

Are there any things that you think it is important for (teacher) to be doing differently than he (she) is in order to help (child) get the most out of school?

[13] Table 12.2 shows that mothers who perceive the teacher as deviating from their expectations much more often desire some modification in the teacher's behavior. Only 15 percent of those who perceive *conformity* desire other behavior, contrasted with 40 percent of those who perceive *deviance*. These figures at once lend credibility to the responses of mothers about preferred teaching styles, and demonstrate the practical value of studying parental preferences.

TABLE 12.2   *MOTHERS' DISSATISFACTION WITH TEACHERS, ACCORDING TO MOTHERS' PERCEPTION OF TEACHERS' CONFORMITY TO PREFERRED STYLES OF TEACHING*

	Teaching styles		Dissatisfaction (% Mothers who say that teacher should be doing something differently)	
	Preferred	Perceived		
Perceived conformity	Control	Control	16% (140)*	
	Content	Content	16% (251)	15% (680)
	Discovery	Discovery	15% (228)	
	Sympathy	Sympathy	13% (61)	
Perceived deviance	Control	(Not control)	27% (134)	
	Content	(Not content)	44% (227)	40% (614)
	Discovery	(Not discovery)	48% (181)	
	Sympathy	(Not sympathy)	33% (72)	

* Numbers in parentheses are the N on which the percentage is based.

[14] Perceived deviance with respect to two of the four styles is especially highly related to dissatisfaction. These styles are the two *intellectual* ones: content-orientation and discovery-orientation. Almost half of the mothers who see the teacher as failing to conform to these desired styles would welcome a change in the teacher's behavior. As we shall see in a moment, these are also the two patterns of teaching that are most commonly preferred at all three grade levels.

In paragraph 13 and Table 12.2 the authors provided an *internal check* on the validity of the mothers' preferences, by determining whether the mothers who were dissatisfied with the teacher's performance also tended to be those mothers who preferred a style different from the style they perceived the teacher to possess. This was the only reported check on response bias or error. One might also question how much and what type of information the mothers possessed on the teaching style of their child's teacher, whether the teachers' self-reported role would match the judgment of a classroom observer, etc. One interesting comparison related to this issue of possible bias that was not reported was the agreement between the tenth grade student perceptions of their teacher and the teacher's own role-definition (Table 12.9 presented only the students' preferred style).

PREFERRED TEACHING STYLES AT DIFFERENT GRADE LEVELS

[15] It is generally assumed that elementary and secondary teachers are expected to perform their teaching roles quite differently. As the pupil passes from lower to higher grade levels, he is expected to become more intellectually serious, and especially so if he wishes to enter college. One would therefore predict that parents with children in the higher grades would place greater emphasis on teaching of *content*. Also, one would expect parents of younger children to desire greater support or sympathy from teachers.

[16] Despite these common impressions, our data show only a slight trend in the direction of parents' placing greatest emphasis on *content*-orientation from lower to higher grade levels, and practically no difference with respect to preferences for the *sympathy*-oriented teacher. As shown in Table 12.3, 33 percent of

TABLE 12.3   *TEACHING STYLES PREFERRED BY MOTHERS WITH CHILDREN IN DIFFERENT GRADE LEVELS*

| | % Mothers | | |
| | Grade level of child | | |
Teaching styles	1st	5th	10th
Control	26%	22%	13%
Content	33	38	43
Discovery	30	29	36
Sympathy	11	11	8
	100%	100%	100%
N mothers	(453)	(494)	(124)

the mothers of first graders would choose a teacher who was content-oriented, compared with 38 percent of the mothers of fifth graders, and 43 percent of the mothers of tenth graders. There is a clear trend, but it is much less pronounced than common sense would predict. The sympathy-oriented style was favored by only 11 percent of first grade mothers, 11 percent of fifth grade mothers, and eight percent of tenth grade mothers.

[17] The greatest difference occurs with respect to preferences for the *control*-oriented teacher: 26 percent of the first grade mothers, 22 percent of the fifth grade mothers, and 13 percent of the tenth grade mothers desire this teaching style. Thus, the younger the child, the more likely are their mothers to want a nonintellectual authoritarian style. This would appear to be in direct conflict with the professional educational ideology that stresses the importance of a permissive classroom climate in the early grades.

[18] To sum up thus far, mothers of older children more often desire the two styles of teaching that emphasize *subject matter*, content-orientation and discovery-orientation. But the overall difference between first and tenth grade mothers is not very pronounced, suggesting that variations in the expectations of parents with children in different grade levels has been overestimated by professional educators.

[19] Perhaps of greater significance is the observation that *within each grade level*, the mothers prefer the *content*-oriented teacher first and the *discovery*-oriented teacher second in order of frequency. Only a small percentage of the mothers opted for the *sympathy*-oriented teacher. In short, it is not true that mothers are only secondarily concerned with the intellectual maturation of their children. Even in the elementary grades, only about a tenth of the mothers prefer a teacher who is primarily oriented to playing a nurturance role with pupils (i.e., the sympathy-oriented teacher). The critics of educational practices who claim that parents are mainly concerned about the intellective aspects of education are by and large correct in their assessment, and especially with reference to the higher grade levels.

PREFERRED TEACHING STYLES AND SOCIAL POSITION

[20] The sample design permits us to examine the expectations of teachers that prevail in different social contexts. In the following discussion we shall use the features of the community to define the characteristics of respondents. In other words, instead of classifying the mothers according to their own socioeconomic position and race, we shall classify them according to the socioeconomic and racial composition of their community. Further analysis will draw upon both sources of classification simultaneously, but for the purposes of this paper it is sufficient to note variations according to community characteristics alone.[10]

---

[10] For stylistic convenience we shall occasionally refer to mothers residing in the various types of social context as "middle-class" or "working-class" mothers; but it should not be overlooked that we are really speaking of mothers who reside in certain types of communities. As previously mentioned, the communities were selected partly on the basis of internal homogeneity of socio-economic characteristics, and therefore this characterization of mothers is accurate in the vast majority of cases.

[21] The variation in preferences of mothers by the social class composition of the communities is at least as great as the variation by grade level; and with respect to certain styles of teaching it is much greater. The most consistent difference between working-class and middle-class communities, controlling for grade level of child, relates to the preference of the middle-class for the *discovery*-oriented style. As shown in Table 12.4, mothers in the middle-class communities much more often prefer this style of teaching. Thus, 23 percent of the working-class residents compared with 38 percent of the middle-class residents with grade school children prefer the discovery-oriented teacher; and the respective figures for mothers of tenth graders are 25 percent and 47 percent.

[22] Evidently, the middle-class emphasis on training for independent effort reasserts itself in the preferences of mothers regarding their children's formal education.[11] One important implication of this finding is that teachers who actually use the "discovery method" will be more successful with middle-class than with working-class children, because of the cultural support for independent effort that middle-class students receive in the home. This is a possibility that has so far been overlooked in psychological literature on the subject.[12]

[23] Mothers located in working-class communities prefer the *control*-oriented and the *sympathy*-oriented styles of instruction more often than do mothers in middle-class communities. (This is mainly the case among grade school mothers.) As mentioned earlier, these two images refer to nonintellectual mechanisms of socialization. Indeed, the two styles refer to socialization sanctions employed by mothers themselves, namely, disciplining and giving affective support. It appears then that working-class mothers, and especially those with grade school children, are more likely to desire a teacher who is a prototypical parent-surrogate. This

TABLE 12.4 *TEACHING STYLES PREFERRED BY MOTHERS WITH CHILDREN IN DIFFERENT GRADE LEVELS ACCORDING TO SES OF COMMUNITY*

Grade of child:	First and fifth grades		Tenth grade°	
Community SES: Teaching styles	Working class	Middle class	Working class	Middle class
Control	30%	17%	12%	8%
Content	32	39	55	40
Discovery	23	38	25	47
Sympathy	15	6	8	5
	100%	100%	100%	100%
N mothers	(495)	(372)	(114)	(129)

° Excludes the city high school because it contains a mixture of social class backgrounds.

---

[11] For a review of research on "independence training" according to social class of parents, see Urie Bronfenbrenner, "Socialization and Social Class through Time and Space," in Maccoby, Newcomb, and Hartley, editors, *Readings in Social Psychology*, 3rd ed., New York: Henry Holt, 1958, pp. 400–25.

[12] See, for example, Jerome S. Bruner, "The Act of Discovery," *Harvard Educational Review*, Vol. 33, No. 1 (Winter 1963), pp. 124–135.

tendency to expect teachers to perform in ways that are similar to informal socialization of the young might stem from the working-class tendency to view the world in more simplistic and personal terms.[13] Isolation from the internal workings of formal organizations and from professional role-playing might limit their understanding of the extent to which teachers are prepared to play a specialized role in dealing with children.

[24] Of the two images more often preferred by working-class mothers of grade school children, it is a preference for the *control*-oriented teacher which more clearly differentiates the two social classes. Seventeen percent of the middle-class mothers of grade school children prefer this teaching style compared with 30 percent of the working-class mothers. At the tenth grade level, however, it is the *content*-oriented style that most clearly distinguishes the working-class from the middle-class (55 percent vs. 40 percent, respectively). These apparent differences between grade levels mask an important underlying similarity. It will be recalled that control- and content-orientation are the two styles which we have designated as *authoritarian*. The proportion of working-class, tenth grade mothers choosing *both* of these styles remains high in comparison with first and fifth grade mothers. Thus, there is simply a shift from one authoritarian stance (control-orientation) to another (content-orientation), although this shift of emphasis crosses the boundary from the nonintellectual, parent-surrogate styles to the intellectual realm of teaching. Stated in relation to the preferences of middle-class mothers, the difference between the two social classes shifts from the question of *whether* subject matter should be emphasized to the question of the appropriate *manner* of emphasis. To sum up, when the working-class mothers choose an intellectual style at the tenth-grade level, they choose "authoritarian intellectualism" (content) rather than "permissive intellectualism" (discovery).

[25] These results are in accord with research that reports a tendency among working-class members to value authoritarian social relationships,[14] and particularly the child-rearing studies that show greater emphasis on parental dominance among working-class mothers.[15]

[26] The social class differences we have observed are not confounded by the different racial compositions of working- and middle-class schools. Table 12.5 makes this quite clear. In this table we show the styles of teaching preferred by mothers of grade school children who are located in the one city in our sample. (As mentioned earlier, the three working-class grade schools in the city were selected according to their racial composition.) Table 12.5 shows that the mothers' desires do not differ systematically according to the proportion of Negroes in the school. But what is more significant, all of the major differences previously noted between middle-class and working-class mothers of grade school children *persist* regardless of racial composition. Working-class mothers more often prefer the control-oriented and the sympathy-oriented teachers, while

---

[13] Seymour M. Lipset, "Democracy and Working-Class Authoritarianism," *American Sociological Review*, vol. 24 (1959), pp. 482–501.

[14] Richard Christie, "Authoritarianism Re-Examined," in *Studies in the Scope and Method of the "Authoritarian Personality,"* Richard Christie and Marie Jahoda, editors, Glencoe, Ill.: The Free Press, 1954, pp. 123–196.

[15] Bronfenbrenner, *op. cit.*

TABLE 12.5 *TEACHING STYLES PREFERRED BY MOTHERS OF GRADE SCHOOL CHILDREN IN THE CITY ACCORDING TO RACIAL COMPOSITION AND SES OF SCHOOL ATTENDANCE AREA*

| Teaching style | Working class | | | Middle class |
	White	*Mixed*	*Negro*	*(Mostly white)*
Control	40%	41%	35%	21%
Content	33	25	26	40
Discovery	17	13	22	30
Sympathy	10	21	17	9
	100%	100%	100%	100%
N mothers	(81)	(92)	(65)	(91)

middle-class mothers more often prefer the content-oriented and the discovery-oriented teachers.[16]

[27] But we have not yet looked at the teachers themselves. In order to determine the amount of consensus between teachers and mothers on styles of classroom teaching, we need to compare the expectations of mothers with the role-definitions of teachers. This question is especially important if we wish to see whether teachers are more likely to conform to the expectations prevailing in the world of professional education than they are to the expectations flowing from outside the system.

---

[16] It is clear from comparing Tables 12.4 and 12.5 that working-class mothers of grade school children in the city prefer the control-oriented style of teaching over the content-oriented style, while the opposite is true for elementary school mothers in working-class settings which are not in the city.

Paragraphs 15 through 27 illustrated the process of *differentiated description.* At first the mothers' preference was described by grade level, then the grade levels were divided according to the socioeconomic status of the community, and finally the two socioeconomic levels were divided by their racial composition. No reason was cited for not presenting all possible breakdowns of grade level, SES, and race, although it is possible that some of the sample sizes may have been too small for meaningful comparisons.

In each table, the authors cited the sample size upon which each percentage was based. For example, in Table 12.3, of the 453 mothers of first grade children, 26 percent preferred a control style, 33 percent a content style, etc.

Sieber and Wilder did not commit the *ecological fallacy*, although it would have been easy to do in the context of this particular study. Despite occasional phrases as "working-class mothers," they very carefully referred to the "preference of mother by social class composition of the communities" (paragraph 21), "mothers located in working-class communities" (paragraph 23), or the "proportion of Negroes in the school" (paragraph 26). In addition, the table headings clearly referred to the socioeconomic level or racial composition of the community, not to that of individuals per se.

CONSENSUS ON STYLES OF TEACHING BETWEEN TEACHERS AND PARENTS

[28] We saw earlier that mothers who believe that teachers are *not* teaching the way they would like them to teach are much more often dissatisfied with teachers. Apparently there is much room for dissatisfaction, for when we compare the teaching styles preferred by parents with the teachers' definitions of their role, we find considerable discrepancy. For example, as we see in Table 12.6, only 30 percent of the grade school mothers desire the *discovery*-oriented style, but 56 percent of the teachers claim that this is the style that best describes them. And even a larger gap occurs between tenth grade mothers and teachers.

[29] Teachers also diverge widely from parents' expectations in the category of *content*-oriented teaching. Thus, 43 percent of the tenth grade mothers prefer this style, but only 16 percent of the teachers describe themselves in this fashion. In short, mothers most often prefer the content-oriented style, while teachers tend to espouse the discovery-oriented style. This contrast confirms the critics of public education who claim that parents want more attention devoted to the basic content of school subjects while school personnel favor a more permissive intellectual approach stressing "independent discovery."

[30] Regardless of the merits of these two instructional patterns, it is obvious that many parents and teachers have quite different educational philosophies. Specifically, *69 percent of the mothers in our study have a teacher for their child whose role-definition is not in accord with their preferences.* The proportions of mothers with various role-preferences whose teachers describe themselves in various ways are shown in Table 12.7.

[31] Mothers whose expectations are most often violated (at least with respect to the teacher's definition of her role) are those who favor a *sympathy*-oriented style. Only 5 percent of these mothers have teachers who describe themselves as sympathy-oriented. But only a small proportion of mothers prefer this style. More serious in terms of possible strain between family and school is the large minority

TABLE 12.6   *TEACHING STYLES PREFERRED BY MOTHERS COMPARED WITH TEACHERS' OWN ROLE-DEFINITIONS (BY GRADE)*

	First and fifth grades		Tenth grade	
Teaching style	*% Mothers who prefer type*	*% Teachers who describe selves*	*% Mothers who prefer type*	*% Teachers who describe selves*
Control	24%	20%	13%	10%
Content	35	18	43	16
Discovery	30	56	36	72
Sympathy	11	6	8	2
	100%	100%	100%	100%
N	(947)	(175)	(424)	(104)

TABLE 12.7   *TEACHERS' ROLE-DEFINITIONS ACCORDING TO THE EXPECTATIONS OF THEIR PUPILS' MOTHERS*

| | | Styles preferred by mothers | | | |
		Control	Content	Discovery	Sympathy
Teachers' self- descriptions	Control	27%	24%	17%	21%
	Content	16	13	12	17
	Discovery	55	59	67	57
	Sympathy	2	4	4	5
		100%	100%	100%	100%
	N mothers	(278)	(510)	(401)	(136)

of mothers (23 percent of the entire sample) who expect the teacher to be *content*-oriented but whose teachers describe themselves as *discovery*-oriented.

[32] The discrepancy between parental and professional role expectations becomes even larger when we compare mothers with *principals*. Table 12.8 shows that teachers occupy a position midway between parents and principals with respect to the proportion espousing the discovery-oriented style. This style, which we earlier characterized as "permissive intellectualism," is preferred by 30 percent of the mothers, 62 percent of the teachers, and 90 percent of the principals. In short, the degree of integration into the educational subsystem determines the extent to which the value of "permissive intellectualism" is held.

[33] The differences observed might not be only due to background differences among the three status groups. The importance of *degree of involvement in the educational structure* is suggested when we examine the role-expectations of *students,* who occupy the overlapping status of "client within the organization." Thus, students stand with one foot in the community and the other in the organization. And as shown in Table 12.9, the teaching styles favored by students reflect their degree of involvement in the educational system.

Whether the emphasis on *discovery* and de-emphasis on *content* of professional educators reflects a functional requirement of our educational system or merely an educational fad cannot be determined here. But whatever the source, "permis-

TABLE 12.8   *PREFERENCES OF MOTHERS AND PRINCIPALS FOR VARIOUS STYLES OF TEACHING, AND TEACHERS' OWN ROLE-DEFINITIONS*

Teaching styles preferred	Mothers	Teachers*	Principals
Control	22%	16%	5%
Content	38	17	5
Discovery	30	62	90
Sympathy	10	5	..
	100%	100%	100%
N	(1334)	(271)	(20)

* Percentages refer to own role-definition.

TABLE 12.9   *PREFERENCES OF TENTH GRADE MOTHERS, STUDENTS,*
AND PRINCIPALS FOR VARIOUS STYLES OF TEACHING,
AND TENTH GRADE TEACHERS' OWN ROLE-DEFINITIONS

Teaching styles preferred	Mothers	Students	Teachers°	Principals
Control	13%	7%	10%	..
Content	43	22	16	14%
Discovery	36	57	72	86
Sympathy	8	14	2	..
	100%	100%	100%	100%
N†	(424)	(418)	(104)	(7)

° Percentages refer to own role-definitions.
† This table contains only 10th grade teachers, mothers of 10th grade students, and principals of high schools, so that results can be compared with the students.

sive intellectualism" is clearly a part of the value system of education, as shown by our data, and is differentially espoused according to the degree of involvement in the educational structure.

This last section focused primarily on comparing the major groupings in the sample: teachers, parents, students, and principals. Such comparisons gave additional meaning to the mothers' preferences. That twice as many mothers as teachers preferred a content teaching style at all grades was clearly shown in Table 12.6, and the overwhelming preference of principals for discovery styles was in sharp contrast to the mothers' preference. Strictly speaking, the data in Table 12.7 examined a question of association—the relationship between mother preferences and teacher role definitions.

CONCLUSIONS

[34] By comparing the preferences of mothers among four typical teaching styles with the self-images of their children's teachers, it was found that mothers prefer a content-oriented style more often than any other, while a majority of teachers see themselves as discovery-oriented. In addition, over two-thirds of the mothers expressed role preferences that were not in accord with the self-descriptions of their child's teacher. A higher proportion of the mothers of tenth graders than mothers of first and fifth graders were found to prefer the two subject matter oriented styles, but somewhat larger differences were found between mothers in communities with different socioeconomic composition. Working-class mothers had a higher preference for the two authoritarian styles of teaching, while middle-class mothers tended to share the preference for a discovery-oriented style with teachers. The latter finding was interpreted as suggesting compatibility between the independence training stressed by middle-class parents and the teaching styles advocated by teachers. It is not clear whether the preference of teachers for the discovery-oriented style is a reflection of professional socialization or a functional requirement of the teaching role in American schools. The high

consensus on teaching styles among teachers, however, and especially the even higher consensus among principals suggest a pervasive educational ideology.

[35] Evidence that instrumental goals of education are potential sources of conflict was shown by the higher dissatisfaction among mothers whose perceived and preferred teaching styles were dissimilar. This demonstrates the importance of studying what teachers do, and are thought to do, in the classroom, as distinct from the more diffuse purposes of education.

[36] In view of the current agitation for increased parental participation in the schools in working-class areas, the especially high preference for the control-oriented teaching style among the mothers of the elementary school children in such areas might be a potential source of parent-teacher conflict. If increased participation results in increased awareness among mothers of their differences with teachers, then the likelihood of conflict should also increase unless (1) the schools are able to legitimate teacher behavior which is not in accord with parental expectations, for example, by persuading parents in working-class areas of the virtues of discovery-oriented teaching, or (2) teachers change their role definitions in accord with the expectations held by the constituency of parents.

Although only a few questions were asked of the participants and the results on even fewer questions were presented in the article, much descriptive information was generated. The conceptualization of teaching styles and the design of the sample contributed greatly to the adequacy of the resulting description. Consider, for example, the nature of the description if only one grade or if only one socioeconomic/racial group had been sampled.

The results of any study, including this one, can be presented in many different ways. Sieber and Wilder's account reflected an analytic style of reporting (e.g., some questions provided checks on the validity of key questions, some comparisons placed the answers to key questions in perspective), rather than a simple report of the distribution of each variable.

12.1.2 OBSERVATION TECHNIQUES

Observations that provide descriptions are usually made in the field or "in situ," that is, in situations in which the participants spend most of their time or in which they are familiar. When the researcher deliberately creates different settings to which the subject is exposed and then observed, the study is probably causal in intent, rather than purely descriptive.

In some cases, observation may be the only feasible technique of data collection. Interviews or questionnaires are not possible with individuals who cannot describe their behavior verbally, such as infants, preschool children, and severely retarded individuals. Sometimes introspective reports are apt to be misleading, inadequate, or impossible to make as in asking counselors to verbalize what types of nonverbal signs they made to their clients and when they made the nonverbal signs. Individuals may be unaware of short events and personal habits. For some researchers, observation is the best technique for providing descriptive data, because observations can preserve events in their entirety.

VARIETY OF BEHAVIORS AND SETTINGS OBSERVED

The range of phenomena that can be observed is indeed great. Six types of social settings can be observed (100): acts, activities, meanings, participation, relationships, and settings. Acts and activities are typical of much psychological research while relationships and settings are typical of sociological and anthropological analyses.

Acts are short in duration, lasting only a few seconds, minutes, or hours. Examples of acts are: nonverbal behavior (facial expressions, body movements, exchanged glances), extralinguistic behavior (pitch and loudness of voice, rate of speaking), and linguistic behavior. Much behavior observed in the classroom consists of linguistic acts. In both the Jackson and Cosca study (Chapter 2) and the Cicirelli and Cicirelli study (Chapter 1) acts were observed.

Activities refer to conduct by groups of individuals which takes days, weeks, or months to occur. Burnett's (23) anthropological description of the ceremonies in a high school is a good example of the activity level. She observed high school activities and ceremonies such as homecoming, the football banquet, pep rallies, the Christmas dance, freshman initiation, and the senior trip in one school for a period of nine months.

Meanings refer to verbal behavior that defines, justifies, and interprets human behavior rather than describes such behavior. More commonly meanings are known as rules, norms, values, ideology, stereotypes, understandings, or world views.

At the *participation* level, the total nature of an individuals' involvement in a social setting is observed, in order to identify what Lofland (100) called "personal types." For example, individuals vary in the way they adapt to new settings and the way in which they establish a career. Smith and Geoffrey (131) identified two roles assumed by some students: the court jester and the nonworker.

Relationships refer to the interrelationships among several persons. Observation at this level includes analyses of hierarchical relationships, patterns of alliance among individuals, and the stages through which interrelationships move. Johnson's (88) observation of the way individual black students were "integrated" or assimilated into a white, middle-class school illustrates this level. Smith and Geoffrey observed four stages in the teacher's establishment of classroom control.

Finally, the entire social *setting* can be described. Such units span the longest time periods and the largest spaces: descriptions of bureaucracies, of high schools, or of the phases of such social settings as the women's movement and the instruction of the gifted. When long time spans are involved, such procedures approach historical analysis.

DEGREE OF STRUCTURE

The degree of structure imposed upon the observer by the observation technique can be small or great. With relatively unstructured techniques, the observer "attempts to provide as complete and nonselective a description as possible" (130, p. 269), and the description is qualitative in nature. At the other end of the continuum, the behaviors to observe are carefully selected beforehand, and the typical description is quantitative. Unstructured techniques are frequently used to generate hypotheses; structured techniques to test hypotheses. *Complete lack of selectivity cannot be achieved* with any observation procedure; the observer always serves as an editor (145).

LOW STRUCTURE Observers can actively participate in the setting they are observing (participant observation) or they may watch from the sidelines (nonparticipant observation). In anthropological research, participant observation usually refers to immersion by the researcher in an alien culture and involves interviewing, obtaining reports from key informants, testing, and collecting documents and records as well as observation. A high degree of participation may allow a more comprehensive picture of the phenomenon of interest, but may also be associated with a loss of observer objectivity.

Smith and Geoffrey (131) used both participant and nonparticipant observation. Smith observed Geoffrey's classroom for almost every day of an entire semester and Geoffrey kept daily notes of his perception of classroom events. The advantages of this two-pronged observation approach were that: (1) the teacher as participant observer (Geoffrey) knew why he proceeded as he did, whereas the nonparticipant observer (Smith) did not, (2) the nonparticipant observer had to observe things as they occurred while the teacher could manipulate events to observe their effects, (3) the teacher generally had access to more information to guide him in interpretation of the data, and (4) the teacher was hindered in real reporting by his participant role, whereas the nonparticipant observer systematically and continually recorded classroom interaction.

The usual techniques for recording unstructured observations are *field notes* and *specimen records*. Both field notes and specimen records are constructed to be as specific as possible and include records of the following elements: the participants, the characteristics of the setting, the purpose of the situation, the social behavior that occurred, and the frequency and duration of the situation. When notes cannot be made while actually observing, they are recorded as soon as possible after the event to reduce forgetting. Observers often record their impressions and interpretations of the data as well. Specimen records are more selective than field notes, and provide a detailed, sequential, narrative description of all behavior that occurs over a relatively brief time period. A record is made of everything the subject says and does, and everything that is said and done to him or her. This may be accomplished by audio-video recording, yielding transcripts of all verbal behavior and a permanent record of nonverbal behavior, or by continuous note taking during data collection.

Two examples of the record produced by unstructured observation techniques are presented below. Johnson (88, pp. 103–104) reported the following classroom incident as illustrative of the fact that the differences between black and white students at a newly integrated school were obvious to everyone. The context was a fourth grade classroom (Mrs. Frank, the teacher) with 28 students, one black male (Jameson) and one black female (Sally). The date of this particular observation was October 18, 1973 and field notes were made while the incident transpired.

> The teacher is talking about classification systems. She talks about things as being either hot or cold, soft or hard, light or heavy. She then asks for some suggestions on how to classify students in the classroom. Sally raises her hand and says, "Some live in southwest and some live in northeast." Mrs. Frank then has the children from the southwest area of town stand up. Every student in the classroom stands up except Sally (Jameson is absent). The teacher then says, "That wasn't very useful to demonstrate the point." Then she says, "Let's classify the class by hair color." She writes down five categories; blond, brunette, brown, black, and red. Then she has all the students with blond hair stand up . . . then red hair . . . when she asks for those with brunette hair to stand up, a white girl who has very black hair stands up. As this girl stands up, some students are saying, "Your hair is black," and the girl responds by saying, "No, no, my hair is brunette." Mrs. Frank then asked for students with brown hair to stand up. At this time, Sally stands up and six different white students say to her, "Your hair is black not brown." Sally responds by saying, "My hair is brown." When the teachers asks for those with black hair to stand up, nobody stands.

The observers in the study by Graves (63) recorded behaviors of children while they composed stories. The incidence of acts other than writing per se were recorded at each step in the child's writing, so that the entire behavior sequence was preserved. A sample of a writing episode is shown in Table 12.10.

Methodological problems associated with unstructured procedures in a field setting include: (1) involvement by the observer in the situation itself, (2) the impossibility of observing everything, (3) the difficulty in recording all that is observed especially when events occur at a fast pace, (4) subjectivity because of observer inferences, and (5) failures by the observer to remember all the events.

HIGH STRUCTURE   More structured procedures are appropriate when investigators can define specifically the behaviors of interest to them. Perhaps one reason for the prevalent use of structured systems for classroom observation is that much is known about the sequence, organization, and dynamics of classrooms, enabling researchers to specify behaviors of interest. Most structured observation systems can be classified as either a sign, category, or rating system.

A *sign* system consists of a list of specific events or behaviors that may or may not occur during a specified period of time. Each behavior is symptomatic (a *sign*) of a dimension of interest. Signs may be quite specific and a large

TABLE 12.10 *EXAMPLE OF A WRITING EPISODE*

A whale is eating the
  1   2   3   4   5
men. A   dinosaur is
6 7 8 ⑨ ⑩ ⑪   12
triing to eat the whale.
 13 14 15 16   17   ⑱
	10:12
	R
		9—Gets up to dictionary. Has the page
		    with pictures of animals.

A dinosaur is frowning ⑲ ⑳ ㉑ 22 23 ㉔	IU R	10—Teacher announcement. 11—Copies from dictionary and returns book to side of room
a tree at the lion. and ㉕26 27 28 29 30 31 32 the cavman too. the men 33 34 35 ㊱ 37 38 are killed. The dinosaur 39 40 41 42 43 killed the whale. The 44 45 46 47 49 ㊽	RR OV OV IS RR RR	18—Stops, rubs eyes. 19—Rereads from 13 to 19. 20—Voices as he writes. 21—Still voicing. 24—Gets up to sharpen pencil and returns. 25—Rereads from 20 to 25. 36—Rereads to 36. Lost starting point.
cavmen live is the roks. 50 51 52 53 54 55 ㊻		48—Puts away paper, takes out again.
	RR 10:20	56—Rereads outloud from 49 to 56.

Key: 1–2–3–4—Numerals indicate writing sequence. ④—Item explained in comment column on the right. T—Teacher involvement; IS—Interruption Solicited; IU—Interruption Unsolicited; RR—Reread; PR—Proofread; DR—Works on drawing; R—Resource use. Accompanying Language: OV—Overt; WH—Whispering; F—Forms letters and words; M—Murmuring; S—No overt language visible.

Source: Donald Graves, 1975. An examination of the writing processes of seven year old children. From the Winter 1975 issue of *Research in the Teaching of English.* Copyright © 1975 by the National Council of Teachers of English. Reprinted with permission.

number (50–70) can be used simultaneously. Each sign defines itself. A sign system can be adapted to the observation of infrequent behavior in which the observer may simply watch for a period of time before any of the specified behaviors occur. Samuels and Turnure (125) used such behaviors as orienting eyes to text or teacher, working on reading follow-up exercises, and observing chalkboard or overhead projection as signs of positive student attention, and such behaviors as failing to follow instructions, closing eyes, and working or playing with nonassigned materials as signs of negative attention.

With a *category* system, categories of behavior are defined that *exhaust the behavior of interest* and are *mutually exclusive.* In contrast with sign systems, categories are usually not self-explanatory and extensive definitions and examples must be given to ensure observer agreement. The sequence of events can be preserved with a category system, but not with a sign system. Although many researchers use the general term of category in describing all observation systems, such terminology does not necessarily mean it is a category system as defined here.

The Flanders (49) system for analyzing the classroom interaction between teachers and pupils is a category system. All possible verbal behavior on the part of either the teacher or pupil is classified into one of ten categories. These categories consist of teacher talk acts (accepts feelings, praises or encourages, accepts or uses ideas of pupils, asks questions, lecturing, giving direction, and criticizing or justifying authority), pupil talk (response and initiation), and a final category of silence/confusion. Associated with this scheme is a sampling procedure that requires the observer to classify verbal acts at a pace of approximately one every three seconds.

Complicated category systems identify several major dimensions and establish a classification system within each. In Miller and Dyer's (107) videotape observation system, each teacher act was classified simultaneously on two major dimensions: (1) interaction with either an individual child or a group of children and (2) giving or requesting of information. The categories of giving and requesting were in turn subdivided into finer categories, e.g., giving linguistic information by modeling, giving linguistic information verbally, requests for linguistic performance, requests to imitate linguistic behavior.

With *rating* systems, observers estimate, rather than record, the frequency or importance of specific events, usually at the end of an observation session. For example, in Rosen's (117) study observers watched teachers for an hour each week over a four-week period and made ratings on such dimensions as "class feeling toward teacher" (as expressed verbally, pictorially, or through gestures by the children) on a nine-point scale from "strong dislike" to "strong liking."

Sign, category, and rating systems can vary on other dimensions. The degree of detail in the system can range from a broad, general description to an intensive analysis of small behavioral units. The signs, categories, or items can demand varying degrees of inference on the part of the observer. Multiple coding may be employed; that is, coding an event on several dimensions such as the speaker, the content of the communication, and the dominant activity at the time.

SAMPLING OF BEHAVIORAL UNITS/SETTINGS

The sampling procedure for observation, in conjunction with the observation scheme itself, determines the description that will be obtained. Some procedures provide good estimates of the duration, frequency, and sequence of interaction; others do not.

Ad libitum, or ad lib, sampling is used with field notes (1). Observers record as much as they can or whatever is most readily observed. No attempt is made to sample systematically, and it is difficult to avoid the bias that results from the observers being attracted to certain types of behavior or individuals.

Time sampling or one-zero sampling (1) is typically associated with sign systems. In each sample period, the simple occurrence/nonoccurrence of a behavior is recorded. Usually the time periods are short (10–15 seconds) and successive. Only statements regarding the number of sample intervals in which a behavior occurred can be made, since time sampling does not honor the beginning and end of natural events. That three occurrences of an event during one sample period must receive a score of one and the continuation of the same event over three sample periods must receive a score of three illustrates the distortion that can occur in both frequency and duration estimates with time sampling.

Instantaneous and scan sampling (1) involves watching an individual just long enough to observe and record one behavior (what the individual is doing at that instant) and then observing the next individual, etc. A large group can be scanned or observed in a very short period of time, and an estimate of the percentage of time spent in an activity by an entire group can be made.

In *event sampling,* the observer waits for a prespecified event to occur and records until the event (e.g., a fight on the school playground) terminates, thereby preserving the continuity of the event. Event sampling can be adapted to the study of phenomena that occur infrequently.

Another procedure is to record *all the occurrences* of some behaviors during the sampling period. Usually only one individual or a small group of individuals can be observed with such procedures and the observation conditions must be excellent. Information can then be obtained on the frequency with which events occur, the pace of events, and the sequence of events. Videotapes can be used to obtain a record of all behaviors. Sproull (135) videotaped children watching an entire hour of "Sesame Street." The tapes were replayed when necessary to record all occurrences and to observe each child in depth.

ANALYSIS OF RESULTS

Analysis of data from observation studies frequently depends on the researcher. With unstructured techniques, the form and content of the final description and its interpretation can be heavily influenced by the observer and researcher, who are usually the same individual. There is no independent check on the accuracy and detail of the original field notes. In addition, it is rarely the case that field notes are condensed and interpreted by a person other than the researchers themselves, reducing the likelihood of alternative analyses and interpretations.

With structured techniques, high agreement among observers is almost routinely required, and the structure of the observation schedule itself eliminates certain sources of bias. However, guidelines for analyzing such data are vague. No good rationale exists as to why one mode of analysis should be preferred to another. With teacher observation, a common procedure is simply to tally the absolute amount or frequency of each category, across all observation sessions. However, when teachers differ in pace, quite a different picture of the classroom could be obtained if the relative frequency of each category were calculated instead. Yamamoto, Jones, and Ross (149) analyzed a set of teacher observation data from classrooms of varying ability levels three different ways. No differences were found between classrooms when the absolute frequency of teacher acts in each category was analyzed. However, differences were found when the sequence of acts and the duration of teacher-initiated and student-initiated sequences were analyzed. Since the complexity of most observation systems makes it infeasible to conduct all possible analyses, researchers must select those that they believe will provide the most appropriate description of the phenomena under study.

12.1.3 EXISTING RECORDS AND DOCUMENTS

Existing records, such as statistical records, personal documents, mass communication, and data records from previous research studies, can also answer descriptive questions. In each instance the *researcher does not control the process of data collection* and is therefore at the mercy of the procedures established by other individuals.

STATISTICAL RECORDS

Much statistical data on individuals and organizations are routinely accumulated by various agencies in a society. Local, state, and federal agencies have records on birthrates and death rates, criminal offenses, automobile accidents, financial transactions, etc. Private economic, industrial, and social institutions often publish indices on rates of economic and population growth, wages, and industrial productivity. Educational institutions maintain records on achievement, school expenses, instructional programs, and number and type of employees.

Glassman and Belasco (57) examined the records of the teachers' organization in an urban school district to determine the nature of appealed grievances (the type, the number of appeals by month, the number of multiple filings, and the final disposition of the grievance). Using a data file supplied by the Personnel Division of the San Diego schools, Greenberg and McCall (64) studied teacher mobility patterns over a two-year period (the background characteristics of newly hired teachers, terminated teachers and transfer teachers; the placement of new teachers; and the initial and new assignments of transfer teachers).

Problems encountered by the researcher in the use of such data and the solutions to the problems are usually discussed in the research report. The researcher must determine the precise definitions employed in the records. For example, how was the variable of "family size" defined? Did it include only children living at home; did it include other relatives such as grandparents who may be in the household; were stepchildren considered in the total figure? Records may vary in accuracy and completeness. Official changes in regulations may affect the records. A school may decide to abolish the policy of retaining students in the same grade. The sudden change in the records could be erroneously interpreted as an improvement in instruction, rather than a change in school policy. Alertness to such possible contaminating factors is essential to the quality of the final description. When the data are not recorded or defined in the manner preferred by researchers, researchers must modify their analyses and qualify their conclusions to correspond with the existing data.

Personal Documents

Letters, diaries, autobiographies, and prize essays are included in the personal documents category. Such documents "permit us to see other people as they saw themselves" (130, p. 381). They provide knowledge of inner experiences relating to both rare and frequent events in human life and can be used to develop theoretical concepts and hypotheses.

Such documents are few in number, and it is extremely difficult to determine what population they represent (e.g., diary writers are probably not typical of the population in general). In addition, such documents may be inadequate in that they often omit necessary background information, are subject to memory errors, may recount only incidents that interest the author, or do not clarify the significance of what is described. Misrepresentations of self may be present, since most communications of this type are written with some particular audience in mind (e.g., teacher, parent, contest judge). However, if the researcher is primarily interested in the author's self-image, the question of whether or not that image agrees with the image held by others is of secondary importance.

Mass Communications

Mass documents such as newspapers, magazines, movies, television broadcasts, and official statements of an organization intend to inform, to entertain, or to influence a segment of society. Analysis of such documents can be used to detect cultural changes, to determine the incidence of a phenomenon, to identify propaganda techniques, and to determine the readability of materials. Fishel (48) examined the comments submitted by both organizations and individuals (university administrators, National Collegiate Athletic Association, state school board associations, American Association of University Women, League of Women Voters, NEA, etc.) to the Department of Health, Education and Welfare on the proposed regulations under Title IX of the Educational Amendments of 1972 that dealt specifically with controversial issues regarding sex discrimination in employment and in the education of students. Cary (28) examined the extent to which the Marxist–Leninist ideology pervaded the questions and assignments in history, geography, and social science texts used in Soviet schools.

Content analysis is frequently used to describe the nature of the communication in written documents. It is a procedure that systematically and objectively identifies specific characteristics of a document (78). The heart of content analysis is the categories into which the raw data, the communication itself, are coded. The categories can be established to reflect either the substance, the style, or the form of the message, although they can also be used to infer either the cause or the effect of the content. Description of content may focus on trends in content, comparisons against standards such as social norms, the relationship of audience characteristics to messages produced for it (e.g., the socioeconomic status of the audience for particular advertisements), techniques of persuasion in the content, or the readability level of the text. The categories must cover every item relevant to the study and be defined so they can be coded with a high degree of reliability.

Although the single word or phrase is often coded, it is not always the most appropriate unit. Sometimes themes, paragraphs, characters in a story, or the entire item (e.g., book, magazine article, speech) are used as the *coding unit*.

In most content analyses every occurrence of a given category is tallied. When the intensity of the communication is of interest, such factors as the relative intensities of verbs, adjectives, and adverbs may be considered. Simple appearance/nonappearance of the category within some definite unit of the material may also be used, ignoring repetition of the category within that unit.

Finally, the *sampling design* of the content must be planned. Three stages may exist: selecting the sources of communication, sampling documents from each source, and sampling within documents. In all cases, a representative sample of content from the universe of interest is desired.

The most recent technical advance in content analysis is the use of computers to code content. Solutions, or partial solutions, have been found to such problems as the multiple meanings of words, searching the text for desired sentences or clusters of words, and examination of semantic as well as syntactic meaning. Some advantages of the computer approach are the rigor imposed on researchers to make their design and categories explicit, the possibility of quick reanalysis of data, complex manipulations of the data not easily done by hand, and exchange of documents for analysis by other scholars for other purposes. Cary (28) used the computer in his analysis of Marxist–Leninist ideology of textbook exercises.

Secondary Analysis of Data

With the existence of banks and archives of data from previous research studies has come a movement to *reexamine such data for information on topics not included in the original focus of the study*. The most extensive examination of the design of such surveys is Hyman's (83) volume on the secondary analysis of survey data. Obviously, such analyses can be conducted for other than descriptive purposes.

A work by Hyman, Wright, and Reed (84) used data from surveys collected over a period of approximately 25 years by the Gallup Poll, the National Opinion Research Center at the University of Chicago, and the Survey Research Center at the University of Michigan to examine "the enduring effects" of education throughout adulthood. The survey samples were divided into three educational groups (elementary school, high school graduates, and college graduates) that were then compared on survey items on public affairs, academic knowledge, and information-seeking behavior (e.g., newspaper and book reading). Age of the respondent and the time period in which the survey was conducted were also used in these educational comparisons. Since the primary question was causal rather than descriptive, controls for variables such as race, sex, religion, and social class origins were imposed.

12.1.4 OTHER TECHNIQUES OF DATA COLLECTION

Description is not limited to questionnaires, observation schedules, and existing records. Attitude scales, standardized tests, projective techniques, etc. can each be used to answer descriptive questions. Guidelines for the construction, application, and interpretation of such techniques can be found in measurement texts and therefore are not discussed at length here. The reliability and validity of such techniques, discussed in Chapters 8 and 9, play a crucial role in the type of description that can be generated and must be considered in any critique of such studies.

12.2 PURPOSE OF STUDY

Some descriptive studies are characterized primarily not by a particular form of data collection but by the inclusion of a specific variable, such as time, or a specific focus, as in the intensive study of a particular individual or institution. Three variations in purpose are described below: studies of change, cross-cultural studies, and case studies.

12.2.1 STUDIES OF CHANGE OVER TIME AND WITH AGE

Perhaps the most obvious way to study *time-related changes* is to follow the phenomenon of interest over the desired period of time. This general approach is referred to as *longitudinal* in psychology and education, as *trend* and *panel* studies in sociology, and as time series in economics. In psychology the variable of time is often a proxy for the variable of age, and the researcher is interested in the changes that occur as the subject matures both psychologically and physically. Because of the time required to implement such developmental studies, a *cross-sectional* design may be used that involves testing subjects of different ages at the same time. In sociology, the age of the subject is often not an important variable. Instead the focus is on determining changes that correspond to particular time periods, as in examining changes in voter preference for presidential candidates during the campaign. In order to examine changes over time with individuals of the same age, a *time-lag* design may be employed. The major types of designs are cited in Table 12.11. At the bottom of the table are the main advantages and disadvantages of each design.

Three dimensions are involved in most studies of time/age changes: the time of measurement itself, which is also associated with changes in the environment; the date of birth of the subjects associated with what are called

TABLE 12.11 *STUDIES THAT EXAMINE CHANGES OVER TIME AND WITH AGE*

Purpose of study	Design of study			
	Test same subjects at different ages or times	*Test equivalent samples at different ages or times*	*Test more than one age group at the same time*	*Test subjects with different birth dates when same age*
To describe age changes	*Longitudinal within* subjects design (subjects of same age)	*Longitudinal between* subjects design (subjects of same age)	*Cross-sectional* (subjects grouped by age)	
To describe time changes	*Panel* study (subjects of many ages)	*Trend* study (subjects of many ages)		*Time-lag* design (test subjects in order of birth)
Advantages	Amount of change for each subject can be determined	No retesting effects	Quick estimate of age changes. No retesting or attrition effects	Changes with time are independent of age
Disadvantages	Retesting effects. Attrition of subjects. Age changes confounded with time changes and unique to generation sampled. Time changes confounded with age	Only change for total group can be determined. Difficult to obtain equivalent samples. Age and time confounding same as longitudinal-within and panel studies	Effects unique to time of testing and to generation sampled. Time changes cannot be determined	Age changes cannot be determined. Time changes unique to generations sampled

cohort or generational differences; and the age of the subject. None of the designs mentioned in Table 12.11 provides independent estimates of each of these effects. For example, with a longitudinal design, changes in the age of the subjects are also associated with changes in time and are unique to the generation of subjects themselves. Similar interpretation problems occur with cross-sectional and time-lag designs. The diagram of these three designs in Table 12.12 illustrates the confounding among the time, cohort, and age dimensions. The illustrated longitudinal design is only one of four that could be chosen (Cohorts 3, 4, 5, 6). The cross-sectional design is only one of four possible choices (Times 1, 2, 3, 4). For age 11, the time-lag design is also only one of four possible choices. Goulet (62) stressed that educators are concerned with both age and time (or school-related) changes. He proposed a more complex design to meet these needs by taking advantage of the fact that chil-

TABLE 12.12   *ILLUSTRATIONS OF POSSIBLE CROSS-SECTIONAL,*
LONGITUDINAL, AND TIME-LAG DESIGNS FOR THREE AGES,
SIX COHORTS, AND SIX TIME PERIODS

		Time of testing (yearly intervals)					
		T_1	T_2	T_3	T_4	T_5	T_6
	C_1	11					
Cohort or	C_2	10	11	←Cross-sectional for T_2			
birth date	C_3	9	10	11			
(yearly	C_4		9	10	11	←Longitudinal for C_4	
intervals)	C_5			9	10	11	
	C_6				9	10	11 ←Time lag for age 11

dren differ in age within each grade and that children increase in age over the school year.

A study by Hilton and Patrick (74) contained both cross-sectional and longitudinal data on achievement in grades 5 through 11. The discrepancies in results from both approaches and the difficulties in the interpretation of each design when applied in isolation were clearly illustrated. As with practically any longitudinal study, subjects were lost. The retention rate was 66 percent over the three-year period, 56 percent over five years, and 43 percent over seven years.

Arthur, Sisson, and Fallis (9) used both cross-sectional and trend approaches in their study of drug knowledge and attitudes among high school students. A cross-sectional survey was made in 1971 of freshmen, sophomores, juniors, and seniors. In 1974, a follow-up cross-sectional survey was made of the same groups in the same school, providing an analysis of trends in drug attitudes and usage over the four-year period.

A problem encountered by all studies of change is the possible nonequivalence of the measurement procedures over all age groups or all time periods. How do you ensure that you are measuring the same dimension at each time or with each age? How do you ensure that a concept such as achievement has similar meanings at ages 6 and 16? Obviously, such problems are not solved easily.

12.2.2 CROSS-CULTURAL RESEARCH

Cross-cultural research encompasses studies within a country as well as studies involving more than one country. Other terms which apply to the same type of research are "cross-national" and "comparative" research. Cross-cultural research can result in descriptions of behavior patterns not present in the researchers' own country, can extend the range of variation in phenomena studied, make the researchers aware of ambiquities in concepts they frequently use in their own society, provide a means of testing the generality of results, and be a source of new concepts and insights even in one's own country.

The usual problems in conducting research, in conceptualizing the study, and in interpreting the results are complicated in cross-cultural research by the fact that a different culture or foreign country is involved. The major challenge is to determine the *real* meaning from culture to culture. For example, some concepts may be irrelevant in some cultures and relevant in others. Even if a concept is salient in all cultures of interest, it may be difficult to devise comparable measures of the concept. Sometimes different indicators are needed to tap the same concept. To attain linguistic equivalence in questionnaires and tests a fruitful approach is that of *back-translation* (19). Bilinguals translate into the target language from English and then other bilinguals working independently of the first group translate back into English. This process is continued until discrepancies are clarified and corrected. Pretesting, by administration of both forms to bilinguals, can also be used to guarantee equivalence in translation.

The International Association for the Evaluation of Educational Achievement has conducted a series of cross-national studies of achievement. Some of the achievement areas studied were mathematics, reading comprehension, geography, science, literature, French, English, and civic education. As many as 19 countries were involved in some studies and usually more than one age group was included. For a review of these cross-cultural studies as well as others within the field of education, read Kerlinger (93, Part II).

12.2.3 CASE STUDIES

Case studies are distinguished by the intensive, detailed investigation of a single unit: an individual, a classroom, a school system, a sorority, a community, etc. The depth of analysis associated with such studies yields important and unique information. This approach is particularly appropriate for (1) studying "pure" cases of phenomena, deviant cases, isolated cases, and cases in transition, (2) generating hypotheses that can be tested more systematically in other settings, and (3) providing information on critical elements of design in major studies conducted on many individuals or units.

The case study approach is not restricted, and should not be restricted, to one mode of data collection. In fact, a variety of data collection techniques is often required in order to adequately investigate all aspects of interest. The usefulness of case studies depends heavily on the investigators: their receptivity to many variations in the phenomenon studied, the extent to which they obtain enough information to characterize and explain the unique features of the case as well as its commonality with other cases, and their ability to integrate diverse bits of information into a unified picture. If investigators are working within a theoretical framework, then they must be able to identify which events contradict the theory and which are consonant with it. Researchers must be constantly aware of when their personal biases distort the data and be cautious in the generalizations they make on the basis of one case.

12.3 HOW TO IDENTIFY AND CRITIQUE TYPES OF DESCRIPTIVE STUDIES

The techniques presented in this chapter are not equally appropriate for all questions of description, and the researcher must determine which technique(s) best answers the question of interest. Guidelines for the identification and critique of descriptive studies are presented in Exhibit 12.1.

EXHIBIT 12.1   *IDENTIFICATION AND CRITIQUE OF TYPES OF DESCRIPTIVE STUDIES*

A. Was the descriptive study characterized primarily by:

1. The method of data collection? If yes, go to Section B.

2. The focus or purpose of the study? If yes, go to Section C.

3. If both purpose and data collection were important, review Sections B *and* C.

B. Was the primary mode of data collection:

1. A descriptive survey (questionnaire or interview)? If so, consider the following questions in critiquing the article.

    Were the types of questions structured or unstructured? What were the advantages and limitations of such questions in the context of the research question and the sample? Did the resulting description present a complete or incomplete picture of the phenomenon of interest? Did the researchers present more than a superficial treatment of the results?

2. Observation?

    What was the scope of the behavior or setting that was observed? Did the observation technique impose much or little structure upon the observer? What precautions were taken to reduce observer bias? If a structured technique was used, was it a sign, category, or rating system? How were the behavioral units sampled for observation? Were estimates of frequency, duration, and/or sequence obtained? Was the observation procedure appropriate for the research question? Did it present an adequate picture of the phenomenon observed?

3. Existing records and documents?

    How were the records/documents selected? What checks were made on the accuracy and validity of the information in the records? Did the authors discuss any biases that could have affected the results?

4. Tests and other techniques?
   What reliability and validity checks were made? Was the resulting description complete?

C. Was the primary focus on:

1. The study of change with age or over time?
   If there was an age focus, was a cross-sectional or a longitudinal approach employed? If there was a time focus, was a trend, panel, or a time-lag design employed? What efforts were made to ensure comparability of tests over all age groups or over all time periods? Did the authors discuss how the limitations of their design could have affected the results? How serious was the attrition rate if a within-subjects longitudinal design or a panel study was employed?

2. Cross-cultural comparisons?
   What procedures were employed to ensure equivalency of meaning across cultures? In what way was the final description unique, different, or more complete because a cross-cultural approach was used? Did the final conclusions appear to be biased in favor of one culture?

3. An individual case?
   Why was a case study approach used? What were its limitations and advantages? Did the researchers limit generalization of the findings? Did the researchers integrate their many observations into a unified picture?
4. A purpose other than those just cited?

12.4 LIST OF DESCRIPTIVE STUDIES

12.4.1 DESCRIPTIVE SURVEYS

Donlan, D., 1974. Teaching writing in the content areas: eleven hypotheses from a teacher survey. *Research in the Teaching of English* 8: 250–262.

Gillo, M. W., M. Landerholm, and D. N. Goldsmith, 1974. Goals and educational trends in community colleges. *Journal of Higher Education* 45: 491–503.

Goslin, D. A., and D. C. Glass, 1967. The social effects of standardized testing in American elementary and secondary schools. *Sociology of Education* 40: 115–131.

Johannson, C. B., and R. S. Fink, 1974. Merit scholars at a liberal arts college. *Journal of College Student Personnel* 15: 177–182.

Lortie, D. C., 1967. The teacher's shame: anger and the normative commitments of classroom teachers. *School Review* **75**: 155–170.

Tamppari, R., and G. Johnson, 1975. Characteristics of the employable science teacher as perceived by school district hiring officials. *Journal of Research in Science Teaching* **12**: 331–339.

12.4.2 OBSERVATION

Becker, F. D., R. Sommer, J. Bee, and B. Oxley, 1973. College classroom ecology. *Sociometry* **36**: 514–525.

Burnett, J H., 1969. Ceremony, rites, and economy in the student system of an American high school. *Human Organization* **28**: 1–10.

Graves, D. H., 1975. An examination of the writing processes of seven-year-old children. *Research in the Teaching of English* **9**: 227–241.

Johnson, D. A., 1976. Treating black students like white students: a definition of school integration. *Urban Education* **11**: 95–114.

McCauley, R. W., R. H. Bruininks, and P. Kennedy, 1976. Behavioral interactions of hearing impaired children in regular classrooms. *Journal of Special Education* **10**: 277–284.

12.4.3 EXISTING RECORDS AND DOCUMENTS

Cary, C. D., 1976. Patterns of emphasis upon Marxist-Leninist ideology: a computer content analysis of Soviet school history, geography, and social science textbooks. *Comparative Education Review* **20**: 11–29.

Glassman, A. M., and J. A. Belasco, 1974. Appealed grievances in urban education: a case study. *Education and Urban Society* **7**: 73–87.

Fishel, A., 1976. Organizational positions on Title IX: conflicting perspectives on sex discrimination in education. *Journal of Higher Education* **47**: 93–105.

12.4.4 OTHER TESTING TECHNIQUES

Dizney, H. F., and R. W. Roskens, 1966. An investigation of certain qualitative aspects of verbalization of gifted children. *American Educational Research Journal* **3**: 179–186.

Griswold, L. E., and J. Commings, 1974. The expressive vocabulary of preschool deaf children. *American Annals of the Deaf* **119**: 16–28.

Van der Veur, B. N., 1975. Imagery ratings of 1,000 frequently used words. *Journal of Educational Psychology* **67**: 44–56.

Wilson, J. D., P. C. Richardson, and P. Chafin, 1976. Mission: audition. *Journal of Special Education* 10: 77–81.

12.4.5 STUDIES OF CHANGE OVER TIME AND WITH AGE

Arthur, G. L., P. J. Sisson, and C. L. Fallis, 1975. Follow-up drug survey: trends in knowledge and attitudes of youth in a typical high school in Georgia. *Journal of Drug Education* 5: 243–249.

Eisenberg, T. A., 1976. Computational errors made by teachers of arithmetic: 1930, 1973. *Elementary School Journal* 76: 229–237.

Hilton, T. L., and C. Patrick, 1970. Cross-sectional versus longitudinal data: an empirical comparison of mean differences in academic growth. *Journal of Educational Measurement* 7: 15–24.

Morris, L. W., C. S. Finkelstein, and W. R. Fisher, 1976. Components of school anxiety: developmental trends and sex differences. *Journal of Genetic Psychology* 128: 49–57.

12.4.6 CASE STUDIES AND CROSS-CULTURAL STUDIES

Harris, D. B., V. DeLissovoy, and J. Enami, 1975. The aesthetic sensitivity of Japanese and American children. *Journal of Aesthetic Education* 9: 81–95.

Stewart, L. H., A. A. Dole, and Y. Y. Harris, 1967 Cultural differences in abilities during high school. *American Educational Research Journal* 4: 19–30.

Of the studies listed above, Burnett, Johnson, and Glassman and Belasco each illustrates a case study of an individual school system.

STUDY PROBLEMS

1. If a researcher wanted to examine the degree to which teachers were satisfied with their jobs by using a questionnaire, what would be the advantages and disadvantages of using closed as opposed to open questions? What type of description would each type of question provide? Would closed or open questions be more likely to provide the more complete description?

2. Read one of the observation studies cited at the end of this chapter or an observation study in an area of interest to you. What type of phenomenon was observed: acts, activities, meanings, participation, relationships, or settings? Was the observation technique unstructured or structured? If it was structured, could the observation system be best described as a sign, category, or rating system? What sampling procedure was used? Did the observation technique provide an adequate description of the phenomenon?

3. Cite four descriptive educational questions that can be studied by using existing records and documents as the primary mode of data collection.

4. A cross-sectional study showed that standardized achievement test scores increased steadily from grades 9 through 12 in Beech High School. Critics said the results were misleading because a longitudinal approach would have been better. Discuss the advantages and disadvantages of using each approach to examine trends in high school achievement. Consider such factors as: if the geographic region served by the school had changed the previous year, would a cross-sectional or longitudinal design be more appropriate; which procedure would be more appropriate if the high school had a high dropout rate.

13

The Design of
Association Studies

Knowing *how and if variables are related to each other* is very important in understanding educational problems. Such knowledge provides information on: (1) whether one variable can be predicted from another, (2) whether one variable can be a proxy for another, (3) the precise nature of the covariation between variables, and (4) the extent to which different variables are part of the same scheme of things. The following are examples of such association questions: do reading readiness tests predict first grade achievement, can results on the Metropolitan Achievement Test be substituted for those on the Iowa Tests of Basic Skills, how strong is the relationship between intelligence and creativity, and how many distinct dimensions are reflected in the subscores of a personality inventory. Although some individuals believe that it is also important to know which variable in a relationship is the causal one and which is the effect, it is premature to examine such causal questions until knowledge about the existence and nature of the relationship itself is determined. This chapter examines the general areas that need to be addressed when studying the association between variables.

13.1 CHARACTERISTICS OF ASSOCIATION

Three primary questions can be asked about the association between variables: the *strength* of the association, its *direction*, and its *shape*. The level of measurement of each variable affects which of these questions can be answered. Questions of strength, the degree to which knowledge of the scores or of a classification on one variable informs us about the scores or classification on another and vice versa, are applicable to all measurement levels. Questions of direction are meaningful only when the scales specify order. Questions regarding the shape (linear, curvilinear) of the relationship have meaning only when distances on the scale also have meaning (interval or ratio scales).

Sometimes it is of interest to determine what happens to the strength of an association when the relationship that one or both of the variables has with a third variable is removed ("held constant" or "partialed out"). A high school principal might be interested in the correlation between physics and chemistry achievement for students in his or her school with the variable of mathematical ability removed; that is, statistically treating all students as though they had the same mathematical ability by calculating what is known as a *partial correlation* coefficient. If math were positively related to each variable, then removal of this common element would decrease the strength of the original association between chemistry and physics. If math were not related to each, then "holding math constant" would not change the strength of the association.

The researcher may focus upon the *asymmetry* of an association; an "If we know X, what can we say about Y?" (not vice versa) question. Although most indices of association are *symmetric* (the information about Y given X is the same as the information about X given Y), some asymmetric indices of association are available and are appropriate when the study's rationale indicates prediction in one direction.

13.2 REASONS FOR ASSOCIATIONS BETWEEN VARIABLES

Why are variables related, or not related, to each other? The rationale for a study may cite any of the following reasons. One variable may cause the other. Both variables may have a common cause. They may each be a partial cause of the other, sort of a "symbiotic" relationship (a teacher asks a question, the students answer, the teacher gives feedback and asks a follow-up question, the students reply—producing an association between teacher questions and student response). The variables may actually be measures of the same phenomenon. Sometimes a researcher deliberately uses several tests that claim to measure the same trait (as in factor analytic studies or in a longitudinal study of intelligence that requires tests of intelligence appropriate for age 6 and for adulthood). In other cases, the researcher may design the study to determine if the tests do, in fact, measure something similar.

13.3 SELECTION OF VARIABLES

13.3.1 THEORETICAL RATIONALE

The variables in association studies should be selected with care. The availability of computers has minimized the problem of statistical analysis, making it tempting to measure a multitude of phenomena, to throw them all into the computer, and to wait and see what relationships emerge. This shotgun approach reflects little theoretical rationale and is to be discouraged, for if enough correlations are calculated, some that appear to be worthwhile will actually be meaningless. The best approach is for the researcher to hypothesize why certain associations should or should not appear in the data rather than to attempt to explain associations after they have occurred.

A good example of a carefully developed rationale for an association study is that by Daly and Miller (40) on the correlates of the two dimensions of fear of writing and verbal aptitude. The basic premise was that fear of writing was not strongly related to verbal aptitude, since the latter deals with vocabulary, reading, and analysis of material rather than with writing skills. Given the difference in these two variables, the major hypotheses were that: (1) verbal aptitude, not fear of writing, would correlate with being in a regular as opposed to a remedial college composition course, and (2) fear of writing, not verbal aptitude, would correlate with perceived likelihood of success in writing courses and with willingness to take future courses in writing. These predictions were supported.

13.3.2 ISSUES OF MEASUREMENT

Measures with high reliability and validity should be chosen. The reliability of a variable places a lower bound on the strength of its association with another variable, and an unreliable measure cannot yield stable or consistent correlations. Validity is also crucial, because researchers usually assume that the measures possess contruct validity when they interpret the results. However, in some instances, the data themselves may force researchers to conclude that the instrument actually measured something other than that claimed by the test developer.

Part–whole relationships frequently occur in association studies and should be interpreted carefully. That the verbal comprehension subscore on an achievement test correlates with the total language score should not be surprising to the reader, since the first is part of the latter. With some personality tests, subscores for "different" traits are necessarily related since the traits are measured by some of the same items.

Another situation you may encounter is that of _ipsative scores_. With such scores, the sum of all the subscores on a test is the same for everyone, placing constrictions on the relative sizes of the subscores. This means that an individual cannot score high on all subtests, but must be low on some if he or she scores high on others. This is the case for some personality and interest inventories. Only the relative position of the subtest scores for each individual are directly comparable; comparison of one student's scores with those of another is not appropriate. This is in contrast to _normative measurement_ in which the total score for each individual can vary (e.g., standardized achievement tests) and cross-student comparisons are legitimate.

Ipsative scores can also occur with some observation techniques. For example, the procedure developed by Flanders (49) requires tallying an act every three seconds; yielding 20 tallies in a one-minute period for each classroom. If 15 of these tallies are categorized as silence/confusion, only five tallies can be distributed into the remaining nine categories. Obviously, this reflects the mutually exclusive structure of the category system itself and the fact that certain behaviors cannot be performed simultaneously (e.g., silence and talk).

When questions regarding the relationships among such variables are posed, the complex dependencies among the observation variables can easily result in misleading correlation coefficients, making interpretation a difficult task.

13.4 SELECTION OF THE SAMPLE

When the full range of the variable of interest does not exist in the sample, then the answers to association questions are incomplete and inaccurate, since the nature of the entire covariation between the variables is unknown. If only highly anxious individuals are in the sample, then the resulting correlation between anxiety and any other variable cannot be assumed to be the same as that resulting if the full range of anxiety were represented. Similarly, exclusion of extreme individuals on a trait will alter the association pattern. Such curtailment frequently results in an underestimation of the degree of association. Sometimes, researchers select individuals only from the tails of a distribution (top and bottom 30 percent). Such loss of the middle group often produces an inflation or overestimation of the association strength.

Sample sizes should be large enough to provide stable estimates of association strength. Different indices of association require different sample sizes. For example, a 5 by 5 contingency table format with 25 cells would need at least 125 subjects (rule of thumb, an estimated 5 subjects per cell), which is a larger sample size than that needed in most situations in which a product–moment correlation is appropriate. When a battery of tests is administered, the sample size must be greater than the number of tests in order to reduce the possibility of spurious dependencies. Recommended ratios of sample size to the number of variables range from 2:1 to 30:1, although the larger the sample size, the better. Another highly recommended approach for determining the stability of associations is to replicate the study with another sample.

13.5 INTERPRETATION OF RESULTS

Although the meaning attached to results from association studies depends to some extent on the particular association indices applied to the data, some general precautions can be cited. First, descriptions of the strength of the association as "high," "moderate," "very strong," "substantial," or "negligible" are inconsistently applied from study to study. Glass and Stanley (56) referred to .50 as a moderate relationship. Using the percentage of shared variance as the criterion (r^2), Fox (50) considered correlations between 0 and .50 as low, from .51 to .70 as moderate, from .71 to .86 as high, and above .86 as very high. In some actual studies, Daly and Miller (40) described a correlation of .19 as low; Lawson, Nordland and Devito (97) called correlations from .11 to .29 as low to moderate. Kurth and Pavalko (95) characterized correlations from .34 to .50 as moderately strong and those from .68 to .83 as strong; Lawson et al. labeled a correlation of .50 as fairly high.

Some researchers determine their descriptive labels on the basis of the percentage of shared variance or reduction in error; others on the basis of the significance level; others in light of previous findings in the area. In comparing and summarizing studies, readers cannot blindly accept the researcher's characterization of association strength, but must examine the numerical values themselves. Then they can make their own judgments of strength, explicitly and consistently, across all studies, even though their decisions may conflict with published conclusions. When different indices of association are used, then direct comparisons of strength frequently cannot be made since the nature of the data varies considerably from study to study.

A second major consideration in interpreting results is that an association coefficient of a given numerical value can reflect more than one association pattern. An illustration of this principle with the product–moment correlation coefficient is presented in Fig. 13.1. Each of the four scatter plots is based on a

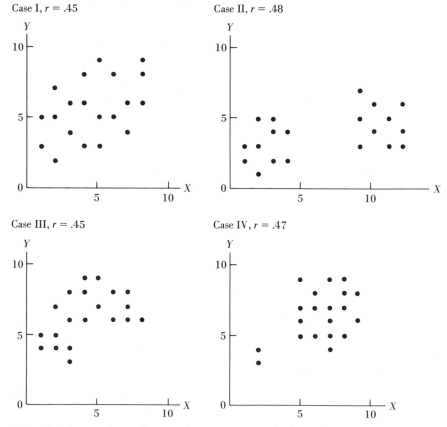

FIG. 13.1 Scatterplots indicating the same numerical relationships, but different patterns of association, between two variables.

sample of 20 and the computed correlation coefficients range from .45 to .48. However, the configurations are each quite different. Case I illustrates the typical picture of a correlation of this size. In Case II, the distribution of the X variable is bimodal (as might result when the middle group is discarded). When the association between variables X and Y is plotted two distinct clusters of points appear; each representing little association. In Case III, the configuration is curvilinear. In Case IV the positive correlation of .47 is produced by the two extreme points. Without these pairs of points the correlation is reduced to a value of .09.

Since scatter diagrams are not published in journal articles, the reader must rely primarily upon the researcher's examination of the data. However, if descriptive information about each variable is presented (means, range, standard deviation, skewness), the reader can judge to some extent whether variables have unusual distributions (skewed, bimodal) that may affect their association with other variables. Without such information, the main recourse for the reader is to be cautious in accepting the reported importance, or lack of importance, attributed to the associations involving such variables.

Ambiguity regarding the pattern of association between qualitative variables can be reduced somewhat by presentation of a cross-tabulation table. However, as the dimensionality of such tables increases, patterns become more difficult to identify.

Finally, the discovery of a relationship between variables should not in and of itself be interpreted as reflecting a causal relationship. Preconceived ideas regarding the direction of influence between variables can affect, sometimes quite subtly, the tone of the researcher's interpretation. In the discussion section of a report, such speculation is often useful and justified. But the researcher should not present such causal arguments as fact, and the reader should feel free to offer alternative explanations. When correlations range between .25 and .75 as is typical of much educational research, a powerful influence of one variable over the other is not indicated, and many explanations of the relationship are possible.

13.6 RESEARCH METHODS THAT FOCUS ON ASSOCIATION QUESTIONS

Any data collection procedure (interviews, questionnaires, observation, tests, attitude scales, existing documents, etc.) can be used to answer questions of association. A good example of a national survey with an association focus is that by Nelson and Sieber (111) on the correlates of the frequency with which innovations are used in urban secondary schools. Seventeen innovations were studied. The frequency of their use in 670 schools in cities with populations over 300,000 was related to four major variables: ratings on the educational quality or worth of the innovation, the administrative difficulty in implementing the innovation, the innovation's durability or resistance to change upon implementation, and innovation cost. Two other questions of interest were the relationship of cost to both quality and administrative difficulty in implementation. None of these relationships reflects differentiated description, making the study's focus one of association rather than description.

Studies with special purposes or special populations such as those described in Chapter 12 do not restrict the basic form of the research question. Longitudinal studies can be predictive or focus on the changing interrelationships among variables with time. Cross-cultural studies can compare the patterns of relationships among variables in different cultures.

13.7 QUESTIONS TO ASK ABOUT THE DESIGN AND INTERPRETATION OF ASSOCIATION STUDIES

A checklist on the design and interpretation of results from association studies is presented in Exhibit 13.1.

EXHIBIT 13.1 *ANALYSIS OF ASSOCIATION STUDY DESIGN*

A. Which aspect(s) of association was (were) of concern in the study?

   1. Strength?

   2. Direction?

   3. Shape or pattern?

   4. Asymmetry?

   5. Strength when another variable was controlled?

B. Why were relationships expected (or not expected) among the variables that were studied?

C. Was information on the reliability and validity of the measure of each variable presented? (High correlations cannot be found between unreliable measures.)

D. Did the sample represent the full range of the trait? If not, was this restriction in range considered in the interpretation of the results?

E. Was the sample size large enough to provide stable estimates of association strength? (As the number of variables increases, the desired sample size also increases.)

F. On what basis did the researcher interpret the nature of the associations: numerical indices, scatterplots, cross-tabulation tables, variable distributions?

G. On what basis did the researcher determine whether the relationships were strong or weak: statistical significance, percentage of shared variance, past research? Was the researcher consistent in applying labels of strength to the indices of association?

H. Did the researcher avoid causal explanations or, at least, exercise caution in applying such explanations?

STUDY PROBLEMS

1. Read one of the association studies investigating the relationship between two variables cited at the end of Chapter 14. Analyze the design of the study using the series of questions in Exhibit 13.1. Evaluate the overall quality of the research design.

2. A teacher hypothesized that there is a positive association between the neatness of exam papers and the grades on the exam. Give four different reasons why this hypothesis might be true.

3. Indicate whether the strength, the direction and/or the shape of an association are indicated in each of the following statements.

a) The correlation between the history and biology exam scores was .82.

b) The beauty contestants who were ranked high by the judges on talent were also ranked high on congeniality, but were not ranked high in the swimsuit competition.

c) In a sample of graduate students at a large midwestern university, the state in which the students were born did not predict the graduate area in which they were majoring.

4. What do you think would be the strength of the relationship between two weekly (or monthly) test scores of students in your classroom? Obtain the scores on two tests and make a scatterplot of the scores. Calculate the correlation coefficient between the sets of scores. Would you describe the strength of the coefficient as strong or weak? Why?

14

Four Types of Association Questions: Research Studies

Association questions vary greatly in complexity. The simplest question examines the relationship between just *two variables*. A more complicated form is the relationship between *several variables and a single criterion*. The *structure or pattern* of association among several variables may be of interest. Finally, associations between *two sets of variables* may be examined. These four types of association questions are discussed in this chapter.

14.1 STUDIES OF ASSOCIATIONS BETWEEN TWO VARIABLES

The most common type of association study is one that examines the relationship between *pairs* of variables. More than two variables may be measured, but both the focus of the study and the analysis are limited to pairwise associations. Not all pairwise associations may be given equal importance in the research report nor will the researcher necessarily expect to find a relationship between each pair. Such factors depend upon the study's rationale.

14.1.1 COMMON STATISTICAL TECHNIQUES

A host of correlational and association indices exist, making it difficult for the uninformed reader to understand the process and meaning of data analysis in association studies. In order to guide you through this maze of indices, the most common ones are listed in Table 14.1. The most common index, the product–moment correlation coefficient, has already been discussed in some detail in previous chapters. Many of the principles and guidelines applicable to it are also applicable to the other indices of association.

The indices in the table are classified by the level of measurement of each variable. Dichotomous, underlying normal, variables occur when a normal distribution has been dichotomized or when it is believed that more extensive measurement of a dichotomous variable could yield a normal distribution.

202

TABLE 14.1 *COMMON INDICES OF ASSOCIATION BETWEEN TWO VARIABLES*

Level of measurement of variables	Symbol	Name of index
Same level		
Dichotomous only	ϕ	*Phi coefficient* (-1 to $+1$; sign is arbitrary)
	Q	*Yule's* Q^a (-1 to $+1$; sign is arbitrary)
Dichotomous-underlying normal	r_{tet}	*Tetrachoric correlation coefficient* (-1 to $+1$)
Nominal or ordered classes	C	*Contingency coefficient* (0 to $+1$)
	V	*Cramér's* V *statistic*[b,c] (0 to $+1$)
	λ	*Lambda*[b,d] (0 to $+1$)
Ordered classes only	γ	*Gamma*[a,d] (-1 to $+1$)
Ranks	r_s	Spearman *rank-correlation coefficient* or *rho* (-1 to $+1$)
	τ	Kendall's *tau* (-1 to $+1$)
Interval or ratio	r_{xy}	Pearson *product–moment correlation* (-1 to $+1$)
	η^2	*Correlation ratio, eta squared*[e] (0 to $+1$; curvilinear relationships)
Mixed levels		
Dichotomous vs. ranks	r_{rb}	*Rank biserial correlation*[e] (-1 to $+1$; sign is arbitrary)
Dichotomous vs. interval or ratio	r_{pb}	*Point-biserial correlation* (-1 to $+1$; sign is arbitrary)
	ω^2	*Omega squared*[b] (0 to $+1$; applied after *t*-test)
Dichotomous-underlying normal vs. interval or ratio	r_b	*Biserial correlation* (usually -1 to $+1$)
Nominal or ordered classes vs. interval or ratio	ω^2	*Omega squared* (0 to $+1$; applied after analysis of variance)

[a] James A. Davis, 1971. *Elementary Survey Analysis.* Englewood Cliffs, N.J.: Prentice-Hall.
[b] William L. Hays, 1973. *Statistics for the Social Sciences,* 2nd ed. New York: Holt, Rinehart and Winston.
[c] Richard J. Light, 1973. Issues in the analysis of qualitative data, In R. M. W. Travers (ed.), *Second Handbook of Research on Teaching.* Chicago: Rand McNally, p. 318–381.
[d] John H. Mueller, Karl F. Schuessler, and Herbert L. Costner, 1970. *Statistical Reasoning in Sociology,* (2nd ed.) Boston: Houghton Mifflin.
[e] Gene V. Glass and Julian C. Stanley, 1970. *Statistical Methods in Education and Psychology.* Englewood Cliffs, N.J.: Prentice-Hall.

Nominal classes refer to qualitative categories, whereas ordered classes refer to groupings along a dimension of increasing magnitude, e.g., low, average, and high ability. Ranks refer to a complete rank ordering of individuals or cases, although occasional ties may appear.

The range of values that each index can assume is also given in Table 14.1. In every instance a value of 0 refers to a lack of association or correlation, and a value of ± 1 refers to the maximum association. In instances in which the numerical coding of the categories is arbitrary, the ± signs are meaningless. For some association indices only positive values occur since direct and inverse relationships (positive and negative signs) cannot be distinguished from each other.

It should be noted that the relationships described in Table 14.1 also include what might often be called group comparisons, since groups or categories of individuals reflect a nominal variable. Different types of mental retardation, overachievers versus underachievers, major in college, the foreign language one speaks, and the type of books one reads are all nominal variables. Therefore, a study that examines the differences in high school grade point average among people with different college majors is an association study between an interval and a nominal variable.

In examining articles on questions of association, first identify the scale of measurement for each variable. Then look at Table 14.1 to determine whch index is appropriate for each pair of variables. The list is not exhaustive but does identify the most frequently used indices of association. More information on these indices is given in Appendix D.

14.1.2 CORRELATION MATRICES

Intercorrelations between more than two variables are usually reported in what is known as a correlation matrix or table. It is important that you be able to interpret such an array of correlation coefficients. Typically, correlations significantly different from zero are indicated by asterisks or are underlined.

Alvord and Glass (2) examined the relationship between self-concept and academic achievement in science among students in grades four, seven, and twelve. Four aspects of self-concept were measured, called general, family, peer, and scholastic. The sum of these subscales yielded a total self-concept score. The science measure was composed of exercises from the National Assessment of Educational Progress. The correlation table presented in the article is reproduced in Table 14.2.

Alvord and Glass indicated that the accessible population was all the students in grades four, seven, and twelve in the state of Iowa. Since the internal consistency reliability coefficients for each of the tests were quite high (.73 to .91), any low correlations between the tests cannot be attributed to unreliability.

As indicated in the correlation matrix, the sample size at each grade level was quite large. Thus there is no need to worry about instability at the correlation coefficients resulting from a small sample size. As mentioned in Chapter 7, the significance test for a correlation coefficient depends on the sample size. Notice that a correlation as low as .0643 was significantly different from zero for the grade seven sample.

How would you describe the patterns of association in the matrix? Alvord and Glass characterized the correlations between science achievement and self-concept as decreasing as the grade level increased, except for the scholastic self-concept subscale. What conclusions might have been drawn if only the

TABLE 14.2   *CORRELATIONS BETWEEN SCIENCE
ACHIEVEMENT AND SELF-CONCEPT*

Grade level	N	Subscales				
		General	Family	Peer	Scholastic	Total
4	1105	.1738†	.2609†	.1846†	.3239†	.2792†
7	1099	.0643*	.1211†	.0085	.3311†	.1759†
12	958	.0613	.0032	.0061	.3823†	.1576†

* $p < .05$.
† $p < .01$.
Source: D. J. Alvord, and L. W. Glass, 1974. Relationships between academic achievement and self-concept. *Science Education* 58(2): 175–179. Reprinted with permission.

correlations between the total score and science achievement had been presented? In this instance, the relationship between total self-concept and science achievement did not reflect the patterns of association that existed with each of the self-concept subscores. Unfortunately, the interrelationships among the subscales and the total self-concept score were not reported, and therefore it is not clear how many separate dimensions were actually measured. An indication that two dimensions might exist comes from the fact that the correlations between the scholastic subscore and science achievement were higher than those between science achievement and the other self-concept subscores.

The following study by Goldman and Hartig illustrates the importance of examining the pattern of association among variables for subgroups within the total sample. The authors used both statistical tests of significance and percentage of shared variance to interpret the strength of the correlation coefficients.

The WISC May Not Be a Valid Predictor of School Performance for Primary Grade Minority Children
ROY D. GOLDMAN AND LINDA K. HARTIG

[1] The use of intelligence tests in nonwhite populations has stirred considerable controversy in recent years (Barnes, 1972; Cleary, Humphreys, Kendrick, and Wesman, 1975; Williams, 1972). This controversy emerges partly from the consistent finding that nonwhite children score about one standard deviation (SD) lower than do white children on standard tests of intelligence (Cleary et al., 1975).

[2] Some psychologists and educators have interpreted the black–white difference in IQ as evidence of a genetic difference between blacks and whites on

Roy D. Goldman and Linda Hartig, 1976. The WISC may not be a valid predictor of school performance for primary grade minority children. *American Journal of Mental Deficiency* 80(6): 583–587. Reprinted with permission.

certain cognitive traits (Garrett, 1961; Jensen, 1969; Shuey, 1966). Others have considered this IQ difference a logical result of the environmental difference between black and white children (Klineberg, 1963; Mercer, 1973). They believe that much of the black–white difference can be attributed to specific and measurable factors such as parental income and years of parental education (Mercer, 1973). Yet, as Jencks (1972) has pointed out, "Explaining a difference environmentally is not sufficient to rule out genetic factors, any more than explaining the difference genetically rules out environmental factors" (p. 82).

[3] While the hereditarian and environmental views of the etiology of the black–white difference in IQ are near opposites, proponents of both views agree on the basic fact of these differences. Yet there are many social scientists and other concerned citizens who question the validity and fairness of the tests themselves (Bay Area Association of Black Psychologists, 1972). Sometimes these criticisms are so strong as to cause public agencies to prohibit the use of individual and group tests of intelligence in the public schools.

[4] These criticisms of the validity of intelligence tests generally take the form of stating that the tests are not valid measures of the biological potential of children of minority ethnic groups (Mercer, 1973). The specific criticisms of intelligence tests often are focused on the manifest content of individual items, particularly information items.

[5] In this way critics attack the content or face validity of the items on intelligence tests. When groups of children have not been exposed to the type of material contained in these items, the test is likely to yield lower scores for those children. While such criticisms appear reasonable, "There is no evidence . . . to support the theory that black children are more disadvantaged on "culture-fair" tests as Raven's Progressive Matrices show larger black–white differences than do conventional verbal tests (Jensen, 1969). Thus, we believe that the critics of the face validity of intelligence tests miss the point; the validity of such tests must be judged on other grounds. To develop this point fully, we shall digress briefly into the historical purposes of intelligence tests.

[6] The origin of complex measures of intelligence, which is usually credited to Alfred Binet, was a response to a practical problem. In 1904, the Society for the Psychological Study of Children (of which Binet was a leading member) recognized the need to separate Paris school children according to their educability. Thus, the original intelligence test had a modest objective—forecasting performance in the Paris public schools. Its success lay in its ability to predict validly the teacher's ratings of school children's academic achievement. Even today, this form of validity is the sine qua non of an intelligence test.

[7] We believe that the intelligence testing controversy would never have achieved its present form had the tests been labeled as "public-school performance predictors" or something similar. Yet, in fact, that is what the original intelligence tests were intended to do—their raison d'être. If intelligence tests do not actually exhibit this simple form of predictive validity, then their construct validity, and hence usefulness, must be questioned. While other correlations seem to support the construct validity of IQ (e.g., correlation of IQ with income, job status, years of education), it may be possible to demonstrate that these correlations are due in each case to a third set of influences.

[8] If it is possible to demonstrate that IQ is not correlated, or is only weakly correlated, with the teachers' ratings of the minority of elementary school children, then such tests may penalize these groups. We base this assertion on the following syllogism:

1. If IQ is correlated with teachers' ratings, then
2. Low (IQ) scoring children generally get low ratings from their teachers, but
3. If IQ is not correlated with teachers' ratings, then
4. Low-scoring children are as likely to receive high as low teachers' ratings, thus
5. A low IQ would not imply poor prospects for educability.

[9] We hope to demonstrate empirically, through the analysis of IQ and teacher rating data for a large number of black, Mexican–American, and Anglo school children, that IQ is a far poorer predictor of elementary school success for black and brown children than it is for white children.

Goldman and Hartig focused on association strength, in particular the degree to which IQ measures predict children's performance in the public school. The rationale stressed the specific criterion of teacher ratings of academic achievement (paragraphs 6 and 8).

The hypothesis in paragraph 9 stated that IQ is a better predictor of school success for white than for nonwhite children. However, no operational definition of a good predictor was cited.

METHOD

Subjects

[10] The subjects were 951 children age 6 to 11 attending public elementary schools in Riverside, Calif., during 1969, from an original sample of 1,310 children attending Riverside schools during the school year 1967–1968. There were 320 Mexican–American, 201 black, and 430 Anglo subjects. The Mexican–American and black children included all the children who attended three de facto segregated elementary schools prior to September, 1966. The Anglo children were randomly selected from the student population of 11 elementary schools which were predominantly Anglo prior to comprehensive school desegregation which began in September, 1966. Of the total sample, 1,270 were enrolled in regular classes and 40 were enrolled in classes for mentally retarded children.

[11] The distribution of socioeconomic statuses (SES's) within each ethnic group for the sample approximated the SES distribution for each ethnic group in the city of Riverside. The distributions by ethnic group were: 18.8 percent of the Anglo children were low status, 55.0 were middle status, and 26.1 were high status; 84.8 percent of the Mexican–American children were low status, 15.1 middle status, and 0 high status; 75.5 percent of the black children were low status, 19.5 middle status, and 5.0 high status. Low-status occupations were those rated 0.29 on the Duncan Socioeconomic Index (Reiss, Duncan, and Hatt, 1961); middle-status occupations were those rated 30 to 69; and high-status occupations were those rated 70 or higher.

Measures

[12] All subjects were tested on the Wechsler Intelligence Scale for Children (WISC) in 1967. Teachers rated each student on a competence scale which was the sum of 11 semantic differential questions scored from 1 to 7 (e.g., slow–quick, disorganized–organized). Social grade point average was calculated from grades recorded from students' cumulative school record for the following subjects: industry, social attitude, mental attitude, work habits, conduct, work and study skills. Academic grade point average score was calculated from the following academic subjects: music, health, art, reading, arithmetic, math, social studies, science, language, spelling, writing, instrumental music, physical education, composition and grammar, history, geography, and foreign language.

Why were the authors concerned about the distribution of socioeconomic status within each ethnic group? Do you think other background characteristics should have been described?

The question of the construct validity of the criterion measures is important in this study since the predictive validity of an IQ test was examined. Despite citing teacher ratings of academic achievement as an important criterion in the introduction, the authors did not use that measure in the study itself. Instead teacher ratings of competence, academic grades, and grades in "nonacademic" areas were used. Only a brief description of the criterion measures was provided. On the basis of this information, do you agree with the author's decision to treat each test as a measure of scholastic performance?

No information on the reliability of the four measures was reported. On which measures should such information have been given?

RESULTS

[13] The means and *SD*s of all measures are shown in Table 14.3; intercorrelations, in Table 14.4. These tables show that IQ seems to be a valid predictor of all three measures of scholastic performance.

Which of the correlations in Table 14.4 were significantly different from zero at the .05 level of significance? Do you agree with the conclusion that IQ is a valid predictor for all three measures of scholastic performance on the total sample?

[14] The means and *SD*s for each ethnic group are shown for all measures in Table 14.5. It seems clear from Table 14.5 that Anglo children scored higher on the measures of scholastic performance and on IQ. Each of these differences among ethnic groups was significant ($p < .0001$). Variances on all variables were significantly ($p < .01$) greater for Anglo children than for black or Mexican–American children. At this point, the reader might be tempted to conclude that since IQ is correlated with scholastic performance, the ethnic differences in scholastic performance might be partly "explainable" by the ethnic differences in IQ. The next analysis will preclude this conclusion.

[15] The correlations of all measures are shown separately for each ethnic group in Table 14.6. It is readily apparent from Table 14.6 that IQ is correlated more

TABLE 14.3   *MEANS AND STANDARD DEVIATIONS (SD'S) FOR ACADEMIC AND SOCIAL GPA,[a] COMPETENCE AND IQ[b]*

Measure	Mean	SD
Academic GPA	218	69
Social GPA	218	61
Competence	47	12
IQ[b]	98	15

[a] Grade point average
[b] Wechsler Intelligence Scale for Children

TABLE 14.4   *INTERCORRELATIONS AMONG ACADEMIC AND SOCIAL GPA,[a] COMPETENCE, AND IQ[b]*

	Intercorrelation		
Measure	2	3	4
1. Academic GPA	.49	.43	.27
2. Social GPA		.69	.57
3. Competence			.50
4. IQ			

[a] Grade point average
[b] Wechsler Intelligence Scale for Children

TABLE 14.5   *MEANS AND STANDARD DEVIATIONS (SD'S) FOR ACADEMIC AND SOCIAL GPA,[a] COMPETENCE, AND IQ[b] FOR ANGLO, MEXICAN–AMERICAN, AND BLACK STUDENTS*

Group/Measure	Mean	SD
Anglo (N = 430)		
Academic GPA	234	74
Social GPA	250	60
Competence	52	12
IQ	107	12
Mexican–American (N = 320)		
Academic GPA	211	66
Social GPA	191	48
Competence	42	11
IQ	89	11
Black (N = 320)		
Academic GPA	194	55
Social GPA	192	43
Competence	42	10
IQ	91	11

[a] Grade point average
[b] Wechsler Intelligence Scale for Children

TABLE 14.6 *INTERCORRELATIONS AMONG ACADEMIC AND SOCIAL GPA,[a] COMPETENCE, AND IQ[b] FOR THE THREE GROUPS*

Group/Measure	Intercorrelation		
	2	3	4
Anglo (N = 430)			
1. Academic GPA	.49	.43	.25
2. Social GPA		.67	.49
3. Competence			.46
4. IQ			
Mexican–American (N = 320)			
1. Academic GPA	.44	.35	.12
2. Social GPA		.58	.28
3. Competence			.26
4. IQ			
Black (N = 201)			
1. Academic GPA	.37	.33	.14
2. Social GPA		.55	.30
3. Competence			.34
4. IQ			

[a] Grade point average
[b] Wechsler Intelligence Scale for Children

with scholastic performance in Anglo than in Mexican–American children. The correlation of IQ with each of the three scholastic performance measures was significantly greater for Anglo students than for Mexican–American students ($p < .05$). Only one of the black–white differences in correlation (IQ–competence) reached significance at the .05 level. These tests were performed by forming a critical ratio of the z scores after an r-to-z transformation of correlation coefficients. This point is more easily envisioned when we speak of proportion of variance associated with IQ which is given by r^2. Here it becomes clear that IQ is associated with more than twice as much variance in scholastic performance in Anglo children than in black or Mexican–American children. In fact, IQ accounts for very little variance in scholastic performance in these children.

Before proceeding to the authors' discussion of their results, you should attempt to arrive at your own conclusions and interpretations. This requires a critical examination of the correlation coefficients.

In paragraph 15, statistical tests of the difference between two correlations were reported. For example, the correlations between IQ and academic GPA for the Anglo and Mexican-American samples were compared, .25 versus .12. In this case a correlation of .25 was found to be statistically higher than that of .12. Although IQ correlated the highest with each of the scholastic performance measures within the Anglo sample, it is important to note that more significant differences were found between the Anglo and Mexican-American samples than were found between the Anglo and black samples.

The authors also examined the correlations in terms of the percentage of shared variance, r^2. The statement that IQ was associated with twice as much variance in scholastic performance in Anglo than in the nonwhite children apparently came from the ratio of two r^2 values; the maximum IQ correlation for the Anglo children (.49) and the maximum IQ correlation for the Mexican-American and black samples (.34). There was a 2 to 1 ratio between these squared values ($.49^2/.34^2 = .24/.11 = 2.2$).

The statement that IQ accounted for very little variance in scholastic performance measures on the nonwhite samples is subject to little dispute since the highest r^2 was 11. However, did the statement adequately reflect all the IQ relationships? The percentage of variance in the academic GPA scores accounted for by IQ scores with the Anglo sample was also very small ($r^2 = .25^2 = .06$). To be consistent, the authors should have added that IQ accounted for very little variance in academic GPA among the Anglo students as well. If the criterion of academic GPA is viewed as a more valid measure of scholastic performance than the other two measures, then this point is particularly important. Other individuals might view the IQ correlations of .49 and .46 with social GPA and competence on the Anglo sample as also accounting for very little variance, at most 24 percent.

DISCUSSION

[16] While it is true that white children score higher on the WISC than black or brown children, there is little reason to presume that this IQ difference "explains" the ethnic difference in scholastic performance. We say this because it appears that the WISC has little or no validity for predicting the scholastic performance of black or brown children.

[17] When the three ethnic groups studied here were combined to form a single group, the WISC IQ appeared to be a valid predictor of scholastic success. This produced the *illusion* that IQ fulfills the basic requirement of predictive validity for scholastic performance. In fact, the WISC IQ appeared to be differentially valid for white vs. minority children. This feature has a number of pragmatic implications since IQ has a function in educational placement. As Mercer (1973) has pointed out. IQ is one of the determinants in educational tracking— particularly assignment to educable mentally retarded (EMR) classes.

[18] There is probably considerable personal and social cost attendant to the misclassification of EMR children. A child who is wrongly assigned to an EMR class may be severely penalized by being denied a full education. Similarly, there is social and personal cost when a student who ought to be placed in an EMR class is wrongly left in a conventional class. Such a student will likely suffer the humiliation that accompanies lagging behind classmates. Thus, correct EMR placement is a critical procedure. If standardized tests such as the WISC can augment the judgments of teachers and school psychologists, then these tests should be employed.

[19] If a test is not a valid predictor of scholastic performance, then, clearly, it should not be used. In the present investigation, it seems we have uncovered a case of differential validity. The WISC is a valid predictor of scholastic success for white children but not for minority children. In a way, this produces a

more pernicious effect than a uniformly invalid test. When minority students are selected for certain educational groupings (such as EMR classes), then selection by an inaccurate method can preclude the use of a better selection method for the minority students.

[20] In addition to the pragmatic issue of selection, the use of an invalid intelligence test can produce a number of other undesirable consequences. Teachers and administrators notice that minority children score lower on the test. This information is rarely tempered with the additional information that the test is virtually uncorrelated with school performance for the minority children. As a result, teachers and administrators may "explain" poor school performance in minority children through reference to low IQ.

[21] There is some evidence in Table 14.6 that the lower validities for minority children may be due, in part, to the smaller variance of grade point average for minority children. In general, a restricted range of a predictor or criterion tends to reduce this correlation. (We corrected for restriction of range in the criterion measures of the black and Mexican–American groups and found small increases in IQ validity for these groups. Using the Anglo variances for academic grade point average and social grade point average, we found that competence resulted in corrected validities in the Mexican–American group of .13 and .34 and .18 and .40 in the black group, respectively. These adjusted coefficients led to the same conclusions as the unadjusted values.) This situation could result if teachers were generally less able to make fine distinctions among minority students—a matter worth investigating in future research. Even if the lower validity of IQ in black and Mexican–American students was due to poor ratings by teachers—a criterion problem—the lack of validity would be no less disappointing. Without the capacity to predict school performance, intelligence tests would have little justification for use. Thus, lower criterion variance is no justification for discounting low-IQ validity in minority groups.

[22] While it is almost certainly true that IQ is correlated with a number of indices of success in adulthood, these correlations do not necessarily support the construct validity of a given intelligence test. As Jencks (1972) has demonstrated, these correlations may be the artifactual correlational baggage of other relationships. Jencks has shown that income is related to years of schooling independent of cognitive abilities. It is possible that IQ determines the educational "track" of the student which, in turn, determines the number of years of schooling. Since the latter strongly affects occupation and income, even an invalid intelligence test can affect adult occupational success and income.

[23] In sum, we urge that the arguments about intelligence testing be examined at the fundamental level of predictive validity (for school performance). If this validity is often absent for minority school children, then the other, more acrimonious arguments become unnecessary. If predictive validity is present, then we can have the other arguments anyway. In short, let us test for the predictive validity of intelligence tests rather than simply assume it.

REFERENCES

Barnes, E. J. Cultural retardation or shortcomings of assessment techniques? In R. L. Jones (ed.). *Black psychology*. New York: Harper & Row, 1972.

Bay Area Association of Black Psychologists. Position statement on use of IQ and ability tests. In R. L. Jones (ed.). *Black psychology*. New York: Harper & Row, 1972.

Cleary, T. A., Humphreys, L. G., Kendrick, S. A., and Wesman, A. Educational uses of tests with disadvantaged students. *American Psychologist*, 1975, 30, 15–41.

Garrett, H. E. The equalitarian dogma. *Mankind Quarterly*, 1961, 1, 253–257.

Jencks, C. *Inequality*. New York: Harper & Row, 1972.

Jensen, A. R. How much can we boost IQ and scholastic achievement? *Harvard Educational Review*, 1969, 39, 1–123.

Klineberg, O. Negro–white differences in intelligence test performance: A new look at an old problem. *American Psychologist*, 1963, 18, 198–203.

Mercer, J. R. *Labeling the mentally retarded*. Berkeley: University of California Press, 1973.

Reiss, A., Duncan, O. D., Hatt, P. K., and North, C. C. *Occupations and social status*. New York: Free Press, 1961.

Shuey, A. *The testing of Negro intelligence*. New York: Social Science Press, 1966.

Williams, R. L. Abuses and misuses in testing black children. In R. L. Jones (ed.). *Black psychology* New York: Harper & Row, 1972.

The authors were aware of the effect that a restricted range on a variable can have upon the value of a correlation coefficient and discussed this problem in paragraph 21. They did not discuss the correlations among the three measures of scholastic performance, although consistent patterns occurred within each ethnic group. Teacher ratings of competence and social GPA correlated the highest, followed by the correlations between the two GPA measures, with academic GPA and teacher rating correlations being the lowest. What additional information do these relationships provide about the nature of the criterion measures?

Although you can disagree with the main conclusion that the WISC IQ is a differentially valid predictor of scholastic success for white and minority children (paragraphs 17 and 18), you cannot disagree with the authors' emphasis upon the necessity to base the use of intelligence tests within schools upon research results rather than upon opinion (paragraph 23).

14.2 ASSOCIATIONS BETWEEN A SET OF VARIABLES AND A CRITERION VARIABLE

To what extent is the prediction of college grades from high school grades improved by adding college entrance exam scores as a predictor? To what extent does sex of child predict first grade reading achievement after the relationships of reading readiness scores and of the child's birth order to first grade achievement have been controlled? These questions focus on the *association between a set or combination of predictor variables* and *one criterion variable*, and are obviously more complex than the one-to-one associations previously discussed. For example, the first prediction question focuses not only on the total relationship between the two predictors and the criterion of

DUNAGIN'S PEOPLE

US WEATHER BUREAU
ESSA

3-27

1975 Sentinel Star
Field Newspaper Syndicate

DUNAGIN'S PEOPLE BY RALPH DUNAGIN,
COURTESY OF FIELD NEWSPAPER SYNDICATE

"WE DEAL IN EXACT SCIENCE HERE, BENTLY...
IF MARCH COMES IN LIKE A LION, THERE'S A
60% CHANCE IT WILL GO OUT LIKE A LAMB."

college grades but also on the extent to which the second predictor contributes nonredundant or new information to the prediction. Not all such multiple-to-one relationships are questions of prediction over time, but may involve the test of a theory, appropriate placement of individuals in jobs or educational programs, or combinations of test scores which maximally discriminate groups of individuals.

The labels of "predictor" and "criterion" are used to characterize the two types of variables examined in association questions at this level. Sometimes the predictor variables are called independent variables and the criterion variable, the dependent variable. However, this independent/dependent terminology is reserved in this text for questions of cause. It is also recognized that many questions of association are not truly predictive and that assignment to criterion or predictor status is often arbitrary.

The most common questions asked of such association data are: (1) what is the strength of the relationship between the criterion variable and all the predictors, (2) how much does the strength of the overall relationship decrease when predictor variables are systematically eliminated from the analysis, (3) after the best predictor variable has been considered, to what extent do additional predictors increase the overall association between the predictors and the criterion, (4) how much does each predictor contribute to the overall association, and (5) what happens to the strength of the association when another sample of individuals is tested.

In selecting predictor variables that will have a strong association with the criterion, the ideal situation is to have high correlations between each predictor and the criterion and to have low correlations among the predictors. Obviously, if a high overall correlation is desired, the predictors must each be correlated with the criterion. But if two predictors are highly related to each other, then the addition of the second will not contribute any new information since essentially the same variable has been included twice in the analysis. Thus it is desirable to have predictors that contribute nonoverlapping, rather than redundant, pieces of information.

The most common technique for examining multiple-to-one associations is called multiple regression analysis. The index of association used with this technique is the multiple correlation coefficient, R. More information on multiple regression is given in Appendix D.

14.3 ASSOCIATIONS WITHIN A SET OF VARIABLES

In some studies researchers administer a series of tests to a sample of individuals. They then examine the nature of the *associations within all the variables* in order to answer such questions as: (1) can the number of variables under study be reduced to a smaller, more manageable number of composite scores, (2) can a structure or pattern be identified which accounts for the interrelationships among the variables, and (3) can different types of individuals be identified on the basis of the similarity of their response patterns on the set of variables. The first two questions just cited are discussed in more detail in the text since they are frequently examined in educational research studies.

When all the relationships among the variables are examined and it is found that the variables are unrelated to each other (each is unique), then the number of variables cannot be reduced and an underlying structure or pattern cannot be identified since no commonality exists among the variables. However, such situations are almost nonexistent in most educational contexts because relationships do exist among the tests typically administered in educational research studies. For example, the subscores on a standardized achievement test are usually related to each other to some degree, as are the items on personality and interest inventories.

Two hypothetical correlation matrices are presented in Table 14.7 to illustrate two different association patterns within a set of variables. The fairly high intercorrelations in Case I indicate that one dimension accounts for much of the variability in the test battery. On the other hand, Case II reflects two dimensions or factors. Variables 1, 2, and 3 seem to be measuring something in common as do Variables 4, 5 and 6, yet the two clusters are not highly intercorrelated. Thus in Case I, the six variables are reduced to one dimension, while in Case II two dimensions exist. In reality, such clear-cut patterns usually do not occur and the number of variables can be much larger, making it very

TABLE 14.7   *TWO HYPOTHETICAL CORRELATION MATRICES ILLUSTRATING DIFFERENT FACTOR STRUCTURES*

	Case I							Case II					
	Variable number							Variable number					
	1	2	3	4	5	6		1	2	3	4	5	6
1	...	.55	.61	.57	.66	.71	1	...	.81	.72	.10	.20	.15
2		...	.63	.65	.73	.58	2		...	.75	.15	.08	.10
3			...	.75	.60	.66	3			...	.05	.13	.15
4				...	.64	.54	4				...	.60	.71
5					...	.72	5					...	.68
6						...	6						...

difficult to mentally analyze the correlation matrix. Various statistical criteria exist for determining the number of dimensions represented by all the variables. Resolving the question of the exact nature or character of each dimension; that is, the underlying structure, often depends greatly on researchers' knowledge of the test battery and their theoretical inclinations.

A general technique that is frequently used to analyze correlational patterns within a set of variables is called factor analysis. More details on this procedure are given in Appendix D. No matter what analytic technique is used, it is important that researchers replicate their results on another sample in order to assess the stability of their findings. However, the most important decision made by researchers is the measures or tests they wish to investigate, for the addition and subtraction of tests to the battery can have profound effects on the analytic solution that is obtained and on the conclusions that are made.

14.4 ASSOCIATIONS BETWEEN TWO SETS OF VARIABLES

It is not surprising that educational researchers frequently investigate questions that involve *two sets of variables.* Darlington, Weinberg, and Walberg (41) cited the following examples of such problems: (1) practical prediction problems—from a test battery to several criterion variables, (2) theoretical problems about relationships between the content in two sets of variables—interests versus academic achievement; interests versus career plans, (3) problems involving variables measured on two occasions, and (4) problems involving paired subjects—teacher/student or husband/wife.

Researchers are often interested in determining the number of independent relationships between the two sets of variables as well as the nature of these independent relationships. If the two sets of variables were the scales from an interest inventory and grades in different school subjects, hypotheses like the following might be tested: that there is no relationship between interests and grades once some measure of overall academic achievement is held constant (i.e., hypothesizing that only one trait or dimension accounts for the relation-ships between the two sets of variables) or that interest and grades have at most three dimensions in common and that once these dimensions are re-moved the two test batteries are unrelated to each other. After the number of dimensions that are common to the two sets of variables has been determined, the researcher will often describe the nature of each dimension (e.g., a general ability dimension, a dimension that reflects creativity, a dimension that reflects potential for achievement in scientific areas).

Two procedures that are used to analyze association data at this level are canonical variate analysis and multivariate analysis of variance. These analytic procedures are quite complex and are only briefly described in Appendix D.

14.5 HOW TO IDENTIFY AND CRITIQUE TYPES OF ASSOCIATION STUDIES

A guide to identifying and evaluating the types of association studies discussed in this chapter is presented in Exhibit 14.1.

EXHIBIT 14.1   *IDENTIFICATION AND CRITIQUE OF TYPES OF ASSOCIATION STUDIES*

A. Which association question(s) was (were) of primary importance in the study?

1. Associations between pairs of variables? If *yes,* go to Section B.

2. Associations between a set of variables and a criterion variable? If *yes,* go to Section C.

3. Associations within a set of variables? If *yes,* go to Section D.

4. Associations between two sets of variables? If *yes,* go to Section E.

5. If *more than one question* was of interest, review all the appropriate sections.

B. 1. What hypotheses were made about the associations between variables? Were these hypotheses supported by the results? Was the author consistent in his or her interpretation of the strength of the relationships?

2. What was the level of measurement of each variable? What indices of associa-tion were applied? (Refer to the list in Table 14.1. Tests of significance such as Chi-square, *t*-test, and analysis of variance may be employed instead of a direct index of association strength.)

C. 1. What was the criterion variable? (A researcher may examine several criterion variables separately.) What were the predictor variables? Were hypotheses made about the strength or nature of the relationship between any of the predictors and the criterion? Were the relationships among each of the predictors presented, as well as relationships between the predictors and the criterion? (If the predictor is a nominal variable, then the relationship between it and the criterion may be investigated by testing for group differences on the criterion variable, rather than using a direct index of association strength.)

2. Did the researcher describe the nature/strength of the relationship between the predictors and the criterion? What was the best single predictor of the criterion? Did the researcher determine whether adding the other variables increased the degree to which the criterion could be predicted?

D. 1. What were the variables of interest? Were the relationships among all the variables in the set presented? What hypotheses were made regarding the nature of the association among the variables? Were these hypotheses supported?

2. How many dimensions were indicated in the analysis of the data? Was this a considerable reduction from the total number of original variables? Was each of the resulting dimensions described?

E. In general, what was the composition of the two sets of variables? What hypotheses, if any, were made regarding the nature of the association between the two sets? Were the two sets of variables actually related? Were associations among the individual variables in each set presented? How many relationships between the two sets were identified? Were these relationships described by the researcher?

14.6 LIST OF ASSOCIATION STUDIES

14.6.1 ASSOCIATIONS BETWEEN TWO VARIABLES

Conway, J. A., 1976. Test of linearity between teachers' participation in decision making and their perceptions of their schools as organizations. *Administrative Science Quarterly* **21**: 130–139.

Daly, J. A., and M. D. Miller, 1975. Further studies on writing apprehension: SAT scores, success expectations, willingness to take advanced courses and sex differences. *Research on the Teaching of English* **9**: 250–256.

Doherty, E. G., and C. Culver, 1976. Sex-role identification, ability, and achievement among high school girls. *Sociology of Education* **49**: 1–3.

Herrmann, R. W., 1972. Classroom status and teacher approval and disapproval

—study of children's perceptions. *Journal of Experimental Education* **41**(2): 32–39.

Kurth, R. W., and R. M. Pavalko, 1975. School resources, social environments, and educational outcomes. *Journal of Research and Development in Education* **9**: 70–81.

Lawson, A. E., F. H. Nordland, and A. DeVito, 1975. Relationship of formal reasoning to achievement, aptitudes, and attitudes in preservice teachers. *Journal of Research in Science Teaching* **12**: 423–431.

Nelson, M., and S. D. Sieber, 1976. Innovations in urban secondary schools. *School Review* **84**: 213–231.

Norfleet, M. A., 1973. The Bender Gestalt as a group screening instrument for first grade reading potential. *Journal of Learning Disabilities* **6**: 383–388.

Prendergast, M. A., and D. M. Binder, 1975. Relationships of selected self-concept and academic achievement measures. *Measurement and Evaluation in Guidance* **8**: 92–95.

14.6.2 ASSOCIATIONS BETWEEN A SET OF VARIABLES AND A CRITERION

Adams, R. S., R. M. Kimble, and M. Marlin, 1970. School size, organizational structure, and teaching practices. *Educational Administration Quarterly* **6**(3): 15–31.

Bergan, J. R., and M. L. Tombari, 1976. Consultant skill and efficiency and the implementation and outcomes of consultation. *Journal of School Psychology* **14**: 3–14.

Janzen, H. L., and H. J. Hallworth, 1973. Demographic and biographic predictors of writing ability. *Journal of Experimental Education* **41**(4): 43–53.

Thorsland, M. N., and J. D. Novak, 1974. The identification and significance of intuitive and analytic problem solving approaches among college physics students. *Science Education* **58**: 245–265.

Tuckman, B. H., and H. P. Tuckman, 1976. The structure of salaries at American universities. *Journal of Higher Education* **47**: 51–64.

14.6.3 ASSOCIATIONS WITHIN A SET OF VARIABLES AND BETWEEN TWO SETS OF VARIABLES

Bean, A. G., and C. K. Mayerberg, 1975. Attitude–aptitude relationships in the quantitative domain: a canonical analysis. *Journal of Experimental Education* **44**(1): 4–8.

Halpin, G., D. A. Payne, and C. D. Ellett, 1975. Life history antecedents of current personality traits of gifted adolescents. *Measurement and Evaluation in Guidance* **8**: 29–36.

Hopkins, K. D., and G. H. Bracht, 1975. Ten-year stability of verbal and non-verbal IQ scores. *American Educational Research Journal* **12**: 469–477.

Pascarella, E. T., 1975. A factor analytic comparison of faculty and students' perceptions of students. *Journal of Experimental Education* **44**(1): 26–32.

STUDY PROBLEMS

1. What are the major distinctions among the four types of association questions?

2. Give two examples of each type of association question, using research problems in an area of interest to you.

3. What are some association indices that can be used to examine the relationship between the following pairs of variables?

a) achievement in reading and in mathematics as determined by scores on a standardized achievement test

b) academic rank in class and sex

c) color of eyes and enrollment in a specific foreign language class (French, Spanish, or German)

d) Socioeconomic status (high, middle, low) and number of books read per year (0, 1–5, 6–10, 11–15, 16–20, over 20)

e) Number of seconds to run 100 meters and number of push-ups completed in 20 seconds

4. Below are two possible sets of correlations among six variables. Assume all correlations are significantly different from zero at the .05 level of significance. For each correlation matrix:

a) what are the strongest correlations?

b) what are the weakest correlations?

c) what are the patterns of association within the matrix?

| | Teacher ratings of ability | | | Standardized tests of ability | | |
	Math	Reading	General	Math	Reading	General
Ratings						
Math	—					
Reading	.55	—				
General	.58	.54	—			
Tests						
Math	.49	.37	.72	—		
Reading	.41	.50	.70	.71	—	
General	.43	.43	.72	.76	.76	—

	Teacher ratings of ability			Standardized tests of ability		
	Math	Reading	General	Math	Reading	General
Ratings						
Math	—					
Reading	.43	—				
General	.41	.39	—			
Tests						
Math	.71	.37	.34	—	—	
Reading	.32	.76	.39	.37	—	
General	.41	.30	.76	.36	.35	—

5. Using the information in the correlation matrix given below, what variables would probably make the best *set* of predictors of college grade point average (GPA)? Explain why you selected or did not select each variable as a predictor.

	College GPA	High school GPA	College entrance exam score	Teacher ratings of college potential	Counselor ratings of college potential
C–GPA	—				
HS–GPA	.56	—			
CEE Score	.57	.20	—		
T–Rate	.57	.71	.70	—	
C–Rate	.39	.45	.20	.23	—

6. Two researchers found that some of the five subtests (verbal comprehension, vocabulary, spelling, mathematical computation, and math problem solving) of a standardized achievement test were correlated with each other. The researchers analyzed the tests to determine how many dimensions actually existed among the subtests. This analysis indicated that the subtests fell into two distinct groups that the researchers called verbal (the comprehension, vocabulary and spelling subtests) and quantitative (the computation and problem-solving subtests). Should they continue to treat each of the five subtests as measuring something unique or should they distinguish only between two dimensions, i.e., verbal and quantitative? Explain your answer.

15

The Design of Studies to Identify Causes

The question of what causes a phenomenon haunts educators and much educational research. The recent attention given to the steady decline in achievement test scores over the past decade raises the question of why once again. The problem of *identifying causes* can easily be raised in other contexts: what causes some teachers to be more effective than others, what determines the career choice of youth, why is one educational program more effective than another, what causes juvenile delinquency, and so on. *Specifying the effects* of a phenomenon is another aspect of the general issue of causation: what are the results of retaining students for one grade, what are the effects of a positive attitude toward schoolwork, what are the consequences of separate educational programs for gifted children and those of lower ability, what are the effects of in-service training for teachers, and so on. Both sides of the causal question are of concern in this chapter.

15.1 CAUSATION

Educational researchers are constantly cautioned about the *problems in inferring causality*. The famous saying that "correlation does not imply causation" is a warning to individuals who would assume causation on the basis that two phenomena are constantly conjoined. The post hoc fallacy is just as easy to commit: "to think that just because something followed or follows something else, it was or is caused by that something else" (22, p. 401). Such cautions are necessary in that they remind both researchers and consumers of research of the importance of maintaining an open mind and of constantly considering other explanations of research findings. However, causal questions should not be avoided and, as specified in Chapter 10, are particularly important in education in which so many decisions are based upon someone's belief about what produces a certain result. *At a minimum,* in order to infer causality, the research evidence must (1) show that the presumed cause preceded the presumed

222

effect, (2) indicate covariation between the cause and effect, and (3) greatly reduce the probability of other causes.

15.1.1 GENERAL AND SPECIFIC CAUSAL STATEMENTS

The computer-assisted-instruction (CAI) program at Greenwood School caused an increase in average math achievement of about two years. CAI programs cause an increase in average math achievement of about two years.

What are the similarities and differences in these two statements? Both are statements about cause. However, the first refers to a *specific* cause and effect relationship that occurred in the past and is of the form "X caused Y" (44). The second is a *general* statement of the form "X causes Y" and refers to cases not covered in the specific statement. The general statement "X causes Y" is a way of saying that events of type Y can be produced by means of producing events of type X; it is a recipe for producing or preventing certain effects. General causal statements are the goal of educational research, although a particular study yields direct evidence only for specific statements.

"Making a specific causal statement is claiming that under the existing conditions the specified cause was sufficient to bring about the effect, and that it was responsible for the effect" (44, p. 10). It is important to note that this definition does not require that the cause be a necessary condition for the effect; that without the first the second could not have occurred. Obviously, some effects can be brought about in several different ways (e.g., an increase in mathematics achievement can be produced by events other than a CAI program).

The *sufficiency* requirement asserts that given the occurrence of the cause, the effect is bound to follow. For example, given two conditions, ideally alike except for X (say an experimental and a control condition), one needs to show that Y occurs only in the condition in which X occurs (the experimental condition). Controlled experiments are specifically designed to rule out alternative causal sequences. Yet even the most tightly controlled experiment cannot guarantee the elimination of all other causes, since unsuspecting causal factors can accidentally accompany the introduction of the experimental condition. The researcher can also use prior knowledge to eliminate other possible causes.

In nonexperimental contexts to say that X is the cause of Y requires evidence that X is always accompanied by Y and that Y never occurs on any other occasions (128). A major problem is to eliminate the possibility that a variable occurring prior to both X and Y is producing both of them. Experiments greatly reduce this problem since the researcher controls the introduction of X, thereby decreasing the likelihood of a third factor being consistently associated with both X and Y.

The *responsibility* condition explains why one particular factor is selected from the total causal sequence as being the cause; why, from among an infinite regression of causes, we stop at one particular point and focus on it. This is the event that we want to hold responsible for the effect. It is the point at which praise or blame, if assigned, is bestowed; the point at which intervention is deemed appropriate. Educators might select the branching capability of the CAI program as the factor responsible for the increase in mathematics achievement, as opposed to the amount of repetition or the content per se. If an increase in mathematics did not occur, then the type of branching would be held responsible for the lack of success and intervention would not imply total removal of the computer-assisted-instruction program, but rather a modification in program branching.

The responsibility condition also "explains the frequent reluctance to label something as *the* cause: We do not want to hold it exclusively responsible" (44, p. 9). Researchers must not only examine results from their particular study but they must also carefully weigh the knowledge in their field in selecting the cause. Obviously, other individuals may disagree with the identification of a particular cause and argue that the causal evidence is inadequate. It then becomes necessary to devise additional studies to examine the validity of the critics' arguments.

15.1.2 PARTIAL AND MULTIPLE CAUSES

Most educators and researchers would agree that it is impossible, even erroneous, to assign a single cause to effects as complex as increases in academic achievement or reductions in juvenile delinquency. Therefore, statements of causality are usually phrased to imply *partial* causes; that the responsibility for the effect is shared. This sharing may take one of two forms: (1) *additive,* where the effects of each partial cause are added together or (2) *conjoint,* where both are required to produce the effect since the occurrence of each alone is not sufficient.

Multiple causes may also occur in which each cause is a sufficient condition for the effect. Whichever occurred is then the cause. If both occurred, then both may have been effective, called simultaneous overdetermination, and neither factor can be identified as *the* cause.

15.2 ELEMENTS OF DESIGN

The rationale for studies asking causal questions should clearly specify the presumed cause(s) and the presumed effect(s). The presumed cause and the presumed effect are called the *independent* and *dependent variables,* respectively. The design should minimize the causal effects of other variables in order to adequately test the hypothesis that changes in the dependent variable are produced by variations in the independent variable. The researcher may cope with such *extraneous variables* through randomization or by experimental or statistical control, although some extraneous variables will always remain uncontrolled. Specific techniques of control are discussed in detail later. It is

important that the researcher discuss the potential impact of extraneous variables in the study's rationale, and that the method section of the report specify
how the design handles such factors.

15.2.1 IDENTIFICATION OF THE INDEPENDENT AND DEPENDENT VARIABLES FROM STATEMENTS OF THE RESEARCH PURPOSE

It is crucial that the reader of causal studies be able to quickly identify the
independent and dependent variables. Confusion may exist at first since statements of the research purpose vary greatly: some are in question form, some
are statements of a research hypothesis, others a version of the statistical null
hypothesis. Rarely does a researcher explicitly state that a particular variable
is expected to cause a certain effect. Some condensed versions of research
purposes are cited below, and the independent and dependent variables are
identified.

1. Mathematics ability is a major determinant of choice of major field at the
   university level (59).
   Independent variable: Mathematics ability
   Dependent variable: Choice of college major
2. A major purpose was to determine whether deaf children find it easier to
   read common words when they are spoken in isolation or when they appear in sentences (45).
   Independent variable: The context in which words are read (in isolation
      or embedded in sentences)
   Dependent variable: Lip reading skills: in particular, children were re-
      quested to write what they thought the speaker had said
3. Are the educational aspirations of students who move between schools of
   different socioeconomic composition affected by that move (7)?
   Independent variable: Change in socioeconomic composition of school
   Dependent variable: Educational aspiration of student
4. Do teachers who are more fully engaged in democratic staff processes (in
   cooperative dialogue and decision making regarding the school's problems)
   have pupils who have more favorable attitudes toward the school, learning,
   and themselves (129)?
   Independent variable: Type of teacher participation in school management
   Dependent variables (3): Students' attitudes toward school, learning, and
      themselves

Statements of purpose usually define the independent and dependent vari- *Purpose*
ables quite broadly. In causal studies much of the method section is devoted
to operationally defining these variables. Such specification is required since *Op. Def*
conclusions and inferences regarding causal factors depend heavily on how
the independent and dependent variables are operationally defined; especially
the specific aspects of the independent variable that the researcher chooses to
hold responsible for the effect.

15.2.2 THE PRESUMED CAUSE–INDEPENDENT VARIABLE

The Locus and Origin of the Independent Variable

The independent variables identified in the previous examples differ greatly. They can be observed or located in different contexts, referred to as the *locus* of the variable by Runkel and McGrath (122). The first independent variable referred to a property that resided in the *subject* (the subject's mathematical ability); the second to the nature of the *stimulus* or task (the context in which words are read); the third was a *characteristic of a setting* or situation (socio-economic composition of a school); and the fourth referred mainly to relationships or *interactions among individuals*. The locus of the independent variable can be determined from a close examination of the operational definition of the variable.

In addition to identifying the locus of the causal property, another distinction must be made; that of the *origin* of the property (122). The independent variable may be *inherent* in the subject, the task, or the behavior at the outset of the study, or it may be *imposed* upon the subject, task, or setting by the investigator. If it is inherent, the researcher must simply identify the property and form aggregates of individuals, tasks, or settings that are alike on the property. If it is imposed, then the researcher must modify the subject, stimulus, or setting. These two processes are quite distinct from each other and strongly influence the degree of control that the researcher possesses over other possible causes and the presumed cause itself. If the origin is inherent, then other variables may be inextricably linked to the independent variable, making it impossible to eliminate them as probable causes.

The locus of the independent variable frequently restricts its origin. For example, characteristics of individuals are usually inherent. In fact, some characteristics (sex, age) cannot be imposed by the researcher. On the other hand, tasks and stimuli are often specifically created by the researcher, rather than being observed in existing settings. When referring to broad behavioral contexts created by society (socioeconomic composition of schools) as independent variables, the researcher works with inherent variables because he or she cannot deliberately establish or impose such conditions.

One characteristic of experiments is that the independent variable is imposed by the investigators. It is crucial that the *researchers determine whether in fact they did create or change that which they intended.* If the independent variable is the number of students in a class, then this process is simple and may seem too obvious to mention. However, if the independent variable is the type of question asked by the teacher during classroom discussion or the participation by teachers in the decision-making process in their school, then the verification process becomes more complex but no less important. In nonexperimental studies in which the independent variable is inherent, researchers must be sure that they have in fact selected the subjects, tasks, or conditions that they intended to select. Frequently this boils down to the question of the construct validity of the tests or observation techniques employed in the selection process.

Most causal studies involve more than one independent variable. Combinations of imposed and inherent variables may be employed in more complex designs. *If at least one of these variables is manipulated or imposed by the researcher, the study is classified in this book as experimental.*

QUALITATIVE VERSUS QUANTITATIVE VARIABLES

The dichotomy of the presence or absence of the presumed cause presented so far is a highly simplified picture of the design of causal studies. Whether the independent variable is qualitative or quantitative, the independent variable must represent distinct variations in the causal factor.

With a quantitative independent variable, such as number of reinforcements given every ten minutes in a computer-assisted instruction program, the researcher can establish a series of experimental conditions that represent systematic variations in the independent variable. The variation along this continuum should be great enough so that the variations are perceived as being different by the subjects.

When the independent variable is qualitative, as in a comparison of counseling techniques, the presence/absence dichotomy is misleading since more than one causal factor often distinguishes the experimental conditions. Techniques of counseling usually differ on a multitude of dimensions. The complexity of a qualitative variable also creates problems in identifying a cause. Nevertheless, even if a hypothesis as vague as "different counseling techniques yield different results" is to be tested, the researcher must establish variations in such techniques that are qualitatively different.

LENGTH OF EXPOSURE TO THE INDEPENDENT VARIABLE

Sometimes the subjects' history affects how rapidly they react to the independent variable. The length of exposure to the independent variable may be particularly crucial in curriculum studies in which students have encountered one mode of instruction for many years. When the school or an investigator institutes a different curriculum, a one-year trial period may be too short for any changes to occur. Similar problems may exist in studies of counseling techniques, teacher training procedures, etc. On the other hand, if enough time is allowed, a point may be reached at which all treatments end up having similar effects, as when students reach mastery on a short learning task. Differences among conditions might have occurred at earlier stages in the investigation and to infer that the independent variable had no effects would be misleading.

15.2.3 THE PRESUMED EFFECT-DEPENDENT VARIABLE

Just as one phenomenon may be the result of multiple causes, so can one event have a multitude of effects. A better understanding of the independent variable will be obtained if both the depth and breadth of its effects are examined. Inclusion of variables contradicted by or even not predicted by theory may be as important as the inclusion of those predicted by theory. Results on variables assumed to be insensitive to the independent variable as well as those presumed to be particularly sensitive to it may be of interest. The duration of an effect may merit consideration.

Any effect of an independent variable can be observed only if the measurement procedure is sensitive to that effect. A standardized test of mathematics achievement will not pick up the same changes in achievement as one developed specifically for a school system. The standardized test may be a measure of transfer of learning and thus be very important, but if it were the only measure employed, it might be concluded that the school's math program had no effect. So at a minimum, researchers must include measures that they believe to be sensitive to variations in the independent variable. This may mean that new tests must be developed since existing measures are often inadequate. However, when researchers are pressed for time and decide they cannot afford to work on test development, they forge ahead with existing, less sensitive, instruments.

An adequate test of a causal hypothesis also demands that the researchers carefully examine the construct validity of the measures they select. It may be desirable to include more than one measure of the same variable so that the effects are not linked to the particular procedures associated with a single test. All the discussions in the previous chapters regarding the quality of measurement procedures apply to the dependent variable. Despite the fact that more journal space is usually devoted to the methodology surrounding the independent variable, the conceptualization and measurement of dependent variable are just as crucial in questions of causation.

15.2.4 EXTRANEOUS VARIABLES

One problem that plagues all researchers examining causal questions is how to eliminate, if possible, or, more realistically, *to reduce the probability of unexpected and unwanted variables from influencing the dependent variable.* In other words, it is necessary to establish that X was indeed a sufficient condition for the occurrence of Y. Without some degree of control over extraneous variables, the researcher cannot determine whether the independent variable did or did not have an effect upon the dependent variable. This concept of control is equivalent to Campbell and Stanley's (27) concept of *internal validity.* Alternative hypotheses become less plausible as the similarity between conditions in which the presumed cause is present and those in which it is absent become more alike. Similarity in experimental conditions is carefully designed by the researcher for it does not occur by accident.

METHODS OF CONTROL

RANDOMIZATION In educational research it is important to ensure the similarity or equivalence of individuals exposed to variations in the independent variable. *When individuals are assigned by chance* (e.g., at random by a table of random numbers) *to each condition, the possibility of initial differences in the groups being compared is reduced.* This process of randomization

> does not mean that the experimental and control groups will be exactly alike, but rather that whatever differences exist before the introduction of the experimental variable are the result of chance alone. The rules of probability make it possible to specify the extent of differences that might be expected by chance in the long run (that is, if the selection were repeated a large number of times). If, after one group has been exposed to the experimental treatment, the two groups are found to differ more than would be expected by chance, one may infer that the experimental variable led to the difference. This inference, of course, is tentative, subject to the possibility that some other factor may have led to the difference (130, p. 130).

Random assignment is the primary way of simultaneously "equating" the groups being compared on all extraneous/unwanted variables. This assurance of "equality is greater [however] for large numbers of random assignments than for small" (27, p. 15).

It is important to recognize that *random assignment of individuals to experimental conditions is distinct from random selection of the sample,* as illustrated in Fig. 15.1. Sequence 1 is "ideal," enabling generalization to the population of interest and ensuring that only chance differences exist among individuals in the experimental conditions, but is rarely attained in practice. The bias in assignment of individuals to conditions in Sequence 2 makes this procedure undesirable for studies of causal questions. Sequence 3 is common in educational research, as illustrated by the many studies in which volunteers

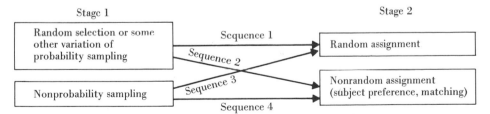

FIG. 15.1 Four possible sequences in the allocation of individuals to experimental conditions (variations in the independent variable). Stage 1: Selection of sample from accessible population. Stage 2: Assignment of subjects from the sample to experimental conditions.

are randomly assigned to treatments. Sequence 4 is the least desirable but is also common, introducing bias at both the selection and assignment stages.

Educational researchers are often confronted with intact groups of individuals, such as classrooms, in which randomization of individuals is impossible, but randomization using the classroom as the experimental unit is feasible. This is *not* equivalent to random assignment of individuals since the original placement of students in classes by the school system is usually not random. When classrooms are randomly assigned to treatments, the unit of statistical analysis should be the classroom rather than the individual student. Since randomization plays such a crucial role in the type of causal inferences that can be drawn from a study, the section of the research report describing the process by which subjects or units were allocated to the experimental conditions must be examined very carefully.

Comparison with matching. Matching of individual subjects on one or more traits (sex, ability, age) and then allocating them to experimental conditions is not equivalent to randomization. It is mistakenly believed that matching assures the initial equivalence of groups. Some of the problems with matching are that: it must be accomplished prior to the experiment thus restricting the matching variables to those on which prior data exist; matching on all relevant variables is impossible; as the number of matching variables increases, a larger pool of potential subjects is required in order to achieve a good match and the small sample that is finally selected is not representative of the original sample; and criteria must be developed for determining when individuals are indeed "matched" or "alike" on each variable. An even less desirable procedure is to match entire groups on group means and standard deviations.

Matching in conjunction with randomization. Use of matching as an adjunct to randomization, however, is often desirable. It may increase the statistical precision of the study and avoid extreme chance fluctuations when the sample size is small. In such instances, subjects are first paired and then randomly assigned to one condition or the other.

Randomization of factors other than subjects. Since differences in individual traits are not the only sources of alternative causes, randomization of other factors may be part of the study's design. The nature of such factors varies with the study. With individualized testing, testers may be randomly assigned to subjects. The stimuli or tasks may be randomized across subjects (e.g., randomizing the sequence of words presented to deaf children in a lip reading task). Teachers may be randomly assigned to instructional conditions, counselors to therapy sessions, etc.

Randomization is therefore an "all-purpose" technique for avoiding bias. Yet it cannot be achieved unless the researcher deliberately introduces it into the design. Although other techniques of control are possible, as discussed below, randomization may be the best control for particular research problems.

Its importance is well known to researchers but it is not well understood by the public. Therefore educational researchers often encounter barriers and resistance to a research design with randomization when conducting studies in the field.

REMOVAL FROM THE DESIGN   The researcher *can remove the effect of an ex-* ⨉ *traneous variable by holding it constant; by not letting it vary.* Including only male subjects removes the effect of sex; the inclusion of a narrow range of ability "holds ability constant." Ensuring that all classrooms have the same lighting and equipment and are painted the same color, that all classes are held at the same time of day, and that students are tested in identical soundproof booths removes the potential contaminating effects of differences in lighting, etc. since these factors are the same for all subjects.

Subjects can also serve as their own control. In other words, each subject is exposed to each variation in the independent variable. Such procedures however are undesirable in studies in which carry-over from one treatment to another is expected, as in studies involving learning. If carry-over is not expected, much can be gained from this technique. The phrases "repeated measures" and "within-subjects" designs describe this procedure.

Controlling a variable by removing it from the design may involve either the selection of subjects, tasks, and settings or the deliberate creation/manipulation of tasks and settings by the researcher. Associated with such controls, however, is frequently a loss in generalization of the findings (e.g., to only one sex or one ability level). In designing a study the researcher must weigh the loss in generalization against the advantages of this form of control.

INTRODUCTION INTO THE DESIGN   In other instances it may be desirable to *de-liberately introduce a variable* other than the presumed cause *into the design to observe its effects.* In essence it then becomes another independent variable. In situations in which such control variables are known to be related to the dependent variable, the precision of the research design is increased.

Ability is often introduced into designs comparing instructional methods since measures of ability are associated with measures of learning. The extent to which the dependent variable of achievement is associated with ability can then be detected and isolated from its association with the method factor. In the lingo of research design, the control variable may be introduced as a "blocking" variable (i.e., subjects are divided into ability groups and randomly assigned to conditions within each block) or as a "covariate" (i.e., each individual's ability score is considered in the statistical analysis).

Instead of eliminating an extraneous variable's effect or allowing chance factors to determine the variable's effects through randomization, researchers "control" its effects by observing them. Being aware of these effects allows researchers to make inferences not possible with the other means of control.

TYPES OF EXTRANEOUS VARIABLES TO CONTROL

In Campbell and Stanley's (27) discussion of the *internal validity* of experimental designs, that is, the extent to which the design controls for extraneous variables, eight classes of variables were cited as particularly relevant to research designs in the behavioral sciences. These classes are described in Table 15.1. Other factors (Classes 9 through 11 in Table 15.1), frequently cited as threats to the generalization of the results (18, 27), are also presented. It is the opinion of this author that these particular factors can also become confounded with the independent variable and therefore represent factors other than the presumed cause and lower the degree of control of the study. However, they are also recognized as threats to the generalizability of the external validity of an experiment and are cited later in that context as well.

Although this list of extraneous factors may seem formidable at first, it is not. Many defects in specific designs are obvious to readers with background in the content being investigated. The task then becomes one of translating these faults expressed in lay terms into the terminology used by researchers. In critiquing an experimental design the *key question is whether an extraneous factor could have in some way affected the dependent variables. If the answer is a probable "yes," then the internal validity of the study has been lowered.*

The major element of design that distinguishes studies with high control from those with low control is randomization of subjects and of other relevant stimuli to variations in the independent variable. Suppose the researcher instituted a simple two-condition experiment in cross-age tutoring: one condition involving seventh graders tutoring first graders on reading problems twice a week for one semester and the other condition being seventh graders who did not tutor. The researcher hypothesized differences in two dependent variables: that the seventh grade tutors would perform at a higher reading level at the end of the study than those who did not tutor, and that they would also exhibit more understanding of the responsibilities of a teacher. In this instance, random assignment of subjects means that the assignment of individual seventh grade students to the tutor and nontutor conditions was determined by chance. Neither counselors, teachers, nor the principal decided who they thought would make the best tutors; the seventh graders were not allowed to volunteer for the tutor group; and the first graders could not choose who they wanted as a tutor. Although the total sample of seventh graders could have been a volunteer one, their assignment to one of the two conditions was determined by a random process, ensuring that the only initial differences between the two seventh grade groups were the result of chance alone.

How does randomization of the tutors (the subjects in this case) make the results easier to interpret? Bias resulting from *differential selection* of subjects (Class 1, Table 15.1) is ruled out as well as any *interaction between selection* and the other threats (Class 8). For example, a critic cannot argue that the results are due to the fact that the seventh grade teachers picked their best or worst readers as tutors. The threat of *statistical regression to the mean* (Class 2) is also reduced since neither tutoring group was selected because

**TABLE 15.1   *DESCRIPTIONS OF CLASSES OF EXTRANEOUS VARIABLES
(THREATS TO THE INTERNAL VALIDITY OF RESEARCH DESIGNS)***

1. *Differential selection:* biases in dependent variable resulting from initial differences in groups being compared when the groups were selected on different criteria (e.g., use of volunteers for experimental group and nonvolunteers for the control group).

2. *Statistical regression to the mean*[*]:* occurs when groups have been deliberately selected because of extreme scores, either high or low. Mean of the extreme group will move toward the mean of the general population from which it was selected irrespective of intervening treatments due to unreliability of measuring instruments or random instability in the population (e.g., as a group, students selected because of high IQ scores will score lower upon a second IQ testing and the opposite will occur for those selected for reason of low ability).

3. *Maturation:* biological and physiological processes that function with the passage of time itself and affect the dependent variable (e.g., getting older, hungry, or tired).

4. *Experimental mortality:* differential loss of subjects in the experimental conditions (e.g., individuals with the highest anxiety scores drop out of the experimental therapy group whereas no mortality occurs in control group).

5. *History:* specific events occurring during the period of the study other than the independent variable that can affect the dependent variable (e.g., laughter, distracting events, news stories).

6. *Pretesting:* the effects of taking a test upon the scores of a second test; the testing process itself is a stimulus to change (e.g., learning that occurs upon taking a pretest and therefore affects responses when the test is administered again).

7. *Instrumentation:* changes in the scoring of a test, in raters, interviewers, observers, etc. that affect the measurements (e.g., observers or raters become more experienced or fatigued with time, making earlier observations or ratings not comparable with later ones).

8. *Interaction of selection and maturation, selection and history, selection and mortality, etc.:* volunteers may maintain interest and motivation over a longer period of time than other subjects, or may be more likely to experience extraneous events related to the experimental conditions.

9. *Reactive effects of experimental arrangements* (Hawthorne effect): factors related to the subject's awareness of being in an experiment which may in turn affect the way he or she responds to the dependent variable (e.g., "I'm a subject" and "I'm a control" effects).

10. *Experimenter effects:* certain characteristics of the experimenter may unintentionally influence the subject's behavior, or the expectations of the experimenter may bias the administration of the treatment.

11. *Interaction between pretest and treatment, history and treatment, etc.:* administration of a pretest may decrease or increase the subject's sensitivity to the experimental conditions; specific events outside of the experimental conditions may decrease or increase the subject's reaction to the treatment.

---

[*] See Campbell and Stanley (27) for a more technical discussion of this issue.

of its extreme position on a trait, such as achievement in reading. Even if students had been selected because of their extreme position, if they were randomly assigned to the experimental conditions, the regression to the mean would be the same for each group and therefore would not contaminate the fiindings. That the two groups of tutors as a whole were of equivalent ages because of randomization means that some *maturation* threats (Class 3) are reduced, since both groups would be at the same stage of maturation, in a developmental sense.

Differential mortality (Class 4) in the two groups could occur, although one could assume that it was not the result of initial differences in any characteristic of the tutors and nontutors (an interaction with selection) because of the random assignment. The key word here is "differential." Loss of subjects per se is not a threat but loss of different types or different numbers in the experimental conditions is of concern.

As the time period for studies increases, the possibility of change-producing events other than the experimental conditions themselves increases (*history*, Class 5). The one-semester period for the tutoring study is much longer than a one- to two-hour experiment. In order for history to be a threat, extraneous events should occur for most subjects in one experimental condition but not in the other conditions. If subjects in all conditions are equally exposed to the event, then no threat exists since the effect should be the same for all groups. Conducting experimental conditions on one individual at a time with the experimental sessions randomized as to time of day and experimenter, as is common to many psychological laboratory experiments, distributes the effects of many extraneous events, as opposed to the one-time only group administration of treatments more common to educational research.

The conditions for measuring the dependent variable must be considered as rival hypotheses (Classes 6, 7, and 11). Obviously *pretesting* is a threat only when a pretest is given. If all groups are given a pretest and subjects are randomly assigned, then any changes in the subjects produced by the initial testing procedure should be constant across all groups. Nevertheless, even with random assignment, interpretation of results can be hindered when the pretest is potentially reactive, resulting in an *interaction between the pretest and experimental treatment* (Class 11). For example, if the tutors and nontutors were given a pretest on their views of the responsibilities of teachers, the tutor group may react to their tutoring experience in a way that is different from the way they would react to tutoring if a pretest had not been given. Any changes from the pretest to the posttest are then likely to be the result of both the experimental condition itself and the sensitizing effect of the pretest to the tutoring experience. Some designs separate these two effects, but most do not. Welch and Walberg (147) concluded that pretest and sensitization effects are less likely to occur with year-long curriculum studies than with shorter units of instruction. Problems of *instrumentation* (Class 7) can often be reduced by randomly assigning the testers/observers to treatments so that any changes in scoring are randomized across treatments. Other controls, such as blind scoring and extensive tester/observer training can be instituted, in order to avoid problems of instrumentation.

The very operation of an experiment often unintentionally creates biases that cannot be separated from the independent variable. The *subject's aware-ness* of his or her role as a subject (Class 9) may have contaminating effects. Generally speaking, increasing the length of a study and decreasing the amount of attention and publicity given to it as an "experiment" will reduce this threat. The *experimenter's expectations or characteristics* (Class 10) may also affect the results, although usually great precautions are taken to minimize such threats.

An important point to understand is that an extraneous variable is a threat only if it is likely to produce different effects in the different experimental conditions being compared. Consider history as a source of invalidity in the tutoring study. If a crash reading improvement program were suddenly instituted in seventh grade during the time of the study, it could affect the students' scores on the reading test administered at the conclusion of the study. But it would have the same overall effect upon both the tutors and nontutors since all were exposed to it and the two groups were initially equivalent. No differences between the two groups would appear as a result of exposure to this factor per se. However, exposure to the reading program could interact with the tutoring experience (*interaction between history and treatment*, Class 11). That is, the experience of tutoring could cause the tutors to be more motivated, more attentive, or to work harder in the reading program, resulting in higher reading scores than the nontutor group even though both had had equal exposure to the reading program. Unless the researcher had planned for such contingencies, it is impossible to separate the effects of the tutoring per se from the interaction it had with such outside events. Finally, if only one group, say the tutors, were exposed to the crash reading program, then the reading scores could be differentially affected. Under these conditions, it is also impossible to attribute any final differences in reading achievement between the tutors and nontutors solely to the tutoring experience, since it is confounded with the existence of the reading program.

If an extraneous variable can be controlled by any of the three methods of control discussed previously, then it no longer can have a differential effect upon the experimental conditions and therefore cannot constitute a rival explanation of the results. History is particularly difficult to control since such events are unexpected and experimental isolation of subjects is usually not possible in educational research. On the other hand, most conditions of testing/instrumentation are directly under the researcher's control and steps can be taken to minimize contaminating effects associated with these sources.

UNCONTROLLED VARIABLES

The impossibility of controlling all extraneous variables means that some will be confounded with the independent variable. It will be impossible to separate their effects. The existence and strength of the controlled variables directly affect the degree to which researchers can make a specific causal claim at the conclusion of the study. The best researchers can do is to control those variables that they believe are relevant. In nonexperimental studies the confounding between the independent and uncontrolled variables is a major source of concern. Some control may be established through selection of subjects, but randomization of subjects and stimuli to variations in the independent variable is by definition impossible.

15.3 GENERALIZATION OF THE RESULTS

Without some degree of control over extraneous variables, results from studies aimed at answering causal questions are meaningless, and any attempt to generalize to other subjects, settings, experiments, and tests is pointless. However, most researchers establish some control, and the issue of generalization can then be raised. This concept has also been referred to as the *external validity* of designs by Campbell and Stanley (27) and Bracht and Glass (18). It is unusual to achieve both a very high degree of control and a high degree of generalizability. For example, experimental subjects can be isolated to avoid the extraneous effects of history, but the degree to which one could generalize beyond that particular setting is limited. Frequently, educational researchers sacrifice some elements of control for a gain in generalization.

Campbell and Stanley's classification of major threats to the external validity of designs was later expanded upon by Bracht and Glass, and this expanded version is presented in Table 15.2. As mentioned previously, some of these threats have a dual role, being sources of both internal and external invalidity.

In critiquing studies, *the key question to ask of each factor is whether it would operate in the same way in other contexts and with other individuals as it did in the study, and/or whether similar effects would be obtained if the factor were absent or modified in other contexts. If the answer is a probable "no," then generalization of the results is hindered* (i.e., external validity is lowered). The following discussion cites a few ways in which designs can be modified to increase the generalizability of results.

One common problem in many highly controlled studies is the use of volunteer subjects or individuals who just happen to be available. Complete descriptions of the sample and the population of interest and/or use of probability sampling procedures for selecting the sample and the accessible population reduce the problems of *inappropriate generalization to the target population* (Threat 1, Table 15.2). If researchers anticipate that the various experimental conditions will have different effects upon different types of individuals (*aptitude–treatment–interaction*, Threat 2), then they should include that particular trait as a factor in the design in order to observe the nature of such

TABLE 15.2   *THREATS TO THE GENERALIZABILITY*
OR THE EXTERNAL VALIDITY OF RESEARCH DESIGNS

Population validity—generalization to populations

1. *Accessible vs. target population:* inappropriate generalization to the target population instead of the accessible population (the concepts of accessible and target populations are discussed in Chapters 6 and 18).

2. *Interaction of personological variables and treatment:* reversal of treatment effects when persons at a different level on some trait are exposed to the treatment (e.g., if a study used only high ability subjects, the same results might not occur for individuals of lower ability).

Ecological validity—generalization to settings

3. *Description of independent variable:* complete description of variations in the independent variable is necessary for replication of the study and appropriate generalization.

4. *Hawthorne (and reverse Hawthorne) effects:* subject's awareness of being in the experimental group (Hawthorne) or of being in the control group (reverse Hawthorne) may affect his or her responses in ways that would not occur if the subject did not perceive himself or herself as a participant in an experiment.

5. *Novelty and disruption effects:* uniqueness of results because of enthusiasm or disruption created by the newness of the treatment.

6. *Experimenter effects:* certain characteristics of the experimenter may unintentionally influence the subject's behavior, or the expectations of the experimenter may bias the administration of the treatment.

7. *Multiple-treatment interference:* when subjects are exposed to more than one treatment, the same results may not hold when generalizing to situations where only one treatment exists.

8. *Interaction of history and treatment effects:* specific events occurring during the experiment may affect the results of the treatment in such a way that the effect would not appear at other times (e.g., occurrence of the historic Viking landing on Mars during a comparison of various astronomy curricula).

9. *Pretest sensitization:* administration of pretest may decrease or increase subject's sensitivity to experimental conditions and results may not apply to contexts in which pretest is not given.

10. *Posttest sensitization:* latent effects of treatment may appear because the subject reacts to or learns from the administration of a formal posttest (e.g., controls may learn in the process of taking a test or become aware of what the study was "all about" and respond accordingly).

11. *Measurement of dependent variable:* results may be unique to specific measurement techniques employed, and to the specific dependent variables that were measured.

12. *Interaction of time of measurement and treatment effects:* results may depend on time of measurement of dependent variable (e.g., immediate posttest scores may not be similar to scores obtained two or eight weeks later).

effects. Otherwise readers and researchers must use their own judgment in deciding if similar results would occur for other types of individuals.

Complete *description of the independent variable* (Threat 3) is not only necessary for making appropriate generalizations but is also essential for understanding what in fact was done in the study and how the independent variable was operationally defined.

Several threats are intimately associated with the fact that the study is an experiment (Threats 4, 5, and 6). Suggestions for minimizing the *Hawthorne effect* include abandoning the experimental–control type of research design completely, emphasizing the value of all experimental conditions so no one group feels it has a unique role to play, including the experimental instructions and treatment as part of the regular classroom when possible, and using a double-blind approach in which neither subject nor experimenter is aware of which subjects are in the experimental condition. A reverse Hawthorne effect, in which the awareness of being in the control group influences the result, has also been identified. The other threats (*novelty/disruption* and *experimenter effect,* Threats 5 and 6) are more serious in some contexts than others. Some of the recommendations for reducing the Hawthorne effect apply to these threats as well (e.g., the double-blind approach as a control for experimenter effects).

In designs that provide for the exposure of subjects to more than one variation of the independent variable, generalizations to settings in which only one treatment exists may be misleading (*multiple-treatment interference,* Threat 7). This threat does not apply, of course, when sequence effects are the focus of the study and any generalization, of necessity, involves the entire sequence of treatments. No research design can eliminate a possible *history-treatment interaction* (Threat 8). However, researchers should report the possibilities for such interaction, and the study can be replicated on other occasions to test for such effects.

The last set of threats involves measurement procedures (Threats 9, 10, 11, and 12). In situations in which tests are routinely administered, *pretest sensitization* (Threat 9) is probably not a major threat, and of course, it is nonexistent when pretests are not given. *Posttest sensitization* (Threat 10) may be reduced by using measures that reduce the subject's awareness of being tested. Administration of more than one measure of a dependent variable, using a measure with convergent validity, and/or measuring more than one dependent variable each will decrease the degree to which the results are unique to a particular measurement procedure (*measurement of dependent variable,* Threat 11). Finally, administration of tests at more than one interval following the treatment is advisable (*interaction of time of measurement and treatment,* Threat 12). Not only does this enhance the understanding of the effects of the independent variable but it more closely approximates educational settings in which tests of learning are not always immediate.

Both the existence of uncontrolled variables and threats to generalizability influence the degree to which general claims of causality can be made. Evidence from one study is insufficient for general claims, although frequently specific causal claims made by the researcher are interpreted in a general way. Replication with other individuals and in other contexts is essential for general statements.

15.4 HOW TO CRITICALLY EXAMINE INDEPENDENT, DEPENDENT, AND EXTRANEOUS VARIABLES IN RESEARCH ARTICLES

Guidelines for critiquing independent, dependent, and extraneous variables in studies of causal questions are presented in Exhibit 15.1.

EXHIBIT 15.1   ANALYSIS OF INDEPENDENT, DEPENDENT, AND EXTRANEOUS VARIABLES

A. What was (were) the presumed cause(s) or independent variable(s)?

B. Did the study's rationale specify whether partial or multiple causes were believed to exist?

C. 1. Describe how each independent variable was operationally defined. Were these definitions adequate; that is, could you come close to replicating the study?

   2. For each independent variable, determine whether its origin was inherent or imposed by the researcher.

     a) If the independent variable was imposed, were any data presented on the degree to which it was successfully manipulated?

     b) If the independent variable was inherent, were any data presented on the reliability and construct validity of the measure?

   3. Identify the locus of each independent variable: in subject, in task, in setting, in relationships among individuals.

D. What was (were) the presumed effect(s) or dependent variable(s)?

   1. Were any data presented on the reliability and construct validity of the measures?

   2. Was an appropriate range of possible outcomes investigated? At the least, measures assumed to be sensitive to the independent variable should have been employed.

   3. Was more than one measure of any dependent variable used?

E. What variables, other than the independent variables, could affect the results? Review the list in Table 15.1. Did the researcher consider these threats in his or her interpretation of the results and in his or her final conclusions and inferences?

F. What factors might hinder the generalizability of the results; that is, what might operate differently in other contexts or with other individuals, or if the factor were absent or modified, different results might occur? Review the list in Table 15.2. Did the researcher consider these threats in his or her final conclusions and inferences?

STUDY PROBLEMS

1. Why are cause-effect statements so difficult to make in research studies? What are the differences between the sufficiency and responsibility requirements for causal statements?

2. Read two of the experimental studies cited at the end of Chapter 16. For each study analyze the independent, dependent, and extraneous variables using the series of questions in Exhibit 15.1. Evaluate the overall quality of the research design.

3. Make five statements regarding cause–effect relationships in schools that you believe are true (e.g., Spelling bee contests are a good way to increase student achievement in spelling, particularly for good spellers). Identify the independent and dependent variables in each of the five statements and determine whether the origin of the independent variable is imposed or inherent. Why is it so important that the origin of the independent variable be imposed rather than inherent in causal studies?

4. What are the advantages and disadvantages of the different ways of controlling extraneous variables?

5. In a typical comparison of teaching methods (e.g., programmed instruction vs. small group discussion vs. lecture with problem solving exercises), the researcher must decide:

    a) which students are to be exposed to each method,
    b) who teaches each method, and
    c) what schools should participate in the study.

At which of these points should randomization be employed? Would any of the other methods of control be appropriate at any of these points, and why? At which points would lack of researcher control present a serious threat to the internal validity of the design? Why?

6. What is the major distinction between the internal and external validity of research designs?

16

The Investigation of Causal Questions with True Experimental Designs: Research Studies

DUNAGIN'S PEOPLE

DUNAGIN'S PEOPLE BY RALPH DUNAGIN, COURTESY OF FIELD NEWSPAPER SYNDICATE

"SURE OUR DRUG PRICES ARE HIGH, KID... BUT YOU GOTTA CONSIDER WHAT WE HAVE TO SPEND ON RESEARCH."

Research designs used to investigate causal questions fall into one of four categories: true experimental designs, quasi-experimental designs, preexperiments, and association studies that have a causal purpose. *These designs fall along a continuum from high control over both the independent and extraneous variables to little or no control over these variables.* In order to determine how to classify a particular study as one of these four types, answer the following series of questions.

Was at least one independent variable imposed by the researcher?

If *no,* then it is an *association study that has a causal purpose,* since all the independent variables are inherent (e.g., explanatory survey, ex post facto study, path analytic study).

If *yes,* then the study is a *form of experimentation.* Were the subjects (or the experimental unit used in the statistical analysis) randomly assigned to the experimental conditions; or if each subject (experimental unit) was exposed to each condition, was the order of exposure random for each subject?

If *yes,* then a *true experiment* exists.

If *no,* were controls such as a series of pretests and posttests, comparison groups that were examined for initial equivalence, matching of subjects, repeated observation of subjects, etc. employed?

If *yes,* then the study is probably a *quasi-experiment.*

If *no,* then it is a *preexperiment* with little or no experimental control.

This chapter focuses on true experimental designs only. The following chapter discusses the three other approaches to the study of causal questions.

Designs with the highest degree of control are referred to as true experimental designs. Researchers control the experimental stimuli (that is, who is exposed to what stimuli and when each individual is exposed) and they control the data collection procedures (who gets what measurements and when an individual is measured). Ideally, researchers have *full* experimental control. In addition to the previously cited *requirements* that *at least one independent variable be imposed by researchers and that subjects be randomly assigned to experimental conditions* (or equivalently, that experimental conditions be randomized across all subjects), such designs also require that *at least two variations* (conditions or levels) *of the independent variable be compared and that measures of the dependent variable occur after the independent variable has been administered.*

16.1 TWO BASIC EXPERIMENTAL DESIGNS

The general form of a true experimental design can be represented as follows:

$$\boxed{R} \quad \begin{matrix} A_1 & O \\ \\ A_2 & O \end{matrix} \qquad \text{Design 1}$$

where $\boxed{R}$ represents random assignment of subjects, "A" represents the independent variable with the subscripts indicating the two variations/conditions, and "O" represents observation of the dependent variable. Subjects are randomly assigned to one of two experimental conditions, and then tested on the dependent variable at the conclusion of the study. The two levels of the independent variable could correspond to the simple dichotomy of the presence vs. absence (A_1 vs. not-A_1) of the causal factor (e.g., drug presence vs. drug absence), to two quantities or strengths of the causal factor (e.g., 5 mg. vs. 20 mg. of a drug), or to two distinct conditions (e.g., computer-assisted instruction vs. lecture-discussion). Given full experimental control over extraneous factors, any differences between the two experimental conditions on the dependent variable can then be attributed to the causal factor. This design has been called the experimental-control group/randomized subjects design (92) or the posttest only control group design (27).

The other basic design includes a fourth component, a component that is not required but is quite common in educational research, that of the administration of a pretest. This design can be diagrammed as follows

$$\boxed{R} \quad \begin{array}{ccc} O & A_1 & O \\ \\ O & A_2 & O \end{array} \qquad \text{Design 2}$$

and is called the pretest-posttest control group design (27) or the before and after control group design (92). This design requires that the pretest be administered *before* the initiation of the experimental treatments.

It is important to understand why *administration of a pretest is not a design requirement*. The randomization process assures the initial equivalence of the comparison groups, especially with large sample sizes. Using a pretest to check on this equivalence is redundant and reflects a basic misunderstanding of the randomization process. Randomization ensures the equivalence, except for chance fluctuations, on any variable imaginable, while pretests can be made on only a few variables.

This is not to say that pretests should never be given, for the researcher may have valid reasons for including this dimension. For example, in a longitudinal study it may be important to document the initial level of key variables in order to examine the direction and rate of change. In Design 1 the key question is whether subjects exposed to the experimental conditions *differ* on the posttest, since randomization allows us to assume they were initially equivalent. Therefore any final differences also imply a change from the initial to final position. Design 2 enables the researcher to document the *amount* of that change and its *direction* (assuming the pretests and posttests are measures of the same variable). When this information is important, pretests are used.

Pretests do have disadvantages. They are associated with the threats of pretesting and sensitization to treatment (discussed in Chapter 15), and create problems in data analysis. Analysis of the difference between pretest and posttest scores (i.e., change) is undesirable since such scores are usually unreliable (usually less reliable than the scores from which they were calculated). Since there is no consensus on how difference scores should be treated, you will encounter many different types of analyses of such scores in research studies.

16.2 VARIATIONS OF THE BASIC DESIGNS

Most educational experiments are more complicated than the two-condition comparison in the designs above. Elaboration of these basic models involve:

1. comparison of more than two levels or variations in the independent variable,
2. inclusion of more than one independent variable,
3. administration of pretests to only some of the subjects, and
4. administration of posttests at more than one time period.

An example of each of these variations is given in Fig. 16.1. The first two design variations are the most common in educational research and are discussed in more detail in the following sections.

16.2.1 NUMBER OF LEVELS OR VARIATIONS IN THE INDEPENDENT VARIABLE

EXAMINING THE VARIATIONS IN THE INDEPENDENT VARIABLE

When the independent variable involves more than two levels, then the researcher compares more than the presence and absence of the causal factor.

$$\boxed{R} \quad \begin{matrix} A_1 & O \\ A_2 & O \\ A_3 & O \\ A_4 & O \\ A_5 & O \end{matrix}$$

Variation 1. Extension of Design 1 to include more than two variations in the independent variable (e.g., 5 variations).

$$\boxed{R} \quad \begin{matrix} A_1 & B_1 & O \\ A_1 & B_2 & O \\ A_2 & B_1 & O \\ A_2 & B_2 & O \end{matrix}$$

Variation 2. Extension of Design 1 to include more than one independent variable. Two variables, A and B, each with two variations, create four experimental conditions.

$$\boxed{R} \quad \begin{matrix} O & A_1 & O \\ & A_1 & O \\ O & A_2 & O \\ & A_2 & O \end{matrix}$$

Variation 3. Combination of Designs 1 and 2 where pretest is given to half the subjects in each experimental condition. Allows for examination of pretesting effects. Is commonly called the Solomon four-group design.

$$\boxed{R} \quad \begin{matrix} A_1 & O & \\ A_1 & & O \\ A_2 & O & \\ A_2 & & O \end{matrix}$$

Variation 4. Extension of Design 1 to include measures of the dependent variable at more than one point in time (immediate and delayed posttests).

FIG. 16.1 Four variations of experimental Designs 1 and 2.

A careful analysis of the exact nature of these variations is central to comprehending and evaluating the entire research report.

The design used by Ryan (123) was a variation of Design 1, in which three experimental conditions were compared and both immediate and delayed tests were given. The independent variable was the cognitive level of teachers' questions in class. The low question condition (LQ) involved lessons written so that 95 percent of the questions asked by the teacher were at the recall or memory level. The high question condition (HQ) involved lessons written so that 75 percent of the teachers' questions required more than memorization. Both of these conditions involved nine daily lessons on a geographical theme covering the reading and interpretation of aerial photographs and the application of the photographs to problems of land use. The control group (C) had nine lessons on South America and no attempt was made to control the level of teacher questions. Posttests on the aerial photography lessons with items at both the high and low levels of achievement were administered to all subjects immediately following the instructional period as well as two weeks later.

Although Ryan did not state any research hypotheses, what hypotheses could be tested with this design? *What role was served by each experimental condition?* Was the control group, as implemented, really necessary to answer the basic question of the effect of different levels of teacher questions upon student achievement?

In reading any experimental study, it is advisable to ask yourself such questions about the design *before proceeding* to the results section. Sometimes a diagram of the design clarifies its correspondence, or lack of correspondence, to the research objectives. *Indicate the conditions that were hypothesized to have an effect upon the dependent variables.* Remember to check these predictions against the actual results. Ask yourself what hypotheses could be tested with the design, irrespective of the author's objectives. *Decide what type of information is needed to verify that the variations in the independent variable were implemented as planned.* Once these steps are taken, you are ready to proceed to the results section.

One of the common statistical techniques you will encounter in the results sections of experimental studies is known as analysis of variance, which is described in more detail in Appendix D. Since it is used to examine differences in means, usually the means on the dependent variables are presented for each experimental condition. You might examine the means before reading the results of the statistical analysis to see if you can predict what, if any, differences occurred between the experimental conditions. Work with the means; graph them; reorganize them to fit your conceptualization of the study and the comparisons that particularly interest you. Ask questions about the author's reporting of the results. *Did he or she report differences that were not significant? Did he or she ignore differences that were significant?* It is important to be an active, not a passive, reader of research results.

Since the researchers have complete access to the data, and you do not, they have an advantage over you in interpreting and explaining the findings. Yet you are still in a position to examine the reasonableness of the researchers' logic and the correspondence between the results of the statistical analysis and the conclusions of the study.

For example, in the Ryan study just discussed, Ryan concluded that the results "suggest that high level questions are more efficient than low level questions for moving students toward low *and* high level understandings" (123, p. 66). This statement implies that the high question condition was significantly higher than the low treatment on both types of tests. However, this was not the case; significant differences occurred only between the two experimental conditions and the control group. If the control group had been omitted from the design, significant results might not have occurred at all.

The researcher must anticipate defects in the design while it is in the planning stages. *Additional control groups and dependent variables are often included for the explicit purpose of examining alternative explanations of the findings.* For example, Rickards and August (115) found it necessary to modify their original explanation of a result, despite the fact that they had correctly predicted it. The new explanation could not have been offered if certain experimental conditions and dependent variables had been omitted from the design. The ability of the researcher to foresee such contingencies depends greatly on his or her experience, objectivity, knowledge, and creativity. A reader must possess some of the same skills if he or she is to effectively evaluate research.

16.2.2 NUMBER OF INDEPENDENT VARIABLES

As the number of independent variables increases, the complexity of the research design also increases and the terminology associated with such designs proliferates. This section is devoted to presenting some of the major concepts associated with these more complex designs.

COMPLETELY CROSSED OR FACTORIAL DESIGNS

TWO INDEPENDENT VARIABLES   The most common design is one that completely crosses the variations or levels of one independent variable with those of the other independent variables; also called a *factorial design.* Consider a design with two independent variables: (1) university teaching method (formal lecture, lecture and discussion, and tutorial) and (2) frequency of testing (weekly, every two weeks [biweekly], and once a month). The dependent variable is the final exam score in the course (the same exam given to all subjects). Ninety students are randomly assigned to the experimental conditions.

Crossing the variable of teaching method with the frequency of testing variable means that weekly, biweekly, and monthly tests must exist in *each* type of teaching method (lecture, lecture/discussion, and tutorial). The complete crossing of the two independent variables, yielding nine experimental conditions, is illustrated in Table 16.1. Going across each row, we find that level B_1 of variable B (weekly testing) exists at all levels of variable A (A_1,

A_2, and A_3), level B_2 exists at all levels of variable A, etc. Conversely, going down each column we find that level A_1 of variable A (formal lecture) exists at each level of variable B (B_1, B_2, and B_3), etc.

Such a design is commonly referred to as a 3×3 factorial (teaching method by frequency of testing) with the "3×3" notation indicating the number of variations or levels of each independent variable. A "2×3" notation indicates one variable with two levels and a second with three levels. A "$2 \times 4 \times 3$" notation indicates one variable with two levels, a second with four levels, and a third with three variations.

With only one independent variable, only one major question can be asked: Did the independent variable produce any differences in the dependent variable? However, when two independent variables, A and B, are employed, three classes of questions can be formulated.

1. *Did independent variable A produce any differences in the dependent variable?* With the present example, this is another way of asking if there was a *main effect* for the teaching method variable. That is, was there a difference in the achievement means for the different instructional methods when all subjects were compared? The answer to this question involves a comparison of the three means corresponding to the lecture (A_1), lecture/discussion (A_2), and tutorial (A_3) conditions.

2. *Did independent variable B produce any differences in the dependent variable?* With the present example, this is another way of asking if there was a *main effect* for the variable of testing frequency. That is, was achievement affected by the frequency of testing variable, as indicated by differences in the average achievement for individuals tested weekly (B_1), biweekly (B_2), and monthly (B_3), irrespective of the teaching method to which the students were exposed?

3. *Did the combination of the two independent variables have a unique effect on the dependent variable?* With the present example, this is another way of asking if there was an *interaction* between the method and testing variables. That is, were the achievement differences produced by the teaching methods

TABLE 16.1 *DIAGRAM OF A COMPLETELY CROSSED OR FACTORIAL DESIGN: A 3×3 FACTORIAL DESIGN (TEACHING METHOD BY FREQUENCY OF TESTING)*

Variable B—Frequency of testing		Variable A—teaching method		
		Formal lecture A_1	Lecture/Discussion A_2	Tutorial A_3
Weekly	B_1	A_1B_1	A_2B_1	A_3B_1
Biweekly	B_2	A_1B_2	A_2B_2	A_3B_2
Monthly	B_3	A_1B_3	A_2B_3	A_3B_3

the same or different for students who were tested weekly, biweekly, and monthly? Or equivalently, were the achievement differences produced by frequency of testing the same or different for students in each of the three instructional methods? If the answer is "different," then an interaction exists. An interaction involves a comparison of the nine cell or combination means (A_1B_1, A_1B_2, etc.).

An examination of the hypothetical data in Table 16.2 will help clarify these questions.

Table 16.2 indicates that the achievement means for the teaching conditions were 50, 60, and 70, with the tutorial condition yielding the highest mean. If we assume that these mean differences were significant, then we can conclude that there was a main effect for the variable of teaching method. Note that these method means were based on *all* subjects in each method. Similarly, a main effect existed for the variable of testing frequency, with weekly testing producing the highest achievement.

Was there an interaction between the two independent variables? Note that the difference between the lecture and lecture/discussion means was 10 points, and the difference between lecture/discussion and tutorial was also 10 points. If this pattern also occurred within *each* of the testing treatments, then there was no interaction. An examination of the weekly, biweekly, and monthly conditions shows that in each the difference between lecture and lecture/discussion was 10 points and the difference between lecture/discussion and tutorial was 10 points. Equivalently the interaction question can be turned around to determine if the overall effect for frequency of testing (10 points between weekly and biweekly; 10 points between biweekly and monthly) held for *each* of the teaching methods. Again the pattern was the same, indicating no interaction. In other words, the combination of the independent variables did not produce a unique result. The means for the method-testing combinations were completely accounted for by the main effects of each variable.

TABLE 16.2   *ACHIEVEMENT MEANS FOR EACH CONDITION OF THE TEACHING METHOD AND FREQUENCY OF TESTING VARIABLES AND FOR THE NINE METHOD AND TESTING COMBINATIONS*

Variable B—Frequency of testing		Variable A—teaching method		
		Formal lecture $A_1 = 50$	*Lecture/Discussion* $A_2 = 60$	*Tutorial* $A_3 = 70$
Weekly	$B_1 = 70$	60	70	80
Biweekly	$B_2 = 60$	50	60	70
Monthly	$B_3 = 50$	40	50	60

The means for the nine treatment conditions are graphed in Fig. 16.2. Note that the set of lines connecting adjacent points are parallel, indicating no interaction.

In Fig. 16.3 three other possible outcomes are presented. In Fig. 16.3(a), the overall means for each independent variable are identical to those in the preceding example in Table 16.2 and Fig. 16.2. However, an interaction among the cell means occurred in Fig. 16.3(a). The overall differences between teaching methods were repeated only for the biweekly testing condition. For monthly testing, the method means were identical and the means for the weekly condition showed larger differences between the instructional methods. Thus the combination of the independent variables had a unique effect; one that could not be accounted for by the main effect of each variable.

In Fig. 16.3(b), no significant main effects occurred, but an interaction existed. In Fig. 16.3(c), teaching methods did not differ, but testing frequency did have an effect upon achievement. Again, an interaction occurred. The diversity in interaction patterns for these three cases is illustrated by the graphs.

These examples illustrate that various combinations of main effects and interactions can exist. The interpretation of a main effect is complicated when there is also an interaction involving that independent variable. In Fig. 16.3(c), the main effect of testing frequency indicated that achievement was highest with weekly testing, followed by biweekly and then monthly testing, with a ten-point difference between each condition. However, a general conclusion to this effect is misleading since the interaction indicated that this particular ordering and degree of discrepancy in means did not hold for all the teaching methods.

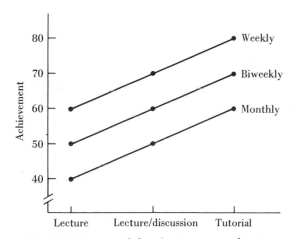

FIG. 16.2 Diagram of the means corresponding to the nine method-testing conditions in Table 16.1, illustrating no interaction between the two variables of teaching method and testing frequency.

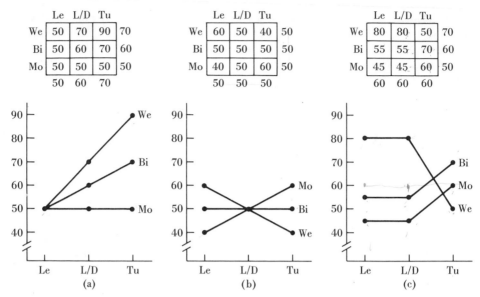

FIG. 16.3 Three other possible outcomes of the teaching method/testing frequency study: (a) Main effects for teaching method and frequency of testing; interaction between method and teaching. (b) No main effects for either teaching method or teaching frequency; interaction between method and teaching. (c) No main effect for teaching method; main effect for testing frequency; interaction between method and teaching.

APTITUDE-TREATMENT INTERACTIONS   A type of interaction particularly relevant to educators is an interaction between instructional methods and individual characteristics, called aptitude-treatment interactions. When educators make the general statement that no single instructional treament is best for all types of students, they are referring to such interactions.

THREE OR MORE INDEPENDENT VARIABLES   The general procedure described for designs with two independent variables can be generalized to designs with more than two variables. The dimensions of student ability (e.g., 3 levels) and sex could be added to the previous design factors of teaching method and testing frequency. The design would then be a $3 \times 3 \times 3 \times 2$ factorial (method by testing by ability by sex), yielding 54 combinations as opposed to the original nine.

Suppose only the ability variable were added to the design, with subjects within each ability level being randomly assigned to the nine method-testing conditions. Now seven questions can be asked of the data. Three questions refer to the main effects for teaching method, for testing frequency, and for ability. Three questions refer to two-way interactions between method and testing, between method and ability, and between testing and ability. Finally, there is the question of a three-way interaction among the three factors of method, testing, and ability.

If the fourth variable of sex were added to the design, then the number of possible effects increases again. There is an additional possible main effect corresponding to the factor of sex; three additional two-variable interactions involving the sex factor; three additional three-variable interactions; and one four-variable interaction. You should be able to list all of the possible effects associated with this four-variable design.

Increasing the number of independent variables allows the researcher to examine their combined effects, which could not be done if the effects of each individual variable were investigated separately. One drawback is that the results may be more difficult to interpret, especially interactions involving three or more variables.

Designs Involving Between-Subjects and Within-Subjects Variables

The designs discussed so far have involved random assignment of subjects to experimental conditions. Comparisons of the experimental conditions were based on *different groups of individuals;* that is, were between-subjects comparisons. In other designs, the *same subjects* may be exposed to all variations in the independent variable. Experimental comparisons then involve the same individuals; that is, are within-subjects contrasts. Sometimes the within-subjects factor is called a repeated measures factor. A design can include any combination of within- and between-subjects comparisons. When researchers test each subject twice (e.g., an immediate and a delayed posttest), the variable of time is a within-subjects factor since the time comparisons involve the same individuals. In Erber and McMahan's (45) study of lip reading, deaf children were exposed to all variations of three independent variables: animate and inanimate nouns, word context (in sentence and in isolation), and placement of a noun in a sentence (initial, medial, and final positions). Thus all independent variables involved within-subjects contrasts in this particular study.

16.3 NUMBER OF DEPENDENT VARIABLES

Typically, educational researchers examine more than one dependent variable, and conduct separate analyses on each. Inferences may then be drawn about the number of different effects or changes produced by the independent variable. However, the reader must keep in mind that some of the dependent variables may not be distinct, and that the researcher may be repeatedly analyzing the same construct disguised by different labels. Researchers guard against such misinterpretations by presenting data on the intercorrelations among the dependent variables and/or by employing statistical techniques that simultaneously consider all the dependent variables.

Criterion variables can be used for different purposes: as a measure of the primary effects of the independent variable, to aid in the interpretation of crucial effects, to measure side effects, as a check on the effectiveness of experimental controls, as a measure of the degree to which the experimental conditions were successfully implemented, etc. Results on such diverse measures safeguard the researcher against broad, unwarranted generalizations, enhance the understanding of the independent variable, and generate ideas for future research.

The following study by Parent, Forward, Canter, and Mohling is a factorial study that focuses primarily on aptitude-treatment interactions. The study is a good illustration of using past research to develop a rationale and to construct an appropriate design.

Statistical Guide. *Analysis of variance* was used in this study. It is a procedure that can be applied to both one-factor and factorial designs. It provides a statistical *test of the differences in dependent variable means for each design factor and a test for interactions among the factors as well.* An *F ratio* is computed that compares the variation in the dependent variable that is associated with a particular design factor to the variation that cannot be accounted for by factors in the design. If this *F* ratio is significant at a preset value of alpha, then differences exist among the means on the factor being examined. If this *F* ratio is not significant, then there are no differences among the means.

Parent et al. used analysis of variance to check the effectiveness of their experimental manipulation of the high and low discipline conditions (one-factor analysis of variance, paragraph 26 and Table 16.3); to examine the effects of the factors of discipline and locus of control (2×2 analysis of variance, paragraph 27 and Table 16.4); and to examine the effects of the discipline and student choice of discipline factors (2×2 analysis of variance, paragraph 28 and Table 16.5). Table 16.3 indicates that the discipline conditions were compared on eight dimensions (i.e., dependent variables). An *F* ratio was computed for each dimension and examined for significance. The level of significance for each *F* ratio was indicated in the table by an asterisk ($*$) and a dagger ($\dagger$). Three *F* ratios were presented in the footnote to Table 16.4; one corresponding to the test for a main effect for the locus of control factor; one to the test for a main effect for the discipline factor; and one to the test for an interaction between the two factors. The numbers in parentheses following the letter "*F*" refer to the degrees of freedom for the test; the notation "ns" indicates "not significant." A similar procedure was followed in Table 16.5.

Interactive Effects of Teaching Strategy and Personal Locus of Control on Student Performance and Satisfaction
JOSEPH PARENT, JOHN FORWARD,
RACHELLE CANTER, AND JUDITH MOHLING

[1] Research on the effects of different teaching strategies on student performances and satisfactions has most often examined two contrasting conditions.

Joseph Parent, John Forward, Rachelle Canter, and Judith Mohling, 1975. Interactive effects of teaching strategy and personal locus of control on student performance and satisfaction. *Journal of Educational Psychology* 67(6): 764–769. Copyright 1976 by the American Psychological Association. Reprinted with permission.

The first condition, labeled high discipline in the present study, is derived from the behavioristic tradition (May, 1965; Skinner, 1953; Watson, 1924) and typically involves high teacher or machine control over both the transmission of information and conditions of learning in the classroom.

[2] The second condition, low discipline, has most often been justified in the conceptual terms of the so-called radical education theorists (Goodman, 1962; Neill, 1960; Rogers, 1969) and has been typified by a low degree of teacher control and a high degree of freedom for the student to select materials and to structure his or her own learning experience.

[3] Reviews by McKeachie (1963) and Stern (1963) of early research on the differential effects of these conditions on student performance revealed generally mixed and disappointing results. For example, Stern found only 7 studies out of the 34 reviewed that demonstrated significant performance effects as a function of discipline condition (5 studies in one direction and 2 in the opposite direction). More significant effects were discovered for student satisfaction (5 in favor of high discipline and 8 favoring low discipline) but again the mixed directionality of the findings was puzzling (Stern, 1963).

[4] In concluding his review, Stern cited three possible sources to account for differences across studies: variations in the operationalization of high and low discipline conditions, uncontrolled interactions between student and teacher characteristics, and differences in performance tasks and achievement criteria used in the studies. Other uncontrolled factors that may have contributed to the mixed results were variations in design (experimental vs. naturalistic), lack of control over initial levels of student competence on the tasks used, and failure to account for possible interactions between student preferences for conditions and student performances and satisfactions.

[5] The most notable area of progress in subsequent research has been the systematic investigation of teacher–student characteristics and their joint effects on performances and satisfactions (cf. Harvey 1970; Harvey, Prather, White, and Hoffmeister, 1968; Mann, Arnold, Binder, Cytrynbaum, Newman, Ringwald, Ringwald, and Rosenwein, 1970; McKeachie, 1967). The present study continues in this tradition by examining the interactive effects of class discipline condition and students' subjective level of internal–external control, as well as systematically attempting to vary or control for the other factors mentioned above.

[6] The theoretical basis of the current study is the "transfer-of-control" paradigm developed by Forward and his colleagues (Forward, Wells, Canter, Parent, Waggoner, and Mohling, 1973). This approach differs from previous thinking in that it takes account not only of the relative "fit" between student characteristics and teaching method in determining student performance, but also incorporates some of the more dynamic aspects of the learning process. For example, most students in beginning a course of study possess relatively low levels of competence in the subject and benefit most from a fairly high level of external discipline. As the student progresses and gains in competence and skills, less and less teacher control should be required for optimal performance. [A continued high level of discipline] may, in fact, become detrimental to performance. The major schools of thought on the debate over the effects of high and low discipline conditions have tended to neglect such simple dynamic aspects of the problem.

[7] One further dynamic aspect of particular interest in the current study is change over time in the student's ability to adopt an active, problem-solving approach to learning as opposed to a passive information-processing mode. This might be conceptualized as a growth process whereby the student gradually moves from dependence on external forms of discipline or structure in learning to the use of more internalized strategies and forms of discipline. Obviously, a concurrent reduction in external forms of discipline over time is necessary in order for the student to maximize performances and satisfactions.

[8] At present, the dynamic variables of change in competence and internalization of discipline are conceived to be independent and additive factors: the former being task or topic specific and the latter being dependent on relatively long-term maturational processes. In the current study, initial level of task competence is controlled for and degree of internalized discipline is varied. In terms of optimal performance conditions in the transfer-of-control paradigm, an interaction is expected between level of internalized discipline and degree of external class discipline, that is, students low on internalized discipline perform better under high external discipline conditions and students high on internal discipline perform better under conditions of low external discipline.

Three independent variables were cited by Parent and his colleagues: degree of classroom discipline, individual's internalized sense of self-discipline or control, and individual's competence for a specific task. The authors chose not to investigate the latter, but controlled it instead. An interaction between the other two variables on the dependent variable of performance was hypothesized. Draw a rough sketch of this predicted result.

[9] Level of internalized discipline is operationalized by the use of the personal control subscale of the Internal–External Locus of Control Scale developed by Rotter (1966) and his colleagues. Several studies using the overall scale have found it to be multifactorial (Forward and Williams, 1970; Gurin, Gurin, Lao, and Beattie, 1969). The personal control subscale seems to measure most closely the individual disposition to attribute the consequences of actions to internal or external sources. However, some previous experimental research using the total scale has been able to provide background support for the predictions made above.

[10] Pines (1973) and Pines and Julian (1972) have shown that persons who score high on internal control are more active information processors and are better able to use previous information in decision-making tasks than are high external persons. These behaviors seem to be ones that should discriminate persons high or low on internalized discipline. In addition, a series of studies have indicated support for the congruence hypothesis stated above (Houston, 1972; Rotter and Mulry, 1965; Watson and Baumal, 1967). However, the nature of the conditions of objective "external" control (time allowed for decision, expectation for future control over shock) and the type of performances used (reaction and decision times, errors in counting digits backward) makes the generality of these results to classroom performance situations an open empirical question. In the present study, an attempt is made to create discipline conditions and per-

formance tasks that are much more ecologically representative (Brunswik, 1956) than the typical experimental situation.

[11] In operationalizing discipline conditions (objective conditions of external control) the present study uses an empirical rather than the typical *a priori* approach. Several hundred students in an introductory level college course were asked to supply open-ended descriptions of the most and least disciplined classes they had ever taken. Coding of the most frequently mentioned responses produced eight dimensions that discriminated high and low perceived discipline. In order of frequency, these were as follows: (a) amount of work assigned, (b) difficulty level of work, (c) amount of class structure, (d) strictness of teacher, (e) work pace, (f) pressure to perform, (g) formality of teacher, and (h) clarity of explanation of material. These dimensions were used as a basis for constructing the discipline conditions used in the study.

[12] Perhaps one of the most difficult problems facing past research studies has been finding performance tasks that were sufficiently controlled and yet at the same time representative of classroom behaviors. On the one hand, some researchers have obtained high representativeness but low experimental control by comparing "natural" classrooms or courses that differed in amount of structure (McKeachie, 1963). On the other hand, as noted above, highly controlled experimentation has tended to use tasks that are only remotely related to classroom performances. The present study seeks a middle ground through the use of a controlled "miniature-course" of two hours length within an experimental design. In this way, the advantages of experimental control and mundane realism can be combined.

Paragraphs 9–12 indicated that only the class discipline variable was imposed (manipulated) by the researcher. The internalized control (I-E) variable was inherent in the subjects. Use of student response to determine the characteristics of a disciplined college classroom was a unique and valuable contribution to the design. The authors wanted to construct experimental conditions that would maximize the external validity of the design and yet maintain a high degree of internal validity or control.

[13] One final variable of interest in the present study is student preference for discipline condition. Especially in the random assignment of subjects to conditions in experiments, the effects of condition on performances and satisfactions may be confounded by whether students obtain their preferred condition. While not a major *a priori* experimental manipulation in the present study, student preferences for high or low discipline learning conditions were obtained by pretesting several weeks prior to the experiment and the effects of preference on the main dependent variables were assessed.

[14] The main expectation concerning the effects of student choice is that choice–condition congruence and incongruence would have a greater effect on student satisfactions than on performances. Part of the rationale for this prediction comes from the results of past studies in which student satisfactions with performances have not matched actual levels of performance (cf. Stern, 1963). Another reason is that in many experiments, satisfaction measures are usually

obtained after performance feedback has been given thereby confounding satisfaction with the learning situation and specific performance-based satisfactions.

[15] In the present study, satisfaction measures were obtained *before* performance feedback and therefore are a more direct index of student reaction to the discipline condition itself. Congruence between student preference for type of teaching method and actually obtaining it may be a common source of satisfaction or dissatisfaction since students cannot always choose the types of courses they must take.

[16] To summarize the hypotheses, two different factors are expected to determine student performances and satisfactions, respectively, under two conditions of external discipline. For performance, students scoring low on internal locus of personal control are expected to perform better under high rather than low class discipline. For satisfaction (measures), students in discipline conditions that are congruent with their preferences of discipline would be more satisfied with the experience than those in preference–incongruent conditions.

The authors introduced another inherent independent variable, student preference for high or low disciplined classrooms, that they predicted would interact with the actual level of classroom discipline on the dependent variable of student satisfaction with the course. Diagram this anticipated result.

METHOD

[17] The design of the experiment is a $2 \times 2 \times 2$ factorial with two levels of external class discipline, two levels of locus of control, and a choice/no-choice condition. For the purposes of analysis, this is decomposed into two 2×2 analyses of variance to test the two hypotheses concerning performance and satisfaction effects, respectively. These are specific tests of hypotheses as recommended by Winer (1962) where only the predicted interactions are tested and where nonpredicted interaction terms are absorbed as within-subjects error. This procedure also helps reduce the possibility of Type 1 errors in multiple F test designs.

Subjects

[18] A pretest instrument containing (a) the total Internal–External Control Scale (Rotter, 1966), (b) the question asking for descriptions of most and least disciplined classes, (c) preferences for type of class discipline for a course in computer programming, (d) level of competence in computer programming, and (e) grade point average was administered to approximately 700 students in an Introductory Psychology class at the University of Colorado. Seven weeks later, students meeting the following criteria were invited to participate in the experiment: no previous computer programming experience and a grade point average of B.

[19] From this group, students were randomly assigned to either the high or low class discipline condition on the basis of scores on the personal control subscale of the Internal–External Locus of Control measure. At the same time, students were assigned so that approximately equal proportions of preference–

congruent and preference–incongruent students occupied each of the cells in the design. No significant difference existed for relative proportions of males and females across conditions. Of the 72 assigned subjects, 9 were lost by attrition, 7 by absenteeism, and 2 by leaving the experiment.

Class Discipline Conditions

[20] The high and low class discipline conditions were based on the empirical dimensions extracted from student descriptions of actual high and low discipline classes obtained on the pretest. Since we were interested in comparing perfor- mance differences between conditions, three of these dimensions—perceived task *controlled* difficulty, amount of work, and clarity of explanations—were equalized rather than varied across conditions. The remaining dimensions constituted the basis for creating the discipline conditions.

[21] In the high discipline condition, the teacher laid down rules concerning not talking in class, not smoking, and not leaving the room without permission (strictness). Also, the teacher went through each step to be learned at a fairly rapid pace and administered brief tests at regular intervals (structure, pressure, pace). The conduct of the teacher was formal and aloof (formality).

[22] In the low discipline condition, students were handed booklets of all ma- terial and quizzes used in the other condition and told to work at their own pace and on their own time. The teacher relaxed at the desk, went to answer questions, and generally displayed a great deal of informality. There were no rules concerning smoking, talking, or leaving the room (two subjects in this con- dition left the room and did not return). The same person taught both the high and low discipline conditions thus controlling for possible differences in teacher personality.

Experimental Task

[23] In order to develop a task that was both representative of college level educational tasks and at the same time permitted some degree of control over the conditions of learning and performance testing, a short two-hour course in computer programming was devised. Initial level of student competence was controlled by selecting students on the basis of responses to this question on the pretest.

Procedures

[24] In both conditions, the task was introduced with some remarks about the importance of computers in the modern world and the necessity for some mini- mal knowledge of programming. In the high discipline condition, the class rules were laid down and the teacher began to guide the class through the program- ming material and quizzes. In the low discipline condition, students were given booklets that contained the same material as in the high condition and which included quizzes and answers to them. They were told to work on their own time. The teacher answered questions and helped with problems.

[25] For both conditions, performance was assessed by a 30-minute "final exam" in which a few questions were asked and a miniature program had to be written.

Preceding the exam, a postexperimental questionnaire assessing interest and satisfaction with the class and perceptions of discipline was completed by the students.

The $2 \times 2 \times 2$ factorial design can be diagrammed

$$
\begin{array}{llll}
A_1 & B_1 & C_1 & O \\
A_1 & B_1 & C_2 & O \\
A_1 & B_2 & C_1 & O \\
A_1 & B_2 & C_2 & O \\
A_2 & B_1 & C_1 & O \\
A_2 & B_1 & C_2 & O \\
A_2 & B_2 & C_1 & O \\
A_2 & B_2 & C_2 & O
\end{array}
$$

$\boxed{R}$

where A represents the classroom discipline condition, B represents the internal-external variable, and C represents the preference measure. Strictly speaking, the $\boxed{R}$ applies only to the manipulated A_1 and A_2 conditions, not to the eight ABC combinations. The description of the randomization process indicated that the different types of students represented by the B and C variables were evenly distributed across the experimental conditions, since only the discipline condition was imposed by the researchers. The variable of competency was controlled by including only students with no previous computer programming experience and who had a GPA of B (paragraphs 18 and 19).

The authors varied only the noncontent aspects of the discipline variable in order to control for the factors that were closely tied to student achievement (paragraphs 20–22). It is this modified definition of high and low classroom discipline that must be used in interpreting the results rather than the definition outlined in paragraph 11.

Measures of the dependent variables of achievement and satisfaction were cited in paragraph 24 as well as measures of student perceptions of classroom discipline. Information on the nature of these measures was inadequate. No reliability or validity data were presented, and there was no information on the form or content of the items.

Before reading the results of an experimental study, it is wise to consider variables which might reduce experimental control and might hinder the generalization of results; that is, the threats to internal and external validity presented in Tables 15.1 and 15.2. An examination of some of the threats to internal validity indicates the following:

1. Differential selection: Not a threat. Subjects were randomly assigned to experimental conditions.

2. Statistical regression: Not a threat, since extreme groups were not selected.

3. Maturation: Not a threat. The variable of time should equally affect all groups.

4. Experimental mortality: Possible threat. Eighteen subjects were lost and no

mention was made regarding whether an equal number of subjects was lost from each treatment or whether they were different in any way from the subjects that were retained.

You should be able to complete the review of the seven other threats to internal validity.

An examination of some of the threats to external validity indicates the following:

1. Accessible vs. target population: As mentioned previously the accessible population was restricted in order to control for the variable of competence. It is difficult to determine the appropriate target population, but given the manner in which the sample was selected, generalizations should be made with caution. The manner of subject selection illustrates how controls that increase the internal validity of the design sometimes reduce its external validity.

2. Interaction of personological variables and treatment: Investigation of such effects was the focus of the study itself.

3. Description of independent variable: Description was good. The questionnaire on student perception of discipline provided additional information on the experimental conditions.

4. Hawthorne effect: A possible threat to generalization since students were aware of their participation in a study.

You should be able to complete the review of the eight other threats to external validity. After checking all internal and external validity threats, how would you rate the study on both control and generalization?

RESULTS

[26] A check on the effectiveness of the experimental manipulation (see Table 16.3) showed significant differences between conditions on all the discipline dimensions that were varied. Two of the three dimensions which we hoped to control for across conditions (perceived difficulty and clarity of explanation) showed no differences but the third, work load, was perceived to be greater under the high discipline condition. This may be due to the rules imposed that students had to take notes and complete the quizzes in this condition.

Parent et al. not only checked for expected differences in the experimental conditions but also the expected similarities. The results in Table 16.3 indicated that the manipulation of the treatments was successful. The one unexpected discrepancy on the work load measure was relatively small. The importance of this verification procedure should not be overlooked for it gives the reader confidence that the presumed cause was actually created by the researcher.

[27] The first hypothesis predicted an interaction effect such that students scoring high on internal control would perform better under the low discipline con-

TABLE 16.3   *DIFFERENCES IN MEAN PERCEIVED LEVEL OF DISCIPLINE BETWEEN CONDITIONS*

Dimension	High discipline (*max: 5*)	Low discipline (*Min: 1*)	F (df $= 1,61$)
Strictness	3.8	1.4	99.9†
Structure	4.6	3.0	43.3†
Pace	3.7	1.8	41.0†
Pressure	2.9	1.6	22.9†
Formality	4.2	1.4	158.5†
Controls			
Difficulty	2.4	2.7	1.8
Work load	2.9	2.3	4.3*
Clarity	4.2	4.0	.6

* $p < .05$.
† $p < .001$.

dition and students high on external control would perform better in the high discipline condition. Table 16.4 provides support for this hypothesis in the rejection of the null hypothesis at the 5% level of confidence ($F = 4.42$, $p < .05$). The performance measure is the grade on the final test (maximum score 100 minus number of errors). Following Rotter's practice, analysis was performed using only the upper- and lower-third scores for locus of control ($n = 43$).

[28] The second hypothesis was that student satisfaction with the class would be a function of preference congruence rather than the performances shown above. Table 16.5 reveals support for this hypothesis in that those students who were assigned to their preferred discipline condition showed greater satisfaction than those who were not ($F = 4.31$, $p < .05$).

[29] To establish the independence between sources for performance and satisfaction effects, two further analyses were performed. These were the obverse of

TABLE 16.4   *MEAN PERFORMANCE SCORES FOR DISCIPLINE AND PERSONAL LOCUS OF CONTROL*

Personal locus of control	High discipline	Low discipline	Total
High internal			
M	84.0	87.6	85.8
SD	10.0	14.7	12.2
Low internal (high external)			
M	93.0	81.3	87.1
SD	7.7	11.4	9.5
Total			
M	88.5	84.5	
SD	8.8	12.9	

Note. For personal locus of control $F(1,39) = .14$, ns; for discipline $F(1,39) = 1.24$, ns; for the interaction between conditions $F(1, 39) = 4.42$, $p < .05$.

TABLE 16.5 *MEAN SATISFACTION RATINGS*
FOR DISCIPLINE AND CHOICE OF CONDITION

Student choice of discipline	High discipline	Low discipline	Total
High			
M	7.7	7.1	7.4*
SD	1.9	1.9	1.9
Low			
M	6.1	7.9	7.0*
SD	2.6	2.4	2.5
Total			
M	6.9	7.5	
SD	2.3	2.1	

Note. For student choice of discipline condition $F(1, 59) = .46$, ns; for discipline condition $F(1, 59) = 1.91$, ns; for the interaction between conditions $F(1, 59) = 4.31$, $p < .05$. reject null ; say was an interaction
* Corrected mean values, communication with Parent and Forward, 1976.

the two above: Performance across Preference × Discipline and Satisfaction across Locus of Personal Control × Discipline. No significant effects were obtained.

In paragraph 17 the authors stated that two 2×2 analyses of variance were conducted. One involved the two factors of class discipline and internal/external locus of control with performance as the dependent variable. These results were shown in Table 16.4. The footnote to this table indicated that the only significant effect was the interaction between the locus of control and discipline factors. The other analysis of variance involved class discipline and student preference with the dependent variable of satisfaction. These results were shown in Table 16.5. The footnote to this table indicated that only the interaction effect was significant. Although a single $2 \times 2 \times 2$ analysis of variance could have been used, the pros and cons of using this procedure instead of the two separate analyses of variance are beyond the scope of this book.

Graph the two significant interactions on the dependent variables of performance and satisfaction as indicated by the four-cell means cited in Tables 16.4 and 16.5. Do these graphs correspond to those you were requested to draw earlier? If you had to decide whether to use high or low classroom discipline techniques on the basis of the results of this study, which would you use?

Two additional analyses were conducted (paragraph 29). Do you think the authors performed all the necessary analyses? Did they present all of the descriptive information that you wanted to see? In other words, did they answer all of your questions about the results?

DISCUSSION

[30] The present results support one of the hypotheses derived from the transfer-of-control paradigm that optimal student performance would be obtained when there is a complementary fit between students' levels of internalized discipline

and the external conditions of discipline in learning settings. By the use of the personal control subscale of the Rotter I–E scale to operationalize internalized discipline, the present study also extends to educational settings the experimental research that has demonstrated the hypothesis under artificial laboratory conditions.

[31] The study contributes also to the profitable line of research in education that investigates interactions between classroom teaching strategies and student characteristics. It is interesting to note that, as in the earlier research, no main effects were obtained for discipline conditions or student characteristics by themselves (cf. Stern, 1963). In addition, the current interactive effects were obtained under more highly controlled conditions than many previous studies, in that control was achieved over assignment of students to conditions, task requirements, achievement criteria, initial levels of competence, and possible variations in teacher personality. However, this level of control was not achieved at the expense of the external validity and representativeness of the experimental situation as is the case with many experimental studies related to this topic (Fry, 1972; Hoffman and Maier, 1964).

[32] One further contribution of the present study is to provide some clarification of the confusing findings on the relationship between student performances and satisfactions in previous research. Past studies that have failed to find a direct relationship between levels of performance and satisfaction have overlooked a possible confound between satisfaction with the teaching condition itself and satisfaction with performance outcomes. In the present design, these two factors are separated by assessing satisfaction before performance feedback. In this way, the effects of congruence between student preference for and assignment to teaching conditions is shown to be an important contributor to student ratings of satisfaction.

[33] However, though student choices influence their rated satisfactions, they do not seem to affect their levels of performance to any great extent. Performance is shown to be much more a function of the fit between the maturational learning skills represented by the personal control I–E subscale and the external conditions of teaching method or class discipline.

REFERENCE NOTE

1. Forward, J., Wells, K., Canter, S., Parent, J., Waggoner, M., and Mohling, J. *Factors inhibiting transfer of control in educational settings* (Project 10626, OEG-8-71-0019-508). Washington, D.C.: Department of Health, Education and Welfare, Office of Education, 1973.

REFERENCES

Brunswik, E. *Perception and the representative design of psychological experiments.* Berkeley: University of California Press, 1956.

Forward, J. R., and Williams, J. R. Internal–external control and black militancy. *Journal of Social Issues,* 1970, *26,* 75–92.

Fry, J. P. Interactive relationship between inquisitiveness and student control of instruction. *Journal of Educational Psychology,* 1972, *63,* 459–465.

Goodman, P. *Compulsory mis-education.* New York: Vintage Books, 1962.

Gurin, P., Gurin, G., Lao, R., and Beattie, M. Internal–external control in the motivational dynamics of Negro youth. *Journal of Social Issues,* 1969, *25,* 29–54.

Harvey, O. J. Belief systems and education: Some implications for change. In J. Crawford (ed.), *The affective domain.* Washington, D.C. Communication Service Corp. 1970.

Harvey, O. J., Prather, M., White, B., and Hoffmeister, J. Teacher's beliefs, classroom atmosphere and student behavior. *American Educational Research Journal,* 1968, *5,* 151–166.

Hoffman, L. R., and Maier, N. R. Valence in the adoption of solutions by problem-solving groups: Concept, method, and results. *Journal of Abnormal and Social Psychology,* 1964, *69,* 264–271.

Houston, B. K. Control over and response to stress. *Journal of Personality and Social Psychology,* 1972, *21,* 249–255.

Mann, R. D., Arnold, S. M., Binder, J., Cytrynbaum, S., Newman, B. M., Ringwald, B., Ringwald, J., and Rosenwein, R. *The college classroom.* New York: Wiley, 1970.

May, K. O. *Programmed learning and mathematical education.* Washington, D.C.: Mathematical Association of America, 1965.

McKeachie, W. J. Research on teaching at the college and university level. In N. L. Gage (ed.), *Handbook of research on teaching.* Chicago: Rand McNally, 1963.

McKeachie, W. J. Significant student and faculty characteristics relevant to personalizing higher education. In W. J. McKeachie and W. J. Minter (eds.), *The individual and the system: Personalizing higher education.* Berkeley: College and University Self-Study Institute, University of California Press, 1967.

Neill, A. S. *Summerhill.* New York: Hart, 1960.

Pines, H. A. An attributional analysis of locus of control orientation and source of informational dependence. *Journal of Personality and Social Psychology,* 1973, *26,* 262–267.

Pines, H. A., and Julian, J. W. Effects of task and social demands on locus of control differences in information processing. *Journal of Personality,* 1972, *40,* 407–416.

Rogers, C. R. *Freedom to learn.* New York: Merrill, 1969.

Rotter, J. B. Generalized expectancies for internal versus external control of reinforcement. *Psychological Monographs,* 1966, *80* (1, Whole No. 609).

Rotter, J. B., and Mulry, R. Internal versus external control of reinforcement and decision time. *Journal of Personality and Social Psychology,* 1965, *2,* 598–604.

Skinner, B. F. *Science and human behavior.* New York: Macmillan, 1953.

Stern, G. G. Measuring non-cognitive variables in research in teaching. In N. L. Gage (ed.), *Handbook of research on teaching.* Chicago: Rand McNally, 1963.

Watson, D., and Baumal, E. Effects of locus of control and expectations of future control upon current performance. *Journal of Personality and Social Psychology,* 1967, *6,* 212–215.

Watson, J. B. *Behaviorism.* New York: Norton, 1924.

Winer, B. J. *Statistical principles in experimental design.* New York: McGraw-Hill, 1962.

In any application of the results from the Parent et al. study, it is important to remember the operational definition of high and low class discipline. The use of such a common word as discipline with its many connotations can easily lead to inappropriate generalizations. In the discussion section the authors summarized the results and emphasized the advantages of the design rather than making broad causal statements. What causal statements do you think could be made on the basis of the results?

16.4 HOW TO CRITIQUE TRUE EXPERIMENTAL DESIGNS

Exhibit 16.1 summarizes points to examine when evaluating reports of true experimental designs.

EXHIBIT 16.1 *IDENTIFICATION AND CRITIQUE OF TRUE EXPERIMENTAL DESIGNS*

A. To determine whether a true experimental design was employed, review the series of questions cited on the first page of this chapter.

B. A review of the questions in Exhibit 15.1 will provide a fairly extensive analysis of the study. Additional questions to consider are cited below.

C. Diagram the design. This diagram should include the following:

1. The number of independent variables,

2. The number of levels of each independent variable,

3. Whether each independent variable was a between-subjects or a within-subjects factor, and

4. The dependent variables and the time(s) at which they were measured. Determine the function of each independent and dependent variable and whether the design corresponded to the research purposes. Indicate the differences between experimental conditions that were expected by the researcher.

D. Determine whether the research hypotheses were supported by the data. Work with the data to become familiar with it; for example, graph the means, order them from high to low, etc. Did the researcher give a complete presentation of the results or was information on some experimental conditions and dependent variables incomplete?

E. Was the researcher's interpretation of the data in accord with the results? Were significant findings ignored or nonsignificant ones emphasized? Were all the data

considered in any attempt to explain the findings? Can you offer other explanations? *Were the concluding causal statements warranted?*

16.5 LIST OF TRUE EXPERIMENTS

16.5.1 ONE INDEPENDENT VARIABLE

Guralnick, M. J., 1976. Solving complex perceptual discrimination problems:
techniques for the development of problem-solving strategies. *American
Journal of Mental Deficiency* **81**: 18–25.

Madsen, C. K., L. G. Dorow, R. S. Moore, and J. U. Womble, 1976. Effect of
music via television as reinforcement for correct mathematics. *Journal of
Research in Music Education* **24**: 51–59.

Paulson, F. L., 1974. Teaching cooperation on television an evaluation of "Sesame Street" social goals programs. *AV Communication Review* **22**: 229–
246.

Rie, H. E., E. D. Rie, S. Stewart, and J. P. Ambuel, 1976. Effects of ritalin on
underachieving children: a replication. *American Journal of Orthopsychiatry* **46**: 313–322.

Rickards, J. P., and G. J. August, 1975. Generative underlining strategies in
prose recall. *Journal of Educational Psychology* **67**: 680–685.

16.5.2 TWO OR MORE INDEPENDENT VARIABLES

Baker, G. P., and L. M. Raskin, 1973. Sensory integration in the learning dis-
abled. *Journal of Learning Disabilities* **6**: 645–649.

Clifford, M. M., and E. Walster, 1972. The effect of sex on college admission,
work evaluation, and job interviews. *Journal of Experimental Education*
41(2): 1–5.

Dwyer, F. M., 1976. The effect of IQ level on the instructional effectiveness of
black-and-white and color illustrations. *AV Communication Review* **24**:
49–62.

Hutson, B. A., and J. Powers, 1974. Reversing irreversible sentences: semantic
and syntactic factors. *Journal of Reading Behavior* **6**: 99–110.

Sheare, J. B., 1974. Social acceptance of EMR adolescents in integrated programs. *American Journal of Mental Deficiency* **78**: 678–682.

Simons, H. D., and K. R. Johnson, 1974. Black English syntax and reading interference. *Research in the Teaching of English* **8**: 339–358.

STUDY PROBLEMS

1. What are the requirements for a true experimental design?

2. What are some advantages of using more than one independent variable and more than one dependent variable in an experimental design?

3.

	Design 1	*Design 2*
$\boxed{R}$	O A_1 O O A_2 O	$\boxed{R}$ A_1 O A_2 O

Sometimes Design 2 is preferred to Design 1. When is this apt to be the case? Design 1 is often used to determine if the experimental and control groups are really "equal." Is this necessary? Why or why not?

4. The design and results of a study were described as follows:

> Prior to student teaching, one group of student teachers was exposed to lectures and discussions on how to teach and another group was exposed to instruction on the same topics that also involved role play of the principles presented in the course. The following semester the classroom teaching performance of the student teachers was rated on three separate occasions. The study design was a 2×3 factorial (teaching method by time) with the time variable being a within-subjects (repeated measures) factor. The results indicated that although the ratings of the classroom performance of the student teachers exposed to the role-playing instruction were generally superior to the ratings obtained by the student teachers in the lecture/discussion only group, this discrepancy increased with time.

This brief description of the results indicates a significant interaction between the time and method variables. Were there also significant main effects? Graph the results in a manner similar to that in Figs. 16.2 and 16.3.

5. The designs discussed in this chapter have a high degree of control over extraneous variables, i.e., high internal validity. Why are they, on the average, likely to have a low degree of external validity, i.e., generalization beyond the experimental setting is often difficult?

6. Read one of the experimental studies cited at the end of the chapter. Examine the study using the series of questions cited in Exhibit 16.1.

17

The Investigation of Causal Questions with Quasi-experimental Designs, Preexperiments, and Association Studies: Research Studies

The experimental designs discussed in the previous chapter provide the *type of control researchers strive for in any causal study.* However, in some cases true experiments with a high degree of control may be removed a step or so from reality, making generalization beyond the experimental setting very difficult. Or it may be extremely difficult or impossible to conduct experiments with a high degree of control. In such cases, a quasi-experimental design, a pre-experiment, or an association study may be the appropriate approach or the only approach to the research question. Preexperiments and association studies are characterized by minimal or no control over the independent and extraneous variables.

When designing a study of causal questions, researchers must weigh the advantages of having high experimenter control and of being able to generalize their findings to other settings. The final design represents the researchers' compromise between these two goals. In critiquing causal studies, you the reader must decide whether the researchers' choice of design was an appropriate or desirable one. Would the study have been improved by a higher degree of control and/or by more attention to the problems of generalization? Could the researchers have changed their design to resolve these problems?

The designs in this chapter represent alternatives to true experimental designs in situations in which such designs are not appropriate, for whatever reason. It must be stressed that *in terms of identifying "the cause"* (which is the primary purpose of causal studies), *true experiments represent the strongest form of causal study, and preexperiments and association studies represent the weakest form.* Quasi-experiments are discussed first, followed by preexperiments, and then association studies.

17.1 QUASI-EXPERIMENTAL DESIGNS

As was the case with true experiments, *quasi-experimental designs require that at least one independent variable be imposed by the researcher*. However, in contrast with true experimental designs, *only partial control over the extraneous and independent variables can be achieved*. The researcher can usually control when the observations are made, when the independent variable is applied, and/or what group receives which experimental condition. But the researcher usually cannot control how subjects are assigned to experimental conditions, which means that random assignment of subjects is not possible.

Although quasi-experiments have lower internal validity than have true experiments, they often have greater external validity. Two basic types of quasi designs are discussed in this chapter: those using comparison groups as a means of control and those using repeated observations to increase control.

17.1.1 NONEQUIVALENT CONTROL GROUP

When random assignment of subjects to experimental conditions is not possible, the addition of either a matched or a nonequivalent control group aids in the interpretation of results. The more similar all the groups are in the way they are recruited, and the more this similarity is confirmed by the scores on a pretest, then the more effective this type of control becomes (27). This design is diagrammed below, with the dashed lines indicating nonequivalent groups of subjects.

$$O \quad A_1 \quad O$$
$$\text{----------} \qquad \text{Nonequivalent control}$$
$$O \quad A_2 \quad O \qquad \text{group design}$$

There are two distinct versions of this design. In one context researchers have intact or naturally assembled groups available to them (classrooms, elementary schools, housing units). In addition they have free choice in determining which group is exposed to which experimental conditions (the treatments may in fact be randomly assigned to the groups) or at least, the researchers have no reason to believe that different recruitment processes created the two groups. Such contexts may approach true experimentation. On the other hand, the group exposed to the primary treatment may be self-selected, may volunteer, or deliberately seek exposure to the treatment whereas individuals in the control group do not seek exposure. Or the researchers themselves may deliberately seek out subjects for the experimental group who possess certain traits. Studies in counseling, remedial education programs of various types, and self-improvement programs exemplify types of research in which this selection process may occur. This version of the nonequivalent control group design is weaker than the intact group version previously described because of the greater possibility of initial group differences.

In comparison with true experimental designs, differential selection of subjects and its attendant problems are always threats to the internal validity of the nonequivalent control group design. The seriousness of selection biases depends, of course, on the particular study.

As discussed previously, use of pretests to check group equivalence is not as satisfactory a control as randomization. Even though groups may be equivalent initially, they may regress toward different means, a common problem when self-selection has occurred. In addition, the use of pretests raises the possibility of a pretesting effect and an interaction between the pretest and treatment.

However, in comparison with true experiments, use of intact groups may reduce the reactive effects of experimental arrangements, thereby increasing the generalizability of the results. Using existing classrooms in which to implement curricula creates fewer disruptions than making special arrangements for random assignment of subjects to curricula, thereby heightening the subject's awareness of his or her role in an experiment.

17.1.2 TIME-SERIES DESIGNS

Another method of control is to increase the number of observations of the dependent variable made both before and after the introduction of the experimental treatment or the assumed cause. The effect of the independent variable can then be judged by the nature of the change in the dependent variable from before to after the treatment. The simplest form of time-series experiment can be diagrammed as follows:

$$O_1 \ O_2 \ O_3 \ O_4 \ A_1 \ O_5 \ O_6 \ O_7 \ O_8 \qquad \text{Single-group time-series design (temporary treatment)}$$

This diagram indicates that four observations were made prior to the initiation of the treatment followed by four observations after the withdrawal of the treatment. (The choice of four observations was arbitrary.) Such designs provide for examination of the pattern of an effect across time; an important question in the study of educational interventions.

An experimental treatment may affect the dependent variable in different ways. There may be an abrupt and permanent change in the level of the dependent variable; the treatment may change the dependent variable only temporarily; or a stable level of performance on the dependent variable may become unstable. Some possible outcomes are presented in Fig. 17.1.

A major uncontrolled factor in time-series designs is history. Some other specific event or a seasonal fluctuation may occur at approximately the same time as the introduction of the independent variable. Although repeated observations provide a check on maturational changes, such changes may not always be regular and may just happen to correspond with the independent variable. In order to avoid the threat of instrumentation, consistent measures should be

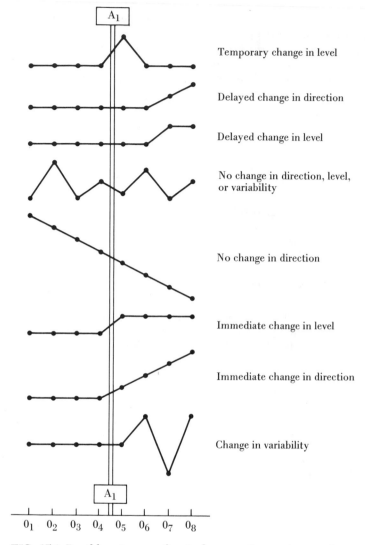

FIG. 17.1 Possible outcomes of a single-group time-series experiment.

obtained on the dependent variable at all time points. If possible, testers and observers should not know when the treatment was introduced.

With the single-group time-series design, selection of subjects per se is not a threat to the internal validity of the study when the same subjects are used at each observation period, since the important comparisons involve changes within the same subjects rather than differences between groups of subjects. On the other hand, when the same subjects are observed repeatedly, the design is more sensitive to a Hawthorne or reactive effect. When the sample is restricted to a few subjects with certain behavior problems, as is the case in many behavior modification or operant conditioning studies, then generalization beyond those particular cases may be difficult (15).

Many variations of the single-group time-series design can be created. One dimension that applies to all time-series designs is the length of the experimental condition. The previous diagram illustrated a temporary treatment that began and terminated between the fourth and fifth observations as opposed to a continuous treatment lasting throughout observations O_5 to O_8. A continuous treatment will be indicated graphically with the notation adopted by Huck, Cormier, and Bounds (80): a continuous line drawn over the O's during which the independent variable is applied. For example, the following diagram indicates that the treatment lasted continuously during the period from O_4 to O_6:

$$O_1 \; O_2 \; O_3 \; A_1 \; \overline{O_4 \; O_5 \; O_6}$$

Other variations of time-series designs involve comparisons of more than one group; introducing more than one variation in the independent variable either simultaneously or at different points in time; and repeatedly introducing the treatment and withdrawing it. A few of these variations are indicated in Fig. 17.2.

Designs that involve a group being exposed to a single treatment more than once, or to more than one treatment followed by testing/observation without the treatment (Variations a, b, and f, Fig. 17.2) usually assume that the treatment effect is reversible, i.e., that when the experimental treatment disappears so does its effect. For example, a man may not smoke if he constantly has another individual at his side preventing him from taking cigarettes, but once that other individual departs he will return to smoking. On the other hand, if the treatment teaches a student to play the trumpet, it is not possible to erase this skill simply by removing the instruction.

Time-series designs can be used with groups or single individuals. In educational research it is common to encounter such designs with small numbers of individuals in behavior modification studies. For example, Walker and Buckley (142) used a single-subject time-series design of the form: $O_1 \; A_1 \; O_2$. The attending behavior of an underachieving nine-year-old boy was first observed to obtain a base rate (O_1); a period of reinforcement for attending was then instituted (A_1); and during the final phase of the study the reinforcement was withdrawn (O_2). A graph of the percentage of attending behavior clearly illustrated changes in behavior from one phase to the next. In another study of attending behavior by Broden, Bruce, Mitchell, Carter, and Hall (21) the following design was employed with a pair of grade two boys: $O_1 \; A_1 \; A_2 \; O_2 \; A_3$. Again, the initial phase constituted obtaining a baseline for attending behavior (O_1); during A_1 the teacher systematically increased the amount of personal attention to one of the boys when he was attending appropriately in class; during A_2 the teacher switched her attention to the other member of the pair; such reinforcement was withdrawn from both boys during O_2; and during A_3 both boys were reinforced with teacher attention.

$$O\ O\ A_1\ O\ O\ A_1\ O\ O$$
(a)

$$O\ O\ A_1\ \overline{O\ O}\ O\ O\ A_1\ \overline{O\ O}\ O\ O$$
(b)

$$O\ O\ A_1\ O\ O\ A_2\ O\ O$$
(c)

$$\begin{array}{c} O\ O\ O\ O\ A_1\ O\ O\ O\ O \\ \hline O\ O\ O\ O\ A_2\ O\ O\ O\ O \end{array}$$
(d)

$$\begin{array}{l} O\ O\ O\ A_1\ O\ O\ O \\ \hline \qquad\qquad\qquad O\ O\ O\ A_2\ O\ O\ O \end{array}$$
(e)

$$\begin{array}{c} O\ O\ O\ A_1\ O\ O\ O\ B_1\ O\ O\ O \\ \hline O\ O\ O\ B_1\ O\ O\ O\ A_1\ O\ O\ O \end{array}$$
(f)

$$O\ O\ A_1\ O\ O\ B_1\ O\ O\ A_1B_1\ O\ O$$
(g)

FIG. 17.2 Variations of the basic time-series design. (a) Single-group, repeated exposure to the same treatment; (b) single-group with two treatment periods, each followed by baseline observation; (c) single-group, multiple levels of A; (d) multiple group, multiple levels of A; (e) Sequential multiple group, multiple levels of A; (f) reversal design, two groups with independent variables, A and B; (g) interaction group, one group with two independent variables, A and B.

17.2 PREEXPERIMENTS

In some cases the researcher may actually impose the presumed cause, but institute minimal or no control over extraneous variables. Such preexperimental designs are to be avoided in studying cause-effect relationships. Causal inferences are not justified, or are extremely tentative at best, with such studies. A better approach is to modify the design to reach the level of control exemplified in quasi-experimental designs.

Three preexperimental designs (27) are described here. A design with virtually no control involves just one group of subjects to which a treatment and posttest are given, the *one-shot case study:* A_1 O. This design provides no comparative data; that is, no before and after measures and no treatment comparisons, which are essential to scientific knowledge. A design that yields before–after comparisons is the *one-group pretest–posttest design:* O A_1 O. It should be obvious that a change from pre to post in this design could be attributed to many factors other than A_1. The pretest does provide a way to check on the type of subjects who drop out of the experiment (mortality) and the type of subjects initially selected, but contributes little additional information for the purpose of causal inference. The third design provides a control group (one not exposed to the experimental treatment) and is called the *static group comparison design:* A_1 O versus not-A_1 O. Since randomization is missing and no pretests exist, this design is much weaker than a true experimental design with randomization (Design 1 in Chapter 16) and the nonequivalent control group design (a quasi design). There is no assurance of equivalent groups nor any means of checking on initial group differences, making selection a major uncontrolled variable.

That such studies are common in social science research was illustrated in a review (91) of process/outcome studies published from 1964 through 1968 in the *Journal of Counseling Psychology.* Of the 73 studies reviewed, 53 percent were judged preexperimental, 23 percent as quasi designs, and 25 percent as true experiments.

17.3 ASSOCIATION STUDIES WITH A CAUSAL PURPOSE

The previous experimental designs required by definition that at least one independent variable be manipulated or imposed by the researcher, and with true and quasi designs, that a substantial degree of control be achieved over extraneous variables. However, for some questions of causation, experiments are not possible and controls are extremely weak. The *independent variable may not be manipulated* because the search may be for the cause of an event that has already occurred. For example, what produced the Legionnaires' disease in Philadelphia during the summer of 1976 or what caused the student riots in the 1960s? Or the presumed cause may be a characteristic of an individual or of a setting that is difficult to modify or create. In other cases it may be unethical to impose a factor that is suspected to have harmful consequences. In many educational contexts the independent variables of interest cannot be modified easily (e.g., parental guidance, teacher personality, and school climate), making association studies the only means of exploring causal relationships. The elimination of rival causal interpretations is made extremely difficult in such contexts by the *lack of direct control over extraneous variables* and by the fact that the *independent variable is inherent* rather than imposed. Such studies are often labeled causal–comparative, explanatory surveys, or ex post facto studies.

When the independent variable is inherent, the researcher has information only on the association or correlation among variables, and it is well known that correlation by itself does not mean causation. With supplementary data, the researcher may be able to infer a causal direction to the relationship. These analyses may proceed from the presumed cause to the effect, or vice versa, from the effect to the presumed cause.

To review the distinctions among the major approaches to causation cited so far, examine the hypothesis that "smoking causes lung cancer." If researchers were to impose or manipulate the independent variable of smoking, as in a true experiment, quasi-experiment, or preexperiment, they would force some subjects to smoke. In a true experiment they would randomly assign subjects to smoking and nonsmoking conditions, and observe the incidence of lung cancer in both groups at the conclusion of the study. However, such procedures are unethical and researchers must treat the independent variable as inherent, making the study one of association. Such an association study could proceed from the presumed cause to the presumed effect. If so, researchers would select a group of subjects who smoke and a group who do not smoke, and then determine the incidence of lung cancer in each. Or researchers could proceed from the effect to the cause. Then they would select subjects who have lung cancer and subjects without lung cancer, and determine the incidence of smokers in each group. Obviously, these two association approaches are not identical and neither are the conclusions that can be drawn from them (65).

Association studies that focus on causal questions can involve: (1) those in which the independent variable or the presumed cause has already produced the effect, and the researchers begin their investigation after "everything" has transpired, (2) those in which the independent variable exists at the initiation of the study, but the researchers do not have any control over it, and (3) those in which researchers initiate the study prior to the existence of the independent variable, but still do not have control over it. Of the three approaches, the last provides the greatest opportunity for control over extraneous variables, although the problems of self-selection of individuals into the groups being compared and of no direct control over the independent variable are common to all approaches.

Fry (51) initiated his study prior to the occurrence of the independent variable. He hypothesized that college graduates who entered employment immediately after graduation would become less negative toward authority figures due to exposure to the occupational world, while those who went on to graduate school would show little decline in their critical attitudes toward authority. Since Fry obtained his subjects during their senior year in college in order to follow them up a year later, he initiated his study prior to the occurrence of the independent variable (i.e., employment vs. graduate school) although he had no control over who entered the work force and who enrolled in graduate school. Yet this approach did allow him to obtain premeasures of attitudes toward authority and to select appropriate curricula to study. Another approach to the same problem would have been to compare a sample of graduate students with a sample of employed college graduates of the same age, thus starting the study while the independent variable is in operation. However, this approach eliminates the opportunity to obtain preattitude measures and to control (or select) the undergraduate curricula. Examples of association studies that were begun after the fact are some of the early follow-up studies of Head Start that were initiated several years after children had been exposed to a three- or six-month Head Start program.

17.3.1 TIME RELATIONSHIP BETWEEN PRESUMED CAUSE AND EFFECT

One of the conditions necessary for causal inference mentioned at the beginning of Chapter 15 was that the *presumed cause occur prior to the presumed effect*. In an experiment this time relationship is enforced since researchers create the independent variable before observing the dependent. However, when the researchers do not control the independent variable, this time relationship may blur, evolving into the chicken and egg question of which came first. When researchers make causal claims, they assume, either explicitly or implicitly, that the dependent variable they are investigating follows the independent variable. This time relationship is particularly important in regard to the various modes of causal analysis that have been developed in sociology.

Time refers to the points at which the independent and dependent variables actually occur, not to when they were measured in the study. For instance, researchers may hypothesize that educational attainment of individuals is a major determinant of their annual income. In order to make causal inferences, they must show that the presumed cause of educational attainment occurs prior to the presumed effect of income, although they may measure both variables simultaneously in the research investigation itself.

17.3.2 SPURIOUS CAUSAL RELATIONSHIPS

Suppose researchers find a relationship between X (independent variable) and Y (dependent variable). If they want to claim that X did in fact produce Y, they *need to show that the differences or variations in Y did not exist prior to the occurrence of X*; that the effect is not related to a factor antecedent to the presumed cause. If the relationship between X and Y disappears when such prior factors are considered or controlled, then the original relationship between X and Y is considered to be *spurious,* and the prior or antecedent variable *explains away* the original relationship between X and Y (43, 58, 82). For the relationship between X and Y to disappear, the antecedent variable must be related to both X and Y. Researchers often "routinely" select control variables such as socioeconomic status, intelligence, sex, and age. However, these variables cannot provide a test of spuriousness unless they are related to the independent and dependent variables.

The beauty of the randomization process in experiments is that it makes the correlation between the independent variable X and any possible antecedent variable (measurable or not, known or unknown) close to zero, so that no antecedent variable can explain the XY correlation. Since, by definition, randomization does not occur in association studies, *researchers must systematically test antecedent variables that are potential threats to their assumption that X causes Y.* Since they cannot measure all relevant variables, such studies never have the validity of controlled experiments, even with elaborate statistical controls.

17.3.3 OTHER RELATIONSHIPS BETWEEN THE PRESUMED CAUSE AND EFFECT

When an antecedent variable is controlled, the original XY relationship may not vanish, but may be repeated instead. Such *replication* of the XY relationship does not guarantee that it is causal, but simply indicates that the relationship was not produced by that antecedent variable. However, when replication rather than a spurious result is the consistent outcome, then the probability that the original relationship is causal is increased (58).

Once the XY relationship has been shown not to be spurious, the researcher may be interested in examining how the assumed cause is related to the effect. One approach to this problem employed in sociology is to identify variables that intervene between the independent and dependent variables. If the researcher finds that the relationship between X and Y disappears when such intervening variables are considered, then such variables are considered to *interpret* or *mediate* the original relationship (58, 82). They provide the link between X and Y. Obviously such intervening variables are related to both X and Y. Some disagreement may then result in deciding what in fact is *the* cause, the intervening or the independent variable. This is primarily a matter of deciding what variable should be held responsible for the effect.

Another possible outcome is that when outside variables are controlled, whether they precede X or intervene between X and Y, the XY relationship is not the same under all conditions or levels of the variable. This statistical result is called *specification* by sociologists. It identifies conditions under which the original relationship is more or less true. On occasion, the XY relationship may be even stronger, indicating that the control variable *suppressed* the "true" strength of the relationship.

An example of an explanatory survey is that by Rehberg and Schafer (114) on the influence of participation in interscholastic athletics upon post high school educational goals. The portions of the article that examined the possible spuriousness of this relationship follow.

Participation in Interscholastic Athletics and College Expectations[1]
RICHARD A. REHBERG AND WALTER E. SCHAFER

INTRODUCTION

[1] James Coleman has remarked that a stranger in an American high school might well suppose, by looking and listening, that "more attention is paid to athletics by teenagers, both as athletes and as spectators than to scholastic matters."[2] Certainly, the vast amounts of spectator and participant time and energy devoted to athletic teams attest to the importance of high school sports, both to the students themselves and to their communities.

[2] Given this importance, the question can be raised as to what effect, if any, interscholastic athletics has upon the educational objectives of the high school. One of these objectives is the preparation of students for college. The question examined in this paper is whether participation in interscholastic sports exerts a positive or a negative influence on boys' educational expectations.

The causal focus on the study was stated in paragraph 2. The remainder of the introduction summarized research that supported a relationship between the two variables of athletic participation and educational expectations.

[3] Since literature on the athletic participation–educational expectation relationship is virtually nonexistent, we cannot approach the construction of hypotheses directly but must do so circuitously, namely, by noting the findings of those studies which have investigated the relationships between athletic participation and those variables linked with educational expectations.

[4] One set of such studies is concerned with athletic participation and academic performance, and academic performance and educational expectations. A positive association between participation and performance has been reported by several investigators, including Eidsmore, Schafer and Armer, and, indirectly,

Richard A. Rehberg and Walter F. Schafer, 1968. Participation in interscholastic athletics and college expectations. *American Journal of Sociology* 73: 732–740. Published by the University of Chicago Press. Reprinted with permission of the University of Chicago Press, R. A. Rehberg, and W. E. Schafer.

[1] The research reported herein was supported by an initial grant from the Cooperative Research Program of the Office of Education, U.S. Department of Health, Education, and Welfare, and a subsequent grant from the Center for the Advanced Study of Educational Administration, the University of Oregon. This paper is a revised version of an earlier draft presented at the annual convention of the American Sociological Association, August, 1967, held in San Francisco.

[2] James S. Coleman, "Athletics in High Schools," *Annals of the American Academy of Political and Social Sciences* 338 (November, 1961), 33–43.

Coleman.[3] In his study of participants and nonparticipants in varsity football teams from twenty-four of the top thirty Iowa high school teams for the year 1962, Eidsmore reported that "the total grade-point average of the 592 players in all subjects carried was 2.523, whereas the grade-point average of their non-participating classmates was 2.085."[4] And, while the tone of Coleman's *The Adolescent Society* suggests that athletic participation is detrimental to educational pursuits, the data of the study suggest otherwise. An inspection of the appropriate tables reveals that in six of the ten midwestern schools surveyed athletes, at least "top athletes," had higher scholastic averages than the male student body as a whole.[5]

[5] Without controls for relevant antecedent variables, it is possible that the grade-point differences reported by Eidsmore and Coleman are spurious. Evidence that such differences are not spurious comes from Schafer and Armer's study of 585 boys from two Middle Western high schools. In that study, controls were invoked for five relevant variables: year in school, measured intelligence, father's occupation, previous grade-point average, and curriculum. While these controls reduced an initial zero-order difference of .52 points on a four-point scale (athletes = 2.35, nonathletes = 1.83) to a fifth-order difference of .11 points (athletes = 2.35, nonathletes = 2.24), the direction of the data still showed a positive association between academic performance and athletic participation.[6]

[6] A positive association between academic performance and educational expectations has been reported in several studies. Berdie and Hood, for example, reported correlations between these two variables averaging about .36.[7]

[7] A second set of relevant studies are those concerned with athletic participation and peer group membership and with peer group membership and educational expectations. One of Coleman's clearest findings was the relationship between athletic participation and membership in the leading crowd. He writes: "The relationship is striking. Going out for football is related to being a member of the various elites more than any other variable in this study."[8] As to the social background of such elites, he reports that "there is a tendency toward control by the higher-educated, more middle-class students in the school, [although] this tendency is sharply diminished when such students become a small minority in the system."[9] Concerning the educational expectation of these elites, Coleman

---

[3] Russell M. Eidsmore, High school athletes are brighter, *School Activities* (November, 1963), pp. 75–77; Walter E. Schafer and J. Michael Armer, On scholarship and interscholastic athletics, *Trans-action* (in press) (a longer version will also appear in Gregory P. Stone (ed.), *Sport, Play, and Leisure* [Indianapolis: Bobbs-Merrill, in press]); and James S. Coleman, *The Adolescent Society* (Glencoe, Ill.: Free Press, 1961), especially pp. 252, 274, and 275.

[4] Eidsmore, *op. cit.* (see n. 3 above), p. 76.

[5] Coleman, *The Adolescent Society* (see n. 3 above).

[6] Schafer and Armer, *op. cit.* (see n. 3 above). GPA's based on all major courses over the high school career.

[7] Ralph F. Berdie and Albert B. Hood, *Trends in Post High School Plans Over an Eleven-Year Period* (Minneapolis: Student Counseling Bureau, University of Minnesota, 1963 [Cooperative Research Project No. 951]), pp. 56–57.

[8] Coleman, *The Adolescent Society* (see n. 3 above), p. 131.

[9] *Ibid.*, p. 109.

states that "the elites more often intend to go to college than do the students as a whole."[10]

[8] That educational expectations of peer groups are positively associated with the expectations of the adolescent himself has been reported by Alexander and Campbell, Krauss, Rehberg, and others.[11]

[9] Given these two sets of findings relating athletic participation to educational expectations via academic performance and membership in college-oriented leading crowds, we suggest that the proportion of athletes expressing expectations to enrol in a four-year college is greater than the proportion of nonathletes expressing such expectations. . . .

DESIGN AND DATA

[10] In the spring of 1965, questionnaire data were gathered from 785 senior males from three public and three parochial schools in three middle-sized Pennsylvania cities. Information for the independent variable, participation or nonparticipation in interscholastic sports, was secured with an item which requested each respondent to list all of his extracurricular activities for his senior year. The dependent variable, educational expectations, was measured with a fixed-response item which requested each respondent to indicate how far he actually *expected* to go in school.[12] The relevant categories for this variable are: (1) expect to enrol in a four-year college, and (2) do not expect to enrol in a four-year college.

It is clear that the independent variable was inherent rather than imposed by the researchers. Students simply reported the extracurricular activities in which they participated. With an inherent independent variable, the researchers have no direct control over the degree or nature of the variation that occurs. Obviously, the range of the independent variable affects the strength of its association with the dependent variable, the adequacy of the test of its effects, and therefore the study's conclusions. The authors did not discuss this issue or present any data on the number of athletic activities in which the subjects participated. As indicated in Table 17.1, athletic participation was simply

---

[10] *Ibid.,* p. 115.

[11] C. Norman Alexander and Ernest Q. Campbell, Peer influences on adolescent educational aspirations and attainments, *American Sociological Review* (August, 1964), pp. 568–75; Irving Krauss, Sources of educational aspirations among working-class youth, *American Sociological Review* (December, 1964), pp. 867–79; and Richard A. Rehberg, *Adolescent Career Plans and the Impact of Chronic Economic Distress upon Adolescent Educational and Occupational Expectations and Aspirations* (University Park: Pennsylvania State University, 1965 [Cooperative Research Project No. S-119]).

[12] Expectations constitute the *realistic* level of a career orientation as distinguished from aspirations which constitute the *idealistic* level. For a further discussion of this conceptual distinction as well as a consideration of specific theoretical and empirical implications, see Richard A. Rehberg, Adolescent career aspirations and expectation: an evaluation of two contrary stratification hypotheses, *Pacific Sociological Review* (Fall, 1967).

coded "yes" or "no." Evidently the authors did not distinguish between subjects who participated in only one sport as opposed to several.

The description of the dependent variable indicated only two variations. However, the data in Table 17.1 indicated that a distinction was also made between four-year and two-year college expectations.

RESULTS

Expectations and Participation: A Zero-Order Analysis

[11] Table 17.1 presents the data for the zero-order relationship between athletic participation and educational expectations. Consistent with the first hypothesis, 62 percent of the athletes expect to enrol in a four-year college compared with 45 percent of the nonathletes. The strength of the association is indicated by a γ value of .28.

[12] This finding does not eliminate the possibility, however, that the relationship is spuriously produced by one or more variables associated with both the independent and the dependent variables. Consequently, the second step in the analysis requires a control for potentially confounding variables.

The XY relationship cited in Table 17.1 was the focus of the study. Any relationships involving control variables were compared to the strength and direction of this association. The remainder of the article focused on the impact of three control variables: socioeconomic status of family, the student's academic performance, and parental encouragement to continue education after high school.

The data in Table 17.1 were percentages of the row totals. For example, the figure of 62 at the intersection of the first column and first row indicated that of the 284 males who participated in athletics, 62 percent or 176 expected to enroll in a four-year college. Of the 490 males who did not participate in athletics, 45 percent or 220 indicated that they expected to enroll in a four-year college. The index of association was gamma (refer to Chapter 14, and Ap-

TABLE 17.1 *PERCENTAGE OF RESPONDENTS REPORTING SPECIFIED EDUCATIONAL EXPECTATIONS, BY ATHLETIC PARTICIPATION (ZERO-ORDER ASSOCIATION)*

Athletic participation	Educational expectations (in years)				Total	N
	16 or more	*14*	*12 or less*	*No response*	*Total*	*N*
Yes	62	20	17	1	100	284
No	45	30	24	1	100	490
No response	73	9	9	9	100	11
Total	52	26	21	1	100	785

* $\gamma = .28.$

pendix D.) You will recall that gamma reflects the association between variables which are ordered classes or categories and ranges in value between −1 and +1, as does a correlation coefficient. The phrase "zero-order analysis" meant that only the relationship between two variables was calculated. A gamma of .28 certainly does not indicate a strong causal relationship. However, since it was positive rather than negative, it does suggest that sports are not detrimental to academic aspirations.

Expectations and Participation: N-order Partial Analysis

[13] Data were gathered for three variables which could theoretically produce a spurious relationship between expectations and participation. The first of those, social status, was measured with the Hollingshead Two Factor Index of Social Position.[13] A positive association between this variable and expectations has been reported consistently in a large number of studies.[14] The findings on the relationship of participation with status are not so consistent, however. Hollingshead implied no association when he wrote: "Athletics attracts boys from all classes in about the same proportion."[15] Schafer and Armer, however, reported a positive association between the two, with 33 percent of white-collar boys participating compared with 22 percent of blue-collar boys.[16] Temporally, we assume that this control variable precedes the independent variable in any kind of causal sequence.

[14] Consistent with virtually all previous studies, expectations and status are positively associated ($\gamma = .50$). The association between status and participation, minimal as it may be, is indicated by a γ of .04, suggesting that for this sample the relationship is more like that reported by Hollingshead than that reported by Schafer and Armer. Partialling out status from the expectation-participation relationship with Rosenberg's test factor standardization technique has no effect on the magnitude of association (for example, both zero- and first-order gammas are .28).[17]

This was the first test of a possible *spurious* relationship between the presumed cause and the presumed effect. In paragraph 13, the authors clearly stated that SES was assumed to precede the independent variable. It can therefore be assumed that it preceded the dependent variable as well. In order

[13] August B. Hollingshead, The two-factor index of social position, (New Haven, Conn.: Yale University, 1957 [mimeographed]).

[14] For a rather comprehensive bibliography of these studies, see William Kuvleksy and George W. Ohlendorf, A *Bibliography of Literature on Educational Orientations of Youth* (College Station:Texas A. and M. University, 1965).

[15] August B. Hollingshead, *Elmtown's Youth* (New York: John Wiley and Sons, 1949), p. 194.

[16] Schafer and Armer, *op. cit.* (see n. 3 above).

[17] Leo A. Goodman and William H. Kruskal, Measures of association for cross classifications, *Journal of the American Statistical Association* (September 1954), pp. 732–64; Morris Rosenberg, Test factor standardization as a method of test interpretation, Social Forces (October, 1962) pp. 53–61.

to control for the variable of SES, the relationships it had with both the independent and dependent variables were statistically removed or partialed out. The resulting relationship between the independent and dependent variable was then examined yielding a first-order gamma of .28. The term "first-order" refers to the fact that one variable was controlled. This first-order gamma was the same as the original gamma value. Thus the original relationship was *replicated* rather than found to be spurious.

[15] The second potentially confounding variable is academic performance, measured with rank in graduating class. Again, positive associations have been reported in previous studies between performance and participation and between performance and expectations. Consistent with previous research, educational expectations and academic performance are highly related ($\gamma = .73$). However, performance and participation are virtually unrelated in this sample ($\gamma = -.02$).[18] As a result, the removal of the effects of academic performance leaves the magnitude of the relationship between expectations and participation virtually unchanged (first-order $\gamma = .29$).

[16] The third control variable is parental educational encouragement, measured according to the respondent's indication of how frequently each parent encourages him to continue his education beyond high school.[19] Kahl, Bordua, Cohen, and Rehberg and Westby have reported moderately strong correlations between expectations and encouragement.[20] We are unaware, however, of any studies

---

[18] One possible explanation for the discrepancy between our findings and that reported by Schafer and Armer is that their sample included adolescents who later dropped out of school. Dropouts, of course, tend to receive lower grades and participate less in interscholastic sports. The sample used for this study includes only students who were still enrolled during their senior year. Had this sample consisted of sophomores, as did Schafer and Armer's sample, we too probably would have found a positive association between academic performance and athletic participation.

[19] The question read: "Which ONE of the following statements is most true about continuing your education beyond high school?

"1. My father [mother] *never* urges me to continue my education.
"2. My father [mother] *sometimes* urges me to continue my education.
"3. My father [mother] *often* urges me to continue my education.
"4. My father [mother] *constantly* urges me to continue my education."

The question was asked separately for each parent. Ordinal scores of 1–4 were assigned to the response for each parent (1 = never and 4 = constantly), then added, and from the total the integer of one was subtracted, yielding a score range of 1–7. Low encouragement consists of scores of 1–4; high encouragement consists of scores of 5–7.

[20] Joseph A. Kahl, Educational and occupational aspirations of "common-man" boys, *Harvard Educational Review* (Summer, 1953), pp. 186–203; David T. Bordua, Educational aspirations and parental stress on college, *Social Forces* (March, 1960), pp. 262–69; Elizabeth G. Cohen, Parental factors in educational mobility, *Sociology of Education* (Fall, 1965), pp. 404–25; Richard A. Rehberg and David L. Westby, Parental educational encouragement, occupation, education, and family size: artifactual or independent determinants of adolescent educational expectations, *Social Forces* (March, 1967), pp. 362–74.

which have investigated the relationship between athletic participation and parental encouragement. As anticipated, expectations and encouragement are rather strongly related in this sample ($\gamma = .58$). Encouragement and participation are moderately associated, with a γ of .28. Removing the effects of this control variable reduces the association between expectations and participation from a zero-order coefficient of .28 to a first-order coefficient of .22.[21]

[17] Parental educational encouragement, then, is the only one of the three control variables which is more than minimally associated with both the independent and the dependent variables. Therefore, it is not surprising that the strength of the original relationship between expectations and participation as displayed in Table 17.2 is only slightly reduced in a third-order partial analysis, that is, from a zero-order gamma of .28 to a third-order γ of .24. This finding thus renders tenable the proposition that athletic participation exerts an independent positive effect on the educational expectations of high school boys. . . .

TABLE 17.2   *PERCENTAGE OF RESPONDENTS REPORTING SPECIFIED EDUCATIONAL EXPECTATIONS BY ATHLETIC PARTICIPATION, WITH SOCIAL STATUS, PARENTAL EDUCATIONAL ENCOURAGEMENT, AND ACADEMIC PERFORMANCE CONTROLLED (THIRD-ORDER ASSOCIATION, STANDARDIZED TABLE)*

| Athletic participation | Educational expectations (in years) | | | | Total | N |
	16 or more	14	12 or less	No response		
Yes	61	19	18	1	99	284
No	46	30	23	1	100	490
No response	70	20	9	1	100	11
Total	52	26	21	1	100	785

* $\gamma = .24$.

No statements were made regarding whether the two control variables of academic rank and parental encouragement occurred prior to the independent and dependent variables, although the Summary and Conclusions section of the report (paragraph 19) indicated that such an assumption was made. Do you agree with this conclusion?

A summary of the relationships cited in the results section is presented in Table 17.3. It is easy to see that the control variables correlated only with the dependable variable. Therefore it is not surprising that the original relationship

---

[21] The positive association between parental educational encouragement and athletic participation is analogous to the finding reported previously by the senior author of this paper that parental educational encouragement correlates positively not only with adolescent educational orientations but with occupational orientations as well. This suggests that educational encouragement represents a form of achievement socialization somewhat more diffuse than that pertinent to educational orientation only (see Rehberg and Westby, *op. cit.* [see n. 20 above]).

TABLE 17.3   *GAMMA COEFFICIENTS CITED IN THE REHBERG AND SCHAFER STUDY*

	Educational expectations (*Dependent*)	*SES*	*Academic rank*	*Parental encouragement*
Athletic participation (Independent)	.28	.04	—.02	.28
Expectations (Dependent)	...	.50	.73	.58

Relationship between participation and expectations with the following
   variables controlled

SES only	.28
Academic rank only	.29
Parental encouragement only	.22
All three variables	.24

did not vanish when the control variables were considered since they did not
also correlate with the independent variable. Are there any other antecedent
variables which should have been examined? Review the list of possible extraneous variables in Table 15.1.

It is important to remember that the tests for spuriousness did not change
the self-selective nature of the independent variable in this study. That is, the
students selected themselves into athletics (or elected not to participate in
athletics). Since this fact cannot change no matter how many additional tests
for spuriousness might be conducted, self-selection remains a possible explanation of the association between athletic participation and educational expectations.

SUMMARY AND CONCLUSION

[18] These data have shown that a greater proportion of athletes than nonathletes expect to enrol in a four-year college, even when the potentially confounding variables of status, academic performance, and parental encouragement
are controlled. This relationship is especially marked among boys not otherwise
disposed toward college, that is, those from working-class homes, those in the
lower half of their graduating class, and those with low parental encouragement
to go to college.

[19] Since the sample of this study is nonrandom and all extraneous variables
have not been controlled, conclusions about the generality and causal direction
of the relationship must be drawn with caution. We suggest, however, that the
positive relationship between educational expectations and athletic participation
is probably not spurious, that is, not produced by "selection" variables but,
rather, is "true," that is, reflects the socialization consequences of participation
in interscholastic sports. . . .

A later study by Spreitzer and Pugh (134) replicated Rehberg and Schafer's findings on a sample of male seniors from 13 Connecticut high schools. In fact, the gamma values were remarkably similar. Spreitzer and Pugh also examined variables that might identify the means by which athletic participation and educational expectations were related. One such variable was the climate of the school. They hypothesized that in schools in which athletic achievement was strongly rewarded, athletes would experience enhanced popularity that in turn would stimulate higher educational goals. On the other hand, in a climate that rewarded primarily academic achievement, athletes would not experience greater popularity and therefore the relationship between athletic participation and educational expectations would be weaker.

The climate of a school was characterized as being either an athletic specialist value climate, an all-around boy value climate, a scholar specialist climate, or a mixed-type, indeterminate climate. Within each of these categories, the relationship between athletic participation and educational expectations was examined. The results are presented in Table 17.4.

The gamma values cited in the table supported Spreitzer and Pugh's expectations. The relationship between athletic participation and educational expectations varied with school climate. It was strongest in schools in which athletics was highly valued and vanishing in schools in which scholarship was the primary means of obtaining status. These results illustrate *specification;* identification of conditions under which the original causal relationship is more or less true.

Other intervening variables could also be investigated. One factor mentioned in both studies was the possibility of greater career counseling and encouragement given to athletes because of their increased prestige and visibility. Another factor could be the opportunity for athletic scholarships. Can you think of other intervening variables that might account for the original relationship between athletic participation and educational goals?

17.3.4 THE CAUSAL MODEL APPROACH

The most elaborate examination of causal relationships from association data involves the development of a causal model to account for the variation in the dependent variable. Causal models can be simple or complex, specifying the causal direction among any number of independent and dependent variables. Usually a path diagram is drawn to illustrate the causal and time relationships among the variables. Three path models are drawn in Fig. 17.3. Unidirectional arrows are drawn from variables taken as causes to variables taken as effects. A string model is depicted in Case I, each preceding variable influencing the next. This model also assumes for instance that variable 1 effects variable 4 only indirectly through variables 2 and 3, and that variable 3 is the only variable that directly affects variable 4. In Case II, variables 1 and 2 are concurrent in time, and are unrelated to each other with each influencing variable 3, which in turn affects variable 4. In Case III, variable 1 affects variable

TABLE 17.4 *EDUCATIONAL EXPECTATIONS BY ATHLETIC*
PARTICIPATION, CONTROLLING FOR SCHOOL VALUE CLIMATE

Educational expectations	Athletic specialist value climate Athletes (%)		Nonathletes (%)
16 or more years	80		57
13–15 years	7		13
12 years	13		30
	(N = 85)		(N = 107)
(3 schools)		Gamma = .47	

All-around boy value climate

Educational expectations			
16 or more years	59		43
13–15 years	23		20
12 years	18		37
	(N = 24)		(N = 60)
(2 schools)		Gamma = .33	

Scholar specialist value climate

Educational expectations			
16 or more years	52		53
13–15 years	23		23
12 years	25		24
	(N = 31)		(N = 53)
(2 schools)		Gamma = .02	

Mixed-type, indeterminate climate

Educational expectations			
16 or more years	58		49
13–15 years	19		17
12 years	23		34
	(N = 130)		(N = 214)
(6 schools)		Gamma = .19	

Source: Elmer Spreitzer and Meredith Pugh, 1973. Interscholastic athletics and educational expectations. *Sociology of Education,* 46: 179. Copyright 1973 by the American Sociological Association. Reprinted with permission.

2, which in turn has two outcomes, represented by variables 3 and 4. In addition, variable 1 is assumed to have a direct effect on variable 3, independent of its indirect influence through variable 2.

The statistical technique used to test causal models against actual data is known as *path analysis.* It provides a "method for determining the direct and indirect effects of each of the independent variables in a causal chain" (47, p. 136). These effects are expressed numerically in path coefficients, which indicate the "amount of expected change in the dependent variable as a result of a unit change in the independent variables" (94, p. 310). Outcomes such as spuriousness, replication, specification, and interpretation can each be examined with path analytic techniques.

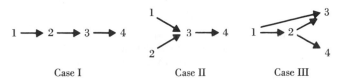

Case I   Case II   Case III

FIG. 17.3 Path diagrams of three causal models.

Even with complex statistical analyses of association data, the axiom that correlation does not mean causation should not be forgotten. "Statistical theory treats only the mechanical problem of the extent to which variates are predictable from each other under various conditions" (68, p. 292). The inference that a variable causes another must be based on other considerations from the particular science which is involved.

17.4 HOW TO CRITIQUE QUASI-EXPERIMENTAL DESIGNS AND OTHER STUDIES OF CAUSE

Exhibit 17.1 provides a guide to the evaluation of quasi-experimental designs and other studies of causal questions.

EXHIBIT 17.1 IDENTIFICATION AND CRITIQUE OF QUASI-EXPERIMENTAL AND PREEXPERIMENTAL DESIGNS AND ASSOCIATION STUDIES OF CAUSE

A. To determine whether the study was a quasi-experiment, a preexperiment, or an association study with a causal purpose, review the series of questions cited at the beginning of Chapter 16.

B. A review of the questions in Exhibits 15.1 *and* 16.1 will provide a fairly extensive analysis of the study. Additional questions regarding association studies are presented in Section C below.

C. 1. Did the analysis proceed from the presumed cause to the effect or vice versa?

2. Did the researcher establish that the independent variable actually occurred *before* the dependent variable?

3. Were *variables that occurred prior* to both the independent and dependent variables introduced to test the possible spuriousness of the causal relationship? Were these variables related to both the independent and dependent

variables? What were the results of such tests? Did the original relationship vanish or become smaller indicating spuriousness; was it replicated; or did it vary in strength with different levels of the control variable (i.e., specification)? What other antecedent variables should have been examined?

4. Were *variables that intervened* between the independent and dependent variables examined? Were such variables related to both the independent and dependent variables? What were the results of such analyses? Did the original relationship vanish or become smaller, indicating that the intervening variable explained how the cause and effect were related (i.e., interpretation)? Did the original relationship vary in strength with different levels of the intervening variables (i.e., specification)? Was the original relationship repeated, indicating that the intervening variable did not explain the relationship? Did the strength of the original relationship increase, indicating a suppression of the relationship by the intervening variable? What other intervening variables should have been examined?

5. Were the concluding causal statements warranted? Can you offer other explanations of the findings?

17.5 LIST OF QUASI-EXPERIMENTS AND OTHER STUDIES OF CAUSAL QUESTIONS

17.5.1 QUASI-EXPERIMENTS

Blizek, W. L., K. Jackson, and J. C. LaVoie, 1974. Short course vs. conventional structures for teaching philosophy. *Journal of Experimental Education* 43(1): 25–33.

Denton, J. J., and F. J. Gies, 1975. The relation between required objective attainment and student-selected objectives: two components in an instructional model for individualization. *California Journal of Educational Research* 26: 225–232.

Porterfield, J. K., E. Herbert-Jackson, and T. R. Risley, 1976. Contingent observation: an effective and acceptable procedure for reducing disruptive behavior of young children in a group setting. *Journal of Applied Behavior Analysis* 9: 55–64.

Sparks, R. L., and E. L. McCallon, 1974. Microteaching: its effect on student attitudes in an elementary science methods course. *Science Education* 58: 483–487.

Wambold, C. L., K. Jedlinski, and L. Brown, 1976. Improving the sequential memory performance of trainable mentally retarded youngsters: a learning strategies approach. *Journal of Special Education* 10: 41–46.

17.5.2 ASSOCIATION STUDIES WITH A CAUSAL PURPOSE

Anderson, J. G., 1975. Strategies of control and their effects on instruction. *Journal of Research and Development in Education* **9**: 115–121.

Balla, D. A., E. C. Butterfield, and E. Zigler, 1974. Effects of institutionalization on retarded children: a longitudinal cross-institutional investigation. *American Journal of Mental Deficiency* **78**: 530–549.

Goldman, R. D., and B. N. Hewitt, 1976. The scholastic aptitude test "explains" why college men major in science more often than college women. *Journal of Counseling Psychology* **23**: 50–54.

Greenberg, D., and J. McCall, 1974. Teacher mobility and allocation. *Journal of Human Resources* **9**: 480–502.

Gruen, G. E., D. R. Ottinger, and T. H. Ollendick, 1974. Probability learning in retarded children with differing histories of success and failure in school. *American Journal of Mental Deficiency* **79**: 417–423.

Kelly, D. H., 1976. Track position, school misconduct, and youth deviance: a test of the interpretive effect of school commitment. *Urban Education* **10**: 366–378.

Kourilsky, M., and E. L. Baker, 1975. An empirical comparison of open and nonopen structured classrooms. *California Journal of Educational Research* **26**: 238–245.

Kuhlman, E. L., and W. K. Hoy, 1974. The socialization of professionals into bureaucracies: the beginning teacher in the school. *Journal of Educational Administration* **12**: 18–27.

Moos, R. H., and J. Otto, 1975. The impact of coed living on males and females. *Journal of College Student Personnel* **16**: 459–467.

Seeman, A. Z., and M. Seeman, 1976. Staff processes and pupil attitudes: a study of teacher participation in educational change. *Human Relations* **29**: 25–40.

STUDY PROBLEMS

1. What are the major distinctions between quasi-experimental designs and true-experimental designs and between quasi-experimental designs and preexperimental designs?

2.

Design 1	Design 2
O A_1 O	A_1 O O
O A_2 O	A_2 O O

What are the major faults of both of these designs? In what situations would you prefer Design 1 to Design 2? In what situations would you prefer Design 2 to Design 1?

3. Read one of the quasi-experiments cited at the end of this chapter. Examine the study using the questions in Exhibits 15.1 and 16.1.

4. What does it mean when the relationship between the independent and dependent variables was found to be spurious?

5. Why are association studies that focus on causal questions the weakest form of causal study? Cite three causal questions likely to be examined by association study techniques. For each question, what might be some possible antecedent variables that would explain away the relationship of interest? What might be some intervening variables that might interpret or mediate the relationship?

PART IV

Views of Educational Research Held by Scientists and Practitioners

Many researchers are concerned with generating knowledge and theories that have general applicability; that will explain or describe a variety of events. On the other hand, most educators are primarily concerned with using research results in their specific professional activities. For instance, while a researcher would probably focus on the general problem of the factors that influence student attention on school tasks, a teacher might be concerned with how to stop Mary from daydreaming in class.

The different viewpoints of the researcher and educator are real and important, because they affect the direction of new research endeavors and how and if research is applied. Chapters 18 and 19 examine how a practitioner can decide if the results of a study might be useful to him or her. The last chapter briefly examines the levels of theory used by researchers.

18

Guidelines for Application
of the Results
of Educational Research

How can educators decide if the results of a study are relevant to their job, if the results will help educators understand themselves or the people with whom they interact, or if the results will give them guidelines for action? Given the immense variety of educational contexts (e.g., 30-student classrooms, individualized instruction at a computer terminal or reading machine, extracurricular activities, counseling sessions, faculty meetings, playground activities, parent–teacher conferences, adult education classes), judging the relevance of a particular study is difficult. What may be of interest or of value to a teacher of mentally retarded children will probably not be of interest to a counselor of senior high students or to a university English professor.

When examining a study, readers can ask the following series of questions to help them decide if the results are relevant to their own situation:

1. Is the *research problem* of potential value or interest to you?
2. If so, how does the *total context in which the research was conducted* limit the degree to which you can generalize the results to your professional role? This issue really involves three separate questions:
   a) To what extent were the *subjects* similar to the individuals with whom you are involved (or, perhaps, to yourself),
   b) To what extent were the *conditions* to which the subjects were exposed similar to the setting in which you work, or to what extent can you duplicate the research setting, and
   c) Were the measurements and the *measurement procedures* similar to those you use or would use?

In general, as the similarity between your setting and the research setting increases, it becomes easier to use the research results.

The final decision regarding the potential usefulness of a study is the reader's. Any factor might override another in making this decision. For example, the reader may find the topic of value because it provides a new perspective, even though it was investigated in a situation quite alien from his or her own.

18.1 THE PROBLEM

General criteria for determining what research problems or topics might be fruitful to a particular educator do not exist. However, some suggestions are offered. Keep an open mind in examining the potential relevance of a study and do not reject it automatically if the results are contrary to your expectations. Clifford (31), in her summary of the impact of research on teaching practices, cited instances in which acceptance of research findings depended not so much on the high quality of the research itself, but rather on whether the results substantiated existing opinion and experience. Acceptance of results also occurred when the research focused on neutral issues; however, few educational issues are neutral.

Readers should attend to what researchers say regarding educational implications of their results, since the researchers themselves are in an excellent position to inform the reader of these applications as well as of the study's limitations. Unfortunately, authors often fail to discuss applications. The weakest section of research reports is usually the section on practical recommendations. Although guidelines for developing appropriate research designs and for selecting the appropriate statistical analysis are systematized, guidelines for generating appropriate recommendations are not. When researchers do not cite any implications for educational practice, this does not mean none exists. When implications are cited, they still must be examined carefully since they may not be applicable to your particular situation. Few, if any studies are conducted in settings identical to the one in which you find yourself.

In an area of research that interests you, you may become frustrated when trying to reconcile disparities in the results from individual studies. Presumably, every researcher builds upon the knowledge generated by other investigators. Yet, close dovetailing of studies and the desired cumulative growth of knowledge is frequently not achieved. Where such growth has occurred, one or two researchers have usually directed the effort (122). Educational research has been criticized for relatively few programs of coordinated research and for a predominance of studies by one-time-only researchers (31). Both factors yield much research with low impact and little direction.

18.2 THE CONTEXT OF RESEARCH

Once you have decided that the focus of a study is of interest to you, the degree to which the subjects, the research environment, and the measurement procedures are similar to or representative of your educational setting determines the applicability of the research results. The extent to which the research environment and measurement procedures could be replicated by you determines whether you could try out the research procedures on individuals with whom you are involved. Although both the subjects and measurement factors can be conceived of as part of the total research environment, they are treated separately here.

18.3 SUBJECTS

The primary question that you must answer is *whether or not you can generalize from the research sample to the individuals or groups with whom you are concerned.* If you are to make such a generalization, not only must the research sample be representative of a larger group, but the individuals of concern to you (labeled the *application group* throughout this discussion) must also be part of that larger group.

18.3.1 SELECTION OF SUBJECTS

As discussed in Chapter 6, *ideally* the *research sample is representative of the population accessible to the researcher, and* in turn, *the accessible population is representative of a target population,* the larger group of ultimate interest to the researcher. If representativeness occurs at both sampling stages, then generalization from the sample to the target population can easily be made. The only way to ensure representativeness is to use some *form of probability sampling* at each stage, such as simple random sampling. Three variations in the sampling procedures that can be employed are described below.

REPRESENTATIVE SAMPLING FROM THE TARGET
AND ACCESSIBLE POPULATIONS

When probability sampling has been employed in the selection of both the accessible population and the sample, *and* when readers conclude that the application group is part of, or at least like, the target population, they can simultaneously *conclude that their application group is like the sample and therefore that the sample results apply to their group.* For example, if a sample of eighth grade students were drawn randomly from all the eighth grade students in City A (the accessible population), and if the accessible population were randomly drawn from all eighth grade students in the United States (the target population), then the sample would represent the target population. If you were a teacher of eighth grade students anywhere in the United States, then your students would be part of the target population and you could generalize from the study sample to your students.

For most social scientists, the sample is rarely attained through such sampling techniques, and the accessible population is rarely attained through such means because of the costs involved. Even in instances in which the resources are sufficient for such sampling procedures, the target population constantly changes with time. However, most scientists assume that, within reasonable time spans, the target population of the past resembles the target population of today, making inferences possible.

REPRESENTATIVE SAMPLING FROM THE ACCESSIBLE POPULATION ONLY

If the sample were representative of only the accessible population, what inferences can be made? The researcher can easily generalize to the accessible population. However, generalization to the target population is made with less confidence. Frequently, the nature of the accessible population can be determined from measurements obtained on the sample itself. *Practitioners* must then *ask whether their application group is similar to the researcher's description of the sample and thus also similar to the accessible population.*

The population accessible to the researcher at the time the study was originally conducted cannot, by definition, include the present application group. In deciding whether the accessible population is similar to the practitioner's group, the factor of time must be considered. It is possible that the time lapse has been too great to assume uniformity in the accessible population over that period. For example, suppose a researcher in the 1920s found that rural and urban teachers both were strongly opposed to teacher unions. The investigator's sample was drawn randomly from the accessible population of teachers defined by geographic areas in Detroit and rural, northern Michigan. If you were a principal in the same geographic area of Detroit or northern Michigan today, would you assume that your teachers are like the corresponding accessible population defined in the 1920 study, and thus that your teachers feel the same way about teacher unions?

No REPRESENTATIVE SAMPLING

In many research studies the sample has not been selected from the accessible population by any form of probability sampling. When this situation occurs, the *sample has actually become the accessible population* (18). Strictly speaking, in this case no inferences or generalizations beyond the sample are warranted; only description of the sample is allowed. However, generalization to an unspecified population "like those observed" has been defended (33, p. 913), despite the possible biases in the selection of the sample. *The crucial issue then becomes that of adequately describing the sample.*

The target population may have been defined very broadly by the researcher as juvenile delinquents in large United States cities. However, the sample was not randomly selected from this target population but consisted of volunteers from the city of St. Louis. The application group of interest fits the target category of juvenile delinquents from large United States cities since it was drawn from the city of Seattle. But without additional information on the unique characteristics of the juvenile delinquents who volunteered in St. Louis, the practitioner will find it difficult to determine whether similar results would occur with his or her Seattle group. The only resolution to this dilemma is to hope that the St. Louis sample was adequately described and that the characteristics of the Seattle group are well known, so that a decision regarding the similarity of the two groups can be made.

18.3.2 DESCRIPTION OF SUBJECTS

No matter how the sample was selected, detailed information on the characteristics of the target population, the accessible population, the research sample, and the application group is necessary in order for you to make an intelligent judgment regarding the application of the research results. In most cases, however, only the sample is described, and frequently the sample description itself is limited. When detailed information on a relevant trait is missing or inadequate, you may find it very difficult to decide if the study sample is similar to the application group.

Discrepancies between the application group and the research sample are important only if those characteristics are related to the variables under investigation. If age is known to be unrelated to the effects of team teaching upon achievement, then the fact that a study is conducted with fifth grade students should not prevent you from applying the results to achievement in a tenth grade class or from attempting to replicate the findings with tenth grade students.

Another factor to consider is that the full range of a trait may not be represented by the student sample. In such instances, you cannot determine whether the results would apply to a group exhibiting a different range of the trait.

In experimental studies, possible interactions between the characteristics of the subjects and the experimental treatments should be considered (the aptitude–treatment interactions discussed in Chapter 16). If an interaction occurred in the study, indicating different effects for different types of individuals, then the practitioner must know how his or her group compares to the study sample on such traits in order to make appropriate use of the results.

18.3.3 GUIDELINES REGARDING SIMILARITY OF SUBJECTS

The major points just discussed have been summarized as a sequence of questions in Exhibit 18.1 to aid you in determining whether you can generalize from the sample results to your application group.

EXHIBIT 18.1   *GUIDELINES: RESEARCH SAMPLE*

A. What are the characteristics of the application group?

B. Was some form of probability sampling, such as random sampling, used not only to select the sample from the accessible population but also to select the accessible population from the target population?

1. If *no,* go to Section C.

2. If *yes,* then the sample represents the target population. Is there a "match" between the characteristics of the application group and the description of the target population?

   a) If yes, since both the sample and the application group are part of, or at least like, the target population, the results on the sample are applicable to the application group.
   b) If no, then generalization of the results to the application group should be made with caution.

   Stop here.

C. Was probability sampling used in selecting the sample from the accessible population?

   1. If *no,* go to Section D.

   2. If *yes,* then the sample represents the accessible population. Is there a "match" between the characteristics of the application group and the description of the accessible population?

      a) If yes, since both the sample and the application group are part of, or at least like, the accessible population, the results on the sample are applicable to the application group.
      b) If no, then generalization of the results to the application group should be made with caution.

      Stop here.

D. Can the sample be considered to be "like" the application group?

   1. Was the sample description adequate to make this decision?

   2. Were discrepancies between the application group and the sample irrelevant to the problem being investigated?

   3. Was the range of the traits similar in both groups?

   4. In experimental studies, were relevant aptitude-treatment interactions examined?

      a) If the answer to questions 1 through 4 is yes, then appropriate application of the results can be made, although such generalization always involves some risk.
      b) If the answer to one or more of questions 1 through 4 is no, then a decision regarding generalization is difficult to make, and the importance of any discrepancies must be determined by your knowledge of and experience in the area.

18.4 RESEARCH ENVIRONMENT

The *research environment,* the time–place–setting in which a study was conducted, *must be described* in order to detect the similarities and differences between it and the educational context of interest. *In experimental studies, the independent variable is the major determinant of the research environment.* Application of experimental results usually means that the practitioner will try out an experimental treatment in the setting in which he or she works. The higher the similarity between the "try-out" conditions and those in the original study, the greater the likelihood that the results will also be similar.

In nonexperimental studies, the environment from which the subjects came should be described. Sometimes characteristics of the subjects (e.g., socioeconomic status) give the reader some idea of this "existing" environment; in other cases, additional information is needed. Description of this existing environment as it relates to both experimental and nonexperimental studies is discussed in this section.

Since few efforts have been made to develop a taxonomy of environments or to develop procedures for analyzing the dimensions of environments, a definitive guide for determining the similarity between research environments and educational environments cannot be provided. However, research efforts to describe environments have been summarized by Moos (108). Each category described below has been shown to have an impact on individual or group behavior. It is important to note that these approaches are interrelated and do not exhaust all possible ways of describing environments.

1. Ecological dimensions: i.e., geographical–meterological characteristics (temperature, rainfall) and architectural–physical design variables (heating, noise level, furniture arrangement).

2. Dimensions of organizational or instructional structure, such as size of institution, staffing ratios, faculty student ratio in educational institutions, and the power structure.

3. Psychosocial characteristics or climate as reflected in how individuals perceive the environment. Some specific variables investigated in university settings have included emphasis upon scholarship, concern for innovation, and institutional spirit.

4. Personal and behavioral characteristics of the inhabitants of the environment that can influence or structure the interpersonal environment of others. Such variables as age, educational attainment, and income level reflect characteristics of subjects as well as the nature of the environment.

5. Behavior settings (as defined by Barker (13, 14)) refer to "natural" settings in which relatively large and distinct patterns of behavior occur. Some behavior settings in high school identified by Barker are: indoor athletic contests (girls' basketball practice, boys' basketball practice, gymnasium for noon–freetime), outdoor athletic contests (track practice, county track meet), food

sales, academic educational groups (English classes—Teacher 1, English classes —Teacher 2), government and school offices, and plays.

6. Potential reinforcing properties of environments; i.e., the types of reinforcers available (money, praise, information, attention) and the types of behavior likely to be reinforced (affiliation, aggression, achievement-oriented behavior, work habits, dependency).

Moos's categories identify rather broad dimensions which create an overall picture of any environment. In a particular research–environment/education–environment comparison, some dimensions will be more important than others. Experience will help determine which dimensions are most relevant.

18.4.1 EXPERIMENTAL SETTINGS

All the factors affecting the external validity of experiments discussed in Chapter 15 influence the degree of generalization beyond the research setting. The primary focus here, however, is upon the importance of detailed description of the experimental treatments, i.e., the independent variable.

In studies in which the experimenter has a high degree of control over the experimental conditions such as when the treatment is quite short, the sequence of events is rigidly controlled, or the instructions to subjects are prescribed, the independent variable is usually described adequately. However, in experiments that attempt to approximate ongoing educational processes such as classroom instruction or student–counselor conferences, the experimental treatments are necessarily complex and the researcher has less control over the treatment. In such cases, summary statements provide inadequate descriptions. A statement saying that the inquiry method, the phonetic approach, the work–study procedure or the usual lecture–discussion technique was implemented provides very incomplete information to the reader on the nature of the treatment. Systematic observation of the treatment is required to describe what actually occurred.

Consider an experimental study comparing different preschool curricula. Probably the first information that the reader needs is descriptions of the curricula. Yet both curricula and the implementation of curricula can vary in so many ways that it is difficult to determine when such description is adequate. Materials, media, content, sequencing of content, physical arrangement of students, what students are allowed to do, the types of cognitive and affective demands made on students, and the time spent on different topics illustrate just a few factors that could be observed. Moos's categories, although general in nature, point to some dimensions that might not be considered if the focus of description were mainly on the curriculum content: (1) ecological—classroom equipment, physical size of rooms, lighting; (2) organizational structure—teacher–student ratio, timing of snack periods, number of teacher assistants; (3) psychosocial characteristics—emphasis upon developing autonomy in children, type of behavior control exerted by the teacher; (4) characteristics of the inhabitants—degree of diversity in the children's backgrounds, ratio of boys to girls; (5) behavior settings—free play, snack time, teacher reading; and (6) reinforcement—frequency of teacher praise for different types of behavior and/or for each child. These examples only skim the surface of what could be observed in a curriculum study.

In order to decide whether the description of the experimental treatment was adequate, ask yourself these questions: (1) *could I replicate (repeat) the study from the information given in the report* and, if not, (2) what additional information do I need for replication. If the list of additional information is rather lengthy, then you will probably find it extremely difficult to judge the similarity between the setting in which you work and the research setting, or to duplicate the treatment in your setting.

Even in experimental studies, it is desirable to describe conditions other than those represented by the independent variable. Moos's categories of climate and personal characteristics of the inhabitants may tap some aspects of this context. For example, in the preschool curriculum study just cited, it may also be important to know the degree to which the parents support the particular curriculum in which their child is enrolled, whether parental behavior in the home conflicts in some way with the focus of the curriculum, how much sleep and food the children receive, etc. Such factors aid readers in determining the similarity between the research context and their own educational setting.

18.4.2 NONEXPERIMENTAL SETTINGS

Generally speaking, description of the environment from which the subjects come in nonexperimental studies is limited. Frequently, demographic data obtained from the subjects themselves provide the only account of the environment. In studies in which description of the environment is the primary purpose, the degree of similarity between the research and the application environments is easy to determine. Moos's categories identify some facets of the environment that are important to examine in determining the degree of this similarity.

18.4.3 GUIDELINES REGARDING SIMILARITY OF RESEARCH ENVIRONMENT

The major points just discussed are summarized in Exhibit 18.2 in a sequence of questions to aid you in determining the similarity between the research environment and the environment to which application is intended, and/or in determining whether you could replicate the experimental treatments.

EXHIBIT 18.2   *GUIDELINES: RESEARCH ENVIRONMENT*

A. If the study was some form of experimentation, go to Section B. If it was not an experiment, go to Section C.

B. Was each experimental treatment or condition adequately described? Two ways of checking on the adequacy of this description are:

1. Could you replicate the treatment? Was enough information presented so that you could create similar environments? Would you know what to do or how to get the information to do it?

2. In describing the treatments, was information presented on the following environmental categories (in some cases, a category may reflect the independent variable itself, as in studying the effects of organizational structure on faculty attitude)?

> Ecological dimensions
> Organizational structure
> Psychological characteristics or climate
> Personal characteristics of the inhabitants
> Behavior settings
> Reinforcement
> Other dimensions

   a) If you could replicate the treatments and general information was given about the context to which the subjects were exposed, then the experimental treatments have been well described.
   Would you be apt to implement the treatment(s) in a similar way?

   (1) If yes, then generalization involves little risk.
   (2) If not, then you must judge the importance of any particular discrepancy on the basis of your knowledge of and experience in the area.

   b) If a description was given, but because of its brevity or high level of abstraction, it did not provide sufficient information to replicate the details of the study, then application may be possible but involves some risk. You must estimate the degree of this risk.

   c) If only a two- or three-word label describing the treatment was given, application of the results is nearly impossible.

3. Was the environment from which the subjects came described? If so, you have additional information to aid you in applying the results.

   Stop here.

C. 1. Was the primary focus of the study to describe a particular environment and perhaps the interactions of its inhabitants as well?

a) If not, go to Section 2.

b) If yes, then description should be rather complete and comparisons with the application environment simplified. The importance of any discrepancies must be judged by your experience in and knowledge of the area.

Stop here.

2. Was the environment from which the subjects came described? Use the checklist cited under Point B.2 to determine the completeness of the description. The more complete the description, then the less risk in applying the results since you can identify important similarities and discrepancies.

18.5 MEASUREMENT PROCEDURES

Just as it is impossible to replicate precisely the research environment, it is impossible to replicate precisely the researcher's measurement procedures. Even if the same instrument were used in the application context, the procedures would be different. It would be administered by a different individual in a different tone of voice at a different time, etc. When different instruments are used by educators and researchers, additional discrepancies exist. The primary question then is the extent to which these inevitable discrepancies in measurement affect the applicability of the research results.

18.5.1 CLASSIFYING MEASUREMENT PROCEDURES

Measurement techniques can be classified into three categories on the basis of two research dimensions, *who recorded and observed the subject's behavior* and the *time period in which the behavior was recorded:*

1. The subject during the time-frame of the study,

2. The researcher, an assistant, or a recording device employed by the researcher during the study, or

3. The subject or a third person at some point in the past for purposes unrelated to the present study.

This classification is a slight modification of that used by Runkel and McGrath (122).

The first category includes instruments by means of which the subject in some way reports, and frequently records, his or her own behavior. Such instruments commonly consist of tests, questionnaires, interviews, attitude scales, interest inventories, sociometric techniques, and physical traces or residues of the subject's behavior (comments, doodles, and underlining in texts). The second category includes observation of the subject during the study, observation during which the subject cannot be considered as "reporting" his or her own behavior, such as participant and nonparticipant observation by the researcher, observation with various forms of hardware, rating scales filled out by individuals other than the subject, and measurement of physiological responses such as eye movements and GSR (galvanic skin response). The last category refers to existing records and documents of the subject's past behavior that are of use to the researcher, but were generated for reasons and under conditions unrelated to the research study itself. Records produced by industry and the government, data from past research projects, and physical traces of subject behavior, such as the remains in archeological digs, all fall into this category.

18.5.2 SIMILARITIES AND DIFFERENCES IN MEASUREMENT TECHNIQUES

Some variables cannot be measured by certain techniques. For example, classroom observation can indicate the number of times a teacher smiled, whereas the teacher cannot report this information. On the other hand, only the teacher can indicate the reason for calling on particular students to answer particular questions. These restrictions on the content tapped by a measurement technique reduce the number of possible discrepancies between the research measures and the applied measures.

Measurement techniques can also restrict the population of subjects that can be sampled. Only part of the population is available for self-administered questionnaires, even if payment for participation is provided. In addition, "a considerable proportion of the populace is functionally illiterate for personality and attitude tests developed on college populations" (143, p. 25). The variety of measurements applicable to children, the mentally retarded, the senile, or the student who speaks a foreign language is necessarily smaller than that available for examining the healthy American adult. *If the researcher used a technique not applicable to the individuals of interest to you, then application of the results should be made with great caution.* Any attempt to replicate the findings on the application group would of necessity involve a different measurement technique and reduce the probability of similar findings.

When different standardized instruments are used, or would be used, by you and the researcher to measure the same variable, answers to questions regarding their similarities and differences can sometimes be found in measurement texts, in critical reviews of tests as in Buros's *Mental Measurements Yearbooks* (24), or in research studies that compare specific tests. Your own experience with different techniques will be quite valuable in this regard as well. The ideal situation is that in which measurement results primarily reflect the trait and not the instrument, so that a variety of techniques are interchangeable. For example, differences in curiosity among children would then order the same whether based on teacher rankings, classroom observation, parental judgment, or a standardized test of curiosity. However, empirical evidence to date suggests that this is frequently not the case.

18.5.3 ARTIFACTS OF MEASUREMENT IN RESEARCH CONTEXTS

With each measurement category, measurement artifacts resulting from either the subject or the investigator may limit generalization of the results. Such *reactive measurement effects* may occur in situations in which "the testing process is itself a stimulus to change rather than a passive record of behavior" (27, p.9).

AWARENESS

The most common form of reactivity is the result of the *subject being aware of the measurement process*—of being a guinea pig so to speak. Awareness of being tested or observed may contaminate the results by producing inaccurate, dishonest, or defensive reporting. Or it may emerge if the subject assumes a role that he or she truly believes is appropriate for the demands of the measurement situation but which is not his or her "natural" role (e.g., playing the role of an expert, the helpful subject, pretending to know what to do when actually the test materials are unfamiliar).

With achievement tests, the fact that the subject is aware that his or her behavior is being recorded is often exactly what the researcher wants, so that the measurement process approximates classroom testing. With questionnaires, interviews, and other forms of self-report, the researcher usually prefers to minimize the reactive effects of awareness. Usually physical remains of the subject's behavior are less susceptible to this form of reactivity.

The effects of subject awareness have been of considerable concern in observation studies. The important element here is not the visible presence of an observer, but whether the subject is psychologically aware of the observer's presence. It is generally believed that an observer, in the process of watching an event, can affect its course; although some argue that it is very difficult to overcome one's attitudes and habits and the observer's presence is soon forgotten.

Little research evidence exists on the reactivity of the observation process in pedagogical settings (105). Mercatoris and Craighead (106) found that observation affected some, but not all, teacher–pupil interactions. They suggested that reactivity may be situation-specific and be less a threat with competent teachers.

Not all behaviors are likely to be contaminated by observation, especially behaviors not under easy conscious control such as physiological responses and characteristic mannerisms. It has also been suggested that children are less bothered than adults by observation; that reactivity with adults is decreased if engrossing tasks are observed (145); that behavior that is highly internalized and related to an individual's feelings of intellectual and interpersonal competence is more resistant to contamination than is behavior that is perceived as inconsequential; and that behavioral acts are more difficult to modify than are subjective reports such as those obtained through questionnaires and interviews (8).

MEASUREMENT AS A CHANGE AGENT

Prior measurements may introduce real changes in what is measured at the end of the study. Two measurement issues are involved: (1) that of simple *practice or repetition effects on later testing or observation,* and (2) that of *pretests sensitizing the subjects to the nature of the experimental treatment* that in turn affects their response to testing at the end of the treatment.

Anastasi (6) concluded that studies investigating the repeated administration of identical intelligence tests showed greater gains upon retest than did administration of parallel forms. In learning studies in which subjects are given repeated trials or practice, end-of-study results may primarily reflect a practice effect. It has been suggested (27) that when generalizing to the classroom, prior measurement of attitudes or personality is more likely to contaminate results than is prior measurement in the area of achievement, since regular achievement testing is an integral part of most common procedures. However, repeated classroom testing may mean posttests, not pretests. In such cases generalization from studies with pretests to situations with none may be dangerous.

Any effect of prior or continued measurement depends greatly on the unique characteristics of the study. It cannot be concluded that all situations with pretests or repeated observations create reactive effects. Usually increasing the time between pretest and posttest or between pretest and the experimental treatment will reduce the magnitude of such effects.

RECORDER CHARACTERISTICS

In addition to the subject's awareness of being observed in a study, his or her *responses may be influenced by specific characteristics of the interviewer, observer, or examiner* (such as age, sex, race). Of particular relevance to educators is whether administration of achievement tests by a teacher differs from administration by an outsider, but little research is available on this subject.

Much information on the effects of interviews is available. Maccoby and Maccoby (102, p. 462) claimed that the interviewer must assume some role, and that,

> Almost always, the role in which the respondent places the interviewer will have some status implication; that is, it will be a role which has more prestige, the same prestige, or less prestige than the respondent's own role, and the nature of the communication which can occur between the respondent and the interviewer will be greatly influenced by the mutual perceptions of status.

In a very well-conducted study replicated in five different areas of a large city, using a large number of interviewers with varying characteristics, Feldman, Hyman, and Hart (46) found few interviewer effects. Those differences that did occur were on open questions that required probing of the respondent's answers and on some items on which the interviewer was required to rate attributes of the respondent or his or her environment. In instances in which

DUNAGIN'S PEOPLE

"HOW CAN I RELAX? I'VE NEVER BEEN INTERVIEWED BY SOMEONE WHO MAKES MORE MONEY THAN I DO!"

answers could be checked against official records, the more experienced inter- viewers obtained more valid responses.

In applying results, the practitioner first must *determine whether discrepan- cies in observer, interviewer, or examiner characteristics exist in the research and application contexts and then whether such differences are serious.* Such decisions are often difficult to make. Suppose a researcher observes the class- room behavior of teachers. Would the same role be assumed by the teachers in an application situation in which they might be observed by a colleague, by their supervisors, or by a hidden camera with only the teachers themselves observing the film? Or consider the situation in which a student is aware that his or her competency is being tested when a researcher administers an achievement test. Are the effects of this awareness substantially different from those when the student's teacher tests the student's competency?

CHANGE IN RESEARCH INSTRUMENT

It is impossible for human observers, examiners, and interviewers to be pre- cisely the same "instrument" at all points of the research, and thus the possibility of contamination exists. Recorders of the data may become bored or more skilled or more relaxed, may make recording errors, interpret behavior differ- ently, or may change the nature of their appearance or dress from interview to interview. Researchers often expend much effort in controlling such errors with extensive training of testers, observers, and interviewers, using standardized procedures for administering tests, and checking on the consistency of observation during the study. All classes of measurement are subject to this type of error.

If researchers did not consider possible contamination from this source in interpreting their data nor attempt to control such factors, the study was probably poorly conducted. If controls were implemented, then you should ask whether similar controls would be or are instituted in the application situation. If not, then you need to estimate the nature and strength of the effects of such variation upon the applied measurement.

18.5.4 GUIDELINES REGARDING SIMILARITY OF MEASUREMENT PROCEDURES

The major points of this discussion of measurement artifacts are summarized in the sequence of questions presented in Exhibit 18.3.

EXHIBIT 18.3   *GUIDELINES: MEASUREMENT PROCEDURES*

A. What variables were measured by the researcher?

Questions regarding research measurement	Questions regarding application measurement
B. For *each* variable, what specific techniques were used to measure it?	For *each* variable, what specific techniques would you probably use, or do you use to measure it? Could you measure it?

C. Into what category of techniques does each of these procedures fall?	Into what category of techniques does each of these procedures fall?
Category I	
Did the subjects themselves report and possibly record their behavior in some way (test, questionnaire, interview, other self-report, physical traces)?	Would the application subjects themselves report and possibly record their behavior in some way (test, questionnaire, interview, other self-report, physical traces)?
Category II	
Was the subjects' behavior recorded or observed by the researcher (non-	Would the application subjects' behavior be recorded or observed by you or a col-

participant observation, participant observation, ratings by researcher or colleague, records of physiological responses)?

league (nonparticipant observation, participant observation, ratings by you or a colleague, records of physiological responses)?

Category III

Was the subjects' behavior recorded in the past by themselves or another party for purposes unrelated to the present research study (records, physical traces, archives of past research data)?

Would information on the subjects' behavior have been recorded in the past by themselves or another party for purposes unrelated to the application context (records, physical traces, archives of past research data)?

D. For each variable, did the research and application contexts indicate different measurement categories (I, II, III) *or* different subclasses of techniques within each category?

1. If *yes,* go to Section E.

22. If *no,* go to Section F.

E. Could the reason for the discrepancy in measurement techniques be that the research measurement restricts the population of subjects that can be measured with that procedure and specifically excludes the population of interest to you?

1. If so, then application should be made only with great caution, if at all.

2. If population restriction is not a feasible explanation for the different procedures, then application is still risky, since frequently the method of measurement has a more powerful effect on scores and behavior than the trait being measured.

F. Were there any *possible sources of error or bias* associated with the research procedure that would hinder generalization to the applied context?

1. Were the research *subjects aware* of being tested or questioned, of being observed, or that public records of their behavior were being made? If so, was this awareness likely to contaminate the record? Did the researcher attempt to determine the existence and degree of contamination?

   a) If subject awareness was not likely to contaminate the research results and awareness is also not a problem for the application measurement, then no problems in application exist.

   b) If contamination was likely with the research instrument, and a similar form of reactivity is possible with the application measurement, then there is little risk in generalization.

2. Were either *pretests or practice trials* given in the research study?

    a) If neither pretests nor practice trials were given, and either the same is true for the application measurement or weak effects are expected, then generalization can be made since measurement cannot act as a change agent in either context.

    b) If similar practice or pretest sensitization effects are expected in both the research and application contexts, then there is little risk to generalization. If different effects are expected, then there are risks to generalizing.

3. Were *characteristics of the interviewer, observer, or examiner* likely sources of measurement error?

    a) If not, would the same condition hold for the application measurement?

    b) If yes, would similar effects be expected in the application context?

4. Did the researcher control for possible *changes in the research instrument—* that the interviewer, observer, or examiner was the same instrument at all points of the study?

    a) If controls exist in both the research and application contexts, generalization can be made.

    b) If changes in the research instrument can easily occur in either or both contexts, then generalization should be made with caution.

G. What other discrepancies exist between the research and application measurements? The final decision regarding application must be based on the answers to the above questions as well as your past experience and knowledge, information from the measurement literature, and the amount of discrepancy you feel you can tolerate before applying the research results.

18.6 APPLICATION OF RESULTS FROM DIFFERENT STUDIES

The application of research results is complicated by the fact that different studies often produce different results. How can you decide which results and/or which procedures are likely to be the most successful for you? There are no guidelines to show you how to make the best decision. However, you should first try to resolve the discrepancies among the studies. The discrepancies may be superficial; you may be able to isolate a group of studies with similar design characteristics that yielded similar results, or you may find that someone else has resolved some of the conflicts. If so, then your decision is not as difficult as it first appeared, since there is a consensus among some studies. If the conflicts cannot be resolved, then your decision is difficult. The best you can do is to apply those results or try out those procedures that you feel have the best chance of success, based on your knowledge of both the research and the application contexts.

19

Determining the Applicability of Specific Research Studies to Educational Contexts

Three studies are reproduced to illustrate the application of the concepts presented in Chapter 18. Two are experimental studies, that, in general, compare whole word with letter–sound (graphic–phonic) approaches to reading. However, the research settings differ in their similarity to reading instruction in the elementary grades. The third study is nonexperimental, focusing on the meaning of integration to senior high school students. In discussing each of these studies, the sequence of questions presented in Exhibits 18.1 through 18.3 in the preceding chapter is followed.

19.1 EXPERIMENTAL STUDIES

Assume for the moment that you are a first grade teacher and one of your main concerns is that of improving the reading skills of your students. You have a class of 30, 15 boys and 15 girls, who come from a rural, light-industrial community of 15,000 in central Illinois. In past years the first grade students in your school have performed slightly below expected end-of-year grade levels on standardized reading tests. Presently you use a combination of reading techniques, attempting to capitalize upon the strengths of each, usually instructing in a small group format with ten students per group.

You encounter the following study by Bishop and examine it for its potential relevance to improving the reading instruction in your classroom. The basic purpose of the Bishop study as stated in paragraph 5 was "to determine the transfer value of training with individual letters as compared with whole words, and to investigate the role of grapheme–phoneme associations in reading." Bishop concluded that letter training had greater transfer value than word training had because it helped individuals to identify grapheme–phoneme correspondences (paragraphs 32–34). As you read the Bishop study, ask yourself if you are justified in inferring that your students should be taught to read by the letter approach or that you should at least try it out in your classroom. What factors might make such application unwarranted?

19.2 EXAMPLE—BISHOP STUDY

Transfer Effects of Word and Letter Training in Reading
CAROL H. BISHOP

[1] The basic process involved in reading is that of "decoding" from graphic to phonic patterns (Hall, 1961; Smith, 1956; Soffietti, 1955). Bloomfield (1942) states, "In order to read alphabetic writing one must have an ingrained habit of producing the sounds of one's language when one sees the written marks which conventionally represent the phonemes" (p. 128). One of the most important criteria of the effectiveness of teaching methods is the amount of transfer which a method yields (Carroll, 1958; Cronbach, 1963). To the psychologist, it is as essential to investigate the basis for transfer of reading training as to find the reading method which yields most transfer.

[2] A point of departure in conducting such an investigation is to distinguish two major respects in which training may vary. One is in regard to the visual-auditory unit employed in training and the other concerns the degree of emphasis upon graphic-phonic associations. Three debated teaching "methods" may be differentiated on this basis: the traditional "phonic" method, which employs individual letters in training and stresses graphic-phonic relationships, i.e., rules of pronunciation (Dougherty, 1923); the traditional "look-and-say" method, which employs entire words and disregards rules of pronunciation (Huey, 1908); and the more recent Bloomfield system, which stresses graphic-phonic relationships but recommends training in the form of entire words (Bloomfield and Barnhart, 1961).

[3] Investigations of the transfer effectiveness of the unit employed in training have produced diverse results (Witty and Sizemore, 1955; Gray, 1955). The different findings may be due to the varying relationships among the studies between training unit and degree of emphasis upon graphic-phonic associations.

[4] It has generally been agreed that a knowledge of graphic-phonic relationships among units smaller than whole words is necessary for transfer to reading new words. At present, a large-scale research project is being undertaken in England on the assumption that one of the major causes of reading disabilities is the irregularities between spelling and pronunciation in the English language, and the presumably resultant difficulty of acquiring graphic-phonic relationships (Downing, 1962). Yet there are few empirical answers to questions concerning the role of component graphic-phonic relationships in reading. Are component graphic-phonic associations necessary to learn to read? Do they facilitate the process of learning to read, and most important, are they in fact necessary for transfer to new words?

[5] The following experiment was designed to determine the transfer value of training with individual letters as compared with whole words, and to investigate

Carol H. Bishop, 1964. Transfer effects of word and letter training on reading. *Journal of Verbal Learning and Verbal Behavior* 3: 215–221. Reprinted with permission of C. H. Bishop and the *Journal of Verbal Learning and Verbal Behavior*.

the role of grapheme-phoneme associations[2] in reading. The child's experience in learning to read was simulated by teaching adult subjects to read several Arabic words.[3] A three-stage transfer design was employed.

METHOD

Material

[6] The graphemes used in the experiment were 12 Arabic characters, each with a one-to-one grapheme-phoneme correspondence. The set of letters contained 8 consonants and 4 vowels. These letters were combined to form 2 sets of 8 Arabic words. The letter set and one of the word sets were used for training in Stage II. The other set of words served as the transfer words in Stage III.

[7] The word lists were so constructed that each of the 12 letters appeared at least once in both lists, all of the words were of a CVCV pattern, and half of the consonants appeared twice each as the beginning letters in one list, with the other half appearing twice each as beginning letters in the second list (thus preventing word differentiation on the basis of first letters only).

[8] A native speaker of the language recorded on tape the 12 letter-sounds in 3 different orders and the 2 sets of words in 4 different orders. The lists were recorded with a 4-sec. interval between each letter-sound or word, and an interval of 20 sec. between each order.

[9] The graphic form of each letter or word was handprinted on a 4 × 6-inch index card. The words deviated from true Arabic writing in several respects: (1) the same character represented a sound whether it appeared at the beginning, the middle, or the end of a word, (2) the vowel-sounds were always represented by their printed symbols, (3) the letters composing a word were disjoined, and (4) the words were written from left to right. These alterations were introduced to prevent interference from pre-existing reading habits. The two lists of Arabic words with their phonetic symbols are shown in Fig. 19.1.

Subjects

[10] Sixty students enrolled in a beginning psychology course at Cornell University participated in the experiment to fulfill partial course requirements. The first 40 Ss were alternately assigned to single-letter training (Group L) or whole-word training (Group W) when they came for testing. The last 20 Ss received no special training, serving as a control group (Group C). The sexes were equated in all groups.

---

[2] This experiment deals only with the smallest component graphic-phonic relationship, the relationship between a single written letter and its speech correlate. This relationship is referred to, hereafter, as a grapheme-phoneme correspondence.

[3] The English translation of the Arabic words were not taught since the associations of meaning to spoken words is a separate learning problem which developmentally precedes reading.

Training words	Phonetic symbols	Transfer words	Phonetic symbols
ڡ ر ا ن	fa:ru:	ى ر ڤ م	mi:ri:
ى د ا ن	fa:di:	ݛ ت ر م	mu:tu:
ا ن ى ت	ti:fa:	ا ش ر ك	ko:ša:
ى ن ر ت	tu:ni:	ى ڤ ا ك	ka:fi:
ا ش ى ش	ši:ša:	ا ڤ ى ن	ni:fa:
ى م ى ش	ši:mi:	ى د ا ن	na:di:
ى ڤ ا د	da:fi:	ا ش ى ر	ri:ša:
ݛ ك ڡ د	do:ko:	ى ڤ ى ر	ri:fi:

FIG. 19.1 Arabic words and phonetic symbols.

[11] Homogeneity of groups was obtained to some extent by testing only freshmen and sophomores who were native English speakers and who were not acquainted with Arabic. After the experiment had concluded, a further check on homogeneity was made by comparing the Ss' SAT verbal scores, which were required prior to college entrance. An analysis of variance revealed no significant difference between the groups at the 0.01 level or better.

Procedure

[12] The procedure was identical for all groups in Stages I and III, but the training procedure in Stage II differed.

[13] *Stage I—Phonic Familiarization.* All Ss were told that the object of the experiment was to learn to read several Arabic words. Each S became familiar with the transfer set of words by listening to the words played on the tape recorder and by repeating each one aloud in the 4-sec. interval which followed it. Correction was given by E if a word was not pronounced properly. The list was repeated 3 times.

[14] *Stage II—Graphic-Phonic Training: Group L.* The S listened to, and repeated, the 12 letter-sounds. The last was repeated once only, and again, E corrected any errors. The S next learned to associate the graphic forms of the letters with their correct sounds. The cards, each with 1 printed letter, were placed one at a time on a stand in front of S. Each card was exposed for 4 sec., at the end of which the correct sound was repeated on the tape recorder.

[15] The S was instructed to try to learn the grapheme-phoneme associations on the first repetition of the list, and to respond with the correct sound as soon as he was able, on all subsequent repetitions. The correct sound was always repeated at the end of the 4-sec. response interval. The list was repeated 16 times in 3 different orders with an interval of 20 sec. between trials.

[16] *Group W.* The procedure was identical to that of Group L except that the 8 training words were employed instead of the 12 letters. It was decided that

the total amount of time spent in training, rather than number of repetitions or degree of learning the training task, was the important factor to equate in order to evaluate the efficiency of the training methods, since this most closely simulates the classroom situation in which a given amount of time is available for reading training. The number of units used in training differed for the groups. The word list, therefore, was repeated twice in familiarizing S with the word sounds and was repeated 24 times in training S to read the words, thereby equalling the time spent in training Group L.

[17] *Group C.* The S participated in a second, unrelated experiment which determined recognition thresholds of three-letter English words or nonsense syllables presented tachistoscopically. The amount of time spent in the experiment varied slightly for Ss, but it was approximately the same as that in Groups L and W.

[18] *Stage III—Testing for Transfer of Training.* All Ss were tested on ability to learn to read the 8 *transfer* words. The cards with the printed words were presented one at a time, and S was to respond with the correct word during a 4-sec. interval. The procedure was identical to that for Groups L and W in Stage II, except that S was instructed to read the words on the first trial if he were able to do so, and the learning trials continued until an individual reached a criterion of 2 perfect trials.[4]

[19] *Testing for Grapheme-Phoneme Associations.* At the close of Stage III, all Ss were tested on their ability to give the correct letter-sound within a 4-sec. interval following the presentation of each printed letter. The letters were presented once only.

[20] *Subdivision of Training Groups.* The Ss in the two training groups (Groups L and W) were asked to explain how they tried to learn to read the *transfer* words. Their explanations were tape recorded, and later two judges listened to their answers and decided on the basis of the Ss' reports whether each S learned the words by applying knowledge of individual grapheme-phoneme correspondence ("sounding out" words) or by associating the spoken words with the printed words by some other means. This was a double-blind method in that the Ss did not know the purpose of the experiment when they reported their method of learning the words, and the judges did not know which type of training was given to a particular S nor how well S performed. Any disagreements between judges were discussed, and if agreement could not be reached, S was not categorized.

RESULTS

Degree of Learning the Training Task

[21] The amount of time spent in training was equated for the experimental groups. Consequently there was variation in the degree to which the two train-

---

[4] The criterion used in the final analyses was one perfect trial. Each S was run to two perfect trials in the event that later playback of the tape recording of S's responses would reveal an undetected error on what had been taken as the first perfect trial. This procedure allowed greater assurance of obtaining at least one perfect trial for each S.

ing lists were mastered. Nineteen of the 20 Ss who received letter training learned the 12 letters within 16 trials. Thirteen of the 20 word-trained Ss learned the 8 training words within 24 trials. The average first correct trial among those Ss in Group L who reached perfection was 9.42 as compared to 18.07 in Group W. These figures represent an average overlearning of 69.85% in Group L and 32.82% in Group W for those Ss who reached perfection. The one S in Group L who did not reach perfection had 1 error on the last trial and the 7 Ss in Group W who did not reach perfection had an average of 2.25 errors on the last trial. Letter training was thus more readily mastered than was word training.

Measurement of Transfer

[22] Two criteria of learning were used in Stage III: number of trials to reach perfection and number of correct responses on the first trial. The means of the three groups are shown in Table 19.1. There was a significant difference in trials due to training ($F = 15.05$, df $= 2/57$, $p < 0.01$). The rank order of the groups from least to most trials is Group L, W, and C. Individual comparisons of the differences between Group L and both Groups W and C are significant at the 0.01 level, but the difference between Group W and Group C is not.

[23] Since there were no correct responses on the first trial in Group C, Groups L and W were tested for a mean different from 0. Both were significantly different ($t = 4.83$, df $= 19$, $p < 0.01$; $t = 3.50$, df $= 19$, $p < 0.01$). The difference between Group L and Group W was in the same direction as in the previous comparison but was not significant ($t = 1.47$, df $= 38$, $p > 0.01$). The failure to find a significant difference on the first trial may have been due to the fact that the letter-trained Ss were seeing the letters in the framework of whole words for the first time. It often took an initial period of adjustment to the new situation before the Ss started to respond.

[24] The results show, therefore, that letter training has more transfer value than word training, but that word training does produce some transfer, at least in the early stages.

Degree of Learning Grapheme-Phoneme Associations

[25] The average numbers of letter-sounds known at the end of the transfer period are given in Table 19.1. There was a significant difference due to training,

TABLE 19.1 *EFFECTS OF UNIT OF TRAINING IN TRANSFER STAGE*

	Group L		Group W		Group C	
	Mean	*SD*	*Mean*	*SD*	*Mean*	*SD*
First correct trial	7.35	5.68	15.20	11.14	24.95	12.95
Number of correct responses on 1st trial	2.90	2.72	1.75	2.35	0.00	0.00
Number of correct letters	11.85	0.50	8.05	3.37	6.75	3.20

the rank order again being Group L, W, and C ($F = 20.15$, df $= 2/57$, $p < 0.01$), and again comparisons of the differences between Group L and both Groups W and C are significant at the 0.01 level, but the difference between Group W and Group C is not.

[26] The number of correct letters in Groups W and C ranged from 0 to 12. Since it was possible to learn grapheme-phoneme associations regardless of the type of training S was assigned, it was necessary to subdivide the training groups in order to evaluate the transfer merits of such associations.

Categorization of Subgroups

[27] Those Ss who learned to read the transfer words by applying knowledge of grapheme-phoneme correspondences were separated from those who did not use such knowledge. Fifteen of the Ss in Group L applied grapheme-phoneme associations, 2 did not and 3 could not be categorized. In Group W, 12 Ss applied grapheme-phoneme associations, 7 did not and 1 could not be categorized.

[28] Since Group W was substantially divided, the responses of the two subgroups in Group W were further analyzed to determine the effect of grapheme-phoneme associations on reading. A subscript 1 signifies the subgroup which used grapheme-phoneme associations and a subscript 0 indicates the subgroup which did not. For all further analyses, the scores of the S who could not be categorized was dropped. SAT verbal scores were again compared, and there was no significant difference between the subgroups at the 0.01 level or better.

[29] *Validation of Categories.* A brief check on the validity of the subdivisions was made by comparing the subgroups on number of correct grapheme-phoneme associations given at the close of Stage III. The means are shown in Table 19.2. In Group W there could have been self-adopted letter-sound training depending upon the approach taken by a S. It is thus reasonable to expect that Group W_1 should know more grapheme-phoneme correspondences than Group W_0. This, in fact, was true ($t = 4.80$, df $= 17$, $p < 0.01$).

[30] *Degree of Learning the Training Task.* Of the 12 Ss in Group W_1, 75% learned the words to perfection during the training period; whereas 57% of the 7 Ss in Group W_0 performed to perfection. The average first correct trial among those reaching perfection in Group W_1 was 17.55 as compared to an average of

TABLE 19.2   *EFFECTS OF GRAPHEME-PHONEME ASSOCIATIONS IN TRANSFER STAGE*

	Group W_1		Group W_0	
	Mean	*SD*	*Mean*	*SD*
First correct trial	9.75	7.15	23.14	12.70
Number of correct responses on 1st trial	2.83	2.51	0.14	0.34
Number of correct letters	10.00	1.66	4.86	3.38

19.25 among the same in Group W_0. The 3 Ss in Group W_1 who did not reach perfection had an average of 1 error on the last trial and the 3 Ss in Group W_0 had an average of 3.33 errors. Word training was therefore more readily mastered when S took a letter-learning approach.

[31] *Measurement of Transfer.* The means of the subgroups on the two previous learning criteria are shown in Table 19.2. Group W_1 took fewer trials to perfection and had more correct responses on the first transfer trial ($t = 3.16$, df $= 17$, $p < 0.01$; $t = 2.89$, df $= 17$, $p = 0.01$). Group W_1 shows substantial transfer, closely resembling the performance of Group L, while Group W_0 reveals essentially no transfer.

DISCUSSION

[32] Four conclusions may be drawn from the results. (1) Letter training is superior to word training in transfer to reading new words. This is consistent with some older findings (Valentine, 1913). Word training, however, does have some value when compared to the control condition of no training. (2) Component grapheme-phoneme associations are not necessary for learning to read. (3) Although words may be read without the aid of grapheme-phoneme associations, application of these associations does facilitate the learning of new words. (4) Grapheme-phoneme associations, in fact, form the bases for transfer in this investigation.

[33] The two training units (word and letter) produced different results in the transfer stage, but the differences in group performance were almost entirely due to the differences in percentage of Ss applying grapheme-phoneme associations in the two groups. Letter training provided a propitious opportunity for Ss to form the associations and probably influenced Ss to apply them to reading words. Word training left open the possibility that Ss might set themselves to learn grapheme-phoneme correspondences. Word training did not have, for individual Ss, transfer value which was only half as effective as letter training, contrary to the apparent results when comparing group means. Instead it had strong transfer value for that portion of the Ss who learned and applied grapheme-phoneme associations and little or no transfer value for those who did not.

[34] The reason for the overall inferiority of word training as compared to letter training was either that it did not direct as many Ss to learn grapheme-phoneme correspondences or that not all Ss were capable of picking out these relationships when embedded in words. Further research is needed to indicate which alternative is true.

[35] The results of this study have clear implications for the teaching of reading. The importance of component grapheme-phoneme relationships has been indicated, and it has been shown that the degree to which these relationships are learned may vary markedly among individuals given the same type of training. Hockett (1960) and Venezky (1962) have recently demonstrated that there are regular (though often complex) graphic-phonic correlates in the English language, and Gibson, Osser, and Pick (1963) have shown that some of these relationships can be learned by children by the end of their first year of reading. Although the present study has dealt with one-to-one grapheme-phoneme correspondences, it is possible that the results of this study might apply to the more global correspondences found by Hockett and Venezky. This finding would

indicate that to obtain a method of teaching children to read which will transfer to new words, further research should be concerned with the most efficient way of teaching children the spelling-to-sound correlates found in the English language. It would be advantageous to test experimentally the transfer values of various methods of teaching these correspondences, and to determine the generality of this transfer for children of a given age.

SUMMARY

[36] The child's process of learning to read was simulated by teaching adults to read several Arabic words. The purposes of the study were to determine the transfer value of training with individual letters as opposed to whole words, and to investigate the role of grapheme-phoneme associations in reading. It was found that letter training had greater transfer value than word training. Knowledge of grapheme-phoneme correspondences was not necessary to read words, but was necessary for transfer to new words. The reason for the overall inferiority of word training was either that it did not direct as many subjects to learn grapheme-phoneme correspondences or that not all subjects were capable of picking out these relationships when the relationships were embedded in words.

REFERENCES

Bloomfield, L., Linguistics and reading. *Elem. English Rev.*, 1942, *19*, 125–130, 183–186.

Bloomfield, L., and Barnhart, C. L. *Let's read: A linguistic approach.* Detroit: Wayne State Univer. Press, 1961.

Carroll, J. B., Chr. Psychological contributions to problems of communication in education, Report of Panel II. *Psychological research in education.* Washington, D.C.: National Academy of Sciences-National Research Council, 1958, 11–14.

Cronbach, L. J. The psychological background for curriculum experimentation. In P. C. Rosenbloom (Ed.), *National conference on curriculum experimentation.* New York: McGraw-Hill, 1963.

Dougherty, M. L. *How to teach phonics.* New York: Houghton Mifflin Co., 1923.

Downing, J. A. The relationship between reading attainment and the inconsistency of English spelling at the infants' school stage. *Brit. J. educ. Psychol.*, 1962, *32*, 166–178.

Gibson, E. J., Osser, H., and Pick, A. D. A study of the development of grapheme-phoneme correspondences. *J. verb. Learn. verb. Behav.*, 1963, *2*, 142–146.

Gray, W. S. Phonic versus other methods of teaching reading. *Read. Teacher,* 1955, *9*, 102–106.

Hall, R. A. Jr. *Sound and spelling in English.* Philadelphia: Chilton Co., 1961.

Hockett, C. N. Analysis of English spelling, Part I. Analysis of graphic monosyllables. Unpublished manuscript, 1960.

Huey, E. B. *The psychology and pedagogy of reading.* New York: Macmillan, 1908.

Pike, K. L. Phonemics: A technique for reducing languages to writing. Vol. 3. *Linguistics.* Ann Arbor: Univer. of Michigan Publications, 1947.

Smith, H. L., Jr., *Linguistic science and the teaching of English.* Cambridge: Harvard Univer. Press, 1956.

Soffietti, J. P., Why children fail to read: A linguistic analysis. *Harv. educ. Rev.*, 1955, **25**, 63–84.

Valentine, C. W. Experiments on the method of teaching reading. *J. exper. Ped.*, 1913, **2**, 99–112.

Venezky, R. A computer program for deriving spelling-to-sound correlations. Unpublished master's thesis, Cornell University, 1962.

Witty, P., and Sizemore, R. Phonics in the reading program: A review and an evaluation. *Elem. English Rev.*, 1955, **32**, 355–371.

19.3 DISCUSSION OF BISHOP STUDY

19.3.1 SUBJECTS

In answer to Section A, Exhibit 18.1, a very brief description of the children in your classroom was given, but it will suffice for purposes of the present discussion. In answer to Section B, Exhibit 18.1, Bishop's sample was not selected by probability sampling techniques from the target population, and thus the sample did not represent the target population. Although the target population was not clearly delineated, it appeared to be children at the early stages of reading (paragraphs 5, 35, and 36). However, Bishop clearly specified (paragraph 5) that the reading experiences of children were not directly examined in the study, but were instead simulated by a sample of college students learning Arabic words. Bishop's sample was not representative of the accessible population of undergraduate college students either (Section C, Exhibit 18.1), since the students volunteered for the experiment in order to fulfill a course requirement.

Thus we must ask if the sample can be considered to be "like" the application group; that is, your first graders (Section D, Exhibit 18.1). It is immediately apparent that the research and application groups differ on such variables as age, prior reading experience in English, and prior experiences in learning how to learn; variables that could affect the results of the study. These discrepancies make generalization to the application group risky.

19.3.2 RESEARCH ENVIRONMENT

The experimental procedures were described in some detail: all the training and transfer words were presented, the size of the stimulus cards specified, the sequence of the word and letter lists, the exact time between the stimuli, the type of feedback, the number of exposures to stimuli, etc. Certainly Bishop presented enough information to replicate the study (Section B.1., Exhibit 18.2).

Would you be apt to replicate the treatments in a similar way (Section B.2a, Exhibit 18.2)? Probably not. In the first place the behavior settings differ, an experimental laboratory setting versus a first grade classroom. Associated with these different behavior settings are discrepancies in Moos's other categories as well (ecological structure of laboratory versus that of classroom, the psycho-social characteristics or climates created in the two environments, reinforcement patterns, etc.). Your instructional setting would probably be longer, less controlled, in a group rather than an individualized format, etc. Of course, the content of the tasks differs. You would use English grapheme and phonemes. The crucial question is whether such discrepancies are important. No information was given on the environment from which the subjects came (Section B.3., Exhibit 18.2).

Interestingly, despite the highly controlled nature of the study and the little variation in external response allowed the subjects, reports on how they learned the grapheme–phoneme relationships (paragraphs 20, 26–31) indicate that even under rigid experimental control, subjects are not always passive. A researcher cannot always assume that the treatment determines the activities of each subject, since subjects sometimes create their own treatments.

19.3.3 MEASUREMENT PROCEDURES

Bishop measured three variables (Section A, Exhibit 18.3): immediate learning, transfer, and the subjects' perceptions of how they learned (paragraphs 18–20). All three variables are self-reports and fall into Category I (Sections B and C, Exhibit 18.3). Measurement procedures for the immediate learning and transfer variables are best classified as tests, and the students' perception of learning as a questionnaire.

Suppose you decided to measure immediate learning and transfer with a similar stimulus card technique. However, you decided that you could not measure the children's reactions to how they learned, since you felt that such self-reflection requires an ability to abstract that is not acquired until a much later age. Such a decision reflects the way in which measurement techniques restrict the population available to be measured (Section E, Exhibit 18.3). It also means that the part of Bishop's report dealing with these results (paragraphs 27–31) is of less value to you.

Since the research measurement procedures for immediate learning and transfer were so similar, they will be treated as one technique. In both the research and the application measurement contexts, you can assume that the subjects are aware of being tested (Section F.1, Exhibit 18.3). Contamination is, of course, possible in the laboratory situation, but you have no way of determining how serious it might be. However, you might want to assume that measurement of the first grade children is less likely to be affected by awareness, especially since the tests would be given by you, their regular teacher, and the children have no apparent reason to assume a role different from their usual one in any classroom testing situation.

Since no pretests were given, pretest sensitization effects cannot occur. However, practice or learning trials were given (Section F.2, Exhibit 18.3). Probably your children would also be allowed to practice. In either case, practice will have an effect on later testings. Bishop's data showed the results of practice on immediate learning (paragraph 21). The problem in comparing the research and application contexts is the almost impossible task of equating for the amount of practice. Bishop equated the amount of practice time in the three groups, rather than the number of learning trials (paragraphs 16–17). The amount of practice in first graders that would produce similar results is an empirical question. However, one can assume that in both cases, the reactivity of practice will have the same general effect, that of increasing achievement in learning, and thereby reducing the risks in generalization.

Effects of tester characteristics (Section F.3, Exhibit 18.3) were possible in the Bishop study, but it is difficult to determine if any occurred. Thus comparisons with the application measurement cannot be made. The testing procedures were highly controlled in Bishop's study (Section F.4, Exhibit 18.3), allowing for little reactivity. It is doubtful whether your testing procedures in the classroom would be so highly controlled. A good example of testing control was the double-blind coding procedure used in categorizing the subjects' perception of how they learned (paragraph 20).

In summary, the main discrepancies between the research and hypothetical application measurement procedures appear to be in the higher reactivity of testing awareness in the research setting, the difficulty in comparing the roles assumed by the subjects in the two contexts, the difficulty in equating the amount of practice, and the weaker control over possible instrument changes in the applied context.

19.3.4 SUMMARY

Of the three areas, Subjects, Research Environment, and Measurement Procedures, the greatest discrepancy between the resarch context and the hypothetical application context was the Subjects. This factor alone makes it difficult to apply the results. This difficulty is compounded in trying to compare the learning of Arabic letters and sounds by college students to the learning of English letters and sounds by first grade children, the first presented in a short laboratory setting and the latter presented by a teacher over a longer period of time. The discrepancies that also existed between the measurement procedures seem small by comparison.

19.4 EXAMPLE—SULLIVAN, OKADA, AND NIEDERMEYER STUDY

Not satisfied with your search of the literature, you locate a study by Sullivan, Okada, and Niedermeyer representing another variation on the single-letter versus whole-word training approaches to reading. In this study, tasks were modified to more closely approximate the sound blends common in the English language (paragraphs 2–3). The research setting approximated normal classroom instruction since "the study was designed to identify a method of word-attack instruction for eventual use in the classroom" (paragraph 6).

Learning and Transfer under Two Methods of Word-Attack Instruction
HOWARD J. SULLIVAN, MASAHITO OKADA, AND FRED C. NIEDERMEYER

[1] The available evidence on word-attack instruction indicates that greater positive transfer (i.e., ability to read new words composed of familiar grapheme-phoneme correspondences) results from single-letter training than from whole-word training (Bishop, 1964; Jeffrey and Samuels, 1967). Nonetheless, sounding out and reading new words on a letter-by-letter basis (the single-letter method) is a very difficult task for the beginning reader. The child must first say or think each letter sound and then say the word, either by blending the sounds together or by figuring out and saying the word "made" by the sounds. Silberman (1964) and Jeffrey and Samuels (1967) report that the task of figuring out the word is particularly difficult for young children, even when they can say each individual sound in the word.

[2] It is hardly surprising that the task of figuring out the word made by a sequence of letter sounds is difficult for the beginning reader using the single-letter word-attack process. The difficulty of this task would appear to be at least partially a function of (1) the number of letters or sounds in the word, since the child presumably must remember each sound that he says or thinks in sounding out the word, and (2) the amount of distortion of the sounds pronounced individually, as contrasted with their pronunciation in the word itself. Even to figure out relatively simple consonant-vowel-consonant (CVC) words, the child must recall a sequence of three sounds and normally must overcome considerable distortion of one or two of the sounds.

[3] One technique for potentially simplifying the task of figuring out a new word involves the teaching of each common VC and VCC word ending as a single grapheme-phoneme unit. For example, the child would be explicitly taught to say "ad" whenever he pronounces the VC combination *ad* either in isolation or in sounding out a word. Thus, in sounding out the word *bad*, he would pronounce the component sounds as "b-ad." This procedure contrasts with the single-letter approach, under which the child would sound out the word as "b-a-d."

[4] Advantages appear to be associated with both the combined-sounds and the single-letter procedures. Potential advantages of learning VC and VCC combinations as single units are (1) the number of separate sounds to be used in figuring out new words is reduced and (2) distortion in the VC or VCC combination is eliminated. These factors should simplify the task of figuring out new words. The primary advantage in the individual-letter procedure, on the other hand, is that a relatively small number of individual letter sounds combine with each other to form many common VC and VCC combinations. Thus, the child who masters the single-letter procedure may be able to sound out and read a greater number of new words than the child who has mastered common letter combinations and relies exclusively upon this approach.

Howard J. Sullivan, Masahito Okada, and Fred C. Niedermeyer, 1971. Learning and transfer under two methods of word-attack instruction. *American Educational Research Journal* 8: 227–239. Copyright 1971 by the American Educational Research Association, Washington, D.C. Reprinted with permission.

[5] The present study was conducted to determine the effectiveness of word-attack instruction based upon a single-letter approach as contrasted with instruction in which common VC and VCC combinations are taught as single grapheme-phoneme units. Effectiveness of the two approaches was evaluated on the basis of subjects' performance in reading (1) new words composed of graphemes taught in the study (i.e., transfer) and (2) graphemes and words practiced in the word-attack instruction during the study. The desired outcome of the study was the identification of the more effective method of work-attack instruction so that this procedure could be incorporated into a beginning reading program currently under development at the Southwest Regional Laboratory.

[6] Because the study was designed to identify a method of word-attack instruction for eventual use in the classroom, experimental conditions were established to closely simulate normal classroom conditions for reading instruction. First grade children were given group instruction in their regular classrooms daily for approximately a six-week period. The letters taught during the study were selected and sequenced by computer as the most appropriate graphemes for use in word-attack instruction in a beginning program. Primary criteria used in selecting and sequencing the letters were grapheme-phoneme regularity and the number of high frequency one-syllable words composed of the letters. All letter combinations were composed of the selected individual letters.

METHOD

Subjects (Ss)

[7] The Ss in the study consisted originally of all pupils in two first-grade classes in a metropolitan southern California elementary school. In the sixth month of the school year (March, 1970), all Ss were pretested with a 32-item pretest described later in this section. Ss within each classroom were formed into matched pairs on the basis of the pretest score and randomly assigned to one of the two treatment groups. Four of the original 56 Ss were lost or dropped due to attrition factors (moving and poor attendance), and the matched pair of each of these Ss was dropped from the data analyses to guard against differential mortality effects. The mean scores of the 24 Ss remaining in each group on the 32-item pretest were 10.71 (S.D. = 9.00) for the single-letter (SL) group and 10.46 (S.D. = 8.92) for the letter-combination (LC) group. There were 11 girls and 13 boys in the SL group and 13 girls and 11 boys in the LC group.

[8] Test scores from the two classes revealed that as a group the participating Ss scored very slightly above the national average on a standardized reading test (Cooperative Primary Reading Test) administered in Grade 1. Thus, the sample was more characteristic of first graders who are average readers than of populations where high rates of reading failure are typically observed.

Procedure

[9] Ss were instructed in four separate groups. One group in each of the two participating classes was an SL group and one was an LC group. The groups originally consisted of 14 subjects each, but group size was modified slightly during the study by attrition. All instruction was conducted in the Ss' regular first grade classrooms. The order of instruction was counterbalanced between

groups both within and between classes to compensate for time-of-day factors which could influence the results.

[10] A single researcher was trained to teach under both SL and LC conditions. To insure that the difference in treatments was exclusively in the length of the ending unit as pronounced both in isolation and in sounding out words, extensive practice sessions employing videotapes were held prior to the study and several lessons were observed by senior research personnel during the experiment. The SL group was taught to say the sound of each individual letter both in isolation and in words, except for ending CC units (consonant blends, digraphs, and geminate consonants) which were taught as single phonemes. The LC group was taught all VC and VCC ending combinations as single grapheme-phoneme units to be pronounced as one unit both in isolation and in words.

[11] The instructional content was organized into 8 lessons, as shown below in the Content Outline (Table 19.3). It can be seen from the Content Outline that the lesson content was the same for each group with two exceptions. The most important exception was that in each lesson the LC group was taught each ending-letter combination used in the practice words, but the SL group was not taught these combinations. A minor variation was that in Lessons 6 & 7 the SL group was taught four CC blends (for use in sounding out and reading CVCC words) that were taught only in the context of VCC combinations to the LC group.

[12] Each group was given 25 minutes a day of instruction for three days on each of the eight lessons except Lesson 1, which required four days because it included more content than the other lessons. In each lesson, children were initially taught the sounds of the new letters and/or letter combinations for the lesson. Instruction and practice in sounding out and reading new words was then provided for the remainder of the lesson. All content was taught with flash cards and word-list booklets in a prescribed sequence that was identical for each group.

[13] For sounding out and reading new words, all Ss were taught to respond to the oral stimulus, "Sound out and read this word" by first saying the sounds in the manner appropriate for their group and then saying the word. In three-letter words, the SL Ss sounded out each letter separately (C-V-C) before attempting to say the word, whereas the LC pupils sounded out each word as C-VC. In CVCC words, the SL group sounded out the word as C-V-CC, and the LC group sounded it out as C-VCC. Thus, in sounding out both three-letter and four-letter words, the SL group always said three separate sounds, and the LC group always said only two separate sounds. These procedures are contrasted below:

Oral Stimulus	Printed stimulus[2]	SL Response	LC Response
"Sound out and read this word"	sit	"s-i-t, sit"	"s-it, sit"
	nest	"n-e-st, nest"	"n-est, nest"

---

[2] Presented on a flash card by the teacher or contained in word-list booklets used by each child under teacher direction.

TABLE 19.3 *CONTENT OUTLINE BY LESSON*

Lesson	New letter sounds (both groups)	New letter combinations (LC group only)	Work-attack practice words (both groups)			
1	s, i, t, p, n, l	it, in ip	sit pit lit	pin tin sin	lip nip sip tip	
2	a, m	at, an, ap	sat mat pat	man pan tan	lap nap tap map	
3	e, d, r, b	et, en, ed	net set met bet pet	pen men den ten	red led bed Ted	
4	h	id, ad, am	lid did hid	sad mad dad bad had	ham ram bam Sam	
5	o, u	ot, op, ut	lot not hot dot	pop top hop	but rut hut	
6	nt[1], st[1]	ent, est, ust	sent tent bent rent	rest nest pest best	rust dust bust	
7	f, w, ll, nd[1], lt[1]	end, elt, ell	send bend lend mend	melt belt felt	sell bell well	
8	k, sh, nk	ish, ink, ank, unk	fish wish dish	sink pink wink	sank bank tank	hunk bunk dunk

[1] Taught to SL group only.

[14] As training in "putting sounds together to make words," two days of oral-oral instruction and practice were provided prior to the initial instruction with printed stimuli. In this instruction, the researcher-teacher pronounced each word in a sequenced list of words taught in the study in either two or three parts (as appropriate for the particular treatment) and the children said the word "made by" the sounds. This activity was judged to be necessary because the Ss' regular reading instruction was based primarily on a whole word approach and they had received little instruction and practice involving component sounds of words.

Materials

[15] Instruction for both groups was conducted with flash cards and word-list booklets. Each lesson included a flash card for each letter sound, letter combination (LC group only), and word-attack practice word taught in the lesson, as shown in the Content Outline. The individual word-list booklets contained one page per lesson listing the content for that lesson. Both the flash cards and word-list booklets differed for the two groups only in that letter combinations were included in the LC materials but not in the SL materials. The same prescribed sequence of instruction was employed in both groups with the instructional materials.

Criterion Measures

[16] Four tests were administered during the study. Each test consisted of four subtests assessing Ss reading of the following content: 1. *Word Elements:* i.e., letters included in the training for both groups and letter combinations included in the LC training; 2. *Practice Words:* words practiced during word-attack instruction; 3. *Transfer 1 Words:* new words containing VC and VCC endings taught as single grapheme-phoneme units to the LC group; and 4. *Transfer 2 Words:* new words containing VC and VCC endings *not* taught as grapheme-phoneme units to the LC group. Thus, subtest 3 consisted of transfer words composed of an initial consonant learned as a single letter by both groups and an ending VC or VCC unit learned as a unit by the LC group, but as separate sounds by the SL group. Subtest 4 consisted of transfer words composed of an initial consonant learned as a single letter by both groups and an ending VC or VCC unit learned as separate sounds by the SL group but not directly taught to the LC group, although all individual letters in the ending unit had been contained in other VC and VCC combinations taught to the LC group.

[17] The pretest and two intermediate tests consisted of 32 items each, with each subtest containing 8 items. Intermediate Test 1 was administered following Lesson 3, or after 12 days of instruction (including the initial 2 days of oral-oral training and the extra day on Lesson 1), and Intermediate Test 2 was administered following Lesson 6 after 21 total days of instruction. The two intermediate tests were administered to permit an analysis of performance trends during the study and included only content taught up to the points at which they were administered. The posttest consisted of 80 items (20 per subtest) and was administered following Lesson 8 at the conclusion of all instruction in the study.

[18] All tests were individually administered to all Ss and consisted entirely of constructed-response items. Each S was required to read the letter combinations and words as presented on separate flash cards in a stratified random order to balance any order effects on item scores. KR-21 reliability coefficients, computed on the sample of 24 Ss within groups, averaged .94 for each of the three 32-item tests and .97 for the 80-item posttest.

Design and Data Analyses

[19] The experimental design was a pretest-treatment-posttest design with random assignment of matched pairs to the two treatment groups. Because performance trends related to pretest scores were noted during the study, the data

were analyzed by treatment (SL and LC) and pretest level of the Ss. The 24 Ss in each treatment were categorized into 3 ability groups (high, middle, low) of 8 Ss each on the basis of their pretest scores. High-ability Ss scored from 13–31 on the 32-item pretest with a mean score of 21.6 (67%); middle group Ss scored from 5–12 and averaged 7.9 (25%); and low-ability Ss scored from 0–4 and averaged 2.25 (7%).

RESULTS

[20] Posttest mean scores by ability level, treatment and subtest are shown in Table 19.4. It is apparent from the table that there was very little difference between the two treatment groups in either overall mean scores (54.33 for the SL group, 54.04 for the LC group) or subtest means. However, examination of the table suggests that the two treatments were differentially effective with high-ability and low-ability Ss. The analysis of variance of posttest total scores (Table 19.5) revealed a significant treatment $\times$ ability interaction effect ($F = 4.17$, $p < .05$). As shown in Table 19.4, high-ability pupils who received LC training scored more than 10 points *higher* than high-ability SL trained learners, but low-ability LC pupils scored 15 points *lower* than their SL-trained counterparts.

[21] Further analyses revealed other important differences related to the significant ability by treatment interaction. The total test variance of the LC group was significantly greater than that of the SL group ($F = 2.56$, $p < .05$). The greater variance of the LC group is reflected in Table 19.4 by the 58 point difference in posttest means between high-ability LC pupils ($\bar{x} = 79.13$) and low-ability LC pupils ($\bar{x} = 21.38$), as contrasted with a difference of only 32 points between high-ability ($\bar{x} = 68.75$) and low-ability ($\bar{x} = 36.75$) SL pupils.

[22] Table 19.4 reveals that the greatest within-group differences by ability occurred among low-ability Ss. The posttest mean score of 36.75 for low-ability pupils who received the SL treatment is significantly higher than the mean of 21.38 for low-ability LC subjects ($F = 5.46$, $p < .05$), based on a simple-effects

---

TABLE 19.4   *POSTTEST MEAN SCORES BY ABILITY LEVEL, TREATMENT, AND SUBTEST*

Ability level	Treat-ment	Subtest Letter combinations	Practice words	Transfer 1 words	Transfer 2 words	*Test totals
High	SL	17.38	17.38	17.50	16.50	68.75
	LC	19.75	19.88	19.75	19.75	79.13
Middle	SL	16.13	15.50	13.38	12.50	57.50
	LC	16.50	15.50	14.63	15.00	61.63
Low	SL	12.38	9.50	7.50	7.38	36.75
	LC	7.88	5.50	4.00	4.00	21.38
Subtest	SL	15.29	14.13	12.79	12.13	54.33
Means	LC	14.71	13.63	12.79	12.92	54.04

* Fractional differences occurring between sums of cells and test totals are due to rounding.
N = 8 per cell.

TABLE 19.5   *ANALYSIS OF VARIANCE SUMMARY TABLE FOR
TOTAL POSTTEST SCORES*

Source of variation	ss	df	ms	F
Between subjects	22,396.81	23		
A (ability)	16,803.50	2	8,401.75	31.54†
Subjects within				
groups	5,593.31	21	266.35	
Within subjects	5,080.50	24		
B (treatment)	1.02	1	1.02	.01
AB	1,443.19	2	722.09	4.17*
B × subjects				
within groups	3,636.31	21	173.16	

* $p < .05$
† $p < .01$

analysis. In addition, the mean score of 14.58 for low-ability SL pupils on only the transfer portion of the test (subtests 3 and 4) significantly exceeded the mean transfer score of 8.00 for low-ability LC subjects ($F = 5.67, p < .05$).

[23] The 10-point difference between the high-ability SL and LC groups on the posttest was not statistically significant. However, the high-ability LC Ss achieved a mean score of 79.13 out of a possible 80, as contrasted with a mean of 68.75 for high-ability SL pupils. The near-perfect score attained by high-ability LC Ss suggests that the failure to detect a significant difference between the high-ability LC and SL groups may be due to a ceiling effect for the LC group.

[24] Test data collected during the study indicate that the differential effectiveness of the two treatments was a trend that began early and continued throughout the study. This trend is illustrated in Fig. 19.2, which shows the standard deviations by treatment on the four tests administered during the study. The standard deviation of the total LC group was larger on each successive test, indicating a steadily increasing difference in achievement between the high-ability and low-ability LC groups. In contrast, the standard deviation of the SL group became smaller as the study progressed.

[25] Also of importance are the achievement gains registered by the children during the study. These gains are summarized in Fig. 19.3, which shows the mean percentage scores by treatment on each of the four tests. Figure 19.3 reveals that the achievement scores of both groups rose from a pretest mean of 33% to a posttest mean of 68%.

DISCUSSION

[26] The present study was conducted to determine whether single-letter training or letter-combination training is the more effective method of word-attack instruction for beginning readers. Evidence yielded by the study did not categorically favor the use of one method with all children. Rather, achievement data from the study provide a rather strong indication that the two methods are differentially effective depending on the ability level of the learner.

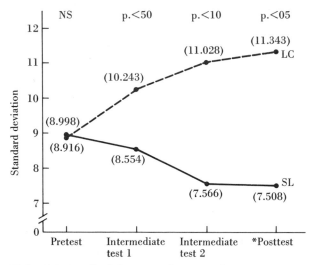

FIG. 19.2 Standard deviations by test and treatment group. The standard deviations for the 80-item posttest were 28.87 for the LC group and 18.27 for the SL group. The posttest S.D.'s shown are estimates for reduced test length (80 to 32 items) to correspond to the length of the other three tests.

[27] High-ability Ss who received letter-combination training during the study achieved a mean score of 79.13 (99%) on the 80-item posttest, as contrasted with a mean of 68.75 (86%) for high-ability Ss who received single-letter training. The 99% average on the posttest is convincing evidence of the effectiveness of the LC approach with high-ability learners within the instructional boundaries of the study.

[28] Achievement of low-ability pupils under the two treatments contrasts sharply with that of high-ability Ss, as indicated by the significant treatment × ability interaction found in the study. Whereas high-ability pupils performed better under the letter-combination approach, low-ability Ss achieved better using the single-letter approach. Low-ability pupils in the SL group achieved significantly higher scores than low-ability LC pupils both on the entire posttest and on the combined subtests requiring reading of transfer words.

[29] It should be noted that the present data do not suggest that higher-ability learners in any first grade class should always receive letter-combination training and the lower-ability learners should always receive single letter training. "High-ability" and "low-ability" are designators that are relative to the particular class or population being studied, and these terms were used in the present study simply to refer to Ss whose pretest scores fell above or below a certain level. The high-ability group in the present study could conceivably be the middle or low group if they were in a very high-achieving class, but this change obviously would not effect the type of treatment that they should receive. Similarly, if all Ss in the study had attained a pretest score of 4 or less (the top score for the "low-ability"

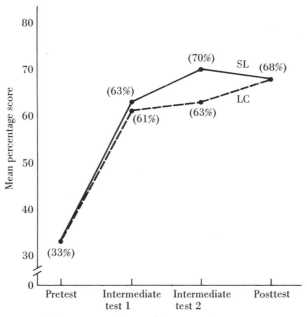

FIG. 19.3 Percentage scores by test and treatment group.

group), then is it likely that the SL method would have been effective with the entire group. The point here is that in cases where assignment to a different instructional treatments is to be made on the basis of entering performance, the child's absolute score on the pretest or placement test (not his performance relative to the class) should serve as the basis for assignment. Thus, to the extent that the results of the present study are generalizable to other instructional situations and word-attack content, pretest or placement scores would serve as better indicators of the appropriate type of word-attack training than would ability level within the class.

[30] There is a definite need for further study of the single-letter and letter-combination methods of word-attack instruction used in the present experiment. Investigations over a longer time period and with a variety of lexical sequences and learner populations will be necessary to assess the generality of the present findings. However, in the absence of a valid predictive measure for a particular instructional sequence, there would appear to be merit in an approach that initially emphasizes single-letter training but switches to a letter-combination emphasis after the early single-letter instruction. Early instruction with the single-letter method should be to the advantage of low-ability learners at a most critical time in the development of their reading skill. The later emphasis on a letter-combination approach would give all learners instruction and practice with a method that is similar to procedures often used by more advanced readers and is efficient for reading graphemes whose pronunciation is contextually determined.

[31] An important aspect of the study is the evident need for more effective word-attack instruction for beginning readers. Although the Ss as a group were reading slightly above the national average for first graders, they achieved a mean percentage score of only 33% on a pretest requiring them to pronounce the sounds of common letters and letter combinations and to read high-frequency, regularly spelled one-syllable words. After nearly six months of school, this would seem to be a very low performance level for first graders. With appropriate training such children can perform much better, as revealed by the posttest scores of 68% overall and 63% on transfer words attained after 25 minutes per day of concentrated word-attack instruction for less than six weeks. The latter figures certainly do not constitute optimal achievement levels, but they do represent important gains in reading performance achieved with first graders in a relatively short period of time. Systematic word-attack instruction by the classroom teacher throughout the school year should result in even higher levels of achievement.

REFERENCES

Bishop, C. H. Transfer effects of word and letter training in reading. *Journal of Verbal Learning and Verbal Behavior,* 1964, 3, 215–221.

Jeffrey, W. E., and Samuels, S. J. Effect of method of reading training on initial learning and transfer. *Journal of Verbal Learning and Verbal Behavior,* 1967, 6, 354–358.

Silberman, H. F. *Exploratory research on a beginning reading program.* Technical Memorandum No. TM-895/100/00. System Development Corporation, Santa Monica, 1964.

19.5 DISCUSSION OF SULLIVAN, OKADA, AND NIEDERMEYER STUDY

19.5.1 SUBJECTS

The nature of the target and accessible populations (paragraphs 7–8) was not clear from the report, although reference (paragraph 8) was made to a population "like" the sample: "the sample was more characteristic of first graders who are average readers than of populations where high rates of reading failure are typically observed." How the sample was selected from the accessible population was also not clear. So the question then becomes is the sample "like" the application group (Section D, Exhibit 18.1). On two variables the two groups can be considered to be alike (first graders and an equal distribution of boys and girls); on two others the groups differ (the research sample was slightly higher on standardized achievement tests and was probably from a more urbanized area). Do you think these four variables provided an adequate description of the sample?

A great plus for this study is that aptitude–treatment interactions were examined (paragraphs 19–23), using an achievement pretest specifically constructed for the study. Thus the reader has some idea of how students with different ability performed under the two instructional settings.

Despite the brief description of the subjects, the sample is clearly more similar to the application group than is the sample in Bishop's study, and application of the results can be made with more certainty.

19.5.2 RESEARCH ENVIRONMENT

Was each instructional method sufficiently described so that you could replicate it (Section B, Exhibit 18.2)? The content of each lesson, the length of each lesson, the instructional procedures for each treatment, and the instructional materials were described (paragraphs 10–15). This description was complete enough that a reader could attempt to replicate each treatment.

How close this replication might actually be to the implementation in the original study cannot be determined since no formal observation procedure was used to determine whether substantial modifications from the instructional plan occurred. (Apparently some informal observations of the lessons were made by the research staff, paragraph 10.) Many questions about the instructional process could have been answered by formal observation. What did the instructor do when students had difficulty with a letter, word, or letter combination? Did each group pronounce each word the same number of times? Apparently, the children were asked to respond in unison (paragraph 13), but did the instructor vary this procedure when individual children did not respond? What types of feedback and reinforcement were given to the children?

Examining Moos's categories, we find no information on the ecological dimensions of the environment or on reinforcement, and little information on the organization structure (the instructor/student ratio was given), psychosocial characteristics (instructor seemed to be in charge), and personal characteristics (although sex and age were cited). The behavior setting involved someone other than the regular teacher, who periodically entered the classroom, divided the class into two groups and gave each group a "reading" lesson.

You could replicate the general procedures, the content, content sequence, materials, and length of the study, but you could not reproduce the details of the instructional process itself. In addition, the behavior setting would be different if you were to give the instruction in your own classroom (a regular teacher giving a "reading" lesson). Since the study was actually conducted in a classroom, the procedures were not "lablike," and the content chosen was judged the "most appropriate graphemes for use in word-attack instruction in a beginning program" (paragraph 6), generalization involves less risk compared with the Bishop study. However, if you actually tried either the single-letter or letter-combination approach, you might make some changes: expand the vocabulary list, be less consistent in instructional procedures across different lessons, or reduce the amount of daily instruction to 20 minutes. The primary question for most readers and researchers is the relative effectiveness of the two word-attack approaches. It is hoped that the effect of such procedural modifications would be small so that the results have some generality.

19.5.3 MEASUREMENT PROCEDURES

Sullivan et al. examined four variables closely related to the two intructional treatments (two pronunciation measures of the letters and words taught in the lessons, and two measures of pronunciation of new words). Tests were given at four times during the study: a pretest, two intermediate tests of learning, and a posttest. Each child was tested individually with a flashcard technique (paragraphs 16–18). Most of the analyses were performed on the total score from the posttest (paragraphs 20–23). If the intermediate tests had not been given, no knowledge of these achievement stages would have existed, and the researchers' conclusion would, of necessity, have been modified (paragraph 24).

How would you measure these variables (Section B, Exhibit 18.3)? Suppose you decide to test pronunciation of the letters and words in a manner similar to that of the researchers, examining each child individually with flash cards. However, you do not give a pretest, only tests during instruction and a posttest.

Reactivity from awareness of being tested (Section F.1, Exhibit 18.3) in the Sullivan et al. study was relatively low due to the length of the study, the repeated testing given as part of the instructional program, and the age of the subjects. If regular testing is part of your usual instructional procedures, then little contamination from this source exists (Section F.2, Exhibit 18.3). One might also assume that your omission of a pretest would not greatly reduce the comparability of the two situations. Since we know nothing about the testers in the study, no conclusion can be reached about recorder characteristics (Section F.3, Exhibit 18.3). Although no direct evidence was presented on the possibility of change in the research instrument (Section F.4); the authors were concerned about its quality, examining test reliability and controlling possible effects associated with only one ordering of the letters and words (paragraph 18). One might assume that your testing procedures would not be so controlled, since most teachers do not examine the reliability of their own tests nor show concern about possible item-order effects. In conclusion, the research and application testings of letter and word pronunciation seem to be comparable.

Suppose you decide to test transfer only at the end of instruction by using words from the vocabulary section of a standardized reading test with the individualized flash-card testing technique. What can be said about the comparability of the two procedures? Both techniques are tests (Section C, Exhibit 18.3). As you review the parts of Section F, the greatest discrepancy you will encounter in the two procedures is the lack of opportunity to practice on transfer words in your classroom. Sullivan et al. did not present data on transfer for each testing period, so we do not know how much transfer scores were affected by practice in comparison to the knowledge scores. However, it is probably safe to assume that the practice had some effect, where there would be no practice effect on transfer in your classroom. The other major discrepancy between the two procedures (Section G) is the content of the tests. Since the transfer tests in the study were based on the lesson content and the vocabulary list you would use for transfer is not, it is logical to assume that different effects might occur (paragraph 22). The degree of similarity would probably depend on the extent to which the same vowel and consonant combinations used in the lessons occurred in your test.

19.5.4 SUMMARY

Since the similarity between the hypothetical application context and the research environment in the Sullivan et al. study is high, try-out of the procedures in your classroom seems quite reasonable. Three major factors reducing the comparability of the two contexts are the special measure of ability used by the researcher, the lack of information regarding the actual implementation of the lessons, and the discrepancies between the transfer measures.

The differences in the research contexts of the Bishop and the Sullivan et al. studies lend strength to the generalizability of the major trend in the results, that for many individuals greater positive transfer (i.e., ability to read new words composed of familiar grapheme–phoneme correspondences) resulted from single-letter or letter-combination training than from whole-word training. Yet the differences between the studies cannot be ignored. Would you, on the basis of these studies, implement the single-letter or letter-combination approach in your first grade classroom, or perhaps view the results as something that might work in your classroom? Or would you, as is often recommended by researchers, say that more research is needed?

The differences in the research contexts illustrate the dilemmas encountered by both researchers and readers of research as they attempt to integrate research results; and the challenges presented to researchers as they determine which factors are important to investigate in a new study.

19.6 A NONEXPERIMENTAL STUDY—MARASCUILO AND DAGENAIS STUDY

Assume for the present that you are a senior high school principal in an urban area of 50,000 in a southern state in the United States. Your school system has been integrated, in response to a court order in 1968, mainly through changes in school boundary lines. The racial composition of the community is approximately 70 percent white and 30 percent black. You are concerned about the effects of integration on students' racial attitudes and the study by Marascuilo and Dagenais is of interest to you. Marascuilo and Dagenais investigated what the word "integration" meant to high school seniors. They intentionally selected a sample of seniors who had attended a school system which had been integrated for six years (paragraphs 5, 6, and 8). Although not directly stated, apparently results were reported only on seniors who had had six years of integration. To what extent do you think their results would also be characteristic of students in your school?

The Meaning of the Word "Integration" to Seniors in a Multiracial High School
LEONARD A. MARASCUILO AND F. DAGENAIS

INTRODUCTION

[1] Since the Supreme Court decision in 1954 that separate schools for different races are "inherently unequal," the nation has moved in the direction of increased racial mixing in the schools. The rhetoric used to bring about or prevent such mixing encompasses the concept of "racial balance" which in turn relies upon the terms desegregation and integration.

[2] These words are often used interchangeably. Sometimes the usage betrays a particular social or political stance wherein either word can be used effectively to trigger an emotional response. Often the words seem to lack precision, as when the National Advisory Commission on Civil Disorders stated that ". . . integration is the only course which explicitly seeks to achieve a single nation rather than accepting the present movement toward a dual society. . . ." The same can be said for the usage of the term integration in a pamphlet which was widely distributed by the Southern Christian Leadership Conference in the 1960s: "The Southern Christian Leadership Conference has the basic aim of achieving full citizenship rights, equality, and the integration of the Negro in all aspects of American life. . . ."[1] Unfortunately, neither the National Advisory Commission nor the Southern Christian Leadership Conference chose to indicate what they meant by their use of the term "integration."

[3] Yet definitions of the term "integration" are readily available. Two are presented here in order to give some perspective on alternative interpretation. Weinberg, who has written an interpretative study of desegregation research, defines integration as the realization of equal opportunity by deliberate cooperation and without regard to racial or other social barriers."[2] Pettigrew, a social psychologist and authority on race, says, "The term 'integrated school' . . . might usefully be reserved for the desegregated school where interracial acceptance is the norm. With these usages, 'desegregation" becomes the prerequisite, but 'integration' is the ultimate goal."[3]

Leonard A. Marascuilo and F. Dagenais, 1974. The meaning of the word "integration" to seniors in a multiracial high school. *Journal of Negro Education* **43**: (Spring): 179–189. Copyright 1974 Howard University Press. Reprinted with permission.

[1] F. L. Broderick, and A. Meier, "This Is SCLC," in *Negro Protest Thought in the Twentieth Century* (Indianapolis: Bobbs-Merrill, 1965).

[2] Meyer Weinberg, *Desegregation Research: An Appraisal* (Bloomington: Ind.: Phi Delta Kappa, 1970).

[3] Thomas F. Pettigrew, "The Negro and Education Problems and Proposals," in Irwin Katz and P. Gurin (eds.), *Race and the Social Sciences* (New York: Basic Books, 1969).

[4] Other distinctions in the meaning of the words integration and desegregation abound. They run from the seemingly flip, but insightful, quip of actor and football star Jim Brown (as quoted by James Farmer)—"To hell with integration. But, man, don't segregate me"—to the considered words of Chicago's South Side delegate to the Illinois Legislature Senator Richard Newhouse, Jr., "Black people . . . must learn that there is nothing contrary to integration by their seeking to develop black dignity and group purpose."4 Given the federal impetus to "integrate" and the Third World desire to maintain ethnic identity along with a striving for equality it is easy to see how the idea of integration can take on different, seemingly contradictory, meanings for different publics.

[5] In a school district where the watchword is integration, the meaning of the term and the expected outcomes of its implementation are vague. During item-writing sessions with a group of black and white high school teachers and counsellors for a larger study of student attitudes toward integration, it became clear that the word could have many nuances of meaning beyond the legalistic administrative effecting of racial balance in the schools. Definitions of integration were sought from many quarters. Eventually, eight definitions emerged which seemed to cover the more salient concepts of the term.

[6] The objective of this paper is to report and interpret the responses of seniors in a desegregated/integrated multiracial school district to eight definitions of the word "integration." Responses are analyzed across such variables as sex, race, socioeconomic status, political affiliation of the students, and attendance at religious services.

METHODS AND SOURCE OF DATA

[7] Eight definitions of the word integration were included in an instrument designed to study the attitudes of students who had been in schools reflecting the racial proportions of the city since the seventh grade and who were about to graduate from the twelfth grade. The students were asked to pick the definition(s) —up to three—which came closest to their own feeling about integration. They were also asked to pick the definition least like their own. The definitions were then ranked with an average of the missing ranks substituted where appropriate. The Friedman test and its appropriate post hoc procedure were applied to group similar definitions.

[8] The data were obtained from the graduating class of Berkeley High School. Usable responses were obtained from 78 Asian, 125 black, and 246 white students. The school district has a single high school which covers the City of Berkeley, a community which has seemingly moved with dispatch to implement the Supreme Court's decision. In 1965 the district systematically integrated its junior high schools. In 1969 the district became the first one in the nation with a population of over 100,000 to effect racial balance in all grades by two-way busing. The students surveyed in this paper entered the seventh grade in 1965 and had thus been beneficiaries of integration in a committed district for a period of six years.

---

4 Nathan Wright, Jr., *Let's Work Together* (New York: Hawthorn, 1968).

RESULTS AND DISCUSSION

[9] The basic statistics of this investigation are shown in Table 19.6. These measures are based on responses made to the following questions by the 449 students who returned usable questionnaires:

The word *integration* often has a different meaning for different people. Here are several possible meanings for the word:

A. Integration is the free association of people of different races on the basis of mutual or like interests.

B. Integration is the forced mixing of people of different races.

C. Integration is the open acceptance of another person and his racial and cultural heritage.

D. Integration is all people having equal social value (may marry outside of their own races, join social clubs, etc.), and receiving equal justice under the law.

E. Integration is accepting the prevailing or common cultural values of the larger society.

F. Integration is all people having equal chances for all things including education, employment, and housing.

G. Integration is the voluntary mixing of people of different races.

H. Integration is the incorporation or inclusion into society, on the basis of equal membership, of people who differ in some group characteristic (like race).

Q_1: Which of these meanings come *close* to your own? (If necessary, use up to three definitions.)

1._____ 2. _____ 3. _____

Q_2: Which of these meanings is *least* like your own? _____

Q_3: What is your sex?   Male   Female

Q_4: Which of the following best describes you?

Asian   Black   Chicano   White   Other

TABLE 19.6   *MEAN RANKS AND FRIEDMAN STATISTICS FOR THREE SEX-RACE GROUPS RANKING EIGHT DEFINITIONS OF THE TERM "INTEGRATION"*

Definition of integration	Mean rank of definitions						Total
	Males			Females			
	Asian	Black	White	Asian	Black	White	
A	4.2	3.7	3.6	3.5	4.2	4.0	3.9
B	5.4	6.2	6.0	6.5	5.8	6.3	6.1
C	3.8	4.2	3.7	3.9	3.7	3.6	3.7
D	4.3	3.8	4.2	3.9	3.6	4.0	4.0
E	5.6	5.4	5.6	5.6	5.7	6.0	5.7
F	4.1	3.9	4.3	3.9	3.6	3.7	3.9
G	4.4	4.1	4.6	3.9	4.6	4.4	4.4
H	4.3	4.9	4.0	4.8	4.9	4.0	4.3
Value of Friedman Statistic	18.4*	48.7*	106.2*	52.5*	69.2*	170.3*	422.3*
Sample size	38	52	119	40	73	127	449
Coefficient of concordance	$.26^2$	$.37^2$	$.36^2$	$.43^2$	$.37^2$	$.44^2$	$.37^2$

* Significant at $\alpha = .05$

[10] In evaluating the responses to the definition of integration, the Friedman test for J matched groups and Kendall's Coefficient of concordance[5] were employed. Since rank data is used throughout this report and since the ranks correspond to a repeated measures variable, these procedures are statistically optimal. The Friedman test was used to determine whether the rank order of choices between the eight definitions of integration are equally likely or whether the differences between the ranks indicate that certain definitions are preferred over other definitions. The hypothesis of no difference between definitions is rejected at $\alpha = .05$ if the Friedman statistic, χ_r^2, exceeds $\chi_7^2(.95) = 14.07$. If the hypothesis is rejected, then Kendall's Coefficient of concordance, W, is evaluated. Kendall's Coefficient measures the agreement in the ranking of the eight definitions by the individual students. If all the students rank the eight definitions in exactly the same order, then the value of $W = 1$. If there is complete disagreement between the students, then $W = 0$. Values of W between 0 and 1 measure the degree of joint agreement or consensus. In this sense the square root of W is analogous to the Pearson product moment correlation coefficient, or to the correlation ratio.

[11] For the analyses of this report, the respondent's first, second, and third choices were ranked 1, 2, and 3, respectively. The definition least like their own was ranked 8. The remaining unknown responses were given a midrank of the average of 4, 5, 6, and 7, or 5.5. Since this produced many tied rank values, the resulting Friedman statistics tend to be small in numerical value and could be increased by correcting for ties. However, since almost all of the Friedman statistics are significant and larger than $\chi_7^2(.95) = 14.07$, the correction for ties is not necessary. Unfortunately, this also means that the reported coefficients of concordance are also lower in numerical value than would be obtained if the values corrected for ties were used.

[12] If sex and race are ignored, it is seen that there is a significant difference in the definitions chosen by the total sample of 449 students since $\chi_r^2 = 422.3$ is considerably larger than the 14.07 value of χ_7^2 needed to reject the hypothesis of no difference at $\alpha = .05$. Even though $\sqrt{w} = .37$ represents a moderate degree of agreement, no one definition stands out as the definition which is acceptable to most of the students. According to Scheffé type post hoc comparisons as described by Marascuilo and McSweeney,[6] definitions A, C, D, F, G, and H are not statistically different from one another in average rank values. Definitions B and E are also not different from one another, but they are statistically different in rank value from the remaining six definitions. The six acceptable definitions of integration are based on the idealistic philosophical ideas of free association of people of different races, acceptance of people on the basis of mutual or like interests, open acceptance of another person, acceptance of another person's racial and cultural heritage, equal social value of each person, equal justice under the law for all people, equal chances for all things, and the voluntary mixing of people. Certainly, these definitions represent the high ideals of people

---

[5] William Hays, *Statistics for Psychologists* (New York: Holt, Rinehart, and Winston, 1963).

[6] L. A. Marascuilo and M. McSweeney, "Nonparametric Post Hoc Comparisons for Trend," *Psychological Bulletin*, LXVII (1967), 401–412.

living in a democratic society where equality of opportunity and justice for everyone is a theoretical goal.

[13] The remaining two definitions of integration emphasize the forced mixing of people and the acceptance on the part of minority groups of the prevailing values of the majority group. These two characteristics of integration definitely do not find favor with the young people of this study. For these youths, integration is voluntary. It does not entail either a forced or voluntary amalgamation into the larger society such as various European groups experienced or desired in the second, third, or later generations after immigration to the U.S. To these contemporary young people, different social customs and different life-styles are acceptable, and the acculturation or assimilation of people into the dominant model is not an acceptable goal of integration.

[14] Essentially, these same conclusions hold for the six sex by race groups also reported in Table 19.6. Definitions B and E cluster together for all six groups. Also, there seems to be little differentiation between definitions A, C, D, F, and G for the six groups. However, definition H stands alone as a response choice for black males, Asian females, and black females. This definition, which was adapted from Webster's *Seventh New Collegiate Dictionary*, is not as acceptable as the other definitions which relate integration to the idealistic concepts of equality of opportunity and justice and acceptance of the individual. Implicit in the dictionary definition of integration is the idea that "incorporation or inclusion into [the larger] society" requires that minority persons must give up their own cultural and racial heritage and thereby be prepared to accept the prevailing or common cultural values of the larger society. In this sense, the dictionary definition is at odds with the way young people choose to define integration. Blacks would be expected to be most sensitive to this point of view especially since they now wish to maintain their identity. It is of some interest that Asian females tend to agree with the blacks in their opposition to this definition. For some unknown reason the Asian male identifies more with the prevailing larger culture than does the Asian female.

[15] In addition to race and sex, respondents were asked to state political party and religious attendance. A measure of social class or socioeconomic status of parents and family was derived by asking students to indicate the census tract in which they resided on a map printed in each questionnaire. Based on a factor analysis performed upon 1960 census tract data by Marascuilo and Penfield,[7] the 28 census tracts of Berkeley were stratified into Low, Medium, and High socioeconomic groups. The analyses for these questions are summarized in Table 19.7.

[16] For political party preference, the Friedman statistics for the Democratic, Republican, Peace and Freedom, and other political parties are given respectively by 184.67, 3.95, 57.56, and 52.60, with the corresponding square roots of the coefficients of concordance given by .36, .15, .50, and .44. The differences in ranking are significant for the students who prefer the Democratic, the Peace and Freedom, and other parties. The rankings parallel those reported in Table 19.6 for the total sample. There is also a clear indication that the students who

---

7 L. A. Marascuilo and K. Penfield, "A Northern Urban Community's Attitudes toward Racial Imbalances in School Classrooms," *The Urban Review*, LXXIV (1966), 359–379.

TABLE 19.7 MEAN RANKS AND FRIEDMAN STATISTICS FOR POLITICAL PARTY PREFERENCE OF THE STUDENTS, THE RELIGIOUS SERVICE ATTENDANCE OF THE STUDENTS, AND THE SOCIOECONOMIC STATUS OF THEIR PARENTS

Definition of integration	Mean rank of definition according to:										
	Political party preference				Religious attendance				SES of parents		
	Demo.	Repub.	Peace and Freedom	Other	Never	Some-times	Often	Reg.	Low	Medium	High
A	3.9	3.8	3.8	3.8	3.8	3.7	4.2	4.2	3.9	3.8	3.9
B	6.1	4.6	7.1	6.8	6.4	6.0	5.6	5.7	6.0	5.9	6.3
C	3.8	4.2	3.5	3.9	3.6	4.0	3.5	3.9	4.0	3.7	3.6
D	3.9	4.9	3.9	3.6	4.0	3.8	3.8	4.3	3.8	3.9	4.1
E	5.9	4.9	5.5	5.6	5.8	5.8	5.6	5.4	5.5	5.7	5.8
F	3.8	4.3	3.9	3.9	3.9	4.0	3.8	3.8	3.9	3.9	3.9
G	4.5	4.9	4.6	4.0	4.4	4.3	5.0	4.6	4.2	4.6	4.4
H	4.3	4.4	4.0	4.4	4.1	4.6	4.6	4.3	4.7	4.6	4.0
Value of Friedman Statistic	184.67*	3.95	57.56*	52.60*	216.59*	150.83*	27.16*	45.68*	102.28*	93.80*	241.91*
Sample size	177	22	30	36	180	163	35	63	122	107	203
Coefficient of concordance	.36[2]	.15[2]	.50[2]	.44[2]	.37[2]	.34[2]	.32[2]	.30[2]	.33[2]	.33[2]	.39[2]

* Significant at $\alpha = .05$

prefer the Peace and Freedom Party politics report that definition B is the one that is most *unlike* their own. For students who show an interest in the politics of the Republican Party, all definitions are of equal value in that none are statistically different from one another.

[17] For the population surveyed, regularity of church attendance has little impact upon student's attitudes toward integration. The rankings of the eight definitions according to the four levels of religious service attendance parallel that shown for the total sample. While all Friedman statistics indicate significant differences in ranking, the square roots of the four coefficients of concordance, .44, .37, .34, and .32, indicate that the variability between the definitions, although monotonically descending with increased church attendance, is statistically uniform across the four levels of attendance.

[18] Finally, it is seen that social class of parents has little bearing on students' definitions of integration. While all three Friedman statistics are significant, the square roots of the three coefficients of concordance, .33, .33, and .39, show that the differences parallel those found for the total sample.

[19] The percentages of students selecting definitions A, C, D, H, G, B, F, and E as their *first choice* were 24, 21, 13, 12, 11, 10, 9, and 1, respectively. In this case the differences between the six sex by race groups can be ignored because the Chi-square test of homogeneity was not significant since the Karl Pearson statistic of $\chi^2 = 40.70$ is considerably less than the significant value of $\chi^2_{35}(.95) = 49.77$. Thus, across all six groups, definition A is preferred by 24 percent of the students. It is followed by definition C which is preferred by 21 percent of the students. For almost half of the students integration connotes free association of people on the basis of interests and the open acceptance of another person's customs. Definition E, accepting the prevailing larger culture, was looked upon favorably by less than 1 percent of the students. Basically, this definition is polar to both definitions A and C and its rejection in the light of acceptance of definitions A and C is not surprising. The percentages of students selecting definitions B, E, G, D, A, F, H, and C as the definition *least* like their own definition was 56, 24, 5, 4, 4, 3, 3, and 2, respectively. According to these figures, it is seen that 80 percent of the students view definitions B and E as least like their own definition.

[20] Students were also asked the following question: "Which of these meanings do you think *most other people* believe?" The percentages of students selecting definitions B, A, F, D, C, G, H, and E as the definitions of integration they thought *most other people* believed were 41, 12, 12, 11, 8, 6, 6, and 4. Since the χ^2 statistic of 51.25 for this response pattern is larger than the tabled $\chi^2_{35}(.95) = 49.77$, statistical differences exist across the six sex by race groups. For the students as a whole, B stands out as the definition which the largest percent (41 percent) reports "most other people believe." Definition B has to do with the forced mixing of people. It is interesting to note that definition B, while ranking highest as *least* like the student's own choice, also ranks highest in the student's estimation as the definition to which *most others* subscribe.

[21] When an examination is made across the six sex by race groupings, it is seen that the major differences are found for the white males. While definition A occupies a second ranking position for all groups, it receives a ranking of seven for the white males. Why this definition of integration, based on the free as-

sociation of people according to individual likes and interests, receives a low ranking by white males could reflect a higher level of self-evaluated liberalism among the white high school males than that given by them to the adults with whom they come into daily contact. As is recalled, for the white males, definition A is the first-ranked definition that comes closest to their own.

[22] It is worth noting that the reported findings are apparent in what the respondents, themselves, had to say about what integration means personally to them since 85 of the 449 responding graduates provided personal comments on the available blank space of the questionnaire. As stated by four students:

1. Integration [is] the acceptance of a person or another race and his racial heritage. (male, Asian)

2. Integration is bringing people together socially and educationally. But in no way changing a person's identity. A black man should think like a black man, and a white must think as a white. (female, black)

3. Integration is the mixing of people from different cultural and racial backgrounds. However, it is not assimilation of minorities into the mainstream; rather each group maintains its own identity while mixing on the basis of their common humanity. (female, white)

4. Integration is seeing everyone as an individual. (male, white)

[23] In general, to these new high school graduates the idea of integration as the voluntary mixing and acceptance of each individual without any adjustments or imposed requirements to conform to or blend in with the larger group was reinforced by these ad hoc comments.

SUMMARY

[24] Eight definitions of integration were examined across sex, race, political preference, religious service attendance, and socioeconomic status for 449 graduating high school seniors. For the most part, these students chose as definitions of integration closest to their own definitions ones based on the idealistic principle of the free association of people of different races on all levels of contemporary life, along with the open acceptance of another person and his racial and cultural heritage. In addition, these students subscribe to the principle that all people have equal social value, that they are entitled to equal justice under the law, and that they should have equal chances for all things. Finally, to these young people, integration does not mean the forced mixing of people or the acculturation or assimilation of minority people into the dominant culture of the contemporary society. Different life-styles are acceptable and the amalgamation into the larger society such as various European groups experienced in the second, third, or later generations after immigration to the U.S. is not required or expected.

[25] Whereas whites and Asians showed no major disagreement with the dictionary definition of integration, blacks reported that they did not accept it as a reasonable definition of integration. Implicit in the dictionary definition of integration is the idea that incorporation or inclusion into the larger society requires that minority persons must give up their own cultural and racial heritage and thereby be prepared to accept the prevailing or common values of the larger

society. Thus, it appears that the dictionary definition is at odds with the way young people, especially blacks, choose to define integration and, with the Black Power and identity movements now in progress, it is not surprising that blacks would not find the dictionary definition too appealing.

[26] Finally, it is of some interest that youth tends to impute to others, mainly adults, the definition of integration that is most unlike their own definition. Thus, youth seems to think that the adult world believes that integration is the forced mixing of people of different races. That they hold this view is not surprising since they have seen whites run for the suburbs with the movement of blacks into the city and have watched whites oppose the movement of blacks into white neighborhoods mainly to protect property values and white schools. In addition, in most cities where school integration has occurred, it has been forced by the courts, rarely having been voluntary in nature. Since society appears to achieve integration mainly through the courts, it is easy to understand that youth attributes to others an acceptance of integration under force, while for itself, it believes that integration is voluntary.

19.7 DISCUSSION OF MARASCUILO AND DAGENAIS STUDY

19.7.1 SUBJECTS

From the introductory paragraphs (4–6) it seems likely that the authors would restrict generalization to a target population of youth from integrated school systems, but it is not clear whether they think generalization would be affected by the type and number of races integrated, whether integration had been voluntary or by court order, the size of the school system, the length of integration, or the region of the country. The Berkeley school district was selected because it was "the first one in the nation with a population of over 100,000 to effect racial balance in all grades by two-way busing" (paragraph 8). Thus the sample was not randomly selected from the target population, and it was not clear what accessible population was available to the researchers. Again we are faced with the question of the degree of similarity between the Berkeley sample and the students in your high school (Section D, Exhibit 18.1).

Marascuilo and Dagenais divided the sample according to the variables of race and sex (Table 19.6) and political party preference, religious attendance, and socioeconomic status of parents (Table 19.7). From these tables the reader can calculate, for example, that 55 percent of the sample was white, 28 percent black and 17 percent Asian; 67 percent expressed a preference for the Democratic party; and 47 percent were classified as coming from a high socioeconomic class.

The racial composition of students in your school is different from the Berkeley sample and they live in a different area of the country in which integration was achieved through means other than busing. But the 1975 seniors in your school would have been exposed to integration for about the same period of time as the Berkeley seniors. Additional information on both groups would make comparisons easier. Even with the information available, you do not know if the discrepancy in the racial composition factor is crucial. If you think it is important, can you predict how the results might change because of this difference? What about the differences in geographic location?

When a topic has been studied extensively, accumulated knowledge in the area can provide educated guesses about the relevance of such discrepancies. But when a new area is explored, as is the case with the present study, it is extremely difficult to make such decisions.

19.7.2 RESEARCH ENVIRONMENT

Was the environment described from which the students came (Section C, Exhibit 18.2)? Some environmental factors can also be called Subject factors; i.e., the racial composition of the sample, the socioeconomic level and size of the community, when the school system was integrated. Moos's categories point to other environmental factors that could be important but were not described; in particular, organizational structure (e.g., change in bus routes, number of additional buses required, racial mixture of the classrooms, racial composition of the faculty and school administration) and psychosocial characteristics (e.g., reaction of the community, teachers or students toward integration before and during the six-year period—voluntary integration does not necessarily mean that all was calm). Such additional description of the Berkeley environment would better enable readers to compare their community and school with Berkeley's.

19.7.3 MEASUREMENT PROCEDURES

The primary variable was the meaning of integration for the students (paragraph 9), although the students were also asked what definition other people would choose (paragraph 20). Five characteristics of the students were also measured (sex, race, socioeconomic status of parents, political party preference, and religious attendance). For purposes of the present discussion only the definition of integration and the social class measure are analyzed.

Suppose you, as the principal, decide to measure students' definitions of integration by asking them to respond in writing to the following request: "Briefly describe what the word 'integration' means to you." Both the researchers' and your measure of integration can be classified as self-report techniques, and some might classify them as questionnaires (Section C, Exhibit 18.3). In both cases the students would be aware of the questioning process. In contrast with the previous reading studies in which most measures were achievement tests given in the context of learning, it is relatively easy to speculate on the possible reactivity of the attitude measure in the present study. For example, students might choose the definition or write a definition that they thought would present a good image rather than one that actually reflected their feelings or concept of integration. If so, would this bias produce similar results with both measures?

No practice or pretest sensitization effects are possible in either context.

Since Marascuilo and Dagenais did not describe how or who administered the questionnaire to the students, no conclusion can be drawn about recorder characteristics. Change in the instrument does not appear to be a source of error with either technique, although in coding the responses to the essay question inconsistencies in classification might occur.

Finally, the discrepancy between the form of the questions must be examined (Section G, Exhibit 18.3). Payne (113) has shown that responses to attitude questions are highly dependent on the phrasing of the question. However, Marascuilo and Dagenais reported that 19 percent of the students voluntarily gave their own definition (paragraph 22), and concluded that these responses agreed with the choice measurement technique. It would seem that these written definitions would correspond closely to your essay question. Nevertheless, can you assume that the remaining 81 percent of the Berkeley students' written definitions, if available, would also correspond to their choices, or that the written responses that were provided were unaffected by prior reading of the eight definitions in the questionnaire?

The measurement of socioeconomic status (paragraph 15) illustrates a nonreactive measure. Some social class indices are based on the occupation and educational level of the head of the household. The map technique avoided problems in coding the prestige level of occupations and any biases or memory errors associated with a student's giving the education and occupation of his or her father.

19.7.4 SUMMARY

In determining the overall similarity between the application context and the research context, the discrepancies in the environments cannot be ignored (voluntary integration through busing in Berkeley versus court-ordered integration through changing of school boundary lines in a southern city). Nor can the different techniques of measuring the meaning of integration be ignored. The ambiguity of the question on what "most other people believe" (paragraph 20) also creates problems in generalization. Although the authors interpreted the results as referring to adults (paragraph 26), some students could have been thinking primarily of their peers, others of their parents, others of adults they knew well, or others of Californians only. If so, it is difficult to assume that responses to the question would produce similar results even on a similar sample of individuals or with the same individuals at a later time.

19.8 CONCLUDING REMARKS

As illustrated in the discussions of the three studies in this chapter, many assumptions must be made in deciding whether the results of a study might be applicable to or be replicated in an applied situation. If similar findings have occurred in a variety of research settings, then the likelihood of obtaining similar results increases. Nevertheless, you can never be 100 percent confident that you will obtain the same results as the researcher did.

Your own expectations might influence the likelihood of obtaining similar results. Rosenthal (118, 119) has suggested that the expectations of the investigator somehow influence the results of the study; that these expectations serve as a self-fulfilling prophecy. Is a teacher, counselor, or principal likely to replicate a research result simply because he or she expects that result, or not replicate it because he or she does not believe it?

Even if a study was conducted in a setting quite different from your own and there is no strong evidence to indicate that you would obtain similar results, the idea behind the study might be so intriguing to you that you would want to examine it anyway. Exploration of ideas generated from research is to be encouraged, not discouraged. The guidelines in this and the previous chapter simply identify factors that can reduce the likelihood of obtaining similar results in an applied setting. They should not be viewed as reasons against attempting to replicate research findings or to implement study procedures.

20
Educational Theory

Researchers often conduct studies for theoretical reasons. A theoretical framework is a guide; it suggests what variables should be examined, aids in the interpretation of results, and makes research cumulative from one study to the next. It is a statement of what is, or might be, important. Above all, it is a network of ideas that relates, explains, and predicts what without this network might appear to be unconnected facts or events.

Educational research has often been criticized for its lack of theory. "Research too often proceeds without explicit theoretical framework, in intellectual disarray, to the testing of myriads of arbitrary, unrationalized hyotheses" (3, p. 657). Although progress has been made since this statement was issued, many individuals would probably still agree with it.

Educational theories do exist, ranging from what might be called speculations or hunches to formal, axiomatic systems (133). Lower levels of theory tend to emphasize the acquisition of facts. Higher levels of theory connect such facts, are more comprehensive, and are broader in descriptive and explanatory power. Higher levels of theory will probably have more impact upon future research in education, since lower levels yield little understanding of educational situations.

Variations in theory are reflected in the rationale for research studies. Some studies are based upon no theory, and are usually characterized by the lack of research hypotheses. The Byalick/Bersoff and Gribbons/Lohnes studies in Chapter 1 illustrate rationales with no theory. At a higher level of theory are studies with research hypotheses based upon little empirical and/or logical rationale, called formative-theories by Snow (133). The Cicerilli/Cicerilli and Sabatino/Dorfman studies in Chapter 1 illustrate this level of theory. At higher levels of theory, the rationale is more intensive and thorough. The researcher attempts to define variables and the relationships among them in terms of very elementary units (called E-theory by Snow) in order to explain why a phenomenon occurs, how it functions, and/or describe it more fully. At another level (called D-theory by Snow) are descriptive theories and taxonomies that systematically classify and discriminate basic concepts. Some well-known examples of this level of theory are the Cognitive Taxonomy (17), Guilford's structure of intellect (66, 67,) Gagné's types of learning (52), and Holland's theory of vocational choice (76, 77).

The highest level of theory which you will encounter in educational research is what Snow called C-theory (conceptual theories and constructs). The goal of C-theory is to explain why something happens, not just to describe it. Special concepts that are not observable are introduced to provide explanations for behaviors that are observed. For example, the concept of anxiety might be introduced to explain why an individual perspires when giving a speech to 1000 people. Anxiety itself is not observable, but the audience of 1000 and the perspiration are. One of the best known and best developed theories at this level in the fields of education and psychology is achievement motivation theory (10, 11, 12). This theory focuses upon explaining why individuals tend either to undertake or to avoid achievement-oriented activities, activities in which each person's performance is evaluated in terms of some standard of excellence. Such explanatory concepts as the motive to approach success (called need for achievement), the motive to avoid failure (reflected in anxiety), the incentive values of success and failure, and the probabilities of succeeding and failing at tasks are embedded in the theory to predict how individuals will perform when faced with achievement-oriented tasks.

Sometimes the interrelationships among the basic concepts of high-level theories can be expressed mathematically. This is true of achievement motivation theory. Higher levels of theory are also sources of many research hypotheses. The variety of educational research topics suggested by achievement motivation theory is indeed great (103, 146).

Just as researchers must be aware of the limitations of their own theory, whatever its level of complexity, so must the practitioner who would use it, in order not be blinded to the potential of alternative points of view. Theories must be tested constantly against factual evidence to determine whether the theoretical predictions are correct; whether the theory is worthwhile; whether it can be applied. Such careful examination of knowledge brings us back to the self-corrective characteristic of research mentioned at the beginning of this book. Self-correction assures the discovery of error, and it is through such discovery that both educators and researchers can protect themselves from sterile ideas.

Appendix A
Guidelines
for Conducting
Research Studies

The actual conduct of research is a very challenging task because it requires many different skills and abilities on the part of researchers. At first glance, you may think that researchers simply need to be knowledgeable in the area they want to study. Although such knowledge is essential, it is certainly not sufficient for the task at hand. As the major stages in conducting research are discussed in this appendix, the diversity of skills researchers are required to have will become evident.

Good *research ideas* are often generated by researchers who are knowledgeable in their area of interest and who also bring a fresh, creative approach to the study of a specific problem. Researchers must also be challenged and intrigued by the problem they intend to study, for many frustrations and hurdles will arise in the process of conducting the study. Without such motivation, researchers may never complete the study.

The *design of studies* requires that researchers think logically and plan ahead. They must determine at this early stage the advantages and disadvantages of alternative research designs. Which one will best answer the research question? Researchers also need to be competent in such specialized areas as measurement/testing, research design, statistics and sampling. They may even need to be able to build special pieces of equipment for the study.

The *data collection process* often means that researchers must be skilled in sales ability; e.g., they must be able to "sell" their research idea to some group in order to obtain subjects, they must convince a funding group that their idea is worthwhile, etc. They must also be educators because they must usually train research assistants for their role in the study. Finally, researchers must play the role of watchdog, making sure that every aspect of the data collection process is conducted as planned.

When it comes to *analyzing the data,* nothing can truly substitute for a good background in statistics. Such knowledge allows an intelligent application of analytic tools. On the other hand, unfamiliarity with such techniques may lead to one of two extreme types of behavior, neither of which is appropriate: a blind dependency upon the ability of statistics to solve all data problems and to answer all research questions or a tendency to avoid use of statistics entirely. Skill in computer programming and the use of computer programs is also desirable since most data are now processed by computers.

Finally, a *report of the study* must be *written*. Good research studies are likely to have more impact if they are written well. Researchers must communicate effectively with their audience, clearly explain the problem and the results, and make the report interesting. The Conclusions section of the report reflects the researchers' ability to integrate all of their research skills, for the final conclusions and inferences must reflect all stages of the research process if they are to be valid.

A.1 HOW DO YOU DETERMINE THE RESEARCH PROBLEM AND RESEARCH HYPOTHESES?

In conducting a study you do not want to reinvent the wheel nor do you want to spin your wheels trying to think up a good research idea. A thorough *review of the research literature and of conceptual articles* in the area will help you avoid both these problems and should be your first step in planning a study.

In order to begin your literature search, you should *delimit the problem.* A one-word topic such as "motivation," "reading," "counseling," "physical education," or "learning disabilities" is simply too general. In order to narrow your topic, state the problem as a question of description, association, or causation. For example, in the area of counseling your interest might really be in (1) describing the high school counseling programs in your school district (description), (2) developing a model that will predict whether an individual decides to be a high school counselor (association), or (3) examining the effects of career counseling on the career aspirations of high school students (causation). Note how each of these problem statements narrows the area of interest and contains key words which can be used in locating relevant articles. Information on locating reports of educational research is given in Appendix B. Guidelines on taking notes of research articles are given in Appendix C.

Although a thorough literature review will take considerable time, it will be time well spent. The review will help you to determine:

a. which aspects of the problem have already been investigated and which have not been investigated.

b. which research hypotheses have been supported by research results and which have not been supported,

c. the controversies in the area,

d. the theories that have been applied to the problem, and

e. the theories that have been developed from research findings.

Once you have completed your review, you are no longer operating in a vacuum. You can now make a *precise statement of the research problem* you want to study and can *explain why* the problem needs to be studied.

You should then go one step beyond the problem statement and formulate *research hypotheses*. Hypotheses specify expected results and demand more than just a statement of the need for a study. They require a *rationale*, i.e., an explanation of why you expect certain results to occur. You cannot expect to find a "ready-made" rationale that will be satisfactory. Instead, you must create a rationale that will fit your particular problem from previous theory, research findings, and your own ideas. The rationale must be carefully constructed, for the end result (the research hypotheses) must be a logical consequence of the assumptions and premises in the argument. One way to improve your rationale is to explain it to someone else and have that person critique it. Ask the person to find rival explanations for the same hypothesized events, to discover hidden assumptions in your rationale, to identify other hypotheses that could be drawn from your rationale, and to determine if your hypotheses are a logical consequence of the rationale. On the basis of this feedback, you should revise your rationale and hypotheses. Then repeat this evaluation process with another person until you are satisfied that the major flaws and ambiguities in the rationale and hypotheses have been eliminated.

A.2 HOW DO YOU DESIGN THE STUDY?

After conducting a review of the literature, you will know how other researchers have investigated the same or similar problems. You will know what type of individuals have been studied, how the samples have been selected, what variables have been measured and how they have been measured, what type of descriptive, association, or causal designs have been employed, and what statistical/analytical techniques were used. Since a thorough review also involves an evaluation of research methods and procedures, you will know the characteristics of the outstanding studies in the field as well as the characteristics of poorly conducted studies. All this information will be immensely helpful as you design your study.

Since the type of study (descriptive, association, causal) is reflected in the problem statement and research hypotheses, you can evaluate alternative designs that you have developed by referring to the guidelines in this text for evaluating studies conducted by other researchers. Now you need to ask whether *your* design meets the criteria in these guidelines. The following topics were covered in the text:

General guidelines—Exhibit 2.1
Reliability and validity of measurement—Exhibits 8.1 and 9.1
Sampling—Exhibits 6.1 and 18.1
Statistical description of variables—Exhibit 5.1
Descriptive studies—Exhibits 11.1 and 12.1

Association studies—Exhibits 13.1 and 14.1
Causal studies—Exhibits 15.1, 16.1 and 17.1

The information presented previously will not be repeated here, although some important points will be elaborated upon.

In designing the study, it is a good idea to develop the *ideal design* first. That is, if you had all the money, time, and resources in the world, how would you design the study to answer the research question? In actually conducting the study you will certainly be forced to make some compromises in this design. A comparison of the actual and ideal designs will indicate whether the problem actually being investigated differs from the problem as originally stated, and will also indicate the extent to which the actual design limits the conclusions that can be drawn from the study.

Pilot studies should be conducted before the final study. In fact, the less research experience you have, the more you will profit from pilot studies. The pilot study will improve the quality of the final study design, and will increase your chances of obtaining clear-cut results in the final study. New approaches to the problem may be revealed. Unforeseen administration problems may occur. You may even decide to abandon your original idea in favor of another on the basis of the pilot study.

The pilot study may be a miniature of the final study, that is, you may conduct the study as you would the final study and analyze the data similarly. If so, then the pilot study provides a check on all the procedures to be used in the final study (testing, experimental treatments, instructions to subjects, statistical analyses), as well as constituting a preliminary test of your hypotheses. The pilot study may examine only certain aspects of the final study, such as the reliability and validity of different measuring instruments or how much the experimental treatments should differ from each other. In some cases, it may be necessary to conduct several successive pilot studies before you feel confident in the procedures and methods to be used in the final study.

In determining the *sampling plan,* first identify the population or group to which you want to apply the results. Once you have precisely defined this group (i.e., the target population), then you need to determine whether you can actually sample from it. If not, then you must determine what population or group is actually available to you (i.e., the accessible population) and what type of sampling plan you can apply to this group. Perhaps you can use some form of probability sampling, such as simple random sampling, because it allows you to generalize beyond the sample. Use of such a representative sampling plan makes the study less subject to the criticism that the results are unique to the study sample; that they might not occur on a different sample.

In determining the appropriate sample size and precise sampling design for a study, you should remember that, in general, large samples are preferable to small samples and probability sampling plans are preferable to nonprobability sampling plans. This is an area in which the advice of a consultant is invaluable unless you have had considerable training in sampling and statistics. In order to help you, a consultant will need information that you may find difficult to provide (e.g., an estimate of the size of the difference among the groups being compared or of the size of a correlation coefficient), unless you have conducted a pilot study and have preliminary results to show to the consultant. The consultant will ask you questions about the purpose of your study and the methods you intend to use, as well as about the subjects themselves, since all these factors have a bearing on the appropriate sample size and sampling plan.

In any study, the researcher must measure at least one variable. In descriptive and association studies, the *measurement process* is the heart of the study. In experimental studies, the researcher must be concerned with manipulation of an independent variable as well as with measurement of the dependent variable. In selecting measuring instruments, the first step is to list every variable that must be measured or tested. For each variable, cite the specific instruments with which you could measure it. This list should not be too hard to construct since your review of the literature has already provided you with information on how other researchers have measured the same or similar variables. In addition, books are available that describe tests in particular areas. Your list may consist of standardized tests or procedures, instruments that have been used for research purposes only, and/or instruments that must be developed specifically for your study.

How do you decide which instruments to use for each variable? You need to obtain much information before selecting a specific instrument. You need to determine the reliability and validity of the alternative instruments you are considering, whether the instruments are appropriate for the subjects in your study, the time it takes to administer the instruments, whether they are likely to yield the type of information you want as indicated by results from previous studies, the type of training required for the individual who gives the test, the type of scores that are produced, and the evaluative comments by reviewers of the instrument. You can also learn much about each instrument by looking at a copy of it, by taking it yourself, and by using it in a pilot study. All these factors should be considered in deciding which instruments would be best in your study. Such information is very important, because you do not want to be forced to conclude that the study did not focus on your research question because you selected the wrong measuring instrument (e.g., it was unreliable, it measured a different variable, or it was too difficult for the students).

If an instrument must be constructed, then you must add another major phase to the study in order to obtain reliability and validity information. This new instrument must be examined carefully before you conclude that it will accurately measure what you want it to measure. A background in test construction is desirable at this point. If the test is to be a measure of achievement, then you should consult a text in tests and measurements and/or take a measurement course. If the instrument is to measure a personal trait, then additional theoretical background in psychology and sociology and in constructing attitude/personality scales is advisable. Presently there are few systematic guidelines for the construction of observation schedules. Your best guides are the types of schedules used successfully in research studies similar to yours and the results you obtain from pilot studies with the observation schedule you develop.

Questionnaires or interviews are usually developed specifically for a study. However, contrary to popular opinion, good questionnaires and interviews are not easily made. The general content of the questionnaire/interview items is determined by the purpose of the study. However, the item format, the item wording, the sequence of the items, and type of response required by the respondent are not dictated by the research purpose. Since these factors can influence the results they must be considered carefully.

You should pretest the questionnaire to determine if it is satisfactory. Administer it under conditions as similar as possible to those anticipated in the final study. You may want to interview the participants to obtain the reasons for their answers and to obtain their overall reaction to the questionnaire (e.g., its length, format, content). This pretest data will indicate such problems as misinterpretations of instructions, items left blank, ambiguities in the items, and unanticipated responses. Revisions can then be made to the questionnaire prior to the final study.

Many suggestions exist for writing questionnaire items. Payne (113) has a concise checklist of 100 considerations that cover nine basic areas: the issue to be studied, the free-response question, the two-way question, multiple-choice question, other types of questions, how respondents should be treated, the words themselves, loading or biasing of items, and the readability of the items. For example, Payne suggests using as few words as necessary, using simple words whenever possible, making sure a word has only one pronunciation, checking the dictionary to see if a word actually means what you intend and that it does not have other meanings that may confuse the issue, etc. Regarding the treatment of respondents, he suggests that you avoid the appearance of talking down to them, use good grammar but do not sound stilted, avoid double negatives, and make the question specific enough without overelaborating.

In experimental studies, not only must you measure the dependent variables, but you must also *create the independent variable*. One crucial issue is whether or not you did in fact create the independent variable that you wanted to create. For example, you might want to compare the amount of learning that occurs in unstructured classroom discussion as opposed to teacher-led, highly structured classroom discussion. You would need to verify that the discussion processes that occurred in these two settings not only differed from each other but also differed along the dimensions you had planned. The other major issue is whether extraneous variables were controlled. How do you verify that these two goals have been achieved or, in other words, that the study has a high degree of internal validity? Your review of the literature should give you some indication of how you can effectively manipulate or create the independent variable. Application of the principles of experimental design (e.g., randomization of subjects and other stimuli across experimental conditions) helps ensure the control of extraneous variables. Instruments can be constructed to measure the effect of experimental controls and the observable differences in the experimental treatments. The crucial test is to conduct a miniature final study, a pilot study, through which you can measure your success in manipulating the independent variable and in controlling extraneous variables. Nothing can really substitute for research experience in learning what experimental variations "work" and what unexpected events you need to anticipate and control for in experimental studies.

In all types of studies you need to plan the *statistical analysis* before you collect the data. If you have limited background in statistics you may want to obtain a statistical consultant to assist you. Since the study design and the scale of measurement of the criterion variables influence the type of statistical analyses that can be conducted, it is best to be aware of any analytical problems that might arise before you conduct the study. In some cases, it may be advisable to change the design and/or the measurement procedures to facilitate the statistical analyses.

A.3 HOW DO YOU COLLECT THE DATA?

No matter how good the design plan, *if the data are collected in a careless manner, the study may be rendered worthless.* For example, a tester may give the wrong instructions, test the wrong subject, or fail to record the subject's full response. An interviewer may misinterpret the sampling plan. A research assistant may give an experimental treatment to the wrong subjects. The responses to a questionnaire may be coded incorrectly or the responses to an achievement test scored incorrectly. Because all sorts of problems can arise during the data collection process, you need to check all aspects of this process very carefully.

Having decided to conduct research, you must carry out the study with respect for the study participants and with concern for their welfare and dignity. The American Psychological Association (4, pp. 1–2) has developed ten *ethical principles* that should be followed in conducting research with participants. These principles are cited below (some have been condensed). For a full discussion and interpretation of these principles, refer to the original publication.

1. In planning a study the investigator has the personal responsibility to make a careful evaluation of its ethical acceptability, taking into account these Principles for research with human beings. . . .

2. Responsibility for the establishment and maintenance of acceptable ethical practice in research always remains with the individual investigator. The investigator is also responsible for the ethical treatment of response participants by collaborators, assistants, students, and employees, all of whom, however, incur parallel obligations.

3. Ethical practice requires the investigator to inform the participant of all features of the research that reasonably might be expected to influence willingness to participate and to explain all other aspects of the research about which the participant inquires. . . .

4. Openness and honesty are essential characteristics of the relationship between investigator and research participant. When the methodological requirements of a study necessitate concealment or deception, the investigator is required to ensure the participant's understanding of the reasons for this action and to restore the quality of the relationship with the investigator.

5. Ethical research practice requires the investigator to respect the individual's freedom to decline to participate in research or to discontinue participation at any time.

6. Ethically acceptable research begins with the establishment of a clear and fair agreement between the investigator and the research participant that clarifies the responsibilities of each. The investigator has the obligation to honor all promises and commitments included in that agreement.

7. The ethical investigator protects participants from physical and mental discomfort, harm, and danger. If the risk of such consequences exists, the investigator is required to inform the participant of that fact, secure consent before proceeding, and take all possible measures to minimize distress. A research procedure may not be used if it is likely to cause serious and lasting harm to participants.

8. After the data are collected, ethical practice requires the investigator to provide the participant with a full clarification of the nature of the study and to remove any misconceptions that may have arisen. Where scientific or humane values justify delaying or withholding information, the investigator acquires a special responsibility to assure that there are no damaging consequences for the participant.

9. Where research procedures may result in undesirable consequences for the participant, the investigator has the responsibility to detect and remove or correct these consequences, including, where relevant, long-term aftereffects.

10. Information obtained about the research participants during the course of an investigation is confidential. When the possibility exists that others may obtain access to such information, ethical research practice requires that this possibility, together with the plans for protecting confidentiality, be explained to the participants as a part of the procedure for obtaining informed consent.

A.4 HOW DO YOU ANALYZE AND INTERPRET THE DATA?

Selection of the appropriate statistical techniques will not be discussed in this appendix for it is simply too large and too complex a topic. It was previously suggested that you obtain some advice regarding the statistical analysis if your background in this area is limited. No matter how sophisticated or unsophisticated your statistical knowledge, you should become very familiar with the data. This can best be accomplished by examining the frequency distribution of each variable, computing indices of central tendency and variability, and by examining the association between variables through cross-tabulation tables or scatter diagrams. The computer centers at most colleges and universities have statistical programs that can be used by students to facilitate the data analysis.

It is one thing to simply report *findings* in a factual, routine way and quite another to *interpret them*: that is, *to determine what they mean in terms of future research, theory and/or practice, and to explain why they occurred.* All stages of the research process influence the interpretation you make. For example, you may conclude that the results may be an artifact of the testing procedure, that they support a different theory, that they apply only to a certain type of individual, or that although the results were statistically significant, the differences were too minor to have any practical educational significance. If different results are found on multiple measures of the same variable, then you should try to explain this discrepancy. When more than one dependent variable is used in an experiment, you should integrate the findings from all variables. When the research hypotheses are not supported, you need to explain why, if possible. In some instances you may be able to verify your explanation with a reanalysis of the data. Since such interpretations are subjective, you should let others critique your position before completing the report.

A.5 HOW DO YOU WRITE THE REPORT?

The exact format of the research report will depend on whether it is to be a thesis, a dissertation, or a journal article. Generally speaking, most universities publish a list of the topics that need to be included in a thesis or dissertation that their students must follow. The editorial policies of the particular research journal to which you intend to send your article should be identified and followed. The thesis and dissertation formats allow more details than a journal article does and you may find it difficult to summarize the study in the journal format. In all instances you must describe as clearly as possible the problem you studied, why you studied it, how you studied it, the pilot studies you conducted, how you analyzed the data, the results of the analysis, and the conclusions you drew from the results. There is no room for ambiguity in scientific writing. General suggestions on writing are given in Appendix C.

Because you can become so involved in your study, you may not be able to be objective about it. Therefore, it is advisable to have others read your report before its completion. Individuals who are familiar with the specific topic can examine the theoretical and technical aspects of the study. Individuals who are not as familiar with the research topic can read the report as would a journal reviewer or editor, that is, evaluate the general quality and the educational value of the study.

A.6 RESEARCH REFERENCES

A.6.1 GENERAL RESEARCH REFERENCES

Borg, W. R., and M. D. Gall, 1971. *Educational Research: An Introduction,* (2nd ed.) New York: David McKay.

Gage, N. L., 1963. *Handbook of Research on Teaching*. Chicago: Rand McNally.

Helmstadter, G. C., 1970. *Research Concepts in Human Behavior: Education, Psychology, and Sociology*. New York: Appleton-Century-Crofts.

Hyman, H., 1955. *Survey Design and Analysis: Principles, Cases, and Procedures*. New York: Free Press.

Isaac, S., and W. G. Michael, 1971. *Handbook in Research and Evaluation for Education and the Behavioral Sciences*. San Diego, Calif.: Robert R. Knapp.

Kerlinger, F. N., 1973. *Foundations of Behavioral Research* (2nd ed.). New York: Holt, Rinehart and Winston.

Lindzey, G., and E. Aronson (eds.), 1968. *The Handbook of Social Psychology*, (2nd ed., Vol. 2), *Research Methods*. Reading, Mass.: Addison-Wesley.

Miller, D. C., 1977. *Handbook of Research Design and Social Measurement* (3rd ed.) New York: David McKay.

Popham, W. J., 1975. *Educational Evaluation*. Englewood Cliffs, N.J.: Prentice-Hall.

Selltiz, C., L. S. Wrightsman, and S. W. Cook, 1976. *Research Methods in Social Relations* (3rd ed.). New York: Holt, Rinehart and Winston.

Stufflebeam, D. I., et al., 1971. *Educational Evaluation and Decision Making*. Itasca, Ill.: Peacock.

Travers, R. M. W., (ed.), 1973. *Second Handbook of Research on Teaching*. Chicago: Rand McNally.

Tuckman, B. W., 1978. *Conducting Educational Research* (2nd ed.). New York: Harcourt Brace Jovanovich.

Underwood, B. J., and J. J. Shaughnessy, 1975. *Experimentation in Psychology*. New York: Wiley.

Warwick, D. P., and C. A. Lininger, 1975. *The Sample Survey: Theory and Practice*. New York: McGraw-Hill.

Worthen, B. R., and J. R. Sanders, 1973. *Educational Evaluation: Theory and Practice*. Worthington, Ohio: Charles A. Jones.

A.6.2 MEASUREMENT REFERENCES

Bloom, B. S., J. T. Hastings, and G. F. Madaus, 1971. *Handbook on Formative and Summative Evaluation of Student Learning*. New York: McGraw-Hill.

Converse, J. M., and H. Schuman, 1974. *Conversations at Random: Survey Research as Interviewers See It*. New York: Wiley.

Cronbach, L. J., 1970. *Essentials of Psychological Testing* (3rd ed.). New York: Harper & Row.

Ebel, R. L., 1965. *Measuring Educational Achievement*. Englewood Cliffs, N.J.: Prentice-Hall.

Edwards, A. L., 1957. *Techniques of Attitude Scale Construction.* New York: Appleton-Century-Crofts.

Guilford, J.P., 1954. *Psychometric Methods* (2nd ed.) New York: McGraw-Hill.

Payne, S. L., 1951. *The Art of Asking Questions.* Princeton: Princeton University Press.

Richardson, S. A., B. S. Dohrenwend, and D. Klein, 1965. *Interviewing: Its Forms and Functions.* New York: Basic Books.

Thorndike, R. L. (ed.). 1971. *Educational Measurement* (2nd ed.). Washington, D.C.: American Council on Education.

Thorndike, R. L., and E. Hagen, 1969. *Measurement and Evaluation in Psychology and Education* (3rd ed.) New York: Wiley.

A.6.3 STATISTICAL REFERENCES

Bennett, S., and D. Bowers, 1976. *An Introduction to Multivariate Techniques for Social and Behavioral Sciences.* London: Macmillan.

Bruning, J. L., and B. L. Kintz, 1968. *Computational Handbook of Statistics.* Glenview, Ill.: Scott Foresman.

Cooley, W. W., and P. R. Lohnes, 1971. *Multivariate Data Analysis.* New York: Wiley.

Conover, W. J., 1971. *Practical Nonparametric Statistics.* New York: Wiley.

Davis, J. A., 1971. *Elementary Survey Analysis.* Englewood Cliffs, N.J.: Prentice-Hall.

Dinham, S. M., 1976. *Exploring Statistics: An Introduction for Psychology and Education.* Monterey, Calif.: Brooks/Cole.

Dixon, W. J., and F. J. Massey, 1969. *Introduction to Statistical Analysis* (3rd ed.) New York: McGraw-Hill.

Glass, G. V., and J. C. Stanley, 1970. *Statistical Methods in Education and Psychology.* Englewood Cliffs, N.J.: Prentice-Hall.

Hicks, C. R., 1964. *Fundamental Concepts in the Design of Experiments* (2nd ed.). New York: Holt Rinehart and Winston.

Huck, S. W., W. H. Cormier, and W. G. Bounds, 1974. *Reading Statistics and Research.* New York: Harper & Row.

Kerlinger, F. N., and E. J. Pedhazur, 1973. *Multiple Regression in Behavioral Research.* New York: Holt, Rinehart and Winston.

Mendenhall, W., 1967. *Introduction to Probability and Statistics* (2nd ed.). Belmont, Calif.: Wadsworth.

Mosteller, F., and R. E. K. Rourke, 1973. *Sturdy Statistics:* Reading, Mass.: Addison-Wesley.

Mueller, J. H., K. F. Schuessler, and H. L. Costner, 1970. *Statistical Reasoning in Sociology* (2nd ed.). Boston: Houghton Mifflin.

Siegel, S., 1956. *Nonparametric Statistics for the Behavioral Sciences*. New York: McGraw-Hill.

Winer, B. J., 1971. *Statistical Principles in Experimental Design* (2nd ed.). New York: McGraw-Hill.

Appendix B
Locating
Educational
Research

Locating reports of educational research can be a time-consuming process if you are not familiar with research journals or the library facilities that can greatly aid you in the search process. This appendix cites various means by which research reports can be located.

B.1 ORIGINAL REPORTS OF RESEARCH

Most research is published in periodicals or journals. However, not all journals contain research articles. Some contain only reviews of research and/or opinion articles. A list of the major journals that publish research within the field of education and related fields is given in Table B.1. Some of these journals are devoted exclusively to research studies and others contain both research and nonresearch articles. You should be able to locate research journals in your area of interest from this list.

Other sources of original research are dissertations/theses and government documents. Most university libraries house dissertations/theses, conducted by their own graduate students, and many government documents. Occasionally the report of a large research project can be found in book form.

B.2 SEARCHING THE RESEARCH LITERATURE

Generally speaking, it is inefficient and unnecessary to page through journal articles in search of a topic of interest to you. Many specially prepared materials are available to aid you in such searches and are cited below.

B.2.1 JOURNAL ARTICLES

Reference to specific journal articles can be found in various abstracting and indexing publications. These services search journals in specific fields and index them under headings or topics that an individual might use in searching for articles of interest. In addition to subject indexes most publications contain author indexes. Some contain abstracts or brief summaries of the articles. Such abstracts can save the user considerable time in determining whether or not an article is relevant to his or her purposes.

In some instances abstracts of the article are also available on computer tape. If such tapes have been purchased by an institution, such as a university, then a search of the abstracts can be made rather quickly by requesting all articles that are classified under a certain heading or only those articles that are classified under several key headings. For instance, if you were interested in articles about the social adjustment of gifted children, you might choose the following descriptive terms: gifted (or related terms such as superior students or talented students) and social adjustment (or related terms such as social isolation, social maturity, social problems, interpersonal competence). A computer listing of the corresponding articles would then be generated.

A list of abstracting and indexing publications of particular importance to educators is given in Table B.2. Some of the publications are highly specialized; others are not. The *Current Index to Journals in Education* abstracts journal articles from education and related fields and is a source that can be used by all educators. With most indexing and abstracting publications, the content index should be consulted first for topics of interest to you. Bibliographic information on publications corresponding to the topics you have selected will be cited in this index. If abstracts are given as well, the content index usually provides an identification number associated with that article in the abstract section, which should then be consulted for further information about the report.

B.2.2 UNPUBLISHED RESEARCH DOCUMENTS

An important source of both research and nonresearch reports in education sponsored by the U.S. government, as well as occasional papers, mimeographed materials, and documents that have not been formally published, is called *Resources in Education* (RIE, formerly *Research in Education*). This service is provided by the Educational Resources Information Center (ERIC) of the National Institute of Education. The RIE volume is published monthly and contains abstracts of the documents cited. The citations are indexed by topics listed in the *Thesaurus of ERIC Descriptors*. Once citations of interest are located in the RIE volumes, the original document can be found in its entirety on microfiche cards that are indexed by the ED number cited in the RIE volume. Most universities have this microfiche collection. A computerized retrieval system of the abstracts exists and hard bound copies of the documents can be obtained.

Other indexing and abstracting publications cite other unpublished government reports and materials such as dissertations and theses. A list of such publications is given in Table B.2.

B.2.3 REVIEWS OF RESEARCH

Another way to identify research studies is to locate reviews of research published in either book or journal form. Textbooks can be a useful source, but are not current with the research literature. Some of the more well-known volumes that periodically review educational and related research are: *Annual Review of Psychology, Encyclopedia of Educational Research,* the *Handbooks of Research on Teaching, National Society for Study of Education* (*NSSE*) *Yearbooks* (one or two volumes are published annually on special topics), and *Review of Research in Education* (American Educational Research Association yearly publication begun in 1973).

Many of the journals listed in Table B.1 contain reviews of research in the form of entire articles or as introductions to research studies themselves. Some other journals that focus on reviews of educational research are: *Harvard Educational Review, Phi Delta Kappan, Review of Educational Research, School Review,* and *Teachers College Record.*

B.2.4 LOCATING A DOCUMENT NOT IN YOUR LIBRARY

If a research report is not in your local library, contact the librarian regarding the means by which you might obtain a copy. Interlibrary loan services are available whereby copies of documents can be obtained from other libraries. Another approach is to write the author directly for a copy of the report. A listing of the addresses of faculty members at major universities throughout the United States is given in the *National Faculty Directory.* Other listings of addresses for faculty in specialized areas can be found in the directories of members for such associations as the American Educational Research Association, National Council on Measurement in Education, American Psychological Association, and American Sociological Association.

TABLE B.1 *RESEARCH JOURNALS IN EDUCATION AND RELATED AREAS*

General Education Journals

Adult Education
Alberta Journal of Educational Research
American Educational Research Journal
Australian Journal of Education
AV Communication Review
British Journal of Educational Psychology
British Journal of Educational Technology
Childhood Education
Classroom Interaction Newsletter
Colorado Journal of Educational Research
Comparative Education
Comparative Education Review
Education

Education and Urban Society
Educational and Psychological Measurement
Educational Broadcasting Review
Educational Research Quarterly (formerly *California Journal of Educational Research*)
Educational Research
Educational Researcher
Elementary School Journal
Gifted Child Quarterly
High School Journal
History of Education Quarterly
Improving Human Performance Quarterly

TABLE B.1 cont.

Instructional Science
Integrated Education
International Journal of Continuing
    Education and Training
Journal of American Indian Education
Journal of Creative Behavior
Journal of Drug Education
Journal of Education for Social Work
Journal of Educational Data Processing
Journal of Educational Measurement
Journal of Educational Psychology
Journal of Educational Research

Journal of Experimental Education
Journal of Negro Education
Journal of Research and Development
    in Education
NASSP Bulletin
NEA Research Bulletin
Peabody Journal of Education
Psychology in the Schools
School Review
Sociology of Education
Urban Education

Curriculum Journals

American Biology Teacher
Arithmetic Teacher
Council of Research in Music Education
    Bulletin
English Language Teaching Journal
Engineering Education
Journal for Research in Mathematics
    Education
Journal of Aesthetic Education
Journal of Band Research
Journal of Business Education
Journal of Chemical Education
Journal of College Science Teaching
Journal of Cooperative Education
Journal of Curriculum Studies
Journal of Dental Education
Journal of English Teaching Techniques
Journal of Reading
Journal of Reading Behavior

Journal of Research in Music Education
Journal of Research in Science Teaching
Language Learning: A Journal of Applied
    Linguistics
Modern Language Journal
Reading Research Quarterly
Reading Teacher
Reading World (formerly Journal of the
    Reading Specialist)
Research in the Teaching of English
Research Quarterly of the AAHPER
School Science and Mathematics
Science Education
Speech Monographs
Speech Teacher
Studies in Art Education
Teaching of Psychology
Teaching Sociology
Two-year College Mathematics Journal

Special Education

Academic Therapy
American Annals of the Deaf
American Journal of Mental Deficiency
American Journal of Orthopsychiatry
Audiology and Hearing Education
Education and Training of the Mentally
    Retarded
Education of the Visually Handicapped
Exceptional Children
Focus on Exceptional Children

Journal of Autism and Childhood Schizo-
    phrenia
Journal of Learning Disabilities
Journal of Mental Deficiency Research
Journal of Special Education
Journal of Speech and Hearing Disorders
Journal of Speech and Hearing Research
Mental Retardation
Volta Review

Guidance and Counseling

Counselor Education and Supervision
Elementary School Guidance and
    Counseling
Journal of Applied Rehabilitation Coun-
    seling
Journal of College Student Personnel

Journal of Counseling Psychology
Journal of Marriage and Family Counseling
Journal of School Psychology
Measurement and Evaluation in Guidance
Vocational Guidance Quarterly

TABLE B.1 cont.

Administration and Higher Education

AAUP Bulletin
Administrative Science Quarterly
Administrator's Notebook
College and University
Educational Administration Quarterly
Educational Administration and Supervision
Educational Leadership
Educational Record
Improving College and University Teaching

Journal of College Student Personnel
Journal of Education Finance
Journal of Educational Administration
Journal of Higher Education
Journal of the National Association of
  Women Deans, Administrators, and
  Counselors
Research in Higher Education

Other Disciplines

Adolescence
American Anthropologist
American Economic Review
American Journal of Community Psychology
American Journal of Sociology
American Sociological Review
Behaviour Research and Therapy
Child Development
Child Study Journal
Child Welfare
Developmental Psychology
Human Development
Human Relations
Journal of Abnormal Psychology
Journal of Applied Behavioral Analysis
Journal of Applied Psychology
Journal of Child Language
Journal of Child Psychology and Psychiatry
  and Allied Disciplines
Journal of Collective Negotiations in the
  Public Sector
Journal of Communication
Journal of Community Psychology
Journal of Consulting and Clinical
  Psychology

Journal of Cross-cultural Psychology
Journal of Experimental Child Psychology
Journal of Genetic Psychology
Journal of Marriage and the Family
Journal of Nervous and Mental Disease
Journal of Personality and Social Psychology
Journal of School Health
Journal of Social Psychology
Journal of the American Medical Association
Journal of Verbal Learning and Verbal
  Behavior
Merrill Palmer Quarterly of Behavior
  and Development
Monographs of the Society for Research in
  Child Development
Organizational Behavior and Human
  Performance
Perceptual and Motor Skills
Public Opinion Quarterly
Science
Scientific American
Sociometry
Youth and Society

TABLE B.2 *PUBLICATIONS WHICH INDEX AND/OR ABSTRACT JOURNAL ARTICLES AND UNPUBLISHED RESEARCH DOCUMENTS*

Name of Index	Coverage	Abstracts	Contents
JOURNAL ARTICLES			
Current Index to Journals in Education (CIJE)	Currently covers 700 journals in education and related fields. Started in 1969. Abstracts can also be retrieved from the ERIC file via computer.	Yes	*Subject* Index is organized by ERIC descriptors. *Abstracts* are in the main entry section which is arranged alphabetically and numerically by ERIC Clearinghouse accession number. *Author* and *Journal Content* Indexes.
Education Index	Over 200 journals in all fields of education	No	*Subject* Index.
Exceptional Child Education	Over 200 journals related to exceptional children	Yes	*Abstracts* are in the abstract section and are ordered by ERIC Clearinghouse accession number. *Subject, Title of Article,* and *Author* Indexes.
Mental Retardation and Developmental Disabilities Abstracts	Medical, psychological, educational, child development, and sociological journals that focus on research and new developments in mental retardation and developmental disabilities.	Yes	*Abstract* section is organized under seven broad headings, e.g., medical aspects, treatment and training aspects, family. *Author* and *Subject* Indexes.
Educational Administration Abstracts	Journals in the field of educational administration and related areas.	Yes	*Abstracts* under headings such as administrative processes and organizational variables, planning, theory and research. *Author* and *Journal* Indexes.
DSH Abstracts	Journals in the areas of deafness, speech, and hearing.	Yes	*Abstracts* under five broad headings: hearing, hearing disorders, speech, speech disorders, and general. *Author* index.

TABLE B.2 cont.

Name of Index	Coverage	Abstracts	Contents
Psychological Abstracts	Covers more than 850 journals, technical reports and scientific documents in psychology. A computerized information retrieval system is available for abstracts beginning in 1967.	Yes	*Abstracts* are classified under 17 broad categories. *Subject* and *Author* Indexes.
Sociological Abstracts	Covers over 90 periodicals in the field of sociology.	Yes	*Abstracts* are in the *Subject* Index section.
Index Medicus	Currently covers approximately 2250 of the world's biomedical journals.	No	*Subject* and *Author* Indexes.
Child Development Abstracts and Bibliography	Journals in psychology, medicine, education, and sociology which contain articles on human development.	Yes	*Abstracts* under headings such as biology, health, medicine, cognition, learning, and educational processes. *Author* and *Subject* Indexes.
Social Sciences Citation Index	An international, interdisciplinary index of literature in the social, behavioral, and related sciences. Covers over 1000 journals. Cites all articles published during the calendar year in the journals covered, as well as the references made in those articles. Useful when searcher has a key article and wishes to find who has cited it and has extended the work in that area.	No	*Source Index* is a complete author index to the journal articles. Complete bibliographic description is given. *Citation Index* alphabetically lists the authors of references cited in the journal articles listed in the Source Index. Under each entry are all authors who referred to the citation article. *Permuterm Subject Index* cites the primary word in the title of the articles in the Source Index and pairs it with all other significant title words. All authors with journal titles with identical primary-coterm pairs are listed under that heading. *Corporate Address Index*.

Science Citation Index	An international, interdisciplinary index of literature in science, medicine, agriculture, technology, and the behavioral sciences.	No	Same format as Social Sciences Citation Index.
Social Sciences Index	Periodicals in such areas as anthropology, economics, law and criminology, medical sciences, political sciences, public administration, psychology, and sociology.	No	*Subject* Index.
Humanities Index	Periodicals in areas such as history, archeology, classical studies, performing arts, philosophy, and religion.	No	*Subject* Index.
Business Periodicals Index	Journals in such areas as accounting, banking, communications, economics, computer technology, management, and personnel administration.	No	*Subject* Index.
Completed Research in Health, Physical Education and Recreation	Reviews about 200 journals in the area of physical education.	No	*Subject* Index.

UNPUBLISHED DOCUMENTS

Resources in Education (RIE, formerly *Research in Education*)	Includes scientific documents and government reports in education that generally have not been formally published. The full document can be obtained on 4″ × 6″ microfiche cards indexed by ED number. Many universities have complete microfiche collections. The abstracts can also be retrieved from the ERIC file via computer.	Yes	*Subject* Index is arranged by ERIC descriptors. *Abstracts* are included in the document section and are arranged by ED number and ERIC Clearinghouse and acquisition number. *Author* and *Institution of Author* Indexes.

TABLE B.2 cont.

Name of Index	Coverage	Abstracts	Contents
Government Reports Annual Index	Cites unclassified federally funded research as it is completed and made available to the public. Includes reports in the behavioral and social sciences. The associated biweekly publication, *Government Reports: Announcements and Index*, does contain abstracts.	No	*Subject, Personal Author, Corporate Author*, and *Contract Number* Indexes.
Research Relating to Children Bulletin	Abstracts of ongoing or recently completed studies in such areas as growth and development, child in the family, educational factors and services, and long-term research.	Yes	Abstracts in the main entry section. *Subject, Investigator*, and *Institution* Indexes.
Completed Research in Health, Physical Education and Recreation	Abstracts of masters and doctoral theses in physical education from 64 institutions are presented.	Yes	*Subject* Index.
Dissertation Abstracts International (formerly *Dissertation Abstracts*)	Abstracts of doctoral dissertations from more than 375 institutions in the U.S. and Canada. Section A, Humanities and Social Sciences, includes the field of education. Section B, Science and Engineering, includes psychology and health and environmental sciences. Complete copies of dissertations can be purchased as microfilm or xerographic prints.	Yes	Abstracts in the main entry section. *Keyword Title* and *Author* Indexes.

Appendix C
Summarizing
and Synthesizing
the Research
Literature

This appendix focuses on writing reviews of research for an undergraduate/ graduate course, for a journal, or for the introduction to a research article, thesis, or dissertation. These guidelines can also assist you in writing up results of an original research study.

C.1 SUMMARIZING STUDIES

Before summarizing research studies in a particular area, you must have a very clear picture of each study. To achieve this goal you must examine each article carefully and take very specific notes. Any quotations from the article should be indicated and the corresponding page number reported. It is also important to check the accuracy of the information in your notes (including the reference itself, i.e., author, title, date, etc.), since you can easily make mistakes in recording information. The major points which should be specified in research notes are described below and are illustrated in Table C.1.

C.1.1 BACKGROUND INFORMATION

1. Put the purpose in question form; that is, what were the major questions asked by the researcher. Sometimes these questions cannot be identified until the entire article has been read.

2. Identify the variables specified in each question (by underlining them or by inserting them in parentheses). A diagram of the research design may also be useful.

3. Classify the study as one of description, association and/or causation; then identify the specific type of descriptive, associative, or causal study.

4. Cite any research hypotheses that were made.

5. Briefly describe the theory and/or previous research upon which the study was based.

C.1.2 RESEARCH METHODOLOGY

1. Describe the characteristics of the sample and how the sample was selected.

2. Determine how the major variables were measured and/or established. For descriptive studies these variables include the background and criterion variables; for association studies, the variables being related; and for causal studies, the independent, dependent, and control variables. In experiments, measurement of the independent variable refers to describing the experimental conditions that were manipulated by the researcher.

C.1.3 RESULTS/CONCLUSIONS/REACTIONS

1. Summarize the answer to each research question; indicate statistical tests used, if possible.

2. Indicate whether the research hypotheses were supported or not supported.

3. Summarize important comments made by the author in his or her discussion and interpretation of the results.

4. Summarize the major conclusions and/or recommendations made by the author.

5. List reactions you have about the study's rationale, the way in which the study was conducted, the analysis of data, and the researcher's conclusions.

This summarization process will take time and will not be easy for every study. However, the time spent will be worthwhile, for you will understand the information in the article better and retain it longer than you will if you do not go through this process.

TABLE C.1   RESEARCH STUDY NOTES: AN EXAMPLE

Reference: Sherman, Julia, and Elizabeth Fennema, 1977. The study of mathematics by high school girls and boys: Related variables. *American Educational Research Journal* **14:** 159–168.

Research questions:

1. To what extent do boys and girls (*sex*) from both high and low *mathematics achievement* groups in the 10th and 11th *grades* intend to take further high school math (*intention-mathematics*)?

2. What are the unique and joint relationships of the four variables of *sex, mathematics achievement, grade level,* and *intention to take further math* to each of the following variables: *verbal ability, spatial visualization,* and eight measures of attitudes toward math—*success in mathematics, stereotyping of math as a male domain, perceived attitude of mother, father,* and *teacher towards one as a learner of mathematics, joy in problem solving, confidence in learning math,* and *usefulness of math?*

3. When the cognitive variables of *math, verbal,* and *spatial ability/achievement* are controlled, what are the unique and joint relationships of *sex, grade level,* and *intention to take further math* to each of the *attitudinal variables?*

Type of study: Association—specifically the relationship between a single variable (several variables taken individually) and a set of variables.

Research hypotheses: None were made.

Theory/previous studies: No theory cited. Reference made only to Maccoby and Jacklin's monograph on sex differences.

Sample: Tenth and eleventh grade students enrolled in nonterminal mathematics courses. No other descriptive information given and no information on how the sample was selected.

Measurement of variables:

Sex and grade level—No information given.

Intention-mathematics—Questions regarding plans for enrolling in math courses the following school year. Answers classified as either Yes, No, or Don't know.

Math achievement—Test of Academic Progress, students divided into upper and lower halves on achievement

Verbal ability—Quick Word Test

Spatial visualization—Differential Aptitude Test, Space Relations subtest

Affective measures—All taken from Fennema–Sherman Mathematics Attitude Scales. No description of scales given.

No information on reliability and validity of any of the measures was given. No indication of whether sex of tester/questioner was controlled.

Answers to research questions:

1. In the 10th grade, proportionately more boys than girls in each math achievement group intended to continue studying math. In the 11th grade, similar proportions of boys and girls of high ability intended to continue math while proportionately more boys than girls of lower ability intended to do so. Chi-square test.

2. In general, students in the upper math group and students who intended to continue math scored higher on the verbal and spatial variables and had more positive attitudes toward math than those in the lower math groups and those who did not intend to continue math. Sex was related to the variable of verbal ability (girls higher) and math as a male domain (boys more stereotyped). No major interactions existed between the background variables and criterion variables. Analysis of variance.

3. Results similar to those in the previous analyses were found: that is, those who intended to study math had more favorable attitudes (except there was no difference between the intend/nonintend groups on the variable of math as a male domain), and boys were more likely to consider math as a male domain. No significant interactions. Analysis of covariance.

Interpretation/discussion:

Girls appeared to deny that math is a male domain. However, they did not elect to study math as often as boys. Viewed as a discrepancy in verbal report and actual behavior by the authors. The verbal report may be a reaction to the ideology espoused by the women's movement; the intended behavior a reaction to pressure from male peers. Authors suggested a need to study the hypothesis that "male teaching of advanced mathematics courses influences students to believe that advanced mathematical thinking is a male province" (p. 166).

Conclusions/recommendations:

Females with relatively low math ability do not intend to continue studying math as often as males of comparable ability. Cognitive variables and the intent to study math re-

TABLE C.1 cont.

late more strongly to various attitudes toward math than sex per se. In order to make appropriate conclusions regarding sex differences in math behavior, researchers should control for sex differences in math ability and attitudes.

Personal comments:

(1) Study rationale inadequate. Study not adequately specify research questions at the beginning. (1) Information about sample was inadequate, making generalization difficult. (3) Need to read more about the mathematics attitude scales that were used. (4) The relationships among the cognitive and affective variables were not shown. (5) A rather complete table of means and standard deviations was given. (6) Disagree with authors' conclusion regarding future studies. Should not cover up sex differences in math by controlling all variables that relate to sex. Instead, rephrase the research question to examine what variables interact with sex to produce math differences. (7) A reexamination of the data indicated two trends: proportion of females above the math median decreased from 10th to 11th grade while proportion of males increased, and the proportion of males above the math median was consistently higher than the proportion of females. (8) Would like to see the study replicated by male researchers.

C.2 SYNTHESIZING STUDIES

After notes have been made on each article, the next task is to construct an *outline* for your paper that cites both the *topics* you are going to discuss and the particular *studies* that pertain to each topic. The choice of topics depends on the purpose of the paper. Frequently, papers concentrate on findings of studies. However, the focus could be on the research methods employed, on the theories applied, or on a combination of these themes.

Since many studies investigate more than one topic, you will probably find a particular study mentioned more than once in your outline. A synthesis of studies is not achieved when each paragraph is devoted to summarizing each study, for such a paper simply represents an annotated bibliography of the studies. In synthesizing studies, the writer must discuss the similarities and differences in the studies, discriminate between relevant and irrelevant portions of a particular study, and discriminate between well-designed and poorly designed studies. The emphasis given to each study depends on the purpose of the paper, and it is uncommon to find all studies receiving equal treatment.

C.3 WRITING THE REPORT

The report should be clearly written, since the reader is usually not familiar with the studies being reviewed. *Clarity* can be enhanced by: (1) defining central terms and concepts when they are first presented, (2) using topic sentences and headings to tell the reader where you are going, (3) avoiding indefinite pronouns such as "it," "one," "this," and "they" whose referents are apt to be ambiguous, (4) making all comparisons and contrasts complete (e.g., The turnover rate of male high school teachers was greater than the turnover of *whom?"*—female high school teachers/male high school principals/male elementary teachers?), (6) rephrasing study results in terms that are meaningful to you instead of relying upon quotations from a study, quotations that can easily lose their meaning once they are extracted from the study, and (6) including summaries where appropriate.

The report should also be *direct.* "Decide what is to be said, say it in the most direct way possible, and stop" (50, p. 711). Avoid jargon and excess verbiage. Be *consistent* and *precise* in the use of terms of quantity, quality, and frequency (e.g., many, most, few). Since researchers are inconsistent in their use of such terms, you must reexamine the results from various studies in order to consistently apply such terms. All other terms should also be used consistently. It is better to define and use a term such as "gifted" throughout the report than to use a variety of terms such as "bright," "above average," "highly intelligent," and "creative" to refer to the same concept. In scientific writing, such inconsistency is more likely to be confusing than boring.

When referring to the content of published reports, the past tense should be used. The present tense can be used when the author "talks" to the reader. The first person ("I" and "my") should not be used.

The *transition* from one section of the paper to another section should be smooth so that new ideas do not appear unexpectedly. Continuity can be enhanced by a closing sentence in a paragraph that prepares the reader for the next section, by an introductory sentence to a new section, by transitional words and phrases, and by repetition of key terms.

Good reports usually require several drafts. Even after you think you have written your last draft, it is advisable to let another individual review your your paper. Select someone who will read the paper carefully and critically, and who can comment on both its style and substance. If such an individual is not available, ignore the paper for one or two weeks and then critically reexamine it yourself. Sometimes faults in the paper will be clearer if you read the paper aloud instead of silently.

C.4 FORMAT OF THE REPORT

Many manuals discuss the general format of papers, theses, and dissertations. Guidelines for the specific format of quotations, footnotes, bibliography, references, tables, figures and appendixes are also given in such publications. Universities and scientific journals usually specify a particular manual which must be followed. Some of the more common style manuals in the social science area are: *A Manual for Writers of Term Papers, Theses, and Dissertations* by Kate L. Turabian, *A Manual of Style* published by the University of Chicago Press, *The Publication Manual of the American Psychological Association,* and *Form and Style in Thesis Writing* by William G. Campbell.

Appendix D
Glossary of Statistical Procedures

D.1 STATISTICAL TESTS/PROCEDURES FREQUENTLY USED IN DESCRIPTIVE RESEARCH

Inferences from the Total Sample

Binomial test
Chi-square one-sample test, goodness of fit
Kolmogorov–Smirnov one-sample test
t-test, one sample

Comparison of Only Two Independent Groups within the Sample

F-test for variances
Mann–Whitney U test
Median test
Proportions, test of
t-test, two sample

Comparison of Two or More Independent Groups within the Sample

Analysis of variance, one-factor
Chi-square test for independence
Discriminant analysis
Kruskal–Wallis analysis of variance by ranks
Median test

Comparison of Dependent or Related Groups

Friedman rank sum test
Sign test
t-test, correlated samples
Wilcoxon matched-pairs, signed-rank test

D.2 STATISTICAL TESTS/PROCEDURES FREQUENTLY USED IN ASSOCIATION STUDIES

Indices of Association between Two Variables

Biserial correlation
Contingency coefficient
Correlation ratio
Cramér's V statistic
Eta squared
Gamma
Kendall's tau
Lambda
Omega squared
Partial correlation coefficient
Phi coefficient
Point-biserial correlation coefficient
Product–moment correlation coefficient
Rank biserial correlation coefficient
Rank correlation coefficient
Rho
Tetrachoric correlation coefficient
Yule's Q

Assessing the Relationship between a Set of Variables and a Criterion Variable

Analysis of variance, factorial
Multiple regression analysis, including multiple correlation

Assessing the Relationships and Patterns among a Set of Variables

Cluster analysis
Factor analysis

Assessing the Relationship between Two Sets of Variables

Analysis of variance, multivariate
Canonical variate analysis

D.3 STATISTICAL TESTS/PROCEDURES FREQUENTLY USED IN STUDIES OF CAUSAL QUESTIONS

Experimental and Quasi-Experimental Designs with One Independent Variable

Analysis of covariance
Analysis of variance, one-factor

Chi-square test for independence
Discriminant analysis
Kruskal-Wallis analysis of variance by ranks
Mann–Whitney U test
Median test
Proportions, test of
t-test

Experimental and Quasi-Experimental Designs with More Than One Independent Variable

Analysis of covariance
Analysis of variance, factorial
Friedman rank-sum test

Experimental and Quasi-Experimental Designs that Simultaneously Evaluate More Than One Dependent Variable

Analysis of variance, multivariate

Association Studies with a Causal Purpose

Variations of multiple regression analysis, such as path analysis
Other indices of association

D.4 ALPHABETICAL LIST AND BRIEF DESCRIPTION OF STATISTICAL TESTS/PROCEDURES CITED IN SECTIONS D.1 THROUGH D.3

Analysis of covariance   A variation of analysis of variance; commonly used in experimental studies. Analysis of covariance is essentially an analysis of variance on the dependent variable scores which have been statistically adjusted for their relationship with a pretest (technically called a *covariate* in such contexts). When the covariate is related to the dependent variable, analysis of covariance yields a more powerful analysis than analysis of variance (i.e., increases the likelihood of significant differences among the experimental groups being compared).

Analysis of variance   Refers to a broad category of statistical techniques used to examine the equality of population *means* on two or more groups. Often abbreviated as ANOVA. See D.5 for more information.
   One-factor   Comparison of means on a criterion or dependent variable is made for just *one* independent variable (experimental studies) or one classification/grouping of subjects (association and descriptive studies)
   Factorial   Comparison on a criterion or dependent variable can be made simultaneously for *more than one* independent variable or more than one classification of individuals. Interactions among independent variables can then be examined.

Multivariate   A variation of analysis of variance that tests for differences in the means on *several dependent variables at one time,* as opposed to a separate analysis of each dependent variable. More than one independent variable can also be examined with this procedure.

Binomial test   Test of the hypothesis that the population proportion equals a specific value.

Biserial correlation coefficient, r_b   An index of association between an interval or ratio variable and a dichotomous variable with an underlying normal distribution. Generally ranges in value from −1 to +1, although it may take on values below −1 and above +1.

Canonical variate analysis   Is used to examine the association between two sets of variables by forming a composite of variables in one set and a composite of variables in the second set in such a way that the resulting correlation between the two composites is a maximum value. This correlation coefficient is referred to as a *canonical correlation.* If there is more than one relationship between the two sets of variables, then more than one significant canonical correlation will be found.

Chi-square one-sample test, goodness of fit   Compares frequencies actually obtained on a one-dimensional classification scheme with frequencies expected on the basis of a specific null hypothesis. For example, the actual distribution of responses to an attitude item with the three categories of agree, indifferent, and disagree can be compared with the distribution that would have occurred if the respondents had shown no preference for any position (i.e., the null hypothesis).

Chi-square test for independence   Test of the hypothesis that two ways of classifying individuals are independent. Refer to Chapters 5 and 7 for details.

Cluster analysis   A broad category of techniques used to classify/group individuals, based upon the similarities and differences in their responses to several variables.

Contingency coefficient   An index of association between two nominal variables. Ranges from 0 to +1, but the maximum value is restricted by the dimensionality of the cross-tabulation table formed by crossing the two variables.

Correlation ratio, η^2   An index of association that reflects the strength of a curvilinear (nonlinear) relationship between two interval or ratio variables. Ranges in value from 0 to +1. Is asymmetric; that is, when a curvilinear relationship exists, the degree to which Y can be predicted from X is not the same as the degree to which X can be predicted from Y: $\eta^2_{xy} \neq \eta^2_{yx}$.

Cramér's V statistic   An index of association between two nominal variables. Ranges from 0 to +1. Refer to Chapter 5 for details.

Discriminant analysis   A procedure that determines the combination of variables that creates the maximum differences among groups and determines the probability of an individual case belonging to each group.

Eta squared   *See* **Correlation ratio.**

Factor analysis   A broad category of techniques that examine the patterns of association within a set of variables to determine whether the total number of variables can be reduced to a smaller number (called factors) or whether there is an underlying structure (called the factor structure) among the variables. See D.5 for more information.

Friedman rank sum test   A test for differences in the location of scores among conditions/treatments related to each other because each subject may have been observed under each condition or because subjects were matched across conditions. Scores for each subject are ranked across conditions.

F-test for variances   Test of the hypothesis that the variances of two populations are equal. The test statistic is simply the ratio of the two sample variances.

Gamma, γ   An index of association between two variables, each of which represents a nominal variable with ordered categories (i.e., can be arranged in magnitude from high to low on a specific dimension). Ranges in value from -1 to $+1$. Gives percentage of guessing errors eliminated by using knowledge of order on one variable to predict categorical order on another variable.

Kendall's tau, τ   An index of association between two variables at the ordinal level of measurement. Ranges in value from -1 to $+1$. Reflects difference in probability that two individuals drawn at random will have the same order on both variables.

Kolmogorov–Smirnov one-sample test   Goodness of fit test. Determines whether sample scores conform to a population which is characterized by a particular distribution, such as the normal or a Chi-square distribution.

Kruskal–Wallis analysis of variance by ranks   Test of the hypothesis that J groups come from populations with the same distribution. The test is particularly sensitive to differences in the location of scores. See D.5 for more information.

Lambda, λ   An index of association between two nominal variables. Ranges in value from 0 to $+1$. Symmetric and asymmetric forms. Symmetric form reflects the degree of reduction in error associated with predicting either variable by knowing the other variable. Asymmetric form may be used in situations in which prediction from one variable to another may be of interest, as when there is a time difference between the two variables.

Mann-Whitney U test   Test of hypothesis that two samples come from populations with the same distribution. Scores are treated as ranks and the null hypothesis is rejected if scores in one group are more likely to precede (or follow) the scores in the other group. Is frequently used in place of the t-test when the t-test assumptions cannot be met.

Median test Test of the hypothesis that two or more groups are from populations with the same median. The median for the total group is determined and then the numbers in each group who are above and below this median are compared.

Multiple regression and the multiple correlation coefficient Multiple regression is a technique for determining the association between a single criterion variable and a set of other variables, commonly referred to as predictors. The strength of this association is reflected in the multiple correlation coefficient, R (which ranges in value from 0 and +1), and in the square of this value, R^2. The relative contribution of each predictor to the criterion is reflected in what are known as regression coefficients. See D.5 for more information.

Omega squared, ω^2 An index of association between a nominal variable and an interval/ratio variable. Ranges in value from 0 to +1. Is sometimes applied after a t-test or analysis of variance has been conducted to provide an index of the percentage of variance that has been accounted for in the criterion variable (interval/ratio variable) by the different groups being compared (the nominal variable).

Partial correlation coefficient Correlation coefficient between two variables where the relationship each of them has to a third variable has been removed statistically ("held constant" or "partialled out").

Path analysis A variation of multiple regression analysis applied to association data for the purpose of identifying causal factors and estimating their strength or influence in a causal chain.

Phi coefficient, ϕ An index of association between two dichotomous variables. Ranges in value from −1 to +1; sign is arbitrary. Is product–moment correlation coefficient applied to dichotomous data.

Point-biserial correlation coefficient, r_{pb} Index of association between a dichotomous and an interval/ratio variable. Ranges in value between −1 and +1; sign is arbitrary. Is product–moment correlation coefficient applied to dichotomous and interval/ratio data.

Product–moment correlation coefficient, r_{xy} An index of the strength of a linear relationship between two interval/ratio variables. Ranges in value from −1 to +1. The square of the correlation coefficient is the proportion of variation in one variable that is associated with the other by a linear relationship. Refer to Chapters 5, 13, and 14 for more details.

Proportions, test of Test of the hypothesis that two population proportions are equal. See D.5 for more information.

Rank biserial correlation coefficient, r_{rb} An index of association between a dichotomous and an ordinal variable. Ranges in value from −1 to +1; sign is arbitrary.

Rank correlation coefficient, r_s Sometimes known as the Spearman rank correlation coefficient and sometimes known as rho (ρ). An index of association between two ordinal variables. Ranges in value between -1 and $+1$; equals 1 only when each person has the same rank on both variables. Is a product–moment correlation coefficient applied to ranked data. See D.5 for more information.

Rho, ρ *See* **Rank correlation coefficient.**

Sign test Test of hypothesis that the difference between all pairs of scores from two related or dependent groups is zero. Considers only whether the sign of the difference between pairs is positive, negative, or zero. The null hypothesis is rejected when the number of pairs with positive differences is greater than the number of pairs with negative differences (or vice versa). For example, the change from one time to another can be recorded as a decrease ($-$) or increase ($+$). Sign test determines whether the change for the total group is positive or negative.

Tetrachoric correlation coefficient, r_{tet} An index of association between two dichotomous variables that have an underlying normal distribution. Ranges in value from -1 to $+1$.

t-test
    One-sample Test of the hypothesis that the population mean equals a specified value. Refer to Chapter 7 for details.
    Two-sample Test of the hypothesis that two population means are equal. See D.5 for more information.
    Correlated/dependent samples Test of the hypothesis that the population means from two related or dependent groups are equal. For example, the same sample may be tested twice, and the t-test is used to examine the amount of change from one time to the next.

Wilcoxon matched-pairs signed-rank test Test of the hypothesis that the differences in ranks between all pairs of scores is zero. Both the sign and the magnitude of the differences are considered, with larger differences given more weight.

Yule's Q An index of association between two nominal variables. Ranges in value from -1 to $+1$; sign is arbitrary. Equals zero when one cell is empty; a special case of the gamma coefficient.

D.5 ILLUSTRATION AND DISCUSSION OF SELECTED STATISTICAL TECHNIQUES

D.5.1 RANK CORRELATION COEFFICIENT

EXHIBIT D.1 CALCULATION OF THE RANK CORRELATION COEFFICIENT

$$r_s = 1 - \frac{6 \, \Sigma_i (X_i - Y_i)^2}{n(n^2 - 1)}$$ where X_i is the rank for the ith individual on variable X
Y_i is the rank for the ith individual on variable Y
n is the total number of individuals

Step 1. Convert scores to ranks on each variable, if the original data are not in the form of ranks.

Step 2. Find the difference between the ith individual's rank on X and Y; that is, $X_i - Y_i$.

Step 3. Square these differences for each individual; $(X_i - Y_i)^2$.

Step 4. Add up all these squared values, Σ_i, and multiply this sum by 6.

Step 5. Divide this product by the following value: $n(n^2 - 1)$.

Step 6. Subtract the result obtained in Step 5 from 1. This gives you the rank correlation coefficient.

Example (Ranked data)

Individual	Academic Rank (X_i)	Musical Ability (Y_i)	Step 2 $X_i - Y_i$	Step 3 $(X_i - Y_i)^2$
A	1	1	0	0
B	2	3	−1	1
C	3	6	−3	9
D	4	2	2	4
E	5	4	1	1
F	6	5	1	1
				$\Sigma_i = 16$

Step 4. $6 \, \Sigma_i (X_i - Y_i)^2 = (6)(16) = 96$

Step 5. $n(n^2 - 1) = (6)(6^2 - 1) = (6)(36 - 1) = (6)(35) = 210$. The sum obtained in Step 4 divided by the above value is .457; that is, 96/210.

Step 6. $1 - .457 = .543$. The rank correlation coefficient is equal to .543.

D.5.2 TEST OF DIFFERENCE BETWEEN TWO PROPORTIONS

EXHIBIT D.2   *STATISTICAL TEST OF THE DIFFERENCE BETWEEN TWO PROPORTIONS*

Test statistic

$$z = \frac{p_1 - p_2}{\sqrt{\left(\frac{f_1 + f_2}{n_1 + n_2}\right)\left(1 - \frac{f_1 + f_2}{n_1 + n_2}\right)\left(\frac{1}{n_1} + \frac{1}{n_2}\right)}}$$

The sampling distribution of z is the normal distribution.

where:

p_1 and p_2 are proportions from the two samples with characteristic X, f_1 and f_2 are the number of individuals from the two samples with characteristic X, and n_1 and n_2 are the two sample sizes.

Statistical hypotheses

$H_0: p_1 = p_2$
$H_1: p_1 \neq p_2$

Sample data

The data are the proportions of high school male and female teachers with more than ten years of teaching experience. From a sample of 125 males (n_1), 35 had more than ten years experience (therefore $p_1 = 35/125 = .28$). Of 200 (n_2) females 125 had more than ten years experience (therefore $p_2 = .625$). The alpha value was set at .05, making the critical z values ±1.96.

Calculation of the statistic

$$z = \frac{.28 - .625}{\sqrt{\left(\frac{35 + 125}{125 + 200}\right)\left(1 - \frac{35 + 125}{125 + 200}\right)\left(\frac{1}{125} + \frac{1}{200}\right)}} = \frac{-.345}{\sqrt{(.492)(.508)(.013)}}$$

$$= -6.05$$

Conclusion

Since the z value of −6.05 was greater than the critical values of ±1.96, the null hypothesis was rejected. The researcher would conclude that there was a statistically significant difference at the .05 level between the two proportions, with more females than males having at least ten years of teaching experience.

D.5.3 t-TEST

EXHIBIT D.3   CALCULATION OF THE t-TEST ON INDEPENDENT SAMPLES

Test statistic

$$t = \frac{\overline{X}_1 - \overline{X}_2}{\sqrt{\left(\dfrac{(n_1 - 1)s_1^2 + (n - 1)s_2^2}{n_1 + n_2 - 2}\right)\left(\dfrac{1}{n_1} + \dfrac{1}{n_2}\right)}}$$

The distribution of this test statistic is that of the t-distribution with $n_1 + n_2 - 2$ df.

where:
$\overline{X}_1$ and $\overline{X}_2$ represent the means on the two samples,
s_1^2 and s_2^2 are the two sample variances, and
n_1 and n_2 are the respective sample sizes.

Statistical hypotheses

H_0: $\mu_1 = \mu_2$ or equivalently $\mu_1 - \mu_2 = 0$.
H_1: $\mu_1 \neq \mu_2$ or equivalently $\mu_1 - \mu_2 \neq 0$.

Sample data

In a cross-cultural study of mathematics achievement, Japanese students ($n_1 = 150$) were compared with United States students ($n_2 = 150$). The math results were as follows: Japanese students: mean of 300, variance of 2500; U.S. students: mean of 290, variance of 2601. The value of alpha was set at .01, making the critical t-values associated with 298 df equal to ± 2.576.

Calculation of the statistic

$$t = \frac{300 - 290}{\sqrt{\left(\dfrac{(149)(2500) + (149)(2601)}{150 + 150 - 2}\right)\left(\dfrac{1}{150} + \dfrac{1}{150}\right)}} = \frac{10}{\sqrt{(2550.5)(.0133)}}$$

$$= 1.72.$$

Conclusion

Since the calculated t-value of 1.72 was smaller than the critical values of ± 2.576, the null hypothesis was not rejected.

Discussion

Note that the value of the t-statistic depends on three quantities: the difference between the sample means, the sample sizes, and the sample variances. It should be fairly obvious that an increase in the difference between the means, other factors held constant, increases the *t*-value and therefore the probability of finding a significant result. An increase in sample size, other factors held constant, will also increase the value of the test statistic. In addition, a decrease in sample variances, other factors held constant, will increase the value of the *t*-statistic.

Directional alternative hypotheses of the form $\mu_1 > \mu_2$ or $\mu_1 < \mu_2$ may be stated in some research studies.

D.5.4 KRUSKAL–WALLIS ANALYSIS OF VARIANCE BY RANKS

EXHIBIT D.4   *CALCULATION OF KRUSKAL–WALLIS "ANALYSIS OF VARIANCE" BY RANKS*

Test statistic

$$H = \left(\frac{12}{N(N+1)} \right) \left(\sum_{j=1}^{J} \frac{T_j^2}{n_j} \right) - \left(3(N+1) \right)$$

where:
N is the total number of cases,
J is the number of groups,
n_j is the number of cases in each group,
and
T_j is the sum of ranks for each group.

For large samples H approximates a Chi-square distribution with $J - 1$ df.

Statistical hypothesis

H_0: That J populations are identical, especially with respect to location.

Sample data

In a study of the self-concept of children, a sample of 20 was divided into three ability groups (low, average, and high). Scores from the three groups on a self-concept test are given below, with each score's rank with respect to the total group in parentheses. High self-concept scores reflect high self-concepts. The scores have been ordered within each group for convenience. The researcher set alpha at .05, making the critical Chi-square value with two df equal to 5.991.

	Low		Average		High	
	29	(7)	49	(18)	55	(20)
	24	(5)	48	(17)	50	(19)
	20	(4)	47	(16)	40	(15)
	19	(3)	37	(14)	35	(12)
	15	(2)	36	(13)	33	(10)
	10	(1)	34	(11)	30	(8)
			31	(9)	28	(6)
T_j	22		98		90	
T_j^2	484		9604		8100	
n_j	6		7		7	

Calculation of the statistic

$$H = \left(\frac{12}{(20)(21)}\right) \left(\frac{484}{6} + \frac{9604}{7} + \frac{8100}{7}\right) - \left(3(21)\right) = 74.56 - 63 = 11.56$$

Conclusion

Since the H of 11.56 was greater than the critical Chi-square value of 5.991, the researcher would conclude that the three samples represented different populations, especially with respect to location. Note that the self-concept ranks for the low ability group were generally below those for the other two groups.

D.5.5 ANALYSIS OF VARIANCE

A one-factor analysis of variance is used to examine the equality of population means from two or more groups. These groups reflect only one independent variable or one status/categorical variable. A factorial analysis of variance is an extension of the one-factor procedure to two or more factors (several independent variables, several status variables, or a combination of independent and status variables).

In a one-factor analysis of variance two sources of variability in criterion or dependent variable scores exist: variation resulting from the fact that individuals are located in *different groups* (as reflected in differences in group means) and variation resulting from differences among individuals *within each group*. To the extent that the group means differ widely and the scores within each group are similar, then the researcher is more likely to infer a difference in the population means. The four diagrams in Fig. D.1 illustrate how the

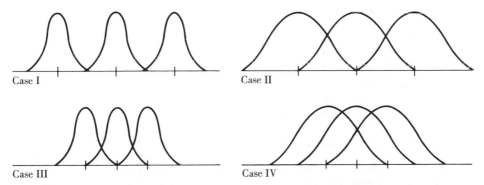

FIG. D.1 Case I: Within group variability is small; group means are far apart. Case II: Within group variability is large; group means are far apart. Case III: Within group variability is small; group means are close. Case IV: Within group variability is large; group means are close.

size of the differences among group means and the degree of individual variation within a group contribute to overall group differences. Case I illustrates
the largest group differences and Case IV, the smallest group differences.

The one-factor analysis of variance procedure tests the significance of the
ratio of the variability of group means to the within group variability. This
ratio is called an *F ratio*. As this *F* ratio increases, the likelihood of rejecting
the null hypothesis of equality of means also increases. The calculations for a
one-factor analysis of variance are presented in Exhibit D.5.

EXHIBIT D.5 CALCULATION OF ONE-FACTOR ANALYSIS OF VARIANCE

Statistical hypotheses

$H_0: \mu_1 = \mu_2 = \cdots = \mu_j$
$H_1:$ Not all the population means are equal.

General outline of one-factor analysis of variance table

Source of variation	SS (Sums of squares)	df	MS (Mean square)	F ratio
Between groups	SS_G	$J-1$	$SS_G/(J-1) = MS_G$	MS_G/MS_W
Within groups or error	SS_W	$N-J$	$SS_W/(N-J) = MS_W$	(with $J-1$ and $N-J$ df)
Total	SS_T	$N-1$		

Definition of symbols

$J =$ Number of groups
$N =$ Total number of individuals
$X_{ij} =$ Score for ith individual in jth group
$\overline{X}_{.j} =$ Mean for jth group
$\overline{X}_{..} =$ Grand mean; Mean for all individuals
$n_j =$ Number of individuals in jth group

Calculation of sums of squares terms

SS_G Find the difference between the first group mean and the grand mean ($\overline{X}_{.j} - \overline{X}_{..}$), square this difference and multiply it by the number of individuals in that group ($n_j(\overline{X}_{.j} - \overline{X}_{..})^2$). Repeat this process for each group mean and then add all these product terms.

SS_W Find the difference between each individual's score and his group mean, square this difference $(X_{ij} - \overline{X}_{.j})^2$, and add up all these squared differences.

SS_T Find the difference between each individual's score and the grand mean, square this difference $(X_{ij} - \overline{X}_{..})^2$, and add up all these squared differences.

Sample data

Attitude scores were obtained in a study of attitudes toward teacher unions. The groups compared were elementary teachers, secondary teachers, principals, and school board members. Scores for each group are given below. A high numerical score represents a more favorable attitude toward teacher unions. The value of alpha was set at .01.

	Elementary	Secondary	Principals	School Board
	9	10	7	6
	8	9	6	5
	8	9	6	4
	7	8	6	3
			5	2
n_j	4	4	5	5
$\overline{X}_{.j}$	8	9	6	4

Calculation

The grand mean, $\overline{X}_{..}$, equals $118/18 = 6.5$; the sum of all the scores divided by the total number of scores.

$SS_G = 4(8 - 6.5)^2 + 4(9 - 6.5)^2 + 5(6 - 6.5)^2 + 5(4 - 6.5)^2 = 66.5$

$SS_W = (9 - 8)^2 + (8 - 8)^2 + (8 - 8)^2 + (7 - 8)^2 + \ldots + (4 - 4)^2 + (3 - 4)^2 + (2 - 4)^2 = 16$

$SS_T = (9 - 6.5)^2 + (8 - 6.5)^2 + (8 - 6.5)^2 + \ldots + (3 - 6.5)^2 + (2 - 6.5)^2 = 82.5$

Analysis of Variance Table

	SS	df	MS	F
Between	66.5	3	22.17	19.45 with 3,14 df
Within	16.0	14	1.14	
Total	82.5	17		

Note that $SS_T = SS_G + SS_W$. The degrees of freedom associated with the F ratio correspond to the df for the numerator and denominator of that ratio. A table of the F distribution is given in Table E.6 of Appendix E. At the intersection of the df corresponding to the numerator (the columns in the table) and to the denominator (the rows in the table) are the critical F-values at both the .05 and .01 levels of significance. You will find that the critical F-value for the data described above is 5.56 (df = 3,14 at the .01 level). If the calculated F-value is larger than the critical value, then the null hypothesis is rejected.

Conclusion

Since the calculated F-value of 19.45 was larger than the critical value, the null hypothesis of equality of population means was rejected, and the alternative hypothesis accepted. The difference in the sample means was great enough to indicate inequality of the population means.

A significant F ratio indicates only that not all of the population means are equal. However, techniques do exist that examine which means or combination of means differ from each other. Some of these procedures are: Newman–Keuls procedure, Duncan's new multiple range test, Tukey's HSD (honestly significant difference) test, Scheffé's S method, Bonferroni t-statistics, Dunnett's test, and the LSD (least significant difference) test. These techniques are sometimes called post hoc comparison techniques.

When more than one factor (independent variable or status/categorical variable) is involved (as in a factorial experimental design), analysis of variance procedures partition the variability in the criterion or dependent variable scores into that associated with *each factor*, that associated with *each* possible *interaction* among the factors, and that which cannot be accounted for by any of the factors in the design, often called *error* variability. F ratios are calculated for each factor and each interaction. Each F ratio is examined for significance, at the alpha value specified by the researcher. If a particular F ratio is significant, then it is concluded that the differences in means associated with that particular factor are larger than what would be expected by chance, and therefore reflect the impact of that particular factor in the design. The formation of these ratios is illustrated with a two-factor design in Exhibit D.6.

D.5.6 MULTIPLE REGRESSION

Multiple regression procedures are used to examine the relationship between a criterion variable and a set of predictors. The criterion variable is usually represented by the symbol Y and the predictor variables by X. The phrase "regression of Y on X" is consistent with this notation.

The association between the predictors and the criterion is reflected in the *multiple correlation coefficient, R*. This coefficient ranges in value between 0 and +1, with 0 indicating no relationship between the criterion and the predictors, and with 1 indicating that the criterion can be completely accounted for by the predictor variables. As with the product–moment correlation, r, one way of examining the strength of the multiple R is to square it, R^2, giving the percentage of variance in the criterion variable that is accounted for by the predictor variables. The multiple correlation can also be tested to see if it is significantly different from zero.

EXHIBIT D.6 FORMAT FOR A TWO-FACTOR ANALYSIS OF VARIANCE TABLE

Source of variability	SS	df	MS*	F ratio	If F ratio is significant, then one can conclude that:
Factor A (Variable A)	SS_A	$a-1$		$\dfrac{MS_A}{MS_E}$	Means corresponding to Factor A differ
Factor B (Variable B)	SS_B	$b-1$		$\dfrac{MS_B}{MS_E}$	Means corresponding to Factor B differ
Interaction (A × B)	SS_{AB}	$(a-1)(b-1)$		$\dfrac{MS_{AB}}{MS_E}$	Factors A and B interact in some way
Error	SS_E	$N-ab$			
Total	SS_T	$N-1$			

* The mean square (MS) for each source of variability is the ratio of its SS to its df; e.g., $MS_A = SS_A/(a-1)$.

Note: The symbol a is the number of levels or conditions of Factor A; b is the number of levels of Factor B; N is the total number of subjects. Any or all of the F ratios can be significant.

In determining the multiple correlation, each of the predictor variables is entered into what is called a regression equation:

$$\text{est } Y = a + b_1 X_1 + b_2 X_2 + \cdots + b_k X_k,$$

where *regressions weights* (the b values) are assigned to each of the predictors (the X values) in order to derive the *estimated* or predicted criterion values (the est Y). An individual's actual criterion score, Y, can then be compared with the score that can be estimated for him or her (est Y) from the predictor variables by use of this regression equation. The regression weights in the equation are determined by what is known as the *principle of least squares*. This principle minimizes the sum of the squared deviations between the estimated Y and the actual Y values; that is, it minimizes the squared errors of prediction.

The simplest case of multiple regression is *simple linear regression,* where there is only one predictor. In this case the product-moment correlation, r, reflects the association between the criterion and the predictor, and the regression equation is simply the equation for the straight line that best fits the swarm of points in the scatter diagram of the two variables ($Y = a + bX$).

Researchers frequently examine the changes in the R or R^2 value as predictors are added to the regression equation. This procedure was used by Lambert, Hartsough, and Zimmerman (96) in their study of the prediction of adolescent functioning in high school from elementary school measures of intellectual and nonintellectual variables. Two longitudinal samples were included in the study: second graders who were in the ninth grade ($n = 81$) and fifth graders who were in the twelfth grade ($n = 87$). The intellectual predictors were WISC IQ scores, grades in reading and math, and achievement test scores in reading and math; the nonintellectual predictors included teacher, peer, and self-ratings of personality. Four criterion variables were investigated. However, only the criterion of successful high school status (a summary of participation in athletics, election to student office, honor roll, and referral for gifted programs) is presented here.

Based upon previous research the authors decided that WISC IQ scores and teacher ratings, consisting of seven rating variables, were most frequently and consistently related to high school status. The first step was to examine the unique and joint predictive effects of these two "variables." Then the separate relationship of the intellectual and nonintellectual batteries to the criterion, and the corresponding increases in R and R^2, were examined. Finally, both batteries of tests were included in the regression analysis in order to determine the maximum multiple correlation. Table D.1 is a reproduction of one table from the original article that illustrates these steps.

TABLE D.1   MULTIPLE CORRELATIONS, PROPORTION OF VARIANCE AND INCREMENTS ASSOCIATED WITH INTELLECTUAL AND NONINTELLECTUAL PREDICTORS. CRITERION: HIGH SCHOOL SUCCESSFUL STATUS—GRADE 2 SUBJECTS

Independent variables	R	R²	Increment (prop. of variance)	F	df	P
A. Teacher rating	.50	.2484		3.46	7/74	<.01
B. WISC IQ	.29	.0862		7.55	1/80	<.01
C. A + B	.55	.3011		3.93	8/73	<.01
			B over A = .0527	8.00	1/72	<.01
			A over B = .2149	5.92	7/72	<.01
D. Teacher rating, peer rating, self-rating	.50	.2516		2.69	9/72	<.01
E. WISC IQ, reading and mathematics achievement, reading and mathematics grade	.40	.1592		2.88	5/76	<.05
F. B + D	.56	.3131		3.24	10/71	<.01
			B over D = .0515	9.55	1/70	<.01
			D over B = .2269	4.77	9/70	<.01
G. D + E	.59	.3523		2.60	14/67	<.01
			E over D = .1007	2.87	5/66	<.05
			D over E = .1931	3.38	9/66	<.01

Source: N. M. Lambert, C. S. Hartsough, and I. L. Zimmerman, 1976. The comparative predictive efficiency of intellectual and nonintellectual components of high school functioning. *American Journal of Orthopsychiatry* 46: 109–122. Copyright © 1976 the American Orthopsychiatric Association, Inc. Reproduced by permission.

The first line in the table can be read as follows. The multiple correlation between the seven teacher ratings of children's personality as second graders and the criterion of successful high school status in ninth grade was .50, with $R^2 = .2484$. The R^2 value was significantly different from zero ($F = 3.46$, df $= 7/74$, p $< .01$). An R^2 value of .25 indicates that 25 percent of the variance in the criterion measure was associated with the teacher ratings. The third line in the table shows the multiple R when both teacher ratings and WISC IQ scores are used as predictors. In this case it was .55. You should be able to interpret the rest of the table.

When a researcher is interested in the relative contribution or weight of each predictor to the criterion (e.g., does one variable contribute twice as much to the prediction as another), he or she usually examines the regression weights. However, interpretation of regression weights is difficult because their size depends not only on the relationship between the criterion and each predictor but also on the correlations among the predictors. They change when a variable is added to the regression equation, and they vary from sample to sample.

Different approaches to multiple regression calculations can be applied. The more common techniques are known as the *backward elimination* procedure (enter all predictors and then remove them one at a time until a significant drop in R^2 occurs), the *forward selection* procedure (the predictor that has the highest correlation with the criterion is entered first, the next variable entered has the highest correlation with the criterion after having considered the first variable, etc.; this process is continued until significant and/or meaningful increases in R^2 have ceased), and the *stepwise* solution (is similar to the forward solution except tests are performed at each step to reexamine the contribution of each variable already in the equation, possibly eliminating a variable previously entered).

D.5.7 FACTOR ANALYSIS

Associations within a set of variables are frequently examined by factor analysis. The dimensions represented by the variables in the set are called *factors*. The typical report of a factor analysis includes what is called a *factor matrix*, a table that indicates the relationship between each of the variables and the underlying factors or dimensions. The entries in the table are called *factor loadings*. They express the associations between the tests and the factors and are interpreted like correlation coefficients, ranging in value from -1 through 0 to $+1$.

The factor matrix presented below was obtained by Covert and Mason [34] in their factor analysis of a 17-item student evaluation of university teaching form. In the first column, the entry of .81 represents the loading of the "command of subject," item 1, on the first factor; .08 represents the factor loading of the "quality of textbooks," item 6, on the same factor. Thus item 1 loaded more strongly on the first factor than item 6. On the other hand, item 6 loaded more strongly on Factor III.

TABLE D.2   *FACTOR MATRIX OF THE STUDENT EVALUATION OF TEACHING*

Variable	I	II	III	Commu- nality
1. Command of subject	.81	.04	.22	.71
2. Clarity of presentation	.81	.01	.19	.70
3. Responsiveness to class	.83	−.11	.13	.72
4. Availability to students	.82	−.12	.13	.71
5. Enthusiasm	.87	−.03	.15	.79
6. Quality of textbooks	.08	.06	.77	.60
7. Quality of supplementary readings	.27	.04	.77	.68
8. Quality of lectures	.76	.07	.39	.74
9. Quality of class discussion	.73	.03	.36	.66
10. Quality of laboratories	.46	−.04	.58	.55
11. Quality of assignments	.49	−.04	.63	.65
12. Quality of examinations	.50	−.10	.57	.59
13. Overall value of course	.71	.04	.47	.72
14. Expected grade	.08	−.34	.29	.20
15. Course difficulty	.06	.81	.05	.66
16. Pace of the course	.05	.78	−.02	.62
17. Workload	−.10	.66	.07	.45

Source: R. W. Covert and E. J. Mason, 1974. Factorial validity of a student evaluation of teaching instrument. *Educational and Psychological Measurement* **34**: 903–905. Copyright © 1974 by Educational and Psychological Measurement. Reprinted by permission.

Sometimes the factor matrix also includes a column labeled *communality* or h^2. These entries are the sums of the squared factor loadings of a test or variable and express the amount of variance of each variable that is accounted for by the set of derived factors (e.g., item 1, communality = .71 = ($.81^2$ + $.04^2$ + $.22^2$)). The communality values indicate, for example, that the three factors accounted for more of the variability in Item 1 than in Item 14.

In determining the nature of a factor, the typical approach is first to identify all tests or variables that load highly on a factor. The criterion for a "high" loading varies considerably from study to study, with minimum values ranging from ±.25 to ±.60. The researcher then examines the nature of the similarity among the variables with high loadings in order to give the factor a name. Since naming factors is a subjective procedure, researchers frequently disagree on the results of a factor analysis.

Cited below is Covert and Mason's interpretation of the first two factors in their course evaluation study. As you check off those variables they reported as loading on each factor, you will discover that the loadings were greater than .50. The one exception to this minimum level was the "expected grade item 14 with a factor loading of −.34, which they said contributed to Factor II. Their approach to naming factors is representative of factor analytic studies.

> The loadings on the first factor included those variables which rate a teacher's command of the subject, e.g., clarity of presentation, responsiveness to the class, availability to students, enthusiasm, quality of lectures, quality of class discussions, and overall quality of the course. Thus, Factor I named the Teacher/ Teaching Factor appeared to measure method and style of teaching. The second factor was made up of variables which measure a student's perception of self as it relates to the course. The variables which loaded highly on this factor were the grade that the student expected, the perceived level of course difficulty, the perceived pace of the course, and the workload required of the student in relation to other courses. Thus Factor II was called the Student Perception Factor (34, p. 904–905).

Covert and Mason identified five items that loaded on the third factor and described it as the concrete characteristics of the course controlled and used by the instructor.

Frequently researchers report the proportion of variance accounted for by each factor (associated with what is called an eigenvalue, characteristic root, or latent root). If two factors were extracted from a battery of 20 tests, the first accounting for 90 percent of the variance, then one strong factor exists. On the other hand, four factors might be extracted, with the first accounting for only 30 percent of the variance, reflecting a much weaker first factor and a different factor structure.

There are many variations of factor analysis. Some of the more common ones you are likely to encounter are principal components, principal factors, alpha, maximum likelihood, and image analysis.

Appendix E
Statistical Tables

TABLE E.1   *RANDOM NUMBERS*

07018	31172	12572	23968	55216	85366	56223	09300	94564	18172
52444	65625	97918	46794	62370	59344	20149	17596	51669	47429
72161	57299	87521	44351	99981	55008	93371	60620	66662	27036
17918	75071	91057	46829	47992	26797	64423	42379	91676	75127
13623	76165	43195	50205	75736	77473	07268	31330	07337	55901
27426	97534	89707	97453	90836	78967	00704	85734	21776	85764
96039	21338	88169	69530	53300	29895	71507	28517	77761	17244
68282	98888	25545	69406	29470	46476	54562	79373	72993	98998
54262	21477	33097	48125	92982	98382	11265	25366	06636	25349
66290	27544	72780	91384	47296	54892	59168	83951	91075	04724
53348	39044	04072	62210	01209	43999	54952	68699	31912	09317
34482	42758	40128	48436	30254	50029	19016	56837	05206	33851
99268	98715	07545	27317	52459	75366	43688	27460	65145	65429
95342	97178	10401	31615	95784	77026	33087	65961	10056	72834
38556	60373	77935	64608	28949	94764	45312	71171	15400	72182
39159	04795	51163	84475	60722	35268	05044	56420	39214	89822
41786	18169	96649	92406	42773	23672	37333	85734	99886	81200
95627	30768	30607	89023	60730	31519	53462	90489	81693	17849
98738	15548	42263	79489	85118	97073	01574	57310	59375	54417
75214	61575	27805	21930	94726	39454	19616	72239	93791	22610
73904	89123	19271	15792	72675	62175	48746	56084	54029	22296
33329	08896	94662	05781	59187	53284	28024	45421	37956	14252
66364	94799	62211	37539	80172	43269	91133	05562	82385	91760

From Rand Corporation, *A Million Random Digits*. Reprinted with permission.

68349	16984	86532	96186	53893	48268	82821	19526	63257	14288
19193	99621	66899	12351	72438	99839	24228	32079	53517	18558
49017	23489	19172	80439	76263	98918	59330	20121	89779	58862
76941	77008	27646	82072	28048	41589	70883	72035	81800	50296
55430	25875	26446	25738	32962	24266	26814	01194	48587	93319
33023	26895	65304	34978	43053	28951	22676	05303	39725	60054
87337	74487	83196	61939	05045	20405	69324	80823	20905	68727
81773	36773	21247	54735	68996	16937	18134	51873	10973	77090
74279	85087	94186	67793	18178	82224	17069	87880	54945	73489
34968	76028	54285	90845	35464	68076	15868	70063	26794	81386
99696	78454	21700	12301	88832	96796	59341	16136	01803	17537
55282	61051	97260	89829	69121	86547	62195	72492	33536	60137
31337	83886	72886	42598	05464	88071	92209	50728	67442	47529
94128	97990	58609	20002	76530	81981	30999	50147	93941	80754
06511	48241	49521	64568	69459	95079	42588	98590	12829	64366
69981	03469	56128	80405	97485	88251	76708	09558	86759	15065
23701	56612	86307	02364	88677	17192	23082	00728	78660	74196
09237	24607	12817	98120	30937	70666	76059	44446	94188	14060
11007	45461	24725	02877	74667	18427	45658	40044	59484	59966
60622	78444	39582	91930	97948	13221	99234	99629	22430	49247
79973	43668	19599	30021	68572	31816	63033	14597	28953	21162
71080	71367	23485	82364	30321	42982	74427	25625	74309	15855
09923	26729	74573	16583	37689	06703	21846	78329	98578	25447
63094	72826	65558	22616	33472	67515	75585	90005	19747	08865
19806	42212	41268	84923	21002	30588	40676	94961	31154	83133
17295	74244	43088	27056	86338	47331	09737	83735	84058	12382
59338	27190	99302	84020	15425	14748	42380	99376	30496	84523

TABLE E.2   *AREAS OF THE NORMAL CURVE FOR VALUES OF z*

Values of z	Area between z and the mean	Larger area beyond z	Smaller area beyond z
0.00	.0000	.5000	.5000
0.01	.0040	.5040	.4960
0.02	.0080	.5080	.4920
0.03	.0120	.5120	.4880
0.04	.0160	.5160	.4840
0.05	.0199	.5199	.4801
0.06	.0239	.5239	.4761
0.07	.0279	.5279	.4721
0.08	.0319	.5319	.4681
0.09	.0359	.5359	.4641
0.10	.0398	.5398	.4602
0.11	.0438	.5438	.4562
0.12	.0478	.5478	.4522
0.13	.0517	.5517	.4483
0.14	.0557	.5557	.4443
0.15	.0596	.5596	.4404
0.16	.0636	.5636	.4364
0.17	.0675	.5675	.4325
0.18	.0714	.5714	.4286
0.19	.0753	.5753	.4247
0.20	.0793	.5793	.4207
0.21	.0832	.5832	.4168
0.22	.0871	.5871	.4129
0.23	.0910	.5910	.4090
0.24	.0948	.5948	.4052
0.25	.0987	.5987	.4013
0.26	.1026	.6026	.3974
0.27	.1064	.6064	.3936
0.28	.1103	.6103	.3897
0.29	.1141	.6141	.3859
0.30	.1179	.6179	.3821
0.31	.1217	.6217	.3783
0.32	.1255	.6255	.3745
0.33	.1293	.6293	.3707
0.34	.1331	.6331	.3669
0.35	.1368	.6368	.3632
0.36	.1406	.6406	.3594
0.37	.1443	.6443	.3557
0.38	.1480	.6480	.3520
0.39	.1517	.6517	.3483

From S. Dinham, 1976. *Exploring Statistics*, Monterey, Calif.: Brooks/Cole, pp. 257–265.

TABLE E.2   (*CONTINUED*)

Values of z	Area between z and the mean	Larger area beyond z	Smaller area beyond z
0.40	.1554	.6554	.3446
0.41	.1591	.6591	.3409
0.42	.1628	.6628	.3372
0.43	.1664	.6664	.3336
0.44	.1700	.6700	.3300
0.45	.1736	.6736	.3264
0.46	.1772	.6772	.3228
0.47	.1808	.6808	.3192
0.48	.1844	.6844	.3156
0.49	.1879	.6879	.3121
0.50	.1915	.6915	.3085
0.51	.1950	.6950	.3050
0.52	.1985	.6985	.3015
0.53	.2019	.7019	.2981
0.54	.2054	.7054	.2946
0.55	.2088	.7088	.2912
0.56	.2123	.7123	.2877
0.57	.2157	.7157	.2843
0.58	.2190	.7190	.2810
0.59	.2224	.7224	.2776
0.60	.2257	.7257	.2743
0.61	.2291	.7291	.2709
0.62	.2324	.7324	.2676
0.63	.2357	.7357	.2643
0.64	.2389	.7389	.2611
0.65	.2422	.7422	.2578
0.66	.2454	.7454	.2546
0.67	.2486	.7486	.2514
0.68	.2517	.7517	.2483
0.69	.2549	.7549	.2451
0.70	.2580	.7580	.2420
0.71	.2611	.7611	.2389
0.72	.2642	.7642	.2358
0.73	.2673	.7673	.2327
0.74	.2704	.7704	.2296
0.75	.2734	.7734	.2266
0.76	.2764	.7764	.2236
0.77	.2794	.7794	.2206
0.78	.2823	.7823	.2177
0.79	.2852	.7852	.2148
0.80	.2881	.7881	.2119
0.81	.2910	.7910	.2090
0.82	.2939	.7939	.2061
0.83	.2967	.7967	.2033
0.84	.2995	.7995	.2005

TABLE E.2   (CONTINUED)

Values of z	Area between z and the mean	Larger area beyond z	Smaller area beyond z
0.85	.3023	.8023	.1977
0.86	.3051	.8051	.1949
0.87	.3078	.8078	.1922
0.88	.3106	.8106	.1894
0.89	.3133	.8133	.1867
0.90	.3159	.8159	.1841
0.91	.3186	.8186	.1814
0.92	.3212	.8212	.1788
0.93	.3238	.8238	.1762
0.94	.3264	.8264	.1736
0.95	.3289	.8289	.1711
0.96	.3315	.8315	.1685
0.97	.3340	.8340	.1660
0.98	.3365	.8365	.1635
0.99	.3389	.8389	.1611
1.00	.3413	.8413	.1587
1.01	.3438	.8438	.1562
1.02	.3461	.8461	.1539
1.03	.3485	.8485	.1515
1.04	.3508	.8508	.1492
1.05	.3531	.8531	.1469
1.06	.3554	.8554	.1446
1.07	.3577	.8577	.1423
1.08	.3599	.8599	.1401
1.09	.3621	.8621	.1379
1.10	.3643	.8643	.1357
1.11	.3665	.8665	.1335
1.12	.3686	.8686	.1314
1.13	.3708	.8708	.1292
1.14	.3729	.8729	.1271
1.15	.3749	.8749	.1251
1.16	.3770	.8770	.1230
1.17	.3790	.8790	.1210
1.18	.3810	.8810	.1190
1.19	.3830	.8830	.1170
1.20	.3849	.8849	.1151
1.21	.3869	.8869	.1131
1.22	.3888	.8888	.1112
1.23	.3907	.8907	.1093
1.24	.3925	.8925	.1075
1.25	.3944	.8944	.1056
1.26	.3962	.8962	.1038
1.27	.3980	.8980	.1020
1.28	.3997	.8997	.1003
1.29	.4015	.9015	.0985

TABLE E.2 (*CONTINUED*)

Values of z	Area between z and the mean	Larger area beyond z	Smaller area beyond z
1.30	.4032	.9032	.0968
1.31	.4049	.9049	.0951
1.32	.4066	.9066	.0934
1.33	.4082	.9082	.0918
1.34	.4099	.9099	.0901
1.35	.4115	.9115	.0885
1.36	.4131	.9131	.0869
1.37	.4147	.9147	.0853
1.38	.4162	.9162	.0838
1.39	.4177	.9177	.0823
1.40	.4192	.9192	.0808
1.41	.4207	.9207	.0793
1.42	.4222	.9222	.0778
1.43	.4236	.9236	.0764
1.44	.4251	.9251	.0749
1.45	.4265	.9265	.0735
1.46	.4279	.9279	.0721
1.47	.4292	.9292	.0708
1.48	.4306	.9306	.0694
1.49	.4319	.9319	.0681
1.50	.4332	.9332	.0668
1.51	.4345	.9345	.0655
1.52	.4357	.9357	.0643
1.53	.4370	.9370	.0630
1.54	.4382	.9382	.0618
1.55	.4394	.9394	.0606
1.56	.4406	.9406	.0594
1.57	.4418	.9418	.0582
1.58	.4429	.9429	.0571
1.59	.4441	.9441	.0559
1.60	.4452	.9452	.0548
1.61	.4463	.9463	.0537
1.62	.4474	.9474	.0526
1.63	.4484	.9484	.0516
1.64	.4495	.9495	.0505
1.65	.4505	.9505	.0495
1.66	.4515	.9515	.0485
1.67	.4525	.9525	.0475
1.68	.4535	.9535	.0465
1.69	.4545	.9545	.0455
1.70	.4554	.9554	.0446
1.71	.4564	.9564	.0436
1.72	.4573	.9573	.0427
1.73	.4582	.9582	.0418
1.74	.4591	.9591	.0409

TABLE E.2   (*CONTINUED*)

Values of z	Area between z and the mean	Larger area beyond z	Smaller area beyond z
1.75	.4599	.9599	.0401
1.76	.4608	.9608	.0392
1.77	.4616	.9616	.0384
1.78	.4625	.9625	.0375
1.79	.4633	.9633	.0367
1.80	.4641	.9641	.0359
1.81	.4649	.9649	.0351
1.82	.4656	.9656	.0344
1.83	.4664	.9664	.0336
1.84	.4671	.9671	.0329
1.85	.4678	.9678	.0322
1.86	.4686	.9686	.0314
1.87	.4693	.9693	.0307
1.88	.4699	.9699	.0301
1.89	.4706	.9706	.0294
1.90	.4713	.9713	.0287
1.91	.4719	.9719	.0281
1.92	.4726	.9726	.0274
1.93	.4732	.9732	.0268
1.94	.4738	.9738	.0262
1.95	.4744	.9744	.0256
1.96	.4750	.9750	.0250
1.97	.4756	.9756	.0244
1.98	.4761	.9761	.0239
1.99	.4767	.9767	.0233
2.00	.4772	.9772	.0228
2.01	.4778	.9778	.0222
2.02	.4783	.9783	.0217
2.03	.4788	.9788	.0212
2.04	.4793	.9793	.0207
2.05	.4798	.9798	.0202
2.06	.4803	.9803	.0197
2.07	.4808	.9808	.0192
2.08	.4812	.9812	.0188
2.09	.4817	.9817	.0183
2.10	.4821	.9821	.0179
2.11	.4826	.9826	.0174
2.12	.4830	.9830	.0170
2.13	.4834	.9834	.0166
2.14	.4838	.9838	.0162
2.15	.4842	.9842	.0158
2.16	.4846	.9846	.0154
2.17	.4850	.9850	.0150
2.18	.4854	.9854	.0146
2.19	.4857	.9857	.0143

TABLE E.2 (*CONTINUED*)

Values of z	Area between z and the mean	Larger area beyond z	Smaller area beyond z
2.20	.4861	.9861	.0139
2.21	.4864	.9864	.0136
2.22	.4868	.9868	.0132
2.23	.4871	.9871	.0129
2.24	.4875	.9875	.0125
2.25	.4878	.9878	.0122
2.26	.4881	.9881	.0119
2.27	.4884	.9884	.0116
2.28	.4887	.9887	.0113
2.29	.4890	.9890	.0110
2.30	.4893	.9893	.0107
2.31	.4896	.9896	.0104
2.32	.4898	.9898	.0102
2.33	.4901	.9901	.0099
2.34	.4904	.9904	.0096
2.35	.4906	.9906	.0094
2.36	.4909	.9909	.0091
2.37	.4911	.9911	.0089
2.38	.4913	.9913	.0087
2.39	.4916	.9916	.0084
2.40	.4918	.9918	.0082
2.41	.4920	.9920	.0080
2.42	.4922	.9922	.0078
2.43	.4925	.9925	.0075
2.44	.4927	.9927	.0073
2.45	.4929	.9929	.0071
2.46	.4931	.9931	.0069
2.47	.4932	.9932	.0068
2.48	.4934	.9934	.0066
2.49	.4936	.9936	.0064
2.50	.4938	.9938	.0062
2.51	.4940	.9940	.0060
2.52	.4941	.9941	.0059
2.53	.4943	.9943	.0057
2.54	.4945	.9945	.0055
2.55	.4946	.9946	.0054
2.56	.4948	.9948	.0052
2.57	.4949	.9949	.0051
2.58	.4951	.9951	.0049
2.59	.4952	.9952	.0048
2.60	.4953	.9953	.0047
2.61	.4955	.9955	.0045
2.62	.4956	.9956	.0044
2.63	.4957	.9957	.0043
2.64	.4959	.9959	.0041

TABLE E.2   (*CONTINUED*)

Values of z	Area between z and the mean	Larger area beyond z	Smaller area beyond z
2.65	.4960	.9960	.0040
2.66	.4961	.9961	.0039
2.67	.4962	.9962	.0038
2.68	.4963	.9963	.0037
2.69	.4964	.9964	.0036
2.70	.4965	.9965	.0035
2.71	.4966	.9966	.0034
2.72	.4967	.9967	.0033
2.73	.4968	.9968	.0032
2.74	.4969	.9969	.0031
2.75	.4970	.9970	.0030
2.76	.4971	.9971	.0029
2.77	.4972	.9972	.0028
2.78	.4973	.9973	.0027
2.79	.4974	.9974	.0026
2.80	.4974	.9974	.0026
2.81	.4975	.9975	.0025
2.82	.4976	.9976	.0024
2.83	.4977	.9977	.0023
2.84	.4977	.9977	.0023
2.85	.4978	.9978	.0022
2.86	.4979	.9979	.0021
2.87	.4979	.9979	.0021
2.88	.4980	.9980	.0020
2.89	.4981	.9981	.0019
2.90	.4981	.9981	.0019
2.91	.4982	.9982	.0018
2.92	.4982	.9982	.0018
2.93	.4983	.9983	.0017
2.94	.4984	.9984	.0016
2.95	.4984	.9984	.0016
2.96	.4985	.9985	.0015
2.97	.4985	.9985	.0015
2.98	.4986	.9986	.0014
2.99	.4986	.9986	.0014
3.00	.4987	.9987	.0013
3.01	.4987	.9987	.0013
3.02	.4987	.9987	.0013
3.03	.4988	.9988	.0012
3.04	.4988	.9988	.0012
3.05	.4989	.9989	.0011
3.06	.4989	.9989	.0011
3.07	.4989	.9989	.0011
3.08	.4990	.9990	.0010
3.09	.4990	.9990	.0010

TABLE E.2 (*CONTINUED*)

Values of z	Area between z and the mean	Larger area beyond z	Smaller area beyond z
3.10	.4990	.9990	.0010
3.11	.4991	.9991	.0009
3.12	.4991	.9991	.0009
3.13	.4991	.9991	.0009
3.14	.4992	.9992	.0008
3.15	.4992	.9992	.0008
3.16	.4992	.9992	.0008
3.17	.4992	.9992	.0008
3.18	.4993	.9993	.0007
3.19	.4993	.9993	.0007
3.20	.4993	.9993	.0007
3.21	.4993	.9993	.0007
3.22	.4994	.9994	.0006
3.23	.4994	.9994	.0006
3.24	.4994	.9994	.0006
3.30	.4995	.9995	.0005
3.40	.4997	.9997	.0003
3.50	.4998	.9998	.0002
3.60	.4998	.9998	.0002
3.70	.4999	.9999	.0001

TABLE E.3   *VALUES OF t-DISTRIBUTIONS FOR CRITICAL PERCENTILE POINTS*

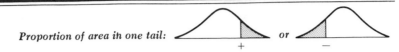

Proportion of area in one tail: *or*

Significance level for one-tailed test—directional alternative hypothesis

.050	.025	.010	.005

Proportion of area in two tails:

Significance level for two-tailed test—nondirectional alternative hypothesis

df	.100	.050	.020	.010
1	6.314	12.706	31.821	63.657
2	2.920	4.303	6.965	9.925
3	2.353	3.182	4.541	5.841
4	2.132	2.776	3.747	4.604
5	2.015	2.571	3.365	4.032
6	1.943	2.447	3.143	3.707
7	1.895	2.365	2.998	3.499
8	1.860	2.306	2.896	3.355
9	1.833	2.262	2.821	3.250
10	1.812	2.228	2.764	3.169
11	1.796	2.201	2.718	3.106
12	1.782	2.179	2.681	3.055
13	1.771	2.160	2.650	3.012
14	1.761	2.145	2.624	2.977
15	1.753	2.131	2.602	2.947
16	1.746	2.120	2.583	2.921
17	1.740	2.110	2.567	2.898
18	1.734	2.101	2.552	2.878
19	1.729	2.093	2.539	2.861
20	1.725	2.086	2.528	2.845
21	1.721	2.080	2.518	2.831
22	1.717	2.074	2.508	2.819
23	1.714	2.069	2.500	2.807
24	1.711	2.064	2.492	2.797
25	1.708	2.060	2.485	2.787
26	1.706	2.056	2.479	2.779
27	1.703	2.052	2.473	2.771
28	1.701	2.048	2.467	2.763
29	1.699	2.045	2.462	2.756
30	1.697	2.042	2.457	2.750
∞	1.645	1.960	2.326	2.576

From Sir Ronald A. Fisher, 1972. *Statistical Methods for Research Workers* (14th ed.). New York: Hafner Press, Division of Macmillan Publishing Co., p. 176.

TABLE E.4   *VALUES OF THE CORRELATION COEFFICIENT,* r, *FOR DIFFERENT LEVELS OF SIGNIFICANCE* (H_0: $\rho = 0$; H_1: $\rho \neq 0$; *TWO-TAILED TEST*)

Proportion of area in two tails

df	.10	.05	.02	.01
1	.98769	.996917	.9995066	.9998766
2	.90000	.95000	.98000	.990000
3	.8054	.8783	.93433	.95873
4	.7293	.8114	.8822	.91720
5	.6694	.7545	.8329	.8745
6	.6215	.7067	.7887	.8343
7	.5822	.6664	.7498	.7977
8	.5494	.6319	.7155	.7646
9	.5214	.6021	.6851	.7348
10	.4973	.5760	.6581	.7079
11	.4762	.5529	.6339	.6835
12	.4575	.5324	.6120	.6614
13	.4409	.5139	.5923	.6411
14	.4259	.4973	.5742	.6226
15	.4124	.4821	.5577	.6055
16	.4000	.4683	.5425	.5897
17	.3887	.4555	.5285	.5751
18	.3783	.4438	.5155	.5614
19	.3687	.4329	.5034	.5487
20	.3598	.4227	.4921	.5368
25	.3233	.3809	.4451	.4869
30	.2960	.3494	.4093	.4487
35	.2746	.3246	.3810	.4182
40	.2573	.3044	.3578	.3932
45	.2428	.2875	.3384	.3721
50	.2306	.2732	.3218	.3541
60	.2108	.2500	.2948	.3248
70	.1954	.2319	.2737	.3017
80	.1829	.2172	.2565	.2830
90	.1726	.2050	.2422	.2673
100	.1638	.1946	.2301	.2540

For a total correlation, df is 2 less than the number of pairs in the sample; for a partial correlation, the number of eliminated variates also should be subtracted. From Sir Ronald A. Fisher, 1972, *Statistical Methods for Research Workers* (14th ed.). New York: Hafner Press, Division of Macmillan Publishing Co., p. 211.

TABLE E.5   *VALUES OF CHI-SQUARE DISTRIBUTIONS FOR CRITICAL PERCENTILE POINTS*

Proportion of area to the right of χ^2:

df	.99	.98	.95	.90	.80	.70	.50	.30	.20	.10	.05	.02	.01
1	.000157	.000628	.00393	.0158	.0642	.148	.455	1.074	1.642	2.706	3.841	5.412	6.635
2	.0201	.0404	.103	.211	.446	.713	1.386	2.408	3.219	4.605	5.991	7.824	9.210
3	.115	.185	.352	.584	1.005	1.424	2.366	3.665	4.642	6.251	7.815	9.837	11.345
4	.297	.429	.711	1.064	1.649	2.195	3.357	4.878	5.989	7.779	9.488	11.668	13.277
5	.554	.752	1.145	1.610	2.343	3.000	4.351	6.064	7.289	9.236	11.070	13.388	15.086
6	.872	1.134	1.635	2.204	3.070	3.828	5.348	7.231	8.558	10.645	12.592	15.033	16.812
7	1.239	1.564	2.167	2.833	3.822	4.671	6.346	8.383	9.803	12.017	14.067	16.622	18.475
8	1.646	2.032	2.733	3.490	4.594	5.527	7.344	9.524	11.030	13.362	15.507	18.168	20.090
9	2.088	2.532	3.325	4.168	5.380	6.393	8.343	10.656	12.242	14.684	16.919	19.679	21.666
10	2.558	3.059	3.940	4.865	6.179	7.267	9.342	11.781	13.442	15.987	18.307	21.161	23.209
11	3.053	3.609	4.575	5.578	6.989	8.148	10.341	12.899	14.631	17.275	19.675	22.618	24.725
12	3.571	4.178	5.226	6.304	7.807	9.034	11.340	14.011	15.812	18.549	21.026	24.054	26.217
13	4.107	4.765	5.892	7.042	8.634	9.926	12.340	15.119	16.985	19.812	22.362	25.472	27.688
14	4.660	5.368	6.571	7.790	9.467	10.821	13.339	16.222	18.151	21.064	23.685	26.873	29.141
15	5.229	5.985	7.261	8.547	10.307	11.721	14.339	17.322	19.311	22.307	24.996	28.259	30.578
16	5.812	6.614	7.962	9.312	11.152	12.624	15.338	18.418	20.465	23.542	26.296	29.633	32.000
17	6.408	7.255	8.672	10.085	12.002	13.531	16.338	19.511	21.615	24.769	27.587	30.995	33.409
18	7.015	7.906	9.390	10.865	12.857	14.448	17.338	20.601	22.760	25.989	28.869	32.346	34.805
19	7.633	8.567	10.117	11.651	13.716	15.352	18.338	21.689	23.900	27.204	30.144	33.687	36.191
20	8.260	9.237	10.851	12.443	14.578	16.266	19.337	22.775	25.038	28.412	31.410	35.020	37.566
21	8.897	9.915	11.591	13.240	15.445	17.182	20.337	23.858	26.171	29.615	32.671	36.343	38.932
22	9.542	10.600	12.338	14.041	16.314	18.101	21.337	24.939	27.301	30.813	33.924	37.659	40.289
23	10.196	11.293	13.091	14.848	17.187	19.021	22.337	26.018	28.429	32.007	35.172	38.968	41.638
24	10.856	11.992	13.848	15.659	18.062	19.943	23.337	27.096	29.553	33.196	36.415	40.270	42.980
25	11.524	12.697	14.611	16.473	18.940	20.867	24.337	28.172	30.675	34.382	37.652	41.566	44.314
26	12.198	13.409	15.379	17.292	19.820	21.792	25.336	29.246	31.795	35.563	38.885	42.856	45.642
27	12.879	14.125	16.151	18.114	20.703	22.710	26.336	30.319	32.912	36.741	40.113	44.140	46.963
28	13.565	14.847	16.928	18.939	21.588	23.647	27.336	31.391	34.027	37.916	41.337	45.419	48.278
29	14.256	15.574	17.708	19.651	22.475	24.577	28.336	32.461	35.139	39.087	42.557	46.693	49.588
30	14.953	16.306	18.493	20.599	23.364	25.508	29.336	33.530	36.250	40.256	43.773	47.962	50.892

For larger values of df, the expression $2\sqrt{2\chi^2} - \sqrt{2df - 1}$ may be used as a normal deviate with unit variance, remembering that the probability for χ^2 corresponds with that of a single tail of the normal curve. From Sir Ronald A. Fisher, 1972. *Statistical Methods for Research Workers* (14th ed.). New York: Hafner Press, Division of Macmillan Publishing Co., pp. 112–113.

TABLE E.6 VALUES OF F-DISTRIBUTIONS AT THE .05 (ROMAN TYPE) AND .01 (BOLDFACE TYPE) SIGNIFICANCE LEVELS. NUMERATOR DEGREES OF FREEDOM FOR THE F-RATIO ARE ACROSS THE TOP, AND DENOMINATOR DEGREES OF FREEDOM ARE ON THE SIDE.

Each cell shows the .05 value (roman) over the .01 value (boldface) as "roman / boldface".

df	1	2	3	4	5	6	7	8	9	10	11	12	14	16	20	24	30	40	50	75	100	200	500	∞
1	16 / 4,052	200 / 4,999	216 / 5,403	225 / 5,625	230 / 5,764	234 / 5,859	237 / 5,928	239 / 5,981	241 / 6,022	242 / 6,056	243 / 6,082	244 / 6,106	245 / 6,142	246 / 6,169	248 / 6,208	249 / 6,234	250 / 6,261	251 / 6,286	252 / 6,302	253 / 6,323	253 / 6,334	254 / 6,352	254 / 6,361	254 / 6,366
2	18.51 / 98.49	19.00 / 99.00	19.16 / 99.17	19.25 / 99.25	19.30 / 99.30	19.33 / 99.33	19.36 / 99.36	19.37 / 99.37	19.38 / 99.39	19.39 / 99.40	19.40 / 99.41	19.41 / 99.42	19.42 / 99.43	19.43 / 99.44	19.44 / 99.45	19.45 / 99.46	19.46 / 99.47	19.47 / 99.48	19.47 / 99.48	19.48 / 99.49	19.49 / 99.49	19.49 / 99.49	19.50 / 99.50	19.50 / 99.50
3	10.13 / 34.12	9.55 / 30.82	9.28 / 29.46	9.12 / 28.71	9.01 / 28.24	8.94 / 27.91	8.88 / 27.67	8.84 / 27.49	8.81 / 27.34	8.78 / 27.23	8.76 / 27.13	8.74 / 27.05	8.71 / 26.92	8.69 / 26.83	8.66 / 26.69	8.64 / 26.60	8.62 / 26.50	8.60 / 26.41	8.58 / 26.35	8.57 / 26.27	8.56 / 26.23	8.54 / 26.18	8.54 / 26.14	8.53 / 26.12
4	7.71 / 21.20	6.94 / 18.00	6.59 / 16.69	6.39 / 15.98	6.26 / 15.52	6.16 / 15.21	6.09 / 14.98	6.04 / 14.80	6.00 / 14.66	5.96 / 14.54	5.93 / 14.45	5.91 / 14.37	5.87 / 14.24	5.84 / 14.15	5.80 / 14.02	5.77 / 13.93	5.74 / 13.83	5.71 / 13.74	5.70 / 13.69	5.68 / 13.61	5.66 / 13.57	5.65 / 13.52	5.64 / 13.48	5.63 / 13.46
5	6.61 / 16.26	5.79 / 13.27	5.41 / 12.06	5.19 / 11.39	5.05 / 10.97	4.95 / 10.67	4.88 / 10.45	4.82 / 10.29	4.78 / 10.15	4.74 / 10.05	4.70 / 9.96	4.68 / 9.89	4.64 / 9.77	4.60 / 9.68	4.56 / 9.55	4.53 / 9.47	4.50 / 9.38	4.46 / 9.29	4.44 / 9.24	4.42 / 9.17	4.40 / 9.13	4.38 / 9.07	4.37 / 9.04	4.36 / 9.02
6	5.99 / 13.74	5.14 / 10.92	4.76 / 9.78	4.53 / 9.15	4.39 / 8.75	4.28 / 8.47	4.21 / 8.26	4.15 / 8.10	4.10 / 7.98	4.06 / 7.87	4.03 / 7.79	4.00 / 7.72	3.96 / 7.60	3.92 / 7.52	3.87 / 7.39	3.84 / 7.31	3.81 / 7.23	3.77 / 7.14	3.75 / 7.09	3.72 / 7.02	3.71 / 6.99	3.69 / 6.94	3.68 / 6.90	3.67 / 6.88
7	5.59 / 12.25	4.74 / 9.55	4.35 / 8.45	4.12 / 7.85	3.97 / 7.46	3.87 / 7.19	3.79 / 7.00	3.73 / 6.84	3.68 / 6.71	3.63 / 6.62	3.60 / 6.54	3.57 / 6.47	3.52 / 6.35	3.49 / 6.27	3.44 / 6.15	3.41 / 6.07	3.38 / 5.98	3.34 / 5.90	3.32 / 5.85	3.29 / 5.78	3.28 / 5.75	3.25 / 5.70	3.24 / 5.67	3.23 / 5.65
8	5.32 / 11.26	4.46 / 8.65	4.07 / 7.59	3.84 / 7.01	3.69 / 6.63	3.58 / 6.37	3.50 / 6.19	3.44 / 6.03	3.39 / 5.91	3.34 / 5.82	3.31 / 5.74	3.28 / 5.67	3.23 / 5.56	3.20 / 5.48	3.15 / 5.36	3.12 / 5.28	3.08 / 5.20	3.05 / 5.11	3.03 / 5.06	3.00 / 5.00	2.98 / 4.96	2.96 / 4.91	2.94 / 4.88	2.93 / 4.86
9	5.12 / 10.56	4.26 / 8.02	3.86 / 6.99	3.63 / 6.42	3.48 / 6.06	3.37 / 5.80	3.29 / 5.62	3.23 / 5.47	3.18 / 5.35	3.13 / 5.26	3.10 / 5.18	3.07 / 5.11	3.02 / 5.00	2.98 / 4.92	2.93 / 4.80	2.90 / 4.73	2.86 / 4.64	2.82 / 4.56	2.80 / 4.51	2.77 / 4.45	2.76 / 4.41	2.73 / 4.36	2.72 / 4.33	2.71 / 4.31
10	4.96 / 10.04	4.10 / 7.56	3.71 / 6.55	3.48 / 5.99	3.33 / 5.64	3.22 / 5.39	3.14 / 5.21	3.07 / 5.06	3.02 / 4.95	2.97 / 4.85	2.94 / 4.78	2.91 / 4.71	2.86 / 4.60	2.82 / 4.52	2.77 / 4.41	2.74 / 4.33	2.70 / 4.25	2.67 / 4.17	2.64 / 4.12	2.61 / 4.05	2.59 / 4.01	2.56 / 3.96	2.55 / 3.93	2.54 / 3.91
11	4.84 / 9.65	3.98 / 7.20	3.59 / 6.22	3.36 / 5.67	3.20 / 5.32	3.09 / 5.07	3.01 / 4.88	2.95 / 4.74	2.90 / 4.63	2.86 / 4.54	2.82 / 4.46	2.79 / 4.40	2.74 / 4.29	2.70 / 4.21	2.65 / 4.10	2.61 / 4.02	2.57 / 3.94	2.53 / 3.86	2.50 / 3.80	2.47 / 3.74	2.45 / 3.70	2.42 / 3.66	2.41 / 3.62	2.40 / 3.60
12	4.75 / 9.33	3.88 / 6.93	3.49 / 5.95	3.26 / 5.41	3.11 / 5.06	3.00 / 4.82	2.92 / 4.65	2.85 / 4.50	2.80 / 4.39	2.76 / 4.30	2.72 / 4.22	2.69 / 4.16	2.64 / 4.05	2.60 / 3.98	2.54 / 3.86	2.50 / 3.78	2.46 / 3.70	2.42 / 3.61	2.40 / 3.56	2.36 / 3.49	2.35 / 3.46	2.32 / 3.41	2.31 / 3.38	2.30 / 3.36
13	4.67 / 9.07	3.80 / 6.70	3.41 / 5.74	3.18 / 5.20	3.02 / 4.86	2.92 / 4.62	2.84 / 4.44	2.77 / 4.30	2.72 / 4.19	2.67 / 4.10	2.63 / 4.02	2.60 / 3.96	2.55 / 3.85	2.51 / 3.78	2.46 / 3.67	2.42 / 3.59	2.38 / 3.51	2.34 / 3.42	2.32 / 3.37	2.28 / 3.30	2.26 / 3.27	2.24 / 3.21	2.22 / 3.18	2.21 / 3.16
14	4.60 / 8.86	3.74 / 6.51	3.34 / 5.56	3.11 / 5.03	2.96 / 4.69	2.85 / 4.46	2.77 / 4.28	2.70 / 4.14	2.65 / 4.03	2.60 / 3.94	2.56 / 3.86	2.53 / 3.80	2.48 / 3.70	2.44 / 3.62	2.39 / 3.51	2.35 / 3.43	2.31 / 3.34	2.27 / 3.26	2.24 / 3.21	2.21 / 3.14	2.19 / 3.11	2.16 / 3.06	2.14 / 3.02	2.13 / 3.00
15	4.54 / 8.68	3.68 / 6.36	3.29 / 5.42	3.06 / 4.89	2.90 / 4.56	2.79 / 4.32	2.70 / 4.14	2.64 / 4.00	2.59 / 3.89	2.55 / 3.80	2.51 / 3.73	2.48 / 3.67	2.43 / 3.56	2.39 / 3.48	2.33 / 3.36	2.29 / 3.29	2.25 / 3.20	2.21 / 3.12	2.18 / 3.07	2.15 / 3.00	2.12 / 2.97	2.10 / 2.92	2.08 / 2.89	2.07 / 2.87
16	4.49 / 8.53	3.63 / 6.23	3.24 / 5.29	3.01 / 4.77	2.85 / 4.44	2.74 / 4.20	2.66 / 4.03	2.59 / 3.89	2.54 / 3.78	2.49 / 3.69	2.45 / 3.61	2.42 / 3.55	2.37 / 3.45	2.33 / 3.37	2.28 / 3.25	2.24 / 3.18	2.20 / 3.10	2.16 / 3.01	2.13 / 2.96	2.09 / 2.98	2.07 / 2.86	2.04 / 2.80	2.02 / 2.77	2.01 / 2.75

The function, $F = e$ with exponent $2z$, is computed in part from Fisher's table VI(7). Additional entries are by interpolation, mostly graphical.
From George W. Snedecor, and William G. Cochran, 1967. *Statistical Methods* (6th ed.). Ames, Iowa: Iowa State University Press, pp. 560–563.

TABLE E.6 (CONTINUED)

df	1	2	3	4	5	6	7	8	9	10	11	12	14	16	20	24	30	40	50	75	100	200	500	∞
17	4.45 / 8.40	3.59 / 6.11	3.20 / 5.18	2.96 / 4.67	2.81 / 4.34	2.70 / 4.10	2.62 / 3.93	2.55 / 3.79	2.50 / 3.68	2.45 / 3.59	2.41 / 3.52	2.38 / 3.45	2.33 / 3.35	2.29 / 3.27	2.23 / 3.16	2.19 / 3.08	2.15 / 3.00	2.11 / 2.92	2.08 / 2.86	2.04 / 2.79	2.02 / 2.76	1.99 / 2.70	1.97 / 2.67	1.96 / 2.65
18	4.41 / 8.28	3.55 / 6.01	3.16 / 5.09	2.93 / 4.58	2.77 / 4.25	2.66 / 4.01	2.58 / 3.85	2.51 / 3.71	2.46 / 3.60	2.41 / 3.51	2.37 / 3.44	2.34 / 3.37	2.29 / 3.27	2.25 / 3.19	2.19 / 3.07	2.15 / 3.00	2.11 / 2.91	2.07 / 2.83	2.04 / 2.78	2.00 / 2.71	1.98 / 2.68	1.95 / 2.62	1.93 / 2.59	1.92 / 2.57
19	4.38 / 8.18	3.52 / 5.93	3.13 / 5.01	2.90 / 4.50	2.74 / 4.17	2.63 / 3.94	2.55 / 3.77	2.48 / 3.63	2.43 / 3.52	2.38 / 3.43	2.34 / 3.36	2.31 / 3.30	2.26 / 3.19	2.21 / 3.12	2.15 / 3.00	2.11 / 2.92	2.07 / 2.84	2.02 / 2.76	2.00 / 2.70	1.96 / 2.63	1.94 / 2.60	1.91 / 2.54	1.90 / 2.51	1.88 / 2.49
20	4.35 / 8.10	3.49 / 5.85	3.10 / 4.94	2.87 / 4.43	2.71 / 4.10	2.60 / 3.87	2.52 / 3.71	2.45 / 3.56	2.40 / 3.45	2.35 / 3.37	2.31 / 3.30	2.28 / 3.23	2.23 / 3.13	2.18 / 3.05	2.12 / 2.94	2.08 / 2.86	2.04 / 2.77	1.99 / 2.69	1.96 / 2.63	1.92 / 2.56	1.90 / 2.53	1.87 / 2.47	1.85 / 2.44	1.84 / 2.42
21	4.32 / 8.02	3.47 / 5.78	3.07 / 4.87	2.84 / 4.37	2.68 / 4.04	2.57 / 3.81	2.49 / 3.65	2.42 / 3.51	2.37 / 3.40	2.32 / 3.31	2.28 / 3.24	2.25 / 3.17	2.20 / 3.07	2.15 / 2.99	2.09 / 2.88	2.05 / 2.80	2.00 / 2.72	1.96 / 2.63	1.93 / 2.58	1.89 / 2.51	1.87 / 2.47	1.84 / 2.42	1.82 / 2.38	1.81 / 2.36
22	4.30 / 7.94	3.44 / 5.72	3.05 / 4.82	2.82 / 4.31	2.66 / 3.99	2.55 / 3.76	2.47 / 3.59	2.40 / 3.45	2.35 / 3.35	2.30 / 3.26	2.26 / 3.18	2.23 / 3.12	2.18 / 3.02	2.13 / 2.94	2.07 / 2.83	2.03 / 2.75	1.98 / 2.67	1.93 / 2.58	1.91 / 2.53	1.87 / 2.46	1.84 / 2.42	1.81 / 2.37	1.80 / 2.33	1.78 / 2.31
23	4.28 / 7.88	3.42 / 5.66	3.03 / 4.76	2.80 / 4.26	2.64 / 3.94	2.53 / 3.71	2.45 / 3.54	2.38 / 3.41	2.32 / 3.30	2.28 / 3.21	2.24 / 3.14	2.20 / 3.07	2.14 / 2.97	2.10 / 2.89	2.04 / 2.78	2.00 / 2.70	1.96 / 2.62	1.91 / 2.53	1.88 / 2.48	1.84 / 2.41	1.82 / 2.37	1.79 / 2.32	1.77 / 2.28	1.76 / 2.26
24	4.26 / 7.82	3.40 / 5.61	3.01 / 4.72	2.78 / 4.22	2.62 / 3.90	2.51 / 3.67	2.43 / 3.50	2.36 / 3.36	2.30 / 3.25	2.26 / 3.17	2.22 / 3.09	2.18 / 3.03	2.13 / 2.93	2.09 / 2.85	2.02 / 2.74	1.98 / 2.66	1.94 / 2.58	1.89 / 2.49	1.86 / 2.44	1.82 / 2.36	1.80 / 2.33	1.76 / 2.27	1.74 / 2.23	1.73 / 2.21
25	4.24 / 7.77	3.38 / 5.57	2.99 / 4.68	2.76 / 4.18	2.60 / 3.86	2.49 / 3.63	2.41 / 3.46	2.34 / 3.32	2.28 / 3.21	2.24 / 3.13	2.20 / 3.05	2.16 / 2.99	2.11 / 2.89	2.06 / 2.81	2.00 / 2.70	1.96 / 2.62	1.92 / 2.54	1.87 / 2.45	1.84 / 2.40	1.80 / 2.32	1.77 / 2.29	1.74 / 2.23	1.72 / 2.19	1.71 / 2.17
26	4.22 / 7.72	3.37 / 5.53	2.98 / 4.64	2.74 / 4.14	2.59 / 3.82	2.47 / 3.59	2.39 / 3.42	2.32 / 3.29	2.27 / 3.17	2.22 / 3.09	2.18 / 3.02	2.15 / 2.96	2.10 / 2.86	2.05 / 2.77	1.99 / 2.66	1.95 / 2.58	1.90 / 2.50	1.85 / 2.41	1.82 / 2.36	1.78 / 2.28	1.76 / 2.25	1.72 / 2.19	1.70 / 2.15	1.69 / 2.13
27	4.21 / 7.68	3.35 / 5.49	2.96 / 4.60	2.73 / 4.11	2.57 / 3.79	2.46 / 3.56	2.37 / 3.39	2.30 / 3.26	2.25 / 3.14	2.20 / 3.06	2.16 / 2.98	2.13 / 2.93	2.08 / 2.83	2.03 / 2.74	1.97 / 2.63	1.93 / 2.55	1.88 / 2.47	1.84 / 2.38	1.80 / 2.33	1.76 / 2.25	1.74 / 2.21	1.71 / 2.16	1.68 / 2.12	1.67 / 2.10
28	4.20 / 7.64	3.34 / 5.45	2.95 / 4.57	2.71 / 4.07	2.56 / 3.76	2.44 / 3.53	2.36 / 3.36	2.29 / 3.23	2.24 / 3.11	2.19 / 3.03	2.15 / 2.95	2.12 / 2.90	2.06 / 2.80	2.02 / 2.71	1.96 / 2.60	1.91 / 2.52	1.87 / 2.44	1.81 / 2.35	1.78 / 2.30	1.75 / 2.22	1.72 / 2.18	1.69 / 2.13	1.67 / 2.09	1.65 / 2.06
29	4.18 / 7.60	3.33 / 5.42	2.93 / 4.54	2.70 / 4.04	2.54 / 3.73	2.43 / 3.50	2.35 / 3.33	2.28 / 3.20	2.22 / 3.08	2.18 / 3.00	2.14 / 2.92	2.10 / 2.87	2.05 / 2.77	2.00 / 2.68	1.94 / 2.57	1.90 / 2.49	1.85 / 2.41	1.80 / 2.32	1.77 / 2.27	1.73 / 2.19	1.71 / 2.15	1.68 / 2.10	1.65 / 2.06	1.64 / 2.03
30	4.17 / 7.56	3.32 / 5.39	2.92 / 4.51	2.69 / 4.02	2.53 / 3.70	2.42 / 3.47	2.34 / 3.30	2.27 / 3.17	2.21 / 3.06	2.16 / 2.98	2.12 / 2.90	2.09 / 2.84	2.04 / 2.74	1.99 / 2.66	1.93 / 2.55	1.89 / 2.47	1.84 / 2.38	1.79 / 2.29	1.76 / 2.24	1.72 / 2.16	1.69 / 2.13	1.66 / 2.07	1.64 / 2.03	1.62 / 2.01
32	4.15 / 7.50	3.30 / 5.34	2.90 / 4.46	2.67 / 3.97	2.51 / 3.66	2.40 / 3.42	2.32 / 3.25	2.25 / 3.12	2.19 / 3.01	2.14 / 2.94	2.10 / 2.86	2.07 / 2.80	2.02 / 2.70	1.97 / 2.62	1.91 / 2.51	1.86 / 2.42	1.82 / 2.34	1.76 / 2.25	1.74 / 2.20	1.69 / 2.12	1.67 / 2.08	1.64 / 2.02	1.61 / 1.98	1.59 / 1.96
34	4.13 / 7.44	3.28 / 5.29	2.88 / 4.42	2.65 / 3.93	2.49 / 3.61	2.38 / 3.38	2.30 / 3.21	2.23 / 3.08	2.17 / 2.97	2.12 / 2.89	2.08 / 2.82	2.05 / 2.76	2.00 / 2.66	1.95 / 2.58	1.89 / 2.47	1.84 / 2.38	1.80 / 2.30	1.74 / 2.21	1.71 / 2.15	1.67 / 2.08	1.64 / 2.04	1.61 / 1.98	1.59 / 1.94	1.57 / 1.91
36	4.11 / 7.39	3.26 / 5.25	2.86 / 4.38	2.63 / 3.89	2.48 / 3.58	2.36 / 3.35	2.28 / 3.18	2.21 / 3.04	2.15 / 2.94	2.10 / 2.86	2.06 / 2.78	2.03 / 2.72	1.98 / 2.62	1.93 / 2.54	1.87 / 2.43	1.82 / 2.35	1.78 / 2.26	1.72 / 2.17	1.69 / 2.12	1.65 / 2.04	1.62 / 2.00	1.59 / 1.94	1.56 / 1.90	1.55 / 1.87
38	4.10 / 7.35	3.25 / 5.21	2.85 / 4.34	2.62 / 3.86	2.46 / 3.54	2.35 / 3.32	2.26 / 3.15	2.19 / 3.02	2.14 / 2.91	2.09 / 2.82	2.05 / 2.75	2.02 / 2.69	1.96 / 2.59	1.92 / 2.51	1.85 / 2.40	1.80 / 2.32	1.76 / 2.22	1.71 / 2.14	1.67 / 2.08	1.63 / 2.00	1.60 / 1.97	1.57 / 1.90	1.54 / 1.86	1.53 / 1.84
40	4.08 / 7.31	3.23 / 5.18	2.84 / 4.31	2.61 / 3.83	2.45 / 3.51	2.34 / 3.29	2.25 / 3.12	2.18 / 2.99	2.12 / 2.88	2.07 / 2.80	2.04 / 2.73	2.00 / 2.66	1.95 / 2.56	1.90 / 2.49	1.84 / 2.37	1.79 / 2.29	1.74 / 2.20	1.69 / 2.11	1.66 / 2.05	1.61 / 1.97	1.59 / 1.94	1.55 / 1.88	1.53 / 1.84	1.51 / 1.81

42	4.07	3.22	2.83	2.59	2.44	2.32	2.24	2.17	2.11	2.06	2.02	1.99	1.94	1.89	1.82	1.78	1.73	1.68	1.64	1.60	1.57	1.54	1.51	1.49
	7.27	5.15	4.29	3.80	3.49	3.26	3.10	2.96	2.86	2.77	2.70	2.64	2.54	2.46	2.35	2.26	2.17	2.08	2.02	1.94	1.91	1.85	1.80	1.78
44	4.06	3.21	2.82	2.58	2.43	2.31	2.23	2.16	2.10	2.05	2.01	1.98	1.92	1.88	1.81	1.76	1.72	1.66	1.63	1.58	1.56	1.52	1.50	1.48
	7.24	5.12	4.26	3.78	3.46	3.24	3.07	2.94	2.84	2.75	2.68	2.62	2.52	2.44	2.32	2.24	2.15	2.06	2.00	1.92	1.88	1.82	1.78	1.75
46	4.05	3.20	2.81	2.57	2.42	2.30	2.22	2.14	2.09	2.04	2.00	1.97	1.91	1.87	1.80	1.75	1.71	1.65	1.62	1.57	1.54	1.51	1.50	1.46
	7.21	5.10	4.24	3.76	3.44	3.22	3.05	2.92	2.82	2.73	2.66	2.60	2.50	2.42	2.30	2.22	2.13	2.04	1.98	1.90	1.86	1.80	1.78	1.72
48	4.04	3.19	2.80	2.56	2.41	2.30	2.21	2.14	2.08	2.03	1.99	1.96	1.90	1.86	1.79	1.74	1.70	1.64	1.61	1.56	1.53	1.50	1.47	1.45
	7.19	5.08	4.22	3.74	3.42	3.20	3.04	2.90	2.80	2.71	2.64	2.58	2.48	2.40	2.28	2.20	2.11	2.02	1.96	1.88	1.84	1.78	1.73	1.70
50	4.03	3.18	2.79	2.56	2.40	2.29	2.20	2.13	2.07	2.02	1.98	1.95	1.90	1.85	1.78	1.74	1.69	1.63	1.60	1.55	1.52	1.48	1.46	1.44
	7.17	5.06	4.20	3.72	3.41	3.18	3.02	2.88	2.78	2.70	2.62	2.56	2.46	2.39	2.26	2.18	2.10	2.00	1.94	1.86	1.82	1.76	1.71	1.68
55	4.02	3.17	2.78	2.54	2.38	2.27	2.18	2.11	2.05	2.00	1.97	1.93	1.88	1.83	1.76	1.72	1.67	1.61	1.58	1.52	1.50	1.46	1.43	1.41
	7.12	5.01	4.16	3.68	3.37	3.15	2.98	2.85	2.75	2.66	2.59	2.53	2.43	2.35	2.23	2.15	2.06	1.96	1.90	1.82	1.78	1.71	1.66	1.64
60	4.00	3.15	2.76	2.52	2.37	2.25	2.17	2.10	2.04	1.99	1.95	1.92	1.86	1.81	1.75	1.70	1.65	1.59	1.56	1.50	1.48	1.44	1.41	1.39
	7.08	4.98	4.13	3.65	3.34	3.12	2.95	2.82	2.72	2.63	2.56	2.50	2.40	2.32	2.20	2.12	2.03	1.93	1.87	1.79	1.74	1.68	1.63	1.60
65	3.99	3.14	2.75	2.51	2.36	2.24	2.15	2.08	2.02	1.98	1.94	1.90	1.85	1.80	1.73	1.68	1.63	1.57	1.54	1.49	1.46	1.42	1.39	1.37
	7.04	4.95	4.10	3.62	3.31	3.09	2.93	2.79	2.70	2.61	2.54	2.47	2.37	2.30	2.18	2.09	2.00	1.90	1.84	1.76	1.71	1.64	1.60	1.56
70	3.98	3.13	2.74	2.50	2.35	2.23	2.14	2.07	2.01	1.97	1.93	1.89	1.84	1.79	1.72	1.67	1.62	1.56	1.53	1.47	1.45	1.40	1.37	1.35
	7.01	4.92	4.08	3.60	3.29	3.07	2.91	2.77	2.67	2.59	2.51	2.45	2.35	2.28	2.15	2.07	1.98	1.88	1.82	1.74	1.69	1.62	1.56	1.53
80	3.96	3.11	2.72	2.48	2.33	2.21	2.12	2.05	1.99	1.95	1.91	1.88	1.82	1.77	1.70	1.65	1.60	1.54	1.51	1.45	1.42	1.38	1.35	1.32
	6.96	4.88	4.04	3.56	3.25	3.04	2.87	2.74	2.64	2.55	2.48	2.41	2.32	2.24	2.11	2.03	1.94	1.84	1.78	1.70	1.65	1.57	1.52	1.49
100	3.94	3.09	2.70	2.46	2.30	2.19	2.10	2.03	1.97	1.92	1.88	1.85	1.79	1.75	1.68	1.63	1.57	1.51	1.48	1.42	1.39	1.34	1.30	1.28
	6.90	4.82	3.98	3.51	3.20	2.99	2.82	2.69	2.59	2.51	2.43	2.36	2.26	2.19	2.06	1.98	1.89	1.79	1.73	1.64	1.59	1.51	1.46	1.43
125	3.92	3.07	2.68	2.44	2.29	2.17	2.08	2.01	1.95	1.90	1.86	1.83	1.77	1.72	1.65	1.60	1.55	1.49	1.45	1.39	1.36	1.31	1.27	1.25
	6.84	4.78	3.94	3.47	3.17	2.95	2.79	2.65	2.56	2.47	2.40	2.33	2.23	2.15	2.03	1.94	1.85	1.75	1.68	1.59	1.54	1.46	1.40	1.37
150	3.91	3.06	2.67	2.43	2.27	2.16	2.07	2.00	1.94	1.89	1.85	1.82	1.76	1.71	1.64	1.59	1.54	1.47	1.44	1.37	1.34	1.29	1.25	1.22
	6.81	4.75	3.91	3.44	3.14	2.92	2.76	2.62	2.53	2.44	2.37	2.30	2.20	2.12	2.00	1.91	1.83	1.72	1.66	1.56	1.51	1.43	1.37	1.33
200	3.89	3.04	2.65	2.41	2.26	2.14	2.05	1.98	1.92	1.87	1.83	1.80	1.74	1.69	1.62	1.57	1.52	1.45	1.42	1.35	1.32	1.26	1.22	1.19
	6.76	4.71	3.88	3.41	3.11	2.90	2.73	2.60	2.50	2.41	2.34	2.28	2.17	2.09	1.97	1.88	1.79	1.69	1.62	1.53	1.48	1.39	1.33	1.28
400	3.86	3.02	2.62	2.39	2.23	2.12	2.03	1.96	1.90	1.85	1.81	1.78	1.72	1.67	1.60	1.54	1.49	1.42	1.38	1.32	1.28	1.22	1.16	1.13
	6.70	4.66	3.83	3.36	3.06	2.85	2.69	2.55	2.46	2.37	2.29	2.23	2.12	2.04	1.92	1.84	1.74	1.64	1.57	1.47	1.42	1.32	1.24	1.19
1000	3.85	3.00	2.61	2.38	2.22	2.10	2.02	1.95	1.89	1.84	1.80	1.76	1.70	1.65	1.58	1.53	1.47	1.41	1.36	1.30	1.26	1.19	1.13	1.08
	6.66	4.62	3.80	3.34	3.04	2.82	2.66	2.53	2.43	2.34	2.26	2.20	2.09	2.01	1.89	1.81	1.71	1.61	1.54	1.44	1.38	1.28	1.19	1.11
∞	3.84	2.99	2.60	2.37	2.21	2.09	2.01	1.94	1.88	1.83	1.79	1.75	1.69	1.64	1.57	1.52	1.46	1.40	1.35	1.28	1.24	1.17	1.11	1.00
	6.63	4.60	3.78	3.32	3.02	2.80	2.64	2.51	2.41	2.32	2.24	2.18	2.07	1.99	1.87	1.79	1.69	1.59	1.52	1.41	1.36	1.25	1.15	1.00

TABLE E.7   *SQUARE ROOTS*

The table can be used to find the square root of numbers from 1 to 998. The square root of numbers from *1.00 to 9.98* can be read directly from the $\sqrt{n}$ column. For example, the square root of 1.44 is 1.20. The $\sqrt{10n}$ column can be used to find the square root of numbers from *10.0 to 99.8*. For example, the square root of 14.4 (or 10 times 1.44) is 3.79. The square root of numbers from *100 to 998* can also be found. Locate such numbers by removing the decimal from the values in the "*n*" column. For example, 1.44 can then be read as 144. The square root of these numbers is then 10 times the value in the $\sqrt{n}$ column. The square root of 144 is 12.0. Some accuracy in the square root values is lost for odd numbers such as 1.01 and 1.03 since the numbers in the *n* column increase in units of two hundredths (1.00 to 1.02 to 1.04 etc.).

n	$\sqrt{n}$	$\sqrt{10n}$	n	$\sqrt{n}$	$\sqrt{10n}$	n	$\sqrt{n}$	$\sqrt{10n}$	n	$\sqrt{n}$	$\sqrt{10n}$
1.00	1.00	3.16	1.80	1.34	4.24	2.60	1.61	5.10	3.40	1.84	5.83
1.02	1.01	3.19	1.82	1.35	4.27	2.62	1.62	5.12	3.42	1.85	5.85
1.04	1.02	3.22	1.84	1.36	4.29	2.64	1.62	5.14	3.44	1.85	5.87
1.06	1.03	3.26	1.86	1.36	4.31	2.66	1.63	5.16	3.46	1.86	5.88
1.08	1.04	3.29	1.88	1.37	4.34	2.68	1.64	5.18	3.48	1.87	5.90
1.10	1.05	3.32	1.90	1.38	4.36	2.70	1.64	5.20	3.50	1.87	5.92
1.12	1.06	3.35	1.92	1.39	4.38	2.72	1.65	5.22	3.52	1.88	5.93
1.14	1.07	3.38	1.94	1.39	4.40	2.74	1.66	5.23	3.54	1.88	5.95
1.16	1.08	3.41	1.96	1.40	4.43	2.76	1.66	5.25	3.56	1.89	5.97
1.18	1.09	3.44	1.98	1.41	4.45	2.78	1.67	5.27	3.58	1.89	5.98
1.20	1.10	3.46	2.00	1.41	4.47	2.80	1.67	5.29	3.60	1.90	6.00
1.22	1.10	3.49	2.02	1.42	4.49	2.82	1.68	5.31	3.62	1.90	6.02
1.24	1.11	3.52	2.04	1.43	4.52	2.84	1.69	5.33	3.64	1.91	6.03
1.26	1.12	3.55	2.06	1.44	4.54	2.86	1.69	5.35	3.66	1.91	6.05
1.28	1.13	3.58	2.08	1.44	4.56	2.88	1.70	5.37	3.68	1.92	6.07
1.30	1.14	3.61	2.10	1.45	4.58	2.90	1.70	5.39	3.70	1.92	6.08
1.32	1.15	3.63	2.12	1.46	4.60	2.92	1.71	5.40	3.72	1.93	6.10
1.34	1.16	3.66	2.14	1.46	4.63	2.94	1.71	5.42	3.74	1.93	6.12
1.36	1.17	3.69	2.16	1.47	4.65	2.96	1.72	5.44	3.76	1.94	6.13
1.38	1.17	3.71	2.18	1.48	4.67	2.98	1.73	5.46	3.78	1.94	6.14
1.40	1.18	3.74	2.20	1.48	4.69	3.00	1.73	5.48	3.80	1.95	6.16
1.42	1.19	3.77	2.22	1.49	4.71	3.02	1.74	5.50	3.82	1.95	6.18
1.44	1.20	3.79	2.24	1.50	4.73	3.04	1.74	5.51	3.84	1.96	6.20
1.46	1.21	3.82	2.26	1.50	4.75	3.06	1.75	5.53	3.86	1.96	6.21
1.48	1.22	3.85	2.28	1.51	4.77	3.08	1.76	5.55	3.88	1.97	6.23
1.50	1.22	3.87	2.30	1.52	4.80	3.10	1.76	5.57	3.90	1.97	6.25
1.52	1.23	3.90	2.32	1.52	4.82	3.12	1.77	5.59	3.92	1.98	6.26
1.54	1.24	3.92	2.34	1.53	4.84	3.14	1.77	5.60	3.94	1.98	6.28
1.56	1.25	3.95	2.36	1.54	4.86	3.16	1.78	5.62	3.96	1.99	6.29
1.58	1.26	3.97	2.38	1.54	4.88	3.18	1.78	5.64	3.98	1.99	6.31
1.60	1.26	4.00	2.40	1.55	4.90	3.20	1.79	5.66	4.00	2.00	6.32
1.62	1.27	4.02	2.42	1.56	4.92	3.22	1.79	5.67	4.02	2.00	6.34
1.64	1.28	4.05	2.44	1.56	4.94	3.24	1.80	5.69	4.04	2.01	6.36
1.66	1.29	4.07	2.46	1.57	4.96	3.26	1.81	5.71	4.06	2.01	6.37
1.68	1.30	4.10	2.48	1.57	4.98	3.28	1.81	5.73	4.08	2.02	6.39
1.70	1.30	4.12	2.50	1.58	5.00	3.30	1.82	5.74	4.10	2.02	6.40
1.72	1.31	4.15	2.52	1.59	5.02	3.32	1.82	5.76	4.12	2.03	6.42
1.74	1.32	4.17	2.54	1.59	5.04	3.34	1.83	5.78	4.14	2.03	6.43
1.76	1.33	4.20	2.56	1.60	5.06	3.36	1.83	5.80	4.16	2.04	6.45
1.78	1.33	4.22	2.58	1.61	5.08	3.38	1.84	5.81	4.18	2.04	6.47

TABLE E.7   (*CONTINUED*)

n	$\sqrt{n}$	$\sqrt{10n}$	n	$\sqrt{n}$	$\sqrt{10n}$	n	$\sqrt{n}$	$\sqrt{10n}$	n	$\sqrt{n}$	$\sqrt{10n}$
4.20	2.05	6.48	5.22	2.28	7.22	6.24	2.50	7.90	7.26	2.69	8.52
4.22	2.05	6.50	5.24	2.29	7.24	6.26	2.50	7.91	7.28	2.70	8.53
4.24	2.06	6.51	5.26	2.29	7.25	6.28	2.51	7.92	7.30	2.70	8.54
4.26	2.06	6.53	5.28	2.30	7.27	6.30	2.51	7.94	7.32	2.71	8.56
4.28	2.07	6.54	5.30	2.30	7.28	6.32	2.51	7.95	7.34	2.71	8.57
4.30	2.07	6.56	5.32	2.31	7.29	6.34	2.52	7.96	7.36	2.71	8.58
4.32	2.08	6.57	5.34	2.31	7.31	6.36	2.52	7.97	7.38	2.72	8.59
4.34	2.08	6.59	5.36	2.32	7.32	6.38	2.53	7.99	7.40	2.72	8.60
4.36	2.09	6.60	5.38	2.32	7.33	6.40	2.53	8.00	7.42	2.72	8.61
4.38	2.09	6.62	5.40	2.32	7.35	6.42	2.53	8.01	7.44	2.73	8.63
4.40	2.10	6.63	5.42	2.33	7.36	6.44	2.54	8.02	7.46	2.73	8.64
4.42	2.10	6.65	5.44	2.33	7.38	6.46	2.54	8.04	7.48	2.73	8.65
4.44	2.11	6.66	5.46	2.34	7.39	6.48	2.55	8.05	7.50	2.74	8.66
4.46	2.11	6.68	5.48	2.34	7.40	6.50	2.55	8.06	7.52	2.74	8.67
4.48	2.12	6.69	5.50	2.35	7.42	6.52	2.55	8.07	7.54	2.75	8.68
4.50	2.12	6.71	5.52	2.35	7.43	6.54	2.56	8.09	7.56	2.75	8.69
4.52	2.13	6.72	5.54	2.35	7.44	6.56	2.56	8.10	7.58	2.75	8.71
4.54	2.13	6.74	5.56	2.36	7.46	6.58	2.57	8.11	7.60	2.76	8.72
4.56	2.14	6.75	5.58	2.36	7.47	6.60	2.57	8.12	7.62	2.76	8.73
4.58	2.14	6.77	5.60	2.37	7.48	6.62	2.57	8.14	7.64	2.76	8.74
4.60	2.14	6.78	5.62	2.37	7.50	6.64	2.58	8.15	7.66	2.77	8.75
4.62	2.15	6.80	5.64	2.37	7.51	6.66	2.58	8.16	7.68	2.77	8.76
4.64	2.15	6.81	5.66	2.38	7.52	6.68	2.58	8.17	7.70	2.77	8.77
4.66	2.16	6.83	5.68	2.38	7.54	6.70	2.59	8.19	7.72	2.78	8.79
4.68	2.16	6.84	5.70	2.39	7.55	6.72	2.59	8.20	7.74	2.78	8.80
4.70	2.17	6.86	5.72	2.39	7.56	6.74	2.60	8.21	7.76	2.79	8.81
4.72	2.17	6.87	5.74	2.40	7.58	6.76	2.60	8.22	7.78	2.79	8.82
4.74	2.18	6.88	5.76	2.40	7.59	6.78	2.60	8.23	7.80	2.79	8.83
4.76	2.18	6.90	5.78	2.40	7.60	6.80	2.61	8.25	7.82	2.80	8.84
4.78	2.19	6.91	5.80	2.41	7.62	6.82	2.61	8.26	7.84	2.80	8.85
4.80	2.19	6.93	5.82	2.41	7.63	6.84	2.62	8.27	7.86	2.80	8.86
4.82	2.20	6.94	5.84	2.42	7.64	6.86	2.62	8.28	7.88	2.81	8.87
4.84	2.20	6.96	5.86	2.42	7.66	6.88	2.62	8.29	7.90	2.81	8.89
4.86	2.20	6.97	5.88	2.42	7.67	6.90	2.63	8.31	7.92	2.81	8.90
4.88	2.21	6.99	5.90	2.43	7.68	6.92	2.63	8.32	7.94	2.82	8.91
4.90	2.21	7.00	5.92	2.43	7.69	6.94	2.63	8.33	7.96	2.82	8.92
4.92	2.22	7.01	5.94	2.44	7.71	6.96	2.64	8.34	7.98	2.82	8.93
4.94	2.22	7.03	5.96	2.44	7.72	6.98	2.64	8.35	8.00	2.83	8.94
4.96	2.23	7.04	5.98	2.45	7.73	7.00	2.65	8.37	8.02	2.83	8.96
4.98	2.23	7.06	6.00	2.45	7.75	7.02	2.65	8.38	8.04	2.84	8.97
5.00	2.24	7.07	6.02	2.45	7.76	7.04	2.65	8.39	8.06	2.84	8.98
5.02	2.24	7.09	6.04	2.46	7.77	7.06	2.66	8.40	8.08	2.84	8.99
5.04	2.24	7.10	6.06	2.46	7.78	7.08	2.66	8.41	8.10	2.85	9.00
5.06	2.25	7.11	6.08	2.47	7.80	7.10	2.66	8.43	8.12	2.85	9.01
5.08	2.25	7.13	6.10	2.47	7.81	7.12	2.67	8.44	8.14	2.85	9.02
5.10	2.26	7.14	6.12	2.47	7.82	7.14	2.67	8.45	8.16	2.86	9.03
5.12	2.26	7.16	6.14	2.48	7.84	7.16	2.68	8.46	8.18	2.86	9.04
5.14	2.27	7.17	6.16	2.48	7.85	7.18	2.68	8.47	8.20	2.86	9.06
5.16	2.27	7.18	6.18	2.49	7.86	7.20	2.68	8.49	8.22	2.87	9.07
5.18	2.28	7.20	6.20	2.49	7.87	7.22	2.69	8.50	8.24	2.87	9.08
5.20	2.28	7.21	6.22	2.49	7.89	7.24	2.69	8.51	8.26	2.87	9.09

TABLE E.7   (*CONTINUED*)

n	$\sqrt{n}$	$\sqrt{10n}$	n	$\sqrt{n}$	$\sqrt{10n}$	n	$\sqrt{n}$	$\sqrt{10n}$	n	$\sqrt{n}$	$\sqrt{10n}$
8.28	2.88	9.10	8.72	2.95	9.34	9.16	3.03	9.57	9.60	3.10	9.80
8.30	2.88	9.11	8.74	2.96	9.35	9.18	3.03	9.58	9.62	3.10	9.81
8.32	2.88	9.12	8.76	2.96	9.36	9.20	3.03	9.59	9.64	3.10	9.82
8.34	2.89	9.13	8.78	2.96	9.37	9.22	3.04	9.60	9.66	3.11	9.83
8.36	2.89	9.14	8.80	2.97	9.38	9.24	3.04	9.61	9.68	3.11	9.84
8.38	2.89	9.15	8.82	2.97	9.39	9.26	3.04	9.62	9.70	3.11	9.85
8.40	2.90	9.17	8.84	2.97	9.40	9.28	3.05	9.63	9.72	3.12	9.86
8.42	2.90	9.18	8.86	2.98	9.41	9.30	3.05	9.64	9.74	3.12	9.87
8.44	2.91	9.19	8.88	2.98	9.42	9.32	3.05	9.65	9.76	3.12	9.88
8.46	2.91	9.20	8.90	2.98	9.43	9.34	3.06	9.66	9.78	3.13	9.89
8.48	2.91	9.21	8.92	2.99	9.44	9.36	3.06	9.67	9.80	3.13	9.90
8.50	2.92	9.22	8.94	2.99	9.46	9.38	3.06	9.68	9.82	3.13	9.91
8.52	2.92	9.23	8.96	2.99	9.47	9.40	3.07	9.70	9.84	3.14	9.92
8.54	2.92	9.24	8.98	3.00	9.48	9.42	3.07	9.71	9.86	3.14	9.93
8.56	2.93	9.25	9.00	3.00	9.49	9.44	3.07	9.72	9.88	3.14	9.94
8.58	2.93	9.26	9.02	3.00	9.50	9.46	3.08	9.73	9.90	3.15	9.95
8.60	2.93	9.27	9.04	3.01	9.51	9.48	3.08	9.74	9.92	3.15	9.96
8.62	2.94	9.28	9.06	3.01	9.52	9.50	3.08	9.75	9.94	3.15	9.97
8.64	2.94	9.30	9.08	3.01	9.53	9.52	3.09	9.76	9.96	3.16	9.98
8.66	2.94	9.31	9.10	3.02	9.54	9.54	3.09	9.77	9.98	3.16	9.99
8.68	2.95	9.32	9.12	3.02	9.55	9.56	3.09	9.78			
8.70	2.95	9.33	9.14	3.02	9.56	9.58	3.10	9.79			

References and
Index of Sources

	Cited in this text on pages
1. Altmann, J., 1974. Observational study of behavior: sampling methods. *Behaviour* **49**: 228–267.	180–181
2. Alvord, D. J., and L. W. Glass, 1974. Relationships between academic achievement and self-concept. *Science Education* **58**: 175–179.	204–205
3. American Educational Research Association, 1953. Second report of the committee on the criteria of teacher effectiveness. *Journal of Educational Research* **46**: 641–658.	348
4. American Psychological Association, Ad Hoc Committee on Ethical Standards in Psychological Research, 1973. *Ethical Principles in the Conduct of Research with Human Participants.* Washington, D.C.: American Psychological Association.	356
5. American Psychological Association, American Educational Research Association and National Council on Measurement in Education, Joint Committee, 1974. *Standards for Educational and Psychological Tests* (Rev. ed.). Washington, D.C.: American Psychological Association.	134
6. Anastasi, A., 1968. *Psychological Testing* (3rd ed.). New York: Macmillan.	306
7. Anderson, B. D., E. J. Haller, and T. Smorodin, 1976. The effects of changing social contexts: a study of students who transferred between high schools. *Urban Education* **10**: 333–355.	225
8. Argyris, C., 1968. Some unintended consequences of rigorous research. *Psychological Bulletin* **70**: 185–197.	305
9. Arthur, G. L., P. J. Sisson, and C. L. Fallis, 1975. Follow-up drug survey: trends in knowledge and attitudes in a typical high school in Georgia. *Journal of Drug Education* **5**: 243–249.	187
10. Atkinson, J. W., 1965. The mainsprings of achievement-oriented activity. In J. D. Krumboltz (ed.), *Learning and the Educational Process.* Chicago: Rand McNally, pp. 25–66.	349
11. Atkinson, J. W., and N. T. Feather (eds.), 1966. *A Theory of Achievement Motivation.* New York: Wiley.	349

Cited in this
text on pages

12. Atkinson, J. W., and J. O. Raynor (eds.), 1974. *Motivation and Achievement*. New York: Winston/Wiley (Halsted Press).   349

13. Barker, R. G., 1968. *Ecological Psychology: Concepts and Methods for Studying the Environment of Human Behavior*. Stanford, Calif.: Stanford University Press.   299

14. Barker, R. G., and P. Gump, 1964. *Big School, Small School*. Stanford, Calif.: Stanford University Press.   299

15. Birnbrauer, J. S., C. R. Peterson, and J. V. Solnick, 1974. Design and interpretation of studies of single subjects. *American Journal of Mental Deficiency* **79**: 191–203.   271

16. Blalock, H. M., 1968. Theory building and causal inferences. In H. M. Blalock and A. B. Blalock (eds.), *Methodology in Social Research*. New York: McGraw-Hill, pp. 155–198.   142

17. Bloom, B. S. (ed.), 1956. *Taxonomy of Educational Objectives, Handbook I: Cognitive Domain*, New York: David McKay.   349

18. Bracht, G. H., and G. V. Glass, 1968. The external validity of experiments. *American Educational Research Journal* **5**: 437–474.   90, 232, 236, 296

19. Breslin, R. W., W. J. Lonner, and R. M. Thorndike, 1973. *Cross-cultural Research Methods*. New York: Wiley.   188

20. Bridgman, P. W., 1945. The prospect for intelligence, *Yale Review* **34**: 444–461.   4

21. Broden, M., C. Bruce, M. A. Mitchell, V. Carter, and R. V. Hall, 1970. Effects of teacher attention on attending behavior of two boys at adjacent desks. *Journal of Applied Behavior Analysis* **3**: 205–211.   271

22. Broudy, H. S., R. H. Ennis, and L. I. Krimerman, (eds.), 1973. *Philosophy of Educational Research*, New York: Wiley.   222

23. Burnett, J. H., 1969. Ceremony, rites, and economy in the student system of an American high school. *Human Organization* **28**: 1–10.   176

24. Buros, O. K., (ed.), 1941–1972 (irregular). *The Mental Measurements Yearbooks*. Highland Park, N.J.: Gryphon Press.   134, 304

25. Byalick, R., and D. N. Bersoff, 1974. Reinforcement practices of black and white teachers in integrated classrooms. *Journal of Educational Psychology* **66**: 473–480.   6–7

26. Campbell, D. T., and D. W. Fiske, 1959. Convergent and discriminant validation by the multitrait-multimethod matrix. *Psychological Bulletin* **56**: 81–105.   132

27. Campbell, D. T., and J. C. Stanley, 1966. *Experimental and Quasi-experimental Designs for Research*. Chicago: Rand McNally. (Also in N. L. Gage (ed.), 1963. *Handbook of Research on Teaching*. Chicago: Rand McNally, pp. 171–246).   229, 232–233, 236, 243, 268, 272, 305–306

28. Cary, C. D., 1976. Patterns of emphasis upon Marxist–Leninist ideology: a computer content analysis of Soviet school history, geography, and social science textbooks. *Comparative Education Review* **20**: 11–29.   183–184

29. Chein, I., 1976. An introduction to sampling. In C. Selltiz, L. S. Wrightsman, and S. W. Cook (eds.), *Research Methods in Social*   91

Cited in this
text on pages

Relations (3rd ed.) New York: Holt, Rinehart and Winston, pp. 512–540.

30. Cicirelli, V., et al. *The Impact of Head Start: An Evaluation of the Effects of Head Start on Children's Cognitive and Affective Development*. Washington, D.C.: Office of Economic Opportunity.   36

31. Clifford, G. J., 1973. A history of the impact of research on teaching. In R. M. W. Travers (ed.), *Second Handbook of Research on Teaching*. Chicago: Rand McNally, pp. 1–46.   294

32. Coleman, J. S., et al., 1966. *Equality of Educational Opportunity*. Washington, D.C.: U.S. Government Printing Office.   36

33. Cornfield, J., and J. W. Tukey, 1956. Average values of mean squares in factorials. *The Annals of Mathematical Statistics* **27**: 907–949.   296

34. Covert, R. W., and E. J. Mason, 1974. Factorial validity of a student evaluation of teaching instrument. *Educational and Psychological Measurement* **34**: 903–905.   393–395

35. Cramér, H., 1946. *Mathematical Methods of Statistics*. Princeton: Princeton University Press.   84

36. Cronbach, L. J., 1970. *Essentials of Psychological Testing* (3rd ed.). New York: Harper & Row.   135

37. Cronbach, L. J., 1971. Test validation. In R. L. Thorndike (ed.), *Educational Measurement* (2nd ed.). Washington, D.C.: American Council on Education, pp. 443–507.   129–132

38. Cronbach, L. J., G. C. Gleser, H. Nanda, and N. Rajaratnam, 1972. *The Dependability of Behavioral Measurements: Theory of Generalizability for Scores and Profiles*. New York: Wiley.   125

39. Cronbach, L. J., N. Rajaratnam, and G. C. Gleser, 1963. Theory of generalizability: a liberalization of reliability theory. *British Journal of Statistical Psychology* **16**: 137–163.   125

40. Daly, J. A., and M. D. Miller, 1975. Further studies on writing apprehension: SAT scores, success expectations, willingness to take advanced courses, and sex differences. *Research on the Teaching of English* **9**: 250–256.   196–197

41. Darlington, R. B., S. L. Weinberg, and H. J. Walberg, 1975. Canonical variate analysis and related techniques. In D. J. Amick and H. J. Walberg (eds.), *Introductory Multivariate Analysis for Educational, Psychological, and Social Research*. Berkeley, Calif.: McCutchan, pp. 91–112.   216

42. Davis, F. B., 1964. *Educational Measurements and Their Interpretation*. Belmont, Calif.: Wadsworth.   120

43. Davis, J. A., 1971. *Elementary Survey Analysis*. Englewood Cliffs, N.J.: Prentice-Hall.   203, 275

44. Ennis, R. H., 1973. On causality. *Educational Researcher* **2**(6): 4–11.   142, 145, 223–224

45. Erber, N. P., and D. A. McMahan, 1976. Effects of sentence context on recognition of words through lip reading by deaf children. *Journal of Speech and Hearing Research* **19**: 112–119.   225, 251

Cited in this
text on pages

46. Feldman, J. J., H. Hyman, and C. W. Hart, 1951–1952. A field   306
study of interviewer effects on the quality of survey data. *Public
Opinion Quarterly* **15**: 734–761.

47. Feldman, K. A., 1970. Some methods for assessing college impacts.   286
Sociology of Education **44**: 133–150.

48. Fishel, A., 1976. Organizational positions on Title IX: conflicting   183
perspectives on sex discrimination in education. *Journal of Higher
Education* **47**: 93–105.

49. Flanders, N. A., 1970. *Analyzing Teacher Behavior.* Reading,   179–180, 196
Mass.: Addison-Wesley.

50. Fox, D. J., 1969. *The Research Process in Education.* New York: 197, 375
Holt, Rinehart and Winston.

51. Fry, P. W., 1976. Changes in youth's attitudes toward authority: 274
the transition from university to employment. *Journal of Counseling
Psychology* **23**: 66–74.

52. Gagné, R. M., 1970. *The Conditions of Learning* (2nd ed.) New   349
York: Holt, Rinehart and Winston.

53. Gallup, G. H., 1973. Fifth annual Gallup poll of public attitudes   99
toward education. *Phi Delta Kappan* **55**: 38–51.

54. Gardner, P. L., 1975. Scales and statistics. *Review of Educational   55
Research* **45**: 43–57.

55. Gellert, E., 1955. Systematic observation: a method in child study.   124
Harvard Educational Review **25**: 179–195.

56. Glass, G. V., and J. C. Stanley, 1970. *Statistical Methods in Edu-   103, 197, 203
cation and Psychology.* Englewood Cliffs, N.J.: Prentice-Hall.

57. Glassman, A. M., and J. A. Belasco, 1974. Appealed grievances in   182
urban education: a case study. *Education and Urban Society* **7**:
73–87.

58. Glock, C. Y., 1967. Survey design and analysis in sociology. In   150, 275–276
C. Y. Glock (ed.), *Survey Research in the Social Sciences.* New
York: Russell Sage Foundation, pp. 1–62.

59. Goldman, R. D., and B. N. Hewitt, 1976. The scholastic aptitude   225
test "explains" why college men major in science more often than
college women. *Journal of Counseling Psychology* **23**: 50–54.

60. Goslin, D. A., and D. C. Glass, 1967. The social effects of standard-   158
ized testing in American elementary and secondary schools. *Sociology of Education* **40**: 115–131.

61. Gottlieb, D., 1974. Work and families: great expectations for col-   149
lege seniors. *Journal of Higher Education* **45**: 535–544.

62. Goulet, L. R., 1975. Longitudinal and time-lag designs in educa-   186
tional research: an alternate sampling model. *Review of Educational Research* **45**: 505–523.

63. Graves, D. H., 1975. An examination of the writing processes of   159, 178–179
seven-year-old children. *Research in the Teaching of English* **9**:
227–241.

64. Greenberg, D., and J. McCall, 1974. Teacher mobility and alloca-   182
tion. *Journal of Human Resources* **9**: 480–502.

	Cited in this text on pages

65. Greenwood, E., 1945. *Experimental Sociology: A Study in Method.* New York: King's Crown Press. — 274

66. Guilford, J. P., 1967. *The Nature of Human Intelligence.* New York: Holt, Rinehart and Winston. — 349

67. Guilford, J. P., and R. Hoepfner, 1971. *The Analysis of Intelligence.* New York: McGraw-Hill. — 349

68. Guttman, L., 1941. An outline of the statistical theory of prediction. In P. Horst (ed.), *The Prediction of Personal Adjustment.* Social Science Research Council Bulletin 48, pp. 251–364. — 287

69. Hanson, N. R., 1961. *Patterns of Discovery: An Inquiry into the Conceptual Foundations of Science.* London: Cambridge University Press. — 32

70. Hays, W. L., 1973. *Statistics for the Social Sciences* (2nd ed.) New York: Holt, Rinehart and Winston. — 84, 114–116, 203

71. Hempel, C., 1966. *Philosophy of Natural Science.* Englewood Cliffs, N.J.: Prentice-Hall. — 35

72. Herriott, R. E., 1969. Survey research method. In R. L. Ebel (ed.), *Encyclopedia of Educational Research* (4th ed.) London: Macmillan, pp. 1400–1409. — 158

73. Heyns, R. W., and A. F. Zander, 1953. Observation of group behavior. In L. Festinger and D. Katz (eds.), *Research Methods in the Behavioral Sciences.* New York: Holt, Rinehart and Winston, pp. 381–417. — 124

74. Hilton, T. L., and C. Patrick, 1970. Cross-sectional versus longitudinal data: an empirical comparison of mean differences in academic growth. *Journal of Educational Measurement* 7: 15–24. — 187

75. Hirschi, T., and H. C. Selvin, 1973. *Principles of Survey Analysis.* (Formerly entitled *Delinquency Research.*) New York: Free Press. — 153–154

76. Holland, J. L., 1966. *The Psychology of Vocational Choice.* Lexington, Mass.: Ginn. — 349

77. Holland, J. L., 1973. *Making Vocational Choices: A Theory of Careers.* Englewood Cliffs, N.J.: Prentice-Hall. — 349

78. Holsti, O. R., 1968. Content analysis. In G. Lindzey and E. Aronson (eds.), *The Handbook of Social Psychology* (2nd ed., Vol. 2), *Research Methods.* Reading, Mass.: Addison-Wesley, pp. 596–692. — 124, 183

79. Hosie, T. W., R. Gentile, and J. D. Carroll, 1974. Pupil preferences and the Premack principle. *American Educational Research Journal* 11: 241–247. — 32, 34

80. Huck, S. W., W. H. Cormier, and W. G. Bounds, 1974. *Reading Statistics and Research.* New York: Harper and Row. — 271

81. Hyman, H. H., 1954. *Interviewing in Social Research.* Chicago: University of Chicago Press. —

82. Hyman, H., 1955. *Survey Design and Analysis: Principles, Cases and Procedures.* New York: Free Press. — 148–150, 152, 275–276

83. Hyman, H. H., 1972. *Secondary Analysis of Sample Surveys: Principles, Procedures, and Potentialities.* New York: Wiley. — 184

Cited in this
text on pages

84. Hyman, H. H., C. R. Wright, and J. S. Reed, 1975. *The Enduring Effects of Education.* Chicago: University of Chicago Press.   184

85. Hyman, I., R. Carroll, J. Duffey, and J. Manni, 1973. Patterns of interprofessional conflict resolution on school child study teams. *Journal of School Psychology* 11: 187–195.   158

86. Jackson, G., and C. Cosca, 1974. The inequality of educational opportunity in the Southwest: an observational study of ethnically mixed classrooms. *American Educational Research Journal* 11: 219–229.   33

87. Jensen, A. R., 1969. How much can we boost IQ and scholastic achievement? *Harvard Educational Review* 39: 1–123.   36

88. Johnson, D. A., 1976. Treating black students like white students: a definition of school integration. *Urban Education* 11: 94–114.   176, 178

89. Jones, L. V., 1971. The nature of measurement. In R. L. Thorndike (ed.), *Educational Measurement* (2nd ed.) Washington, D.C.: American Council on Education, pp. 335–355.   53

90. Kaplan, A., 1964. *The Conduct of Inquiry: Methodology for Behavioral Science.* San Francisco: Chandler.   4, 32, 48

91. Kelley, J., S. J. Smits, R. Leventhal, and R. Rhodes, 1970. Critique of the designs of process and outcome research. *Journal of Counseling Psychology* 17: 337–341.   273

92. Kerlinger, F. N., 1973. *Foundations of Behavioral Research* (2nd ed.) New York: Holt, Rinehart and Winston.   5, 48, 55–56, 114–115, 243

93. Kerlinger, F. N., (ed.), 1975. *Review of Research in Education* (Vol. 3). Itasca, Ill.: Peacock.   188

94. Kerlinger, F. N., and E. J. Pedhazur, 1973. *Multiple Regression in Behavioral Research.* New York: Holt, Rinehart and Winston.   286

95. Kurth, R. W., and R. M. Pavalko, 1975. School resources, social environments, and educational outcomes. *Journal of Research and Development in Education* 9: 70–81.   197

96. Lambert, N. M., C. S. Hartsough, and I. L. Zimmerman, 1976. The comparative predictive efficiency of intellectual and nonintellectual components of high school functioning. *American Journal of Orthopsychiatry* 46: 109–122.   392

97. Lawson, A. E., F. H. Nordland, and A. Devito, 1975. Relationship of formal reasoning to achievement, aptitudes, and attitudes in preservice teachers. *Journal of Research in Science Teaching* 12: 423–431.   197

98. Lennon, R. T., 1956. Assumptions underlying the use of content validity. *Educational and Psychological Measurement* 16: 294–304.   130

99. Light, R. J., 1973. Issues in the analysis of qualitative data. In R. M. W. Travers (ed.), *Second Handbook of Research on Teaching.* Chicago: Rand McNally, pp. 318–381.   84, 203

100. Lofland, J., 1971. *Analyzing Social Settings.* Belmont, Calif.: Wadsworth.   176

101. Lortie, D. C., 1967. The teacher's shame: anger and the normative commitments of classroom teachers. *School Review* 75: 155–170.   159

Cited in this
text on pages

102. Maccoby, E. E., and N. Maccoby, 1954. The interview: a tool of   306
social science. In G. Lindzey (ed.), *Handbook of Social Psychology* (Vol. 1), *Theory and Method*. Reading, Mass.: Addison-
Wesley, pp. 449–487.

103. Maehr, M. L., and D. D. Sjogren, 1971. Atkinson's theory of   349
achievement motivation: first step toward a theory of academic
motivation? *Review of Educational Research* **41**: 143–161.

104. McGaw, B., J. L. Wardrop, and M. A. Bunda, 1972. Classroom   122, 124
observation schemes: where are the errors? *American Educational
Research Journal* **9**: 13–27.

105. Medley, D. M., and H. E. Mitzel, 1963. Measuring classroom be-   122, 124, 305
havior by systematic observation. In N. L. Gage (ed.), *Handbook
of Research on Teaching*. Chicago: Rand McNally, pp. 247–328.

106. Mercatoris, M., and W. E. Craighead, 1974. Effects on nonpartici-   305
pant observation on teacher and pupil classroom behavior. *Journal
of Educational Psychology* **66**: 512–519.

107. Miller, L. B., and J. L. Dyer, 1975. Four preschool programs: 149, 180
their dimensions and effects. *Monographs of the Society for Research in Child Development* **40**: (5–6, Serial No. 162).

108. Moos, R. H., 1973. Conceptualizations of human environments.   299–301
American Psychologist **28**: 652–665.

109. Mueller, J. H., K. F. Schuessler, and H. L. Costner, 1970. *Statis-   69, 203
tical Reasoning in Sociology* (2nd ed.) Boston: Houghton Mifflin.

110. Nagel, E., 1961. *The Structure of Science: Problems in the Logic   36
of Scientific Explanation*. New York: Harcourt, Brace and World.

111. Nelson, M., and S. D. Sieber, 1976. Innovations in urban sec-   151, 199
ondary schools. *School Review* **84**: 213–231.

112. Nunnally, J. C., 1975. Psychometric theory 25 years ago and now.   82, 120
Educational Researcher **4**(10): 7–14, 19–21.

113. Payne, S. L., 1951. *The Art of Asking Questions*. Princeton: Prince-   122, 346, 355
ton University Press.

114. Rehberg, R. A., and W. E. Schafer, 1968. Participation in inter-   276
scholastic athletics and college expectations. *American Journal of
Sociology* **73**: 732–740.

115. Rickards, J. P., and G. J. August, 1975. Generative underlining   246
strategies in prose recall. *Journal of Educational Psychology* **67**:
860–865.

116. Rokeach, M., 1968. *Beliefs, Attitudes, and Values*. San Francisco: 159
Jossey-Bass.

117. Rosen, J. L., 1968. Personality and first-year teachers' relationships   180
with children. *School Review* **76**: 294–311.

118. Rosenthal, R., 1966. *Experimenter Effects in Behavioral Research*.   347
New York: Appleton-Century-Crofts.

119. Rosenthal, R., 1969. Interpersonal expectations: effects of the ex-   347
perimenter's hypothesis. In R. Rosenthal and R. L. Rosnow (eds.),
Artifact in Behavioral Research. New York: Academic Press, pp.
181–277.

Cited in this
text on pages

120. Rosenthal, R., and L. Jacobson, 1968. *Pygmalion in the Classroom: Teacher Expectation and Pupils' Intellectual Development.* New York: Holt, Rinehart and Winston. — 36

121. Rubin, Z., 1970. The birth order of birth-order researchers. *Developmental Psychology* **3**: 269–270. — 33

122. Runkel, P. J., and J. E. McGrath, 1972. *Research on Human Behavior: A Systematic Guide to Method.* New York: Holt, Rinehart and Winston. — 226, 294, 303

123. Ryan, F. L., 1973. Differentiated effects of levels of questioning on student achievement. *Journal of Experimental Education* **41**(3): 63–67. — 245–246

124. Sabatino, D. A., and N. Dorfman, 1974. Matching learning aptitude to two commercial reading programs. *Exceptional Children* **41**: 85–90. — 15–18

125. Samuels, S. J., and J. E. Turnure, 1974. Attention and reading achievement in first-grade boys and girls. *Journal of Educational Psychology* **66**: 29–32. — 179

126. Scott, W. A., 1955. Reliability of content analysis: the case of nominal scale coding. *Public Opinion Quarterly* **91**: 321–325. — 124

127. Scriven, M., 1972. Objectivity and subjectivity in educational research. In L. G. Thomas (ed.), *Philosophical Redirection of Educational Research.* 71st Yearbook of the National Society for the Study of Education, Part I. Chicago: University of Chicago Press, pp. 94–142. — 5

128. Scriven, M., 1973. Causes, connections, and conditions in history. In H. S. Broudy, R. H. Ennis, and L. I. Krimerman (eds.), *Philosophy of Educational Research.* New York: Wiley, pp. 439–458. — 223

129. Seeman, A. Z., and M. Seeman, 1976. Staff processes and pupil attitudes: a study of teacher participation in educational change. *Human Relations* **29**: 25–40. — 225

130. Selltiz, C., L. S. Wrightsman, and S. W. Cook, 1976. *Research Methods in Social Relations* (3rd ed.) New York: Holt, Rinehart and Winston. — 154, 177, 183, 229

131. Smith, L. M., and W. Geoffrey, 1968. *The Complexities of an Urban Classroom: An Analysis Toward a General Theory of Teaching.* New York: Holt, Rinehart and Winston. — 176–177

132. Snow, R. E., 1974. Representative and quasi-representative designs for research on teaching. *Review of Educational Research* **44**: 265–291. — 90

133. Snow, R. E., 1973. Theory construction for research on teaching. In R. M. W. Travers (ed.), *Second Handbook of Research on Teaching.* Chicago: Rand McNally, pp. 77–112. — 18, 348–349

134. Spreitzer, E., and M. Pugh, 1973. Interscholastic athletics and educational expectations. *Sociology of Education* **46**: 171–182. — 285

135. Sproull, N., 1973. Visual attention, modeling behaviors, and other verbal and nonverbal meta-communication of prekindergarten children viewing "Sesame Street." *American Educational Research Journal* **10**: 101–114. — 181

	Cited in this text on pages

136. Stanley, J. C., 1971. Reliability. In R. L. Thorndike (ed.), *Educational Measurement* (2nd ed.). Washington, D.C.: American Council on Education, pp. 356–442. — 118

137. Stevens, S. S., 1946. On the theory of scales of measurement. *Science* 103: 667–680. — 53

138. Thorndike, R. L., 1951. Reliability. In E. F. Lindquist (ed.), *Educational Measurement*. Washington, D.C.: American Council on Education, pp. 560–620. — 118

139. Thorndike, R. L., and E. Hagen, 1969. *Measurement and Evaluation in Psychology and Education* (3rd ed.) New York: Wiley. — 119, 135

140. Trow, M., 1967. Survey research and education. In C. Y. Glock (ed.), *Survey Research in the Social Sciences*. New York: Russell Sage Foundation, pp. 315–375. — 143

141. Walker, H. M., and J. Lev, 1953. *Statistical Inference*. New York: Holt, Rinehart and Winston. — 107

142. Walker, H. M., and N. K. Buckley, 1968. The use of positive reinforcement in conditioning attending behavior. *Journal of Applied Behavior Analysis* 1: 245–250. — 271

143. Webb, E. J., D. T. Campbell, R. D. Schwartz, and L. Sechrest, 1966. *Unobtrusive Measures: Nonreactive Research in the Social Sciences*. Chicago: Rand McNally. — 304

144. Weber, M., 1973. The scientist as scientist cannot make value judgments. In H. S. Broudy, R. H. Ennis, and L. I. Krimerman (eds.), *Philosophy of Educational Research*. New York: Wiley, pp. 504–512. — 48

145. Weick, K. E., 1968. Systematic observational methods. In G. Lindzey and E. Aronson (eds.), *The Handbook of Social Psychology* (2nd ed., Vol. 2), *Research Methods*. Reading, Mass.: Addison-Wesley, pp. 357–451. — 122, 177, 305

146. Weiner, B., 1967. Implications of the current theory of achievement motivation for research and performance in the classroom. *Psychology in the Schools* 4: 164–171. — 349

147. Welch, W. W., and H. J. Walberg, 1970. Pretest and sensitization effects in curriculum evaluation. *American Educational Research Journal* 7: 605–614. — 234

148. Wright, H. F., 1960. Observational child study. In P. H. Mussen (ed.), *Handbook of Research Methods in Child Development*. New York: Wiley, pp. 71–139. — 124

149. Yamamoto, K., J. P. Jones, and M. B. Ross, 1972. A note on the processing of classroom observation records. *American Educational Research Journal* 9: 29–44. — 181

Index[1]

---

[1] *Research study* refers to the fact that one of the reprinted studies illustrates the concept cited in the index entry.